Painting her pleasure

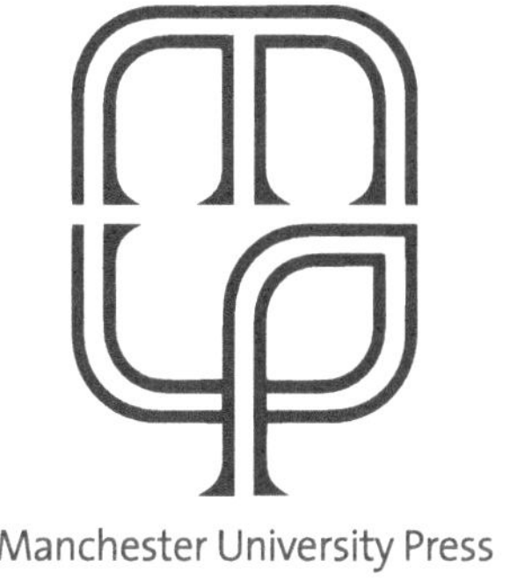

Manchester University Press

Painting her pleasure

Three women artists and the nude in avant-garde Paris

Lauren Jimerson

Manchester University Press

Published by Manchester University Press
Oxford Road, Manchester M13 9PL

www.manchesteruniversitypress.co.uk

British Library Cataloguing-in-Publication Data
A catalogue record for this book is available from the British Library

ISBN 978 1 5261 5983 0 hardback
ISBN 978 1 5261 8496 2 paperback

First published 2023
Paperback published 2025

Typeset
by Cheshire Typesetting Ltd, Cuddington, Cheshire
Printed in Great Britain
by TJ Books Ltd, Padstow

Contents

Plates

Figures

Acknowledgements

From London, New York and Paris to smaller towns across Europe, this venture has unfurled across two continents and has spanned over a decade. Each chapter of this journey was made possible by the unwavering support and shared wisdom of professors, artists' descendants, archivists, curators, family and friends. To each one of them, I owe a debt of gratitude. The idea for this book was ignited in 2010 at Musée Maillol in Paris, where I first saw Suzanne Valadon's drawings. Her images of maladroit female bathers captivated me. I am infinitely appreciative of Christopher Green at The Courtauld, whose expert guidance not only accelerated my research but afforded me the unique opportunity to access curatorial departments. This enabled me to view Valadon's work firsthand, leading to several discoveries detailed in chapter three, and was instrumental in steering my research from initial fascination to the completion of this book.

This project expanded during intensive research periods in and around France. My profound gratitude extends to my advisor at Rutgers University, Susan Sidlauskas, who served as a beacon of inspiration during this crucial stage in the project's development. Her steadfast enthusiasm, astute input and unwavering confidence fostered both my ideas and academic voice. My work in Paris would not have been possible without the support of professors Rémi Labrusse at Université Paris Nanterre and Arnauld Pierre at Université de Paris IV Sorbonne. Additionally, Paula Birnbaum of the University of San Francisco offered critical insight and connected me with scholars in both the US and France, acting not only as a key mentor but as a dear friend.

I am extremely appreciative of the financial support from Rutgers University as well as outside fellowships. A Fulbright Fellowship to France in 2015 enabled me to conduct in-depth research essential for this book, while an exchange with the École Normale Supérieure provided me with lodging in Paris and enabled me to meet a fascinating group of scholars. Andrew W. Mellon Fellowships offered essential financial backing to execute this project, including summer research grants and a year-long fellowship. I am sincerely grateful for the enthusiastic support, sage perspectives, and prudent advice of Joan Marter, Jane Sharp, and Mary Shaw at Rutgers. Their guidance was crucial not only in attaining fellowships and opportunities in Paris, but also in shaping this book. Charlotte Goodwin and the late Arnaud Roujou de Boubée at the Franco-American Fulbright Commission provided steadfast and crucial aid in both academic matters and immigration challenges. In completing this book, I am immensely indebted to Alun Richards, my diligent editor, whose patience and acuity have been instrumental, and the entire team at Manchester University Press who brought this book to life.

I wish to express my heartfelt thanks to the private collectors and artist's descendants who graciously welcomed me into their homes and showed me their collections. The time I spent with each of them was not only critical in carrying out my research, but also highly memorable and enriching in fostering ideas for this book. I would especially like to thank the collectors, Tatiana and Georges Khatsenkov, who kindly invited me to their home in Monaco to see their important collection of Russian artists, including Vassilieff. Similarly, Pamela and the late William Royall shared their fervent admiration for Charmy's work, generously offering me a glimpse into their collection in Richmond. Equally welcoming were Marcel and Isabelle Bernet, who, on numerous occasions, warmly allowed me into their Parisian home to study the Vassilieff works they possess. In London, viewing the Charmy collection of the late Patrick Seale and his daughter, Yasmine Seale, was remarkable. Charmy's grandson, Bernard Bouche, warrants a special mention for sharing valuable insights, images and archival materials about his grandmother throughout the years. Claude Bernès, who maintains the largest archive and collection devoted to Vassilieff, played an instrumental role in aiding my research on the artist. I extend my deepest gratitude to him for his invaluable assistance. I also want to express my thanks to Benoît Noël, who willingly shared a wealth of resources, images and insights about Vassilieff. My appreciation also extends to Cyril Debrailly, the artist's grandson, for his enthusiastic support of this project. Lastly, I am indebted to Jeanine Warnod, daughter of art critic André Warnod. As the only surviving historian who personally knew Vassilieff, Charmy and Valadon, her shared insights were enlightening.

I especially appreciate the curators who pulled artwork and germane materials from storage, and the archivists and librarians who assisted me in finding the materials on which I built this study. I would like to specifically thank Sylvie Carlier, previously at Musée Municipal Paul-Dini and now curator at Musée Marmottan Monet, as well as Matthew Affron, former curator at the Fralin Museum of Art, presently at the Philadelphia Museum of Art. Their assistance was instrumental, and I treasure their dedicated contribution to my work. I would also like to extend a warm appreciation to Stéphane Paccoud and Ewa Penot at Musée des Beaux-Arts de Lyon, Nelly Maillard at Musée National Fernand Léger and the curators at Musée des Beaux-Arts de Limoges, Musée des Beaux-Arts de Nancy, Musée de Grenoble, the Petit Palais in Geneva, Musée des Beaux-Arts de Menton and the Centre Pompidou. I must express my sincere gratitude to Nancy Ireson, who provided me with the opportunity to contribute to the Suzanne Valadon exhibition at the Barnes Foundation, an experience that significantly enriched my perspective on Valadon's *Black Venus*. Likewise, my appreciation extends to Saskia Ooms from the Musée de Montmartre for inviting me to participate in an exhibition on Fernande Olivier. Furthermore, I am thankful to Camille Morineau and Lucia Pesapane for granting me the chance to contribute to the *Pionnières* exhibition at the Musée du Luxembourg. These illuminative experiences have greatly shaped my research and understanding on the roles of Vassilieff, Charmy and Valadon within the Parisian avant-garde.

Wonderful friends on both sides of the Atlantic helped transform what could have been a lonely experience into the most extraordinary and memorable period of my life. Although they are too numerous to mention individually here, I am eternally thankful for them all. I am particularly grateful to Cathy Jarrige, for twice welcoming me into her family's home in Limoges and guiding me to important sites in the area, including Valadon's birthplace. Invaluable allies such as Kit Heintzman and Amanda Herold-Marme came to my aid with ideas and editing for my book at crucial times. I cannot overlook the significant role Estelle Schwalb played; her selfless contribution to copyediting the manuscript was truly indispensable. Kristen Hoey was a remarkable woman whom I met while conducting research in Paris. This book stands as a monument to her memory and a celebration of the unwavering spirit of independent womanhood that she so brilliantly embodied.

My family has been a bedrock of support throughout this endeavor. Their steadfast belief in me has been a source of motivation and strength. I owe a deep sense of gratitude to my father, Douglas Jimerson, who was a vital participant in this project, reading drafts, providing critical feedback and encouraging me through challenging moments. My appreciation extends equally to my mother, Ellen Jimerson, and my sisters, Kirsten and Maddy, who bolstered me with their encouragement and celebrated each achievement, illuminating every step of the way. Finally, the legacy of my late grandfather, Dr. Cedric Jimerson, has been an enduring beacon of inspiration. His fortitude, strength and love have been my guiding light throughout this journey.

Lastly, I would like to extend my most sincere appreciation to the dynamic Art *with* Friends community, a stimulating forum where I have had the privilege of sharing my research journey while crafting this book. This platform, which I founded and nurtured during the book's completion phase, has been an incubator for thoughtful discussions and fruitful interactions around women artists and those traditionally marginalized in art history. The community's perceptive insights, critical feedback and enthusiasm for learning significantly influenced the final shape of this book, and for that I am immensely grateful. Though it is impossible to individually acknowledge each member within this growing group of art enthusiasts, their stimulating dialogues and constructive critiques were essential in refining this manuscript. I want to extend a special mention to Phyllis Cela and Sumi Shohara, whose unwavering encouragement and keen interest in my work catalyzed the creation of this flourishing art community. Their contributions to our collective endeavor are a testament to the enduring vitality and passion that defines Art *with* Friends. This shared passion, inherent within our community, has been instrumental in bringing this book to fruition.

In memory of KRISTEN ANNE HOEY (1985–2017), a *femme moderne* of the twenty-first century.

Note on text

The author's choices about terminology reflect both historical contexts and modern sensitivities. While the term 'prostitute' is used for historical accuracy, it's important to note that the preferred and more inclusive term today is 'sex worker'.

For a more comprehensive view of the works of Marie Vassilieff, Émilie Charmy, Suzanne Valadon, and their contemporaries, we invite you to scan the QR code or visit www.laurenjimerson.com. This dedicated online gallery serves as a supplement to the images presented within these pages and also showcases additional works not included in this book, providing a more complete understanding of these artists' extensive oeuvres.

Introduction: Naked ambition – women artists and the modern nude

At the dawn of the twentieth century, the nude was the subject of ambition and the gateway to artistic prominence. However, the genre was historically sanctioned as the prerogative of male artists. For women painters to approach the nude in a bold or innovative manner was considered socially objectionable. In France, women were barred from studying live nude models in public art institutions until the end of the nineteenth century, with few exceptions. Social mores discouraged women from gazing at their own naked bodies, let alone another woman's. To paint and exhibit the male nude was a transgressive act. With the rise of modern art, the female body became an instrument through which male artists explored new modes of representation while competing for primacy in the avant-garde. Conversely, women who opposed masculine or heteronormative conventions of the nude faced a variety of obstacles, ranging from *ad hominem* attacks to hostile critical reception to outright censorship.

Yet, Marie Vassilieff (1884–1957), Émilie Charmy (1878–1974) and Suzanne Valadon (1865–1938) painted the nude without inhibition, rupturing conventions and reversing gender roles. Stylistically distinct, each artist recast the nude in accordance with her own perception of gender, sexuality and the self. They explored new territory for female artists: the male body, the Black female nude and the nude self-portrait, a genre which few artists, male or female, dared to tackle until the latter half of the twentieth century.[1] Charmy's pregnant nude self-portraits painted in 1915 are the first of their kind. She portrays the pregnant body in the throes of pleasure, daringly expressing a woman's sexual voice. Through their representations of their own bodies as well as those of others, they spurned bourgeois mores and unhinged normative conceptions of womanhood. Well before feminist and gender studies emerged as areas of critical debate, these artists pushed the limits of gender in representation, expressed self-awareness and introduced female sexuality through their paintings.

This book sheds light on three pioneering artists who have heretofore been marginalized within the history of modernism. Vassilieff, a Russian émigré, was directly involved with avant-garde circles in Paris. In 1905, with a grant from the Tsarina, Alexandra Feodorovna, Vassilieff traveled to the French capital to study art. After training with Matisse, she founded her own vanguard art academy in 1912 and a canteen in 1914 to feed starving artists during the war. In her Cubist nudes, Vassilieff captured the body in accordance with a dynamic experience of time and space, a key Cubist objectives. Unlike her male peers, she subverted gender norms and re-presented gender and race as shifting and non-binary. From the outset, Charmy's treatment of modern and uncommon subject matter was evident – a portrait of a pregnant woman, a brothel scene, a woman in a morphine-induced daydream – along with her vigorous application of paint and bold palette. She moved to Paris from Lyon in 1903 and became connected with the Fauve movement through the artist Charles Camoin. But by 1912, she branched out on her own and remained untethered from major art movements. In 1913, she was one of only fifty women who exhibited in the seminal Armory Show in New York. She attained success in the 1920s and was awarded the Legion of Honor in 1926. Critics referred to her as the "Colette of Painting," a reference to the prominent novelist. Charmy reshaped visual representations of female sexuality in accordance with her own subjective perspective as a woman. Many of these works remained hidden in her studio, including radical pregnant nude self-portraits. Valadon entered the art world as a model for Pierre Puvis de Chavannes, Pierre-Auguste Renoir and Henri de Toulouse-Lautrec. She then made the rare transition from model to artist and gained prominence within the bohemian society of Montmartre. Of lower-class background, Valadon treated subject matter that was off limits for bourgeois female painters, and she exposed, authenticated and bore witness to the conditions of the working class in her representations of bathers and nudes. Influenced and encouraged by her friend Edgar Degas, she depicted the body in awkward poses and from unflattering angles in hundreds of drawings, prints and paintings. She employed the human form as a means of dissent against the archetypal standards of beauty and artistic conventions, both traditional and vanguard. In certain instances, she painted the nude from the dual vantage point of seer and seen and captured the figure as lived and embodied.

Vassilieff, Charmy and Valadon share certain similarities. First, they were all painters who created an impressive body of work devoted to the modern nude. They were active in the decades preceding and succeeding World War One – an exciting and ambiguous period for women, marked by an emergence of new opportunities as well as new limitations. Embodying the *femme nouvelle* and its later reincarnation, the *femme moderne*, they worked outside the home in a male-dominated field and led independent and unconventional lifestyles.[2] Each had a mentor or teacher, but none of them received extensive formal art training; they were primarily self-taught. They chose to forgo the customary role of housewife and supported themselves financially. Each became a single parent and juggled motherhood and career concurrently. They participated in important exhibitions, including the annual Salon des Indépendants and Salon d'Automne, as well as in private galleries and artist-organized shows.

Each achieved recognition in France, especially during the 1910s and 1920s. This acknowledgment was short-lived; all three artists have been overlooked posthumously.

They were acquainted with one another and ran in similar circles, and on occasion their work was shown together. Vassilieff and Valadon participated in artists' charity balls in support of L'Aide Amicale Aux Artistes, which frequently took place in the famed dance hall Le Bal Bullier in Montparnasse. Each designed posters for these events – Vassilieff in 1924 and Valadon in 1927. Vassilieff expressly noted her admiration for Valadon's art in her memoir. Valadon likewise appreciated Vassilieff's work and purchased at least one of her *poupée-portraits* for her own collection.[3] Valadon and Charmy both exhibited regularly at Berthe Weill's gallery and later in the salons of the Société des Femmes Artistes Modernes. Valadon even inscribed one of her still lifes, "to E. Charmy for her fine talent."[4] Nevertheless, they did not collaborate with each other in any significant way, and the art that they produced could not be more distinct. Born roughly a decade apart, they represent three succeeding generations, which in part contributes to the stylistic differences inherent in their work. They came from unique social backgrounds, and they rose to prominence in distinct artistic neighborhoods – Valadon was a core member of the turn-of-the-century Montmartrois art world, while Vassilieff was a key figure in the social fabric of the Montparnasse avant-garde. From her arrival in 1903, Charmy launched herself into the Parisian art scene. Her studio was centrally placed within the developing artistic milieu of Place de Clichy. But by the early 1910s, she dissociated herself from other artists. This trio did not benefit from sororal networks that gained momentum during the feminist art movement. Instead, their existence, as Vassilieff's memoir reveals, was at times exceedingly lonely. Nevertheless, each resiliently forged her own singular path through the exhilarating but hostile twentieth-century art world.

In defiance of the French cultural and social values of their era, the "*déstin féminin*," later termed by Simone de Beauvoir, Vassilieff, Charmy and Valadon divorced themselves from expectations of bourgeois womanhood in their life and work. They occupied the roles of working woman, single parent and divorcée, at a time when these positions were not well regarded. However, they never proclaimed themselves as feminists. It is uncertain how Valadon would have felt toward women's suffrage in 1944, which only Charmy and Vassilieff lived to witness. Vassilieff does not broach the topic in her memoir. Valadon, in fact, disliked "women's art," and refused to participate in the Salon des Femmes Artistes Modernes until 1933, when she was finally persuaded by the organization's President, Marie-Anne Camax Zoegger.[5] She was skeptical of women's artist groups and was cautious of identifying her work with them. On the other hand, Charmy was friends with Camax Zoegger, as well as some of France's prominent writers who advocated for women's rights, including the journalist Andrée Viollis and the author and politician Louise Weiss.

Vassilieff, Charmy and Valadon do not constitute a homogeneous unit. I focus on these artists because they are rare and outstanding examples of women in early twentieth-century France who traversed gender boundaries, confronted issues of sexuality head-on and painted the body in a daring manner. They breached assumptions about "feminine" art in terms of style, and unhinged expectations about the subject matter a woman could paint. They developed a sexual self-awareness which informed their work and thoroughly defied turn-of-the-century scientific discourses and social stereotypes. They forged alternative methods for the representation of the nude steered by their own idiosyncratic desires and sensitivities to gender, race and identity. In highlighting this heterogeneous but contemporaneous trio, I reveal how each artist participated in the avant-garde transformation of the nude by pioneering a conception of the body informed by a liberated, sexually conscious self, while also exposing gender biases entrenched in the artworld and society at large. In so doing, they staked their claim as agents in modernism.

Women artists, the avant-garde and the nude

The phenomenon of the avant-garde and its mythologization in the annals of art is complex and multifarious, but art historians concur that it was largely impervious to women, both in its nascence and in its later theorization.[6] James Martin Harding observes, "with regard to questions of gender, studies of the vanguard have decisively remained in the rearguard."[7] Griselda Pollock writes:

> The initial institutionalization of modernism not only failed to acknowledge the centrality of gender to both modernity and its modernisms; it actively fabricated a monogendered, selective narrative of modern art, even in the living presence of the women who defined their moment of modernity through their massive participation in all areas of culture … museum curators and art historians produced a heroic and exclusively masculine legend of the avant-garde that is only being rectified invitationally.[8]

Despite their key and active role, women artists in early twentieth-century France remain grossly understudied and excluded from avant-garde history and theory, now, as then.[9] Over thirty years ago, Gill Perry established the necessary foundations for this book in *Women Artists and the Parisian Avant-garde.*[10] In the introduction, she observed that although the Impressionist period of the late nineteenth century and the twentieth-century movements of Constructivism and Surrealism had garnered significant attention by scholars who critically analyzed representations of and work by women, the early twentieth century languished for feminist scholarship. This book addresses this persistent omission with a focus on three modern women. Vassilieff,

Charmy and Valadon demonstrate the formative role women played in the avant-garde landscapes of Montmartre and Montparnasse, both within and against the movements of Post-Impressionism, Fauvism and Cubism.

In illuminating select women modernists, the aim is not merely to add to the roster of European avant-garde artists, but rather to shift the discourse around what constitutes and characterizes the avant-garde nude. This subject is pivotal because it is inherently gendered and rooted in the body – literally – and is thus never fully divested from matters of human sexuality. Politics of the body, decisively central to this book, and a series of core inquiries, steer the analysis of each artist's oeuvre. What are the consequences for women painting the body in a bold manner with utter disregard for artistic convention or "feminine" styles? What are the implications of a woman's intervention into the traditional practice and display of the nude and expression of desire in art? What happens when a woman disrupts the sanctioned gendered relationship between the viewer and the body in art? Furthermore, this book looks beyond the standard white female nude, and addresses how diverse bodies of different gender are represented. Pushing past a "monogendered" history of modern art, the myth of the masculine avant-garde begins to unravel.

That few women painted nudes in the early twentieth century is a falsehood that has been perpetuated in studies of modern art.[11] Rather, the female nude genre was as significant to women as to male artists at this time. Indeed, women as early as the Renaissance had managed to maneuver around obstacles and gain access to nude and anatomical education, especially on a private basis. Scholars such as Tamar Garb, Paula Birnbaum and Margaret Oppenheimer have shed light on women artists' access to the study of the live nude model in institutions and private academies as well as their exhibition of nudes in state-funded Salons and other exhibition venues in France.[12] Their findings topple long-held assumptions that women did not study or depict the naked body in any sustained or concerted manner. There are myriad exceptions in both academic and private settings beginning in the eighteenth century in France where brazen female artists gained access to the nude despite impediments and discouragement from institutions, social mores and their male peers. This book builds upon and expands this scholarship, not through an extensive overview of educational practices for women artists, nor through an exhaustive list of women who painted nudes in early twentieth century Paris, but through three specific case studies on painters who defied the odds of their era.

Already by the 1890s, women were increasingly engaging with the female nude, as Garb's seminal book cogently argues. The Union of Women Artists and Painters, founded in Paris in 1881, fought for women's rights to public art education that went hand in hand with nude study. Garb demonstrates that in most cases women who depicted the nude in the late nineteenth century did so in accordance with academic strictures.[13] Their nudes appear delicately modeled and in traditional settings and poses. Naturally, academically trained artists aspired to the tradition of *le grand art*. They strove to transform the body from its naked state into the elevated form of the nude, by rendering the figure with established techniques.[14] Consequently, women's depictions of the nude habitually conformed to "the standard erotic economy of their time."[15] When painted following longstanding methods, the female body was typically an object of the male gaze. One artist who resisted academic standards in her representations of the nude was Paula Modersohn-Becker. In her book *Paula Modersohn-Becker: The First Modern Woman Artist*, Diane Radycki posits that Modersohn-Becker introduced the subject of the "Mother Nude" in art.[16] Maternity was not a theme that Valadon, Charmy or Vassilieff dealt with at any length in their oeuvres. Although Charmy painted herself nude and pregnant, her work is expressive of autoeroticism, rather than motherly bliss, and she did not treat the subject of Mother Nude. Still, Radycki's work is instrumental to my own, especially her analyses of Modersohn-Becker's nude self-portraits. The artists in this book likewise depicted their own bodies from their independent viewpoints as individual women. That the outcomes were quite different further underscores the significance and complexity of this topic.

By the interwar period, nudes by women were readily visible in gallery and salon exhibitions. The French group la Société des Femmes Artistes Modernes, commonly known as FAM, founded in 1931 by Marie-Anne Camax-Zoegger, organized important exhibitions featuring art by women, including nudes in myriad styles.[17] Both Valadon and Charmy were members. Others included Tamara de Lempicka, Louise Hervieu and Mariette Lydis, all of whom painted eroticized female nudes discussed in Chapter 2.[18] Mela Muter, a Jewish artist from Poland who painted boldly realistic female nudes in the teens and twenties, exhibited with FAM. These are only a few examples, however. There are countless others, many of whom have been neglected in art historical literature but whose names will emerge as more scholars turn their attention to this subject.[19] By the 1930s and 1940s, a subsequent generation of women artists confronted the body in an increasingly audacious way as part of the Surrealist movement. Informed by Freudian psychoanalysis, they sought to give voice to their unconscious and unspoken desires. Female Surrealists were first spotlighted by Whitney Chadwick in the 1980s.[20] Chadwick's indispensable book on Surrealism commences at the point when this book concludes, at the end of the 1920s.

The male nude is rarely found in art by women during the first half of the twentieth century.[21] When opportunity allowed it, the initial step for women to study the male model seldom resulted in large-scale works for exhibition. Valadon was among the first women to exhibit male nudes before a French audience. In the uncommon instance where women exposed male nudes to the public, they were denounced by critics. They also had to contend with censorship, as is the case with

Valadon. Sometimes the police intervened. Before her arrival in France, Natalia Goncharova was arrested on charges of pornography for exhibiting male nudes in Moscow in 1910.[22] Women artists risked severe repercussions by painting the male nude. The scarcity of documented male nude studies by women prior to the twentieth century is partly because, historically, access to a fully naked male model was largely off limits for female art students in both institutional and private educational settings.[23] Oppenheimer traces the dynamic changes in artistic study for women in France to reveal that, contrary to scholarly assumptions, anatomical and life study in mixed-sexed, state-sanctioned settings was available to women during the fourth quarter of the eighteenth century. Women artists at that time benefitted from the reform and subsequent abolition of the Academy during the French Revolution.[24] Eventually, "the unusual access to coeducational anatomy and life study permitted to women during the Revolution and First Empire was ultimately repressed," Oppenheimer concedes.[25] During the nineteenth century in Paris, affluent women could enroll in private academies, which permitted life study with varying constraints, but it was nearly always a female model or a fully or partially clothed male model who posed.[26] When the École des Beaux-Arts officially opened its doors to women in 1897, academic nude training was being replaced with new approaches, exemplified by Vassilieff's modern art academy in Montparnasse, that spearheaded novel and egalitarian tactics to life study.

In addition to the male nude, Valadon and Vassilieff both engaged with the black model. Vassilieff hired Black men and women to pose at her academy, and her painting *Homme et femme* may feature a Black male nude. While Vassilieff primitivizes the Black body in her Cubist work, Valadon does not. Valadon worked closely with one Black model for her "Black Venus Series," an ignored portion of her oeuvre. Following a thesis by Ebonie Pollock devoted to this series, and in concurrence with a scholarly dialogue on Valadon's *Vénus noire*, I examine the painting within its racial and colonialist context in Chapter 3.[27] Moreover, I am indebted to Denise Murrell's *Posing Modernity*, a comprehensive and sustained analysis of the Black model in Western art, which prioritizes race, along with gender and class, as key issues in the study of Modern painting.[28] Integrating new avenues of analysis and inquiry, Murrell's research offers a springboard for critically dissecting portrayals of the Black model and inspired a quest into the identity of the woman in Valadon's *Vénus noire*.

La forme féminine or its antipode

Vassilieff, Charmy and Valadon experienced the turn-of-the-century turbulence that wholly altered art and life – an evolution of gender roles and social processes, which afforded new liberties as well as restrictions. The decade before World War

One was one potentially teeming with possibilities for women as educational and career opportunities grew. As of 1897, equal art education was afforded to women in Paris, at least nominally, and the numbers of women artists – French and foreign – multiplied.[29] Nevertheless, this remained a highly complex and unstable period for women, especially by the end of World War One.[30] In the 1910s and 1920s, women's social and political freedoms, compounded with new theories on gender and sexuality, threatened conservative bourgeois values and threw society into a quandary. The writer Pierre Drieu la Rochelle famously claimed that France in 1927 was a "civilization without sexes," describing it as a "disturbingly feminized place in the wake of the war's violence."[31] At the same time, writers saw "women were becoming more like men."[32] For many, distinctions between the sexes seemed to be dissolving.

The cultural figure *la garçonne* (the tomboy) emblematized the anxiety about the nebulousness of gender during the interwar period. Making her début in Victor Margueritte's *La Garçonne*, this modern personage represented the sexually open-minded woman who elected neither to marry nor to procreate.[33] The novel centers on the protagonist, Monique, and her quest for sexual freedom. This young, bourgeois woman rejects middle-class familial obligations, choosing to lead a promiscuous life with partners of both sexes. The book caused an uproar: it was banned by the Catholic Church, and its sale was forbidden throughout France. Margueritte's name was then expunged from the roll of the Legion of Honor. *La Garçonne* may have been shocking to contemporary readers, but it was not a demonstration of female emancipation. On the contrary, the book promoted a regressive view of woman and her sexuality, revealing more about the persistence of nineteenth-century values than the emergence of new ones.[34] Monique's uninhibited sexual lifestyle leaves her unfulfilled in the end. She decides to rescind her libertine ways, grow out her hair, and couple with an older man, thus accepting a traditional, feminine role. In retrospect, the tumult and controversy that Margueritte's novel sparked demonstrates a fierce repudiation of equality and anxiety towards women's sexuality. Women could experiment sexually, but only *inconspicuously* – public display of social or sexual freedom was intolerable. They were to be designated as demure wives and mothers, or as sex objects by bourgeois men.[35]

The 1925 edition of Margueritte's *La Garçonne* included illustrations by Kees Van Dongen. In these images, Monique is depicted in the form of a lithe *forme féminine* (feminine form).[36] The *forme féminine* was stylish and graceful, had white porcelain skin, an elongated body, adolescent form and girlish manner.[37] She appeared frequently in both popular imagery and magazines as well as in fine art, surfacing in works by male and female painters alike – Van Dongen, Marie Laurencin and Jacqueline Marval, as well as in fashion plates by Georges Barbier, René Bouché and

Jean Pagès.[38] Freed from the corset and restrictive fashions of the nineteenth century, she represented a progressive woman to popular French audiences. The façade of the *forme féminine*, like that of *la garçonne*, was made to seem liberated, yet carried obscurantist stereotypes. Indeed, the *forme féminine* was not very modern at all. This cultural phenomenon promoted a vision of femininity marked by youthfulness, prettiness and fragility. Vulnerable, childlike and completely unthreatening, the *forme féminine* assuaged societal gender anxieties.

Often, critics conflated female artists with the *forme féminine* depicted in their art. Louis Vauxcelles did so in his account of Laurencin, using the terms "*une forme féminine*" and "*un Marie Laurencin*" together.[39] Critics called attention to the delicate and graceful physical appearances of the artist and the female figures in their canvases – fusing the woman artist with her work. Moreover, they simultaneously merged this female type with a quintessential "feminine" style, a gendered mode of painting, which consisted of delicate color harmonies and soft, floating forms. Marval was lauded for her "feminine" approach. Celebrated for her "delicate" compositions, she was frequently compared with Laurencin. Apollinaire, for example, wrote in a glowing review: "Mme Marval has offered painting amateurs an altogether treat … Abstraction in not her strong point but she has a marvelous way of showing the poetical reality of the subjects she paints … Grace is the very French artistic quality that women like Mme Marval and Mlle Laurencin have preserved in art."[40] Rather than ingenuity, Marval's art is marked by "grace," leaving those "masculine" forays of "technical innovation" to men. Apollinaire concludes that even amateurs (presumably female viewers) can delight in her confectionary creations.

Vassilieff, Charmy and Valadon did not easily win over critics. Laurencin and Marval were extolled by Vauxcelles in his grand art survey, *Histoire générale de l'art français de la révolution à nos jours*, from which Valadon (except for a cursory mention) and Vassilieff are noticeably absent. Only Charmy is described in the text.[41] A few years later, all three were excluded from the momentous exhibition *Cinquante ans de peinture française* in 1925. Organized by Vauxcelles during the *Exposition International des arts décoratifs et industriels modernes*, it served as a showcase of French modern art.[42] When Berthe Weill confronted Vauxcelles about these omissions, he professed, "I don't like Valadon's painting; not more than Charmy's!"[43] Recounting this exchange in her memoir, Weill lamented:

> The history of painting of women is made according to what the [male] author likes or admits is valid; artists who do not appeal to him should be erased from the history of art. Simply put, 'Art' is too abused at the mercy of the agio.[44]

Their art was often seen as "masculine." Critics typified Valadon's use of thick contours outlining the body as "virile." This characterization reflects a larger tendency in art criticism to classify linear styles as male. According to the established *disegno* versus *colorito* binary, a tradition going back to the Renaissance, the former was associated with masculine painting styles and the latter with a female approach. As Norma Broude argues, and as Valadon's case attests, this conservative viewpoint persisted in art writing well into the twentieth century.[45] At the same time, rough, impasto-laden surfaces and vivid color also denoted masculinity for early twentieth-century critics. When Roland Dorgelès declared in 1921 that "Émilie Charmy … sees like a woman and paints like a man," he signaled her masterful and vigorous execution as contradictory to gendered notions of painting.[46] Moreover, technical innovation, scientific approaches and brutal forms were allegedly not the purview of women painters. Apollinaire made this clear in his snide tribute to Marval. The same critic had earlier hinted at the harshness and acidity of Vassilieff's Cubist paintings, without fully avowing it. He writes that with "voluptuous science" her art "imbues charms that sometimes redeem the brutality of forms."[47] In pursuing Cubism, Vassilieff trespassed on male terrain and posed a threat.

Male critics defended the domain of male artists by diminishing the artistic achievements of women. They went as far as insulting them. Of Valadon, Georges Charensol states, "If I name Marie Laurencin it seems to me that she represents the most qualified representative of feminine painters, since Suzanne Valadon owes almost nothing to her sex." He then states, "It is evident that Suzanne Valadon's painting is entirely virile."[48] According to Charensol, Valadon, who "paints like a man," is the opposite of Laurencin, a true "feminine painter." As Perry explains, "Valadon's strong, bold use of form and colour was seen to transgress the boundaries of femininity."[49] Evidently, women artists whose styles were not excessively feminine were considered manly. Moreover, Charensol insinuates Valadon's anomalous aberration from her gender. While virility, when applied to a male artist, could imply intellect, dexterity, and originality, in the case of a female artist, such adjectives were not acclamatory but implied abnormality or deviance. This tendency to ascribe sexuality and virility to artistic creativity was identified in Carol Duncan's seminal essay, "Virility and Domination in Early Twentieth-Century Vanguard Painting" in 1973.[50] Decades later, Natasha Staller's description of the avant-garde female nude "painted large in scale, painted aggressively, painted in a resolutely androgynous or anti-feminine manner" evinces the perpetuation of this proclivity in the histories of early twentieth-century art.[51] Women artists do not surface in Staller's important book on Picasso. Contrariwise, Vassilieff, Charmy and Valadon painted nudes "aggressively" on a grand scale, and in many cases "in a resolutely androgynous or anti-feminine manner." Their art refutes the existence of distinct or essential "feminine" or "masculine" styles of painting.

Case studies on three modern women in reverse chronological order

Painting Her Pleasure demonstrates how the formation of an embodied and sexually conscious self is inflected in complex and myriad ways in artwork by Vassilieff, Charmy and Valadon. It highlights the interdependence of this sexually conscious self with specific socio-historical discourses on the evolving views of gender, sexuality, age, class and race. We can view with a fresh eye the subject of female artists and the nude by expanding beyond the customary theories applied when examining this topic, such as the gaze. Attentive to intersectional feminisms, there is no "singular" gaze in *Painting Her Pleasure*. These artists' works involve various types of gazes in their production and reception beyond the hegemonic male gaze; these include the model's gaze, homoerotic gaze and androgynous gaze. Similarly, no single theory or concept could succinctly illuminate all of their oeuvres. Any attempt to compare these artists and identify a shared style or technique further underscores the diversity between them. Here, each artist is the subject of a vivid case study, with a catered methodological approach. Literary criticism along with theories of embodiment, touch and perception inform these analyses. I remain cognizant of the fact that these artists lacked a feminist agenda, as they were working in an era when current arguments about gender roles were not yet formulated.

The chapters in this book are purposefully organized in reverse chronological order. As well as a nod to Bergson's theories broached in Chapter 1, this achronological approach is meant to foreground the artists who have undeservedly escaped art historical study. Accordingly, the book commences with the least well-known of the trio and concludes with the most recognized. Vassilieff is thus the focus of Chapter 1. An active member of the Parisian avant-garde, she ran an academy promoting the latest techniques and concepts, concurrently generating her own Cubist drawings and paintings. Being of Russian origin, her career was impacted by xenophobia rampant in early twentieth-century Paris. During World War One, she was falsely accused of being a Bolshevik spy and imprisoned, and her studio was ransacked. *Homme et femme* (c. 1910–14) is one of the few pre-war Cubist works which miraculously survived. The painting presents a female and a male nude of different skin tone, painted recto-verso. In this double-sided work, Vassilieff pronounces the interchangeability between gender and race stylistically as well as across time and space. Although resonating with Salon Cubism, the painting counters the misogynist notions permeating vanguard circles. Bergson's concept of *élan vital* informed Salon Cubists' representations of the nude and *retardataire* gender views. Experimenting with the male and female nude simultaneously, Vassilieff merged and conflated their characteristics into androgynous bodies in defiance of such theories. After World War One, she continued to explore gender disruption in her self-portraits, while breaking down the barriers between craft and fine art. In *Poupée-autoportrait*, a mixed-media nude self-portrait doll, she counters the designations of "low" and "high" art forms, elevating a household object to the realm of sculpture. Simultaneously, she extracts the doll from its associations with girlhood and femininity, to disrupt gender conventions. Through her doll self-portrait, she reconsiders her own manifold identity as she pushes past binaries of gender and race. Vassilieff's work attests that fluidity, rather than division, delineates the modern nude.

The second chapter centers on Charmy's varied approaches to the body. Her most sensual renderings were intended not for public viewership, but for her own private pleasure. Charmy forged innovative artistic methods for the expression of her desires, some of which resonate with rhetorical strategies in Colette's novels. During her lifetime, Charmy was frequently compared to the author. This book is the first to analyze the equivalences in their works. Examining Charmy's art and Colette's literature in tandem uncovers ways in which Charmy through brushwork, and Colette through rhetoric, probed the subject of woman's sexual satisfaction and same-sex sexuality. Uniquely, Charmy's work is distinguished by its tactility. Painting the nude in a provocative manner with luscious impasto and striking applications of color, her paintings are as much tactile as they are visual representations of the body. Analyzing Charmy's work in relation to feminist theorist Luce Irigaray's psychoanalytic writings and phenomenological concepts, I posit that Charmy crafted an *aesthetic of female jouissance*. Aware of the avant-garde preoccupation with touch that concerned male painters, I contend that Charmy's emphasis on feminine *jouissance* negates the implications of possession of the female body that touch and paint have traditionally inferred. Many of Charmy's erotic nudes are, in fact, self-portraits. She often substituted her own body for a model's in the studio. Only subtly recognizable as self-portraits, these nudes collapse the long-established division between artist and model and subject and object. Through these paintings, Charmy expressed autoeroticism and feminine erotics. She redefined the boundaries of self-representation and introduced a new subject to the history of art – the pregnant nude self-portrait.

Chapter 3 examines Valadon's dissident practice, focusing on select nudes and examining them in relation to issues of race, gender, embodiment and sexuality. Throughout her career, Valadon consciously broke societal taboos. This chapter expands upon the earlier contributions of Mathews and Betterton, to consider the lesser-studied aspects of Valadon's oeuvre.[52] Acknowledging variations in Valadon's work and its provocative nature, I highlight her most contentious works, while resisting broad generalizations about her oeuvre in its entirety. Although not divorced from its racist and colonialist context, Valadon's *Vénus noire* is one of the earliest known examples of a single, idealized Black female nude in Western European painting.

This controversial work is discussed at length, as well as her series of aged nude self-portraits – among the first to frankly document the unique aging process for women. Valadon portrays her own maturation as an enabling process rather than stressing the deterioration of physical, mental and sexual capabilities. She also dauntingly turned to the male form with intensity, capturing different materializations of the male body – idealized and unidealized, active and passive. With André Utter as her muse, she rendered her unhindered sexual desires on canvas, unnerving male spectators. In certain images, she succeeded in capturing the embodied presence of her subjects.

The absent archive

In the absence of diaries, artist notebooks, ample correspondence and comprehensive accounts recorded during her epoch, Valadon's past has been transformed into the stuff of legends. Her extraordinary metamorphosis from model to artist and her ties with male artists often eclipse any thorough account of her work. The details of her biography, which is plagued with gaps and inconsistencies, have been repeated in reduced and celebratory form in both academic and popular literature – from exhibition catalogues to monographs, and from novels to guidebooks – which in turn have been perpetuated in the oral history of Montmartre. Equipped with only a rudimentary education, Valadon did not write profusely about her art or life. Her extant written statements include two brief essays: "Suzanne Valadon ou l'absolu" and "La nature et la peinture." An interview with the critic Adolphe Tabarant details her experience as a model posing for Puvis de Chavannes, Renoir and other artists, but reveals little about her art. Scant correspondence remains. While the Association Maurice Utrillo reportedly maintains an archive, its utility cannot be measured, as few scholars are granted access.[53] One of the most important primary sources on Valadon is an unpublished manuscript by her partner, André Utter, held in the Kandinsky library at the Musée National d'Art Moderne. Utter was an artist deeply connected with Valadon as her former husband, dealer and manager. Told from his perspective, the text illuminates lesser-known aspects of her life and work. Recognizing that this document is not entirely accurate or complete, it is nevertheless a chief source for Chapter 3.

Known to alter information about herself, including her birthdate, Valadon played a role in mythologizing herself. On paintings, she would sometimes add dates and inscriptions years later. This jeopardizes any researcher's quest for "truth." In a recent doctoral thesis, Yelin Zhao acknowledges these difficulties.[54] She discusses the implications of Valadon's mythologization on the reception and reading of her work. She explains how her fabled identity perpetuates in biographies. Although there are many biographies, few of them are of scholarly merit, and most repeat rumors and overemphasize her sexual relations with other art-world figures. Catherine Hewitt's biography is a recent and well-researched account of Valadon's life.[55] Considering the extant and accessible archival documentations, the main aspects of Valadon's early life and work are laid out succinctly, before segueing to in-depth and nuanced art historical analyses.

Vassilieff's unpublished memoir reveals how an artist can employ autobiography to claim or infer a status or intention. Although this account gives vital insights into her life and work, particularly her studies with Matisse, the formation of her academy, life-modeling sessions and canteen, it is replete with embellishments and unverifiable anecdotes. Writting in 1929 after the highpoint of her career, she emphasizes her relationships with key artists of the period as she attempts to secure a voice for herself within the Parisian avant-garde. Unfortunately, her efforts to publish the manuscript failed along with her aim to forge a legacy, as her name subsequently fell into obscurity. Her archive, maintained by an enthusiastic collector, Claude Bernès, offers a wealth of material as well as her works in myriad media – drawings, posters, sculpture, masks, furniture and more. For more than four decades, Bernès has devotedly amassed a collection of Vassilieff's art and germane material. His Parisian apartment serves as her archive and resembles a shrine. Without this essential depository, it would not have been possible to conduct research on this artist. As for Charmy, rather than mythologization, her case is one of incompleteness or erasure. Privately held, her archive is not readily accessible and is highly fragmented. The materials are not collected in one place but are revealed piecemeal to the researcher. The guarded nature of the archive as well as the inaccessibility of a great number of her works in storage precludes a full understanding of her oeuvre. The heightened concealment creates an aura of secrecy, which the artist herself seems to have endorsed during her lifetime. More vitally, it hampers scholars' attempts to research the artist; correspondingly, it perpetuates the artist's anonymity in the histories of modernism. Charmy's extant correspondence is limited and is mostly from the latter part of her life. No trace of a written exchange with Colette was found in the hands of the descendants or in the various Colette archives in France. An assortment of newspaper clippings of laudatory reviews exposes a fleeting moment of fame, but no depth of understanding. No written statements by Charmy have survived.

The paucity of archival information on Vassilieff, Charmy and Valadon raises numerous insoluble questions regarding who, besides the artist, accumulated and safeguarded the material at the time of their death, and what were their principal motivations. In Charmy's case, one wonders if the artist had a hand in discarding letters or documents throughout her life. She seems to have been intentionally vague and elusive, in her temperament as well as in her art. In Valadon's case it is vexing why certain extraneous details were safeguarded, while other critical documents were erased or excluded. The Valadon archives at the Musée National d'Art Moderne were donated by her patron and friend, Docteur Robert le Masle. One finds a more seemingly whole composite of letters and documents from diverse periods of the artist's life. But there are many holes in the archive. Much of the documentation relates to Utrillo, his drunken escapades and his arrests. If one delves deeper in search of specific details, such as a model's name, the information is often lacking. Superfluous surprises are made instead. While mining the archives, in the very last box, I discovered the most curious of objects – a lock of Valadon's hair from her deathbed. This relic reveals more about the non-objectivity and non-neutrality of the archive. It demonstrates the initial archivist's reverence toward Valadon but tells us virtually nothing about the artist herself.

In Jacques Derrida's *Archive Fever: A Freudian Impression*, the philosopher theorizes the formation of historical knowledge. "Archive fever" he argues is "a compulsive, repetitive and nostalgic desire for the archive."[56] The converse, but essential for the desire to archive to exist, is the "archive drive," which follows the logic of Freud's "death drive" in its will to eradicate. In the case of the three artists studied in this book, "archive fever" and "archive drive" are held in a tenuous, unequal balance. Those who shaped the archive made critical decisions, from assembling the documentation and determining what can and cannot be accessed, to deciding what is preserved and what is destroyed. These choices led to a fragmentary record of the artists' lives, and consequently, gaps in our knowledge of their work as well as their intentions. An archivist's decisions lay the basis for collective memory and historical knowledge, but they also lay the foundations for authority because, ultimately, those who control the archive control the memory. Here, the archive reveals its ambivalence for women artists, as a contradictory phenomenon which makes their agency both visible and invisible. This book carefully navigates through the silences and absences in the archive to recount the histories of three lesser known but important artists. Rather than scrutinize each piece of extant documentary evidence with a magnifying glass, I remain highly vigilant of errors, elaborations, and archival omissions. Although they exerted little if any control over the collection and preservation of material now constituting their respective archives, Vassilieff, Charmy and Valadon nevertheless played a critical role in their own historicization in one poignant way – by painting self-portraits. In so doing, they enacted a form of self-documentation. In the face of the archive's and Modernist history's omissions, their self-portraits serve as testaments of individual memory and lived experience.

Notes

1 One of the earliest known nude self-portraits painted by a woman is Jacqueline Marval's *Odalisque au guépard* (1900, oil on canvas), purchased by Ambroise Vollard in 1901. Collection Comité Jacqueline Marval, Paris. Another early example is Paula

Modersohn-Becker's *Self-Portrait on the 6th Wedding Anniversary* (1906, oil and tempera on cardboard). Museen Böttcherstraße, Paula Modersohn-Becker Museum, Bremen.

2 The female identities, *la femme nouvelle* and *la femme moderne*, and the differences between them are myriad and complex. The former is largely associated with the *fin-de-siècle* and the latter with the interwar period in France. See: Mary Roberts, *Disruptive Acts: The New Woman in Fin-de-Siècle France* (Chicago: University of Chicago Press, 2005), 3; Mary Roberts, *Civilization without Sexes: Reconstructing Gender in Postwar France, 1917–1927* (Chicago: University of Chicago Press, 1994), 19.

3 This is noted in Vassilieff's unpublished memoir. Marie Vassilieff, *La Bohème du XXe siècle* (unpublished memoir), 1929, Vassilieff archives, Paris. See also Marie Vassilieff, "Au poteau de torture: Marie Wassilieff par Marie Wassilieff," in *Paris-Montparnasse*, March 15, 1929, 12.

4 *Charmy* (Paris: Galerie Paul Pétridès, 1963).

5 Gill Perry, *Women Artists and the Parisian Avant-garde* (Manchester: Manchester University Press, 1995), 141.

6 Key sources which examine and theorize the avant-garde broadly include Peter Bürger, *Theory of the Avant-Garde*, translated by Michael Shaw (Minneapolis: University of Minnesota Press, 1984); Clement Greenberg, "Avant-Garde and Kitsch," *Partisan Review* 6 (1939), 34–49; Renato Poggioli, *The Theory of the Avant-garde*, translated by Gerald Fitzgerald (Cambridge: The Belknap Press of Harvard University Press, 1969).

7 James Martin Harding, *Cutting Performances: Collage Events, Feminist Artists, and the American Avant-Garde* (Ann Arbor: University of Michigan Press, 2012), 8.

8 Griselda Pollock, "Moments and Temporalities of the Avant-garde 'in, of, and from the feminine,'" *New Literary History* 41, no. 4 (2010), 795.

9 A select list of publications which address the absence of women from the European avant-garde includes Whitney Chadwick, *Women Artists and the Surrealist Movement* (New York: Thames & Hudson, 2002); Carol Duncan, "Virility and Domination in Early Twentieth-century Vanguard Painting," in *Feminism and Art History: Questioning the Litany*, ed. Norma Broude and Mary D. Garrard (New York: Harper & Row Publishers, 1982), 293–313; Perry, *Women Artists and the Parisian Avant-garde*.

10 Perry, *Women Artists and the Parisian Avant-garde*.

11 Perry criticizes Betterton and Matthews for stating that Valadon's choice to paint the female nude was unusual for a woman artist by 1900. Ibid., 127; Rosemary Betterton. "How Do Women Look? The Female Nude in the Work of Suzanne Valadon," in *Looking On: Images of Femininity in the Visual Arts and Media* (London: Pandora Press, 1987); Patricia Mathews, "Returning the Gaze: Diverse Representations of the Nude in the Art of Suzanne Valadon." *The Art Bulletin* 73, no. 3 (1991), 415–30.

12 Paula J. Birnbaum, *Women Artists in Interwar France: Framing Femininities* (Farnham: Ashgate, 2011); Tamar Garb, *Sisters of the Brush: Women's Artistic Culture in Late Nineteenth Century Paris* (New Haven: Yale University Press, 1994); Margaret A. Oppenheimer, "'The Charming Spectacle of a Cadaver': Anatomical and Life Study by Women Artists in Paris, 1775–1815." *Nineteenth-Century Art Worldwide* 6, no. 1 (Spring 2007), www.19thc-artworldwide.org/spring07/142-qthe-charming-spectacle-of-a-cadaverq-anqthe-charming-spectacle-of-a-cadaverq-anatomical-and-life-study-by-women-artists-in-

paris-17751815atomical-and-life-study-by-women-artists-in-paris-17751815. Accessed May 20, 2023).

13 Garb, *Sisters of the Brush*, 133.

14 Kenneth Clark, *The Nude: A Study in Ideal Form* (New York: Pantheon Books, 1956).

15 Garb, *Sisters of the Brush*, 134.

16 Diane Radycki, *Paula Modersohn-Becker: The First Modern Woman Artist* (New Haven: Yale University Press, 2013), 172.

17 Birnbaum, *Women Artists in Interwar France: Framing Femininities*, 1.

18 Ibid., 189–220.

19 A recent exhibition sheds light on women artists active in Paris during the interwar period. For information on nudes and nude self-portraits by women at this moment, see Lauren Jimerson, "Les Nus et auto-portraits nus des pionnières du XXe siècle," in *Pionnières: artistes dans le Paris des années folles*, edited by Camille Morineau and Lucia Pesapane (Paris: Editions de la Réunion des Musées Nationaux – Grand Palais, 2022).

20 Chadwick, *Women Artists and the Surrealist Movement*. Also see Whitney Chadwick, *Farewell to the Muse: Love, War and the Women of Surrealism* (New York, New York: Thames & Hudson, 2017).

21 One of the earliest known examples of a male nude by a woman artist in France is a drawing of the back of a male nude done by Marie-Anne Pierrette Lavoisier (1758–1836) in 1786, as well as a series of undated life drawings of male models by Pauline Auzou (1775–1835). Oppenheimer, "'The Charming Spectacle of a Cadaver,'" 79.

22 Jane Sharp, *Russian Modernism between East and West: Natal'ia Goncharova and the Moscow Avant-garde* (Cambridge: Cambridge University Press, 2006), 103.

23 Garb, *Sisters of the Brush*, 82.

24 Oppenheimer, "'The Charming Spectacle of a Cadaver,'" 68.

25 Ibid., 81.

26 Garb, *Sisters of the Brush*, 80.

27 Ebonie Pollock, "Suzanne Valadon's *Black Venus:* The Representation and Reception of the Black Artist's Model in Interwar Paris" (BA thesis, Washington University in St. Louis, 2019), Adrienne L. Childs, Nancy Ireson, Lauren Jimerson, Denise Murrell, Ebonie Pollock, "Disrupting Tradition: Suzanne Valadon's *Black Venus*," transcribed and edited by Corrinne Chong. In *Suzanne Valadon: Model, Painter, Rebel*, edited by Nancy Ireson (Philadelphia: The Barnes Foundation in association with London: Paul Holberton Publishing, 2021), 30–41.

28 Denise Murrell, *Posing Modernity: The Black Model from Manet and Matisse to Today* (New Haven: Yale University Press, 2018).

29 Laurence Madeline, *Women Artists in Paris, 1850–1900* (New Haven: Yale University Press, 2017).

30 Whitney Chadwick and Tirza Latimer, "Becoming Modern," in *The Modern Woman Revisited: Paris between the Wars* (New Brunswick: Rutgers University Press, 2003), 4–5.

31 Pierre Drieu la Rochelle quoted in Amy Lyford, *Surrealist Masculinities: Gender Anxiety and the Aesthetics of Post-World War I Reconstruction in France* (Berkeley: University of California Press, 2007), 115.

32 Lyford, *Surrealist Masculinities*, 115.

33 The Surrealists were fascinated with *la garçonne*, which inspired the creation of the androgyne. Depicted by Breton, Masson and others, the androgyne functioned as a figure through which male artists could appropriate facets of femininity for themselves. Whitney Chadwick and Dawn Ades, *Mirror Images: Women, Surrealism, and Self-Representation* (Cambridge: MIT Press, 1998), 35.
34 Christine Bard, *Les Garçonnes: modes et fantasmes des années folles* (Paris: Flammarion, 1998), 78; Marcelline Hutton, *Russian and West European Women, 1860–1939: Dreams, Struggles, and Nightmares* (Lanham: Rowman & Littlefield, 2001), 144.
35 Philippe Ariès and Michelle Perrot (eds), *A History of Private Life: From the Fires of Revolution to the Great War*, vol. 4 (Cambridge, MA: Belknap Press of Harvard University Press, 1990), 590–611.
36 Illustrated in Jan Juffermans, *Kees Van Dongen: The Graphic Work* (Aldershot: Lund Humphries, 2003), 132–5.
37 For a comprehensive discussion of *la forme féminine*, see: Perry, *Women Aritsts and the Parisian avant-garde*, 107–15.
38 Ibid.
39 Louis Vauxcelles, *Histoire générale de l'art français, de la Révolution à nos jours* (Paris: Librarie de France, 1922), 321.
40 Guillaume Apollinaire, "Les Peintresses, Chroniques d'Art," *Le Petit Bleu*, April 5, 1912.
41 Vauxcelles, *Histoire générale de l'art français*, 321.
42 *Cinquante ans de peinture française, 1875–1925* (Paris: Éditions Albert Lévy, 1925). Valadon's work was excluded but a painting by her son, Maurice Utrillo, was shown.
43 Berthe Weill, *Pan! Dans l'oeil!* ... (Paris: Librairie Lipschutz, 1933), 294.
44 Ibid., 294–5.
45 Norma Broude, *Impressionism: A Feminist Reading: The Gendering of Art, Science, and Nature in the Nineteenth Century* (Boulder: Westview Press/Icon Editions, 1997), 14.
46 Henri Béraud, Roland Dorgelès et al., *Émilie Charmy* (Paris: Galeries d'Oeuvres d'Art, 1921).
47 Guillaume Apollinaire, "Les Peintres russes Impasse Ronsin. La vérité sur l'affaire Steinheil," *L'Intransigeant*, October 31, 1910. In Apollinaire, *Chroniques d'art, 1902–1918*, ed. Leroy Breunig (Paris: Gallimard, 2002), 162.
48 Georges Charensol, "Suzanne Valadon," *L'Art Vivant* 3 (1927), 75.
49 Gill Perry, "Women Painting Women: Gender, Modernism and 'Feminine' Art c. 1910–c. 1930," in *Rethinking Art between the Wars: New Perspectives in Art History*, edited by Hans D. Christensen, Niels Jensen-Marup and Øystein Hjort (Copenhagen: Museum Tusculanum Press: University of Copenhagen, 2001), 47.
50 Duncan, "Virility and Domination in Early Twentieth-Century Vanguard Painting."
51 Natasha E. Staller, *A Sum of Destructions: Picasso's Cultures & the Creation of Cubism* (New Haven: Yale University Press, 2002), 318.
52 Betterton, "How Do Women Look?"; Patricia Mathews, *Passionate Discontent: Creativity, Gender, and French Symbolist Art* (Chicago: University of Chicago Press, 1999), 207.
53 Association Maurice Utrillo, Pierrefitte sur Seine.

54 Yelin Zhao. "Ambitious Model, Ambiguous Artist: Three Case Studies of Victorine Meurent, Suzanne Valadon and Alice Prin." Ph.D. dissertation, The University of Leeds, 2018.

55 Catherine Hewitt, *Renoir's Dancer: The Secret Life of Suzanne Valadon* (New York: St. Martin's Press, 2017).

56 Jacques Derrida, *Archive Fever: A Freudian Impression*, translated by Eric Prenowitz (Chicago: University of Chicago Press, 2005), 91.

1 "Ni homme, ni femme":[1] Marie Vassilieff's androgyny

On a sunny afternoon in August of 1916, Jean Cocteau photographed a group of friends on boulevard Montparnasse (figure 1.1). He captured them before the iconic Art Nouveau metro entrance and the popular café La Rotonde. The Chilean painter Manuel Ortiz de Zárate lights a cigarette and next to him the writer Henri-Pierre Roché appears in uniform. The poet Max Jacob sports a polka-dotted bow tie, while Pablo Picasso holds an envelope perhaps containing samples of his work.[2] In front of this motley crowd stands a petite woman with her face engulfed in shadow. She appears as a dapper dandy with her tailored jacket and wide-brimmed hat. Clothed entirely in black except for a white collared shirt, she blends harmoniously with her male comrades. Who is she?

Marie Vassilieff is a rare example of a female Cubist who was at the critical nexus of the avant-garde, and one of the few who pursued an intensive study of the body in art. This chapter explores androgyny as it permeates Vassilieff's oeuvre. In the decade before World War One, Vassilieff captured the body in accordance with a dynamic experience of time and space, central to the Cubists' objectives. However, unlike her male peers, Vassilieff directly challenged misogynist ideas, overthrew hegemonic binaries and represented gender as shifting and equivocal. Experimenting with the male and female nude together, she conflated their characteristics into ambiguous bodies and underscored the interchangeability between gender. After World War One, she invented the self-portrait doll as an apparatus of gender disruption. Through her paintings and mixed-media sculptures, Vassilieff flouted gender norms and asserted a self-image that was subversive and modern.

From Russia to Paris

Little is known about Vassilieff's early life in Russia.[3] She was born Maria Ivanovna Vassilieva on February 12, 1884 in Smolensk, to a bourgeois family.[4] Vassilieff was exposed as a child to art through a neighboring artist's colony, Talashkino, established in the late nineteenth century by Princess Tenisheva to save and promote peasant arts and crafts.[5] The influence of traditional Russian folk art would surface in certain works such as *The Dance* (c. 1910–13) (Plate 3) (painted recto-verso

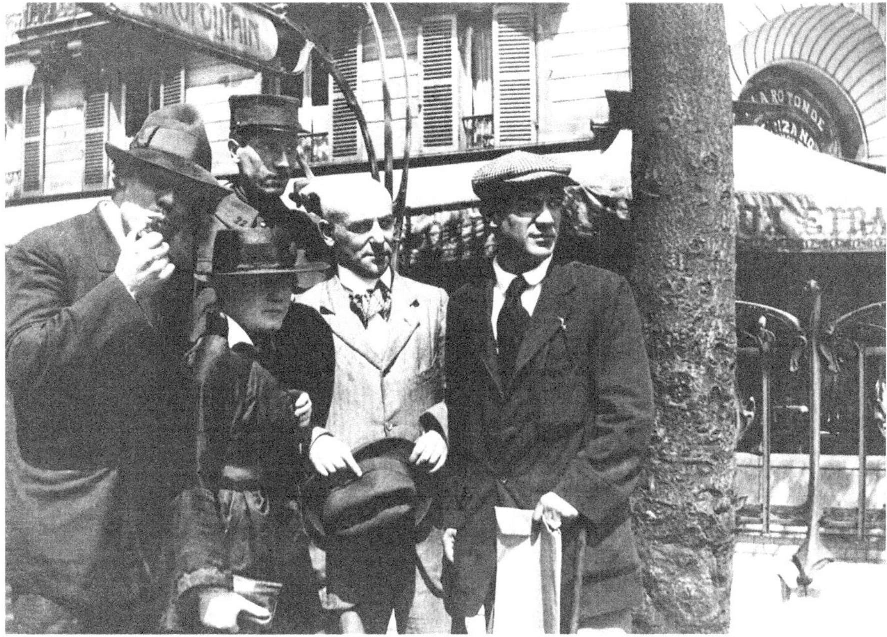

Figure 1.1 Jean Cocteau, Photograph of Marie Vassilieff with Picasso and other artists, August 12, 1916

with *Portrait de Femme*). Vassilieff left Smolensk to attend medical school in Saint Petersburg, presumably at the Women's Medical Institute, opened in 1897 under Tsar Nicholas II.[6] In 1903, Vassilieff changed course. She left medical school and enrolled in the Imperial Academy of Fine Arts in Saint Petersburg, which had opened admissions to women in 1891.[7] The details of her artistic study in Saint Petersburg remain unknown.[8] In 1905, with a grant from the Tsarina Alexandra Feodorovna, Vassilieff traveled to Paris to study art.[9] Her memoir, written in 1929, begins at this moment.[10] On her way to the mecca of the art world, she stopped in Germany, Italy and Spain. She wrote in her memoir that while in Munich she cut her hair short and distributed revolutionary leaflets in the streets – ironically, on the empress's dime. In Munich, she met the artist Jules Pascin, who was involved with the satirical German journal, *Simplicissimus*. She described herself as she embarked on her adventure across Europe:

> Yes, it's me, Marie Vassilieff, very small, all blonde, all round, gray eyes, very short, slightly curly hair, who for twenty years already, lives in this hell, this paradise, the only, unique Paris. I still remember my comic arrival, straight from the provincial Munich, and my very short brown velvet skirt, my darker brown velvet jacket, my black and white checkered cap, my child's shoes, yellow and very shiny … [an] appearance neither man nor woman.[11]

Vassilieff embodied a gender-neutral appearance. Photographs by Cocteau and Man Ray (1923) demonstrate that she frequently dressed in men's attire. Through dress, demeanor, lifestyle and artistic practice, Vassilieff flaunted androgyny. She divorced herself from expectations of bourgeois womanhood and asserted her individuality.

The details of her earliest years in Paris from 1905 to 1908 are muddled, including where she lived and studied.[12] Scholars suggest that Vassilieff, along with Sonia Terk (Delaunay) and Kruglikova, took courses at La Palette. This private art academy was popular among Russian artists.[13] Sofia Dymshits-Tolstaya studied there in 1910 and from 1912 to 1913 Nadezhda Udaltsova and Liubov Popova joined the ranks of Russian students.[14] Unfortunately, none of this information is relayed in Vassilieff's memoir. Her autobiography is a blend of fact and fiction. Written after the height of her career, it reads partly as a nostalgic recollection as well as an attempt to mythologize her persona and to solidify her artistic legacy. She likely omitted certain details about her early years in order to emphasize Matisse as her chief teacher.

Vassilieff first saw Matisse's work at the 1908 Salon d'Automne. She dramatically recounts the episode in her memoir. Enamored by his painting, she bravely decided to pay the artist a visit. She knocked on his door and said, "I would be happy if you could grant me the favor of correcting my studies after the nude." Matisse replied, "Well, come tomorrow to my school and I will be your teacher."[15] He ran an academy at that time and had a spare room that Vassilieff rented along with another Russian artist, Olga Markusovna Meerson.[16] This was an intensive period of artistic study for Vassilieff. She appears in a group photograph with Matisse and his other students in the spring of 1910.[17] At his academy, Vassilieff absorbed Matisse's approach to still life, the nude and portraiture as evidenced by her earliest extant works: *La Statue et le comptoir bleu* (1910–12) and *Nature morte à la cruche* (c. 1909). With its loud colors, *Portrait d'une femme au chapeau* (c. 1908) is reminiscent of Matisse's Fauve work with a similar title, *Femme au chapeau* (1905).[18] In spring 1909, she translated Matisse's "Notes of a Painter" (1908) for the Russian journal *La Toison d'Or*.[19] Much to her dismay, the editor did not give her credit for her work, signing his own name instead.

By translating "Notes of a Painter," Vassilieff was introduced to the theories of Henri Bergson. Matisse refers to the concept of *la durée* (duration), an intuitive perception of time in his essay, stating, "a rapid rendering of a landscape represents only one moment of its duration."[20] Art historians have highlighted the influence of Bergson on Matisse beginning around 1908.[21] This interest deepened from 1909 onward through his connection with the mathematician Matthew Stewart Prichard.[22] As Matisse's student and tenant, Vassilieff likely had access to the Bergson books in his library.[23] Exposed to these concepts through her teacher, they would later inform her Cubist nudes.

Outgoing and garrulous, Vassilieff quickly became acquainted with other members of the avant-garde, including Serge de Diaghilev. She may have seen his monumental exhibition on Russian art at the Salon d'Automne in 1906. She frequented La Ruche (the beehive), an affordable and dilapidated artists' residence in Montparnasse adjacent to an abattoir. There, she encountered Marc Chagall, Chaïm Soutine, Diego Rivera, Alexandre Archipenko, Ossip Zadkin and Fernand Léger. According to her memoir, Henri Rousseau proposed marriage to her, but she firmly refused. She became especially close with Léger and his wife, Jeanne. She also befriended Max Jacob, Georges Braque, Picasso, Blaise Cendrars, Marie Vorobieff (Marevna), Suzanne Valadon, Erik Satie, the critic André Salmon and the fashion designer Paul Poiret. The latter would become an important advocate of Vassilieff's art, especially her *poupées portraits*. Portraits of her by Amedeo Modigliani (c. 1916) and Tsugouharu Foujita (1925) attest to her close bonds with the painters and involvement in the avant-garde.[24] Letters to Picasso and Robert Delaunay in 1912 validate her efforts to promote these artists in Russia.[25] Still, she remained distinctly isolated from her peers in manifold ways. In the catalogue of a posthumous exhibition, André Salmon wrote,

> She saw a lot of people, but essentially had few friends. She systematically presented her eccentric side to others, and it would have been very difficult for me to have an exchange with her to discuss, among other things, her art. Beneath her thin veneer of sociability, she was terribly wild.[26]

Vassilieff was at once immersed in the avant-garde and on the fringe. In this chapter, I demonstrate how this paradox is reflected in her oeuvre, in both her paintings and her doll sculptures.

Académie Marie Vassilieff

Beginning in 1909, Vassilieff exhibited regularly at the Salon d'Automne as well as at the Salon des Indépendants. When the Salon Cubists ignited a *succès de scandale* in salle 41 (room 41) of the 1911 Salon des Indépendants, Vassilieff's paintings were displayed in a nearby room dedicated to Russian artists.[27] Unfortunately, the six paintings she exhibited are now lost.[28] Thus, what Apollinaire meant by his terse and peculiar comment, "Madame Vassilieff loves the exotic," is unclear.[29] When Matisse closed his academy in 1910, Vassilieff founded her own modern painting school. She rented the Villa Steinheil for this purpose and created a supportive community of artists.[30] In her memoir, she writes:

> I founded a large Academy of modern painting ... in order to be able to realize my ambition: to unite all artists, that is to say, to found a society based on liberty, equality, fraternity, on the republican ideal in short, which could give very good results. Then I choose, in agreement with my dear comrades, twelve of them to form the Committee, of which I was elected president, one and only woman among these democrats, these communists.[31]

She advocated an egalitarian vision based on French republican principles. That year, she organized an exhibition entitled *Exposition artistique franco-russe*, in collaboration with the Société Russe Artistique et Littéraire.[32] In April 1911, Vassilieff curated another exhibition at Villa Steinheil entitled *L'Art du livre*, with Russian artists associated with the magazine *Mir iskusstva* (World of Art).

Vassilieff left Villa Steinheil in November 1911 and became the secretary, and then director, of the Académie Russe de Peinture et de Sculpture located at 54 avenue du Maine. Drawing classes were offered for artists of both sexes at a very affordable price. Individuality was encouraged. There were more than eighty members, including Chagall, Soutine, Orloff and Zadkine.[33] In November 1912, she founded yet another academy, this time under her own name, Académie Marie Vassilieff, at 21 avenue du Maine.[34] Its members were an international group of artists: Nathan Altman (Russian), Maria Blanchard (Spanish), Kseniya Boguslavskaya (Russian), Hunt Diederich (Hungarian-American), Jacques Lipchitz (Lithuanian), Amedeo Modigliani (Italian), Chana Orloff (Ukrainian) and Ossip Zadkine (Russian). Art historian Felix Marcilhac states that Orloff acquired her knowledge of modern painting at this academy and notes that Vassilieff's Cubist paintings had an impact on her early work.[35]

At Vassilieff's academy, hierarchy was abandoned.[36] Instruction was particularly *laissez-faire*. Instead of exams, the students corrected each other.[37] More established artists provided critiques and, on occasion, lectures. Léger presented his methodologies in two speeches, and Apollinaire also gave a talk.[38] Writers and theorists such as Jean Cocteau, Paul Fort, André Gide and Max Jacob were involved with the intellectual life of her academy as well.[39] "A great movement of ideas began at that time, especially in art," Vassilieff writes.[40] She may have modeled her academy after other semi-professional studios in Munich, Moscow and elsewhere.[41] She was less of a teacher, and more of a collaborator, and maintained convivial relationships with her students. She often accompanied them for a drink at the café La Rotonde. She even took a group of students, including Maruschka de Anders and Diederich, to paint landscapes in northern Spain (Fontarrabie, Pasajes and San Sebastián) during the summer of 1913.

The most important aspect of instruction at Académie Marie Vassilieff was life drawing. Women had only recently gained access to this fundamental artistic practice in France and Russia. In formal settings at the end of the nineteenth century and early twentieth century, study from the live nude model was limited and highly restricted. Consequently, women were barred from developing the skills necessary for demonstrating mastery in history painting, of which the body, clothed and unclothed, along with anatomy training, were integral.[42] The prestigious Paris institution École Nationale des Beaux-Arts, which equipped artists with the training and skills to portray the nude, was not open to women until 1897. Instead, for much of the nineteenth century, the only state-funded art school for women in Paris was the École Nationale de Dessin pour les Jeunes Filles. In order to study life drawing, they could attend a small number of private academies which accepted women, including the Académie Julian and the Académie Colarossi.[43] Typically, only middle- and upper-middle-class women could afford tuition, which was usually double that charged for male students.[44] The Union des Femmes Peintres et Sculpteurs, founded 1881, fought for entry into the École Nationale des Beaux-Arts, a battle which lasted nearly two decades. But by the time women were admitted by the École in 1897, the art world had changed. The time-honored establishment, including the state-run academy and the Salon, along with the conventional styles and techniques they promulgated, were becoming obsolete.[45] The official artistic structure in France was rapidly replaced with another largely male preserve – the avant-garde.

Vassilieff waged her own war against the antiquated Parisian art establishment, while positioning herself firmly within the Parisian avant-garde milieu. By opening her art academy, she broke outmoded rules, rebelled against restrictions imposed on women, advanced modern styles and promoted gender equality in art study. Vassilieff allowed students of both sexes to study from the live model together, and she hired male and female models. There was a rising demand for studio classes in Montparnasse, and, with low prices, Vassilieff made hers accessible for even the most impecunious students.[46] Study after the nude occurred daily. Modigliani, Soutine and Zadkine were regular participants.[47] In her memoir, *Laughing Torso*, the Welsh artist Nina Hamnett provides a rare glimpse into the day-to-day activities at Vassilieff's academy:

> There worked Russians, Germans, and Scandinavians, but no English or Americans. There were very good models posed with draperies and mimosa. Every afternoon from five to seven there was a sketch class with poses lasting from five minutes to half an hour. On Fridays two models posed together.[48]

Vassilieff's academy became an integral part of life in Montparnasse. Hamnett notes how popular the life drawing classes were, recalling that forty to fifty people gathered each evening to sketch the nude.[49] She also recounts amusing details which attest to an informal and liberated atmosphere. For instance, one evening Hamnett undressed and danced naked before all the students:

> Everyone suspected that I had a good figure and they asked me to take my clothes off and dance … I still had feelings of modesty, but being inordinately vain and proud of my figure, one day I took off all my clothes. Somebody played Debussy's "Golliwog's Cakewalk" on the piano and I improvised a dance. This was a great success and so was the figure.[50]

The academy was a site where artists, male and female, novice and experienced, could congregate and learn the latest developments in modern art in a hospitable and sexually open setting. This was not only an art school but also a fertile meeting ground for the exchange of ideas, and a setting where gender equality was endorsed.

Vassilieff made a deliberate effort to find models of different races and paid them handsomely. She explains, "I often organized big model competitions and the most beautiful came to pose in my academy. I paid them more than the other academies in Montparnasse."[51] She notes that male models were particularly hard to come by, but she managed to find men of African descent who agreed to pose.[52] Unfortunately, she does not elaborate further; she does not pinpoint the models' exact origins or disclose their names. She states that she posed models of different race and gender side by side: "Every Friday, the sketching session was accompanied by music and there were two models at a time, a man and a woman, often a white woman and a Black man."[53] At the time, a new interest in posing the Black female model was expanding among modern artists. Examples of Black female models in turn-of-the-century Paris include Laure (last name unknown), who posed for Édouard Manet's *Olympia* (1863), and Aïcha Goblet who was employed by Van Dongen, Kisling, Soutine, Modigliani, Foujita, Matisse, Félix Vallotton, among others. Simone Luce sat for numerous artists, notably Jules Pascin, and Adrienne Fidelin appears in works by Man Ray and Picasso.[54] However, working with Black male models was quite rare at this time.[55] Vassilieff's goal was twofold: her academy enabled all artists regardless of gender or financial means to study the nude, and she proposed a life-drawing practice that was inclusive of various types of bodies – Black and white, male and female – studied uniformly.

As an enterprising founder and director of a modern art academy with a curiosity and openness toward gender, ethnicity and race, Vassilieff assumed an atypical role for a woman in Paris in the early twentieth century. Her entrepreneurial drive to educate young artists and endorse her peers' work evinces her egalitarian vision. Although she did not explicitly declare herself a feminist, she sympathized with the European left and was obviously progressively minded. In the face of a prejudiced patriarchal art world, she promoted equality and camaraderie. While conventional history assumes that women took a secondary role in the libertine, bohemian milieu of the Left Bank, Vassilieff demonstrates that this is a misconception. In tune with the openness extolled at her academy, she once organized a ball featuring nudes. She writes, "Some time later, I organized a big costume ball with nude extras," among them Black nudes.[56] The "bal travesti," or costume ball, associated with Mardi-Gras and Mi-Carême, was popular during the pre-war years in Paris. Traditionally, one would dress up for the occasion as a person of a different social status, age and sex. This custom proliferated after the war in the form of elaborate costume balls organized by artists. Many of these were philanthropic fundraisers for organizations such as the Aide Amicale Aux Artistes. Vassilieff played an active role in coordinating these events. She frequently designed flyers, posters, programs, tickets and décor, along with Delaunay, Natalia Goncharova, Mikhail Larionov, Valadon, Utter, Utrillo and others as a member of the Union des Artistes Russes (figure 1.2).

With the declaration of war in August 1914, the mood in Paris quickly changed to one of agitation and unrest. Vassilieff momentarily turned her attention away from her academy and enrolled in nursing school with the aim of becoming a paramedic for the Red Cross (figure 1.3).[57] She passed her exam with honors and waited for her placement. Unfortunately, her application was rejected without explanation. Xenophobia was likely to blame. Undeterred, she decided to serve the needs of the artistic community of Paris. Vassilieff especially wished to help the expatriate artists who were among the most destitute. She closed her academy in December 1914 and opened a canteen, henceforth sealing her legacy as "la Mère Courage de l'avant-garde parisienne."[58]

Her canteen became a key gathering place for artists of all nationalities in Paris. In *Kiki et Montparnasse*, Billy Klüver provides a rich description:

> Considered by the police to be a private club, the canteen is not subject to a curfew. In the evening, it is always full. Conversations in a dozen different languages are interrupted only by some musical improvisation. Scandinavian musicians play piano and violin. Van Hoorn sings old French songs while accompanying himself on the guitar. Vassilieff performs Cossack dances and we spin to the rhythm of "Zadkine mad music, the camel's tango." Saturday's concerts are more popular. Despite some police raids, the canteen will operate for most of the war.[59]

It was a lively atmosphere with regular concerts and other performances. The Swedish composer H.M. Melchers directed musical evenings.[60] The canteen was furnished with chairs and stools from the flea market and decorated with paintings by Chagall and Modigliani, with drawings by Picasso and Léger, and with sculpture by Zadkine.[61] In her memoir, Hamnett writes that the nightly dinners were offered at "one

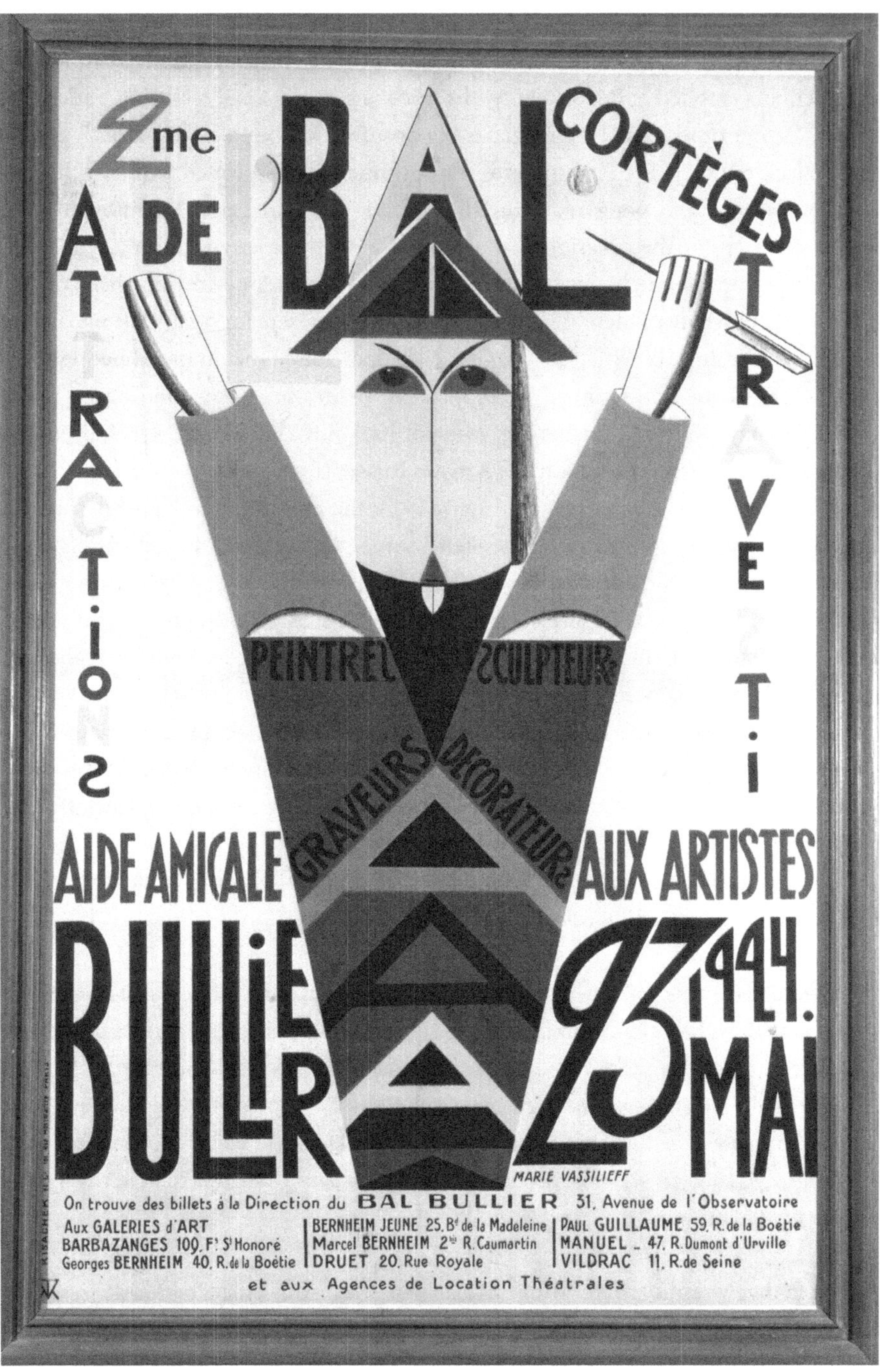

Figure 1.2 Marie Vassilieff, Poster for the Bal Bullier

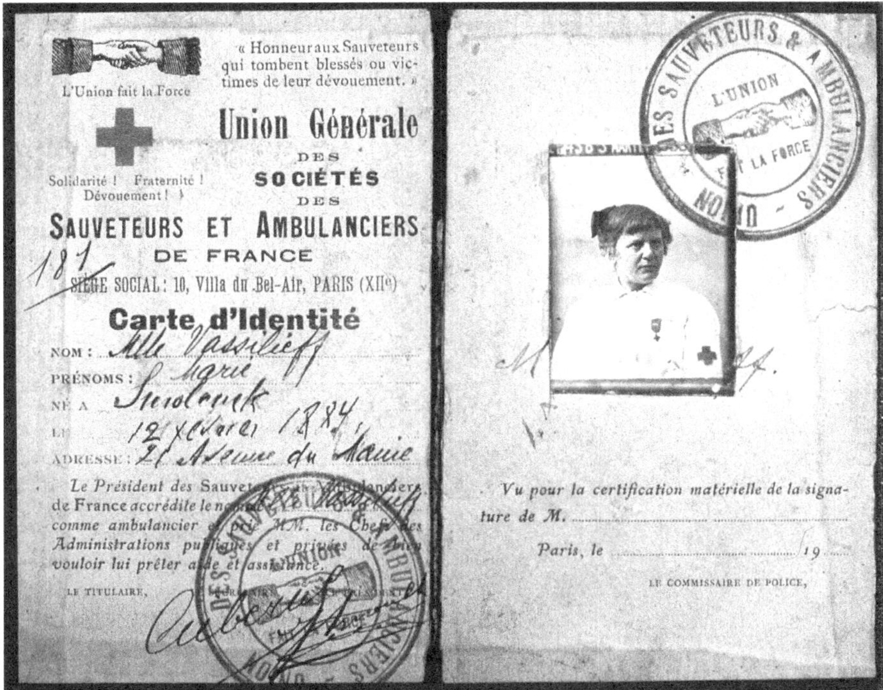

« Honneur aux Sauveteurs qui tombent blessés ou victimes de leur dévouement. »

L'Union fait la Force

Union Générale des Sociétés des Sauveteurs et Ambulanciers de France

Solidarité ! Fraternité ! Dévouement !

181

Siège Social : 10, Villa du Bel-Air, PARIS (XIIe)

Carte d'Identité

NOM : Mlle Vassilieff

PRÉNOMS : Marie

NÉ A Smolensk

LE 12 février 1884

ADRESSE : 21 Avenue du Maine

Le Président des Sauveteurs et Ambulanciers de France accrédite le n... comme ambulancier et prie MM. les Chefs des Administrations publiques et privées de vouloir lui prêter aide et assistance.

LE TITULAIRE,

L'UNION FAIT LA FORCE

Vu pour la certification matérielle de la signature de M.

Paris, le 19

LE COMMISSAIRE DE POLICE,

Figure 1.3 Red Cross certificate

franc-fifty, with one Caporal Bleu cigarette and one glass of wine thrown in."[62] Vassilieff helped impoverished artists, writers and musicians survive this bleak period providing cheap meals, alcohol and cigarettes, while also spreading joy. Her canteen allowed the avant-garde community to assemble and exchange ideas even as the war raged. Inside its walls, the artistic life of Montparnasse thrived during the darkest of days.

The most famous event to occur at Vassilieff's canteen was the "Banquet Braque," held on January 14, 1917, to celebrate Braque's return from the war. He received a head wound in 1915, was trepanned, and in 1916 was discharged after a long convalescence. He was awarded the *croix de guerre*.[63] The list of banquet attendees included Apollinaire, Blaise Cendrars, André Derain, Juan Gris, Jacob, Léger, Matisse, Picasso, Beatrice Hastings, Alfredo Pina and Ortiz de Zárate.[64] Vassilieff recounted the event in detail in her memoir. Modigliani arrived uninvited, causing a ruckus. Fortunately, the wise and calm Matisse mollified the situation, and the feast was saved. Artists wrote about this memorable event afterwards in correspondence. Picasso mentioned it in a letter to Gertrude Stein.[65] In *Banquet Braque* (figure 1.4), Vassilieff depicts the soirée. Braque boasts a crown of laurel leaves, Matisse carries a turkey and Vassilieff holds a paring knife. Cendrars, also wounded in battle, lifts his truncated right arm,

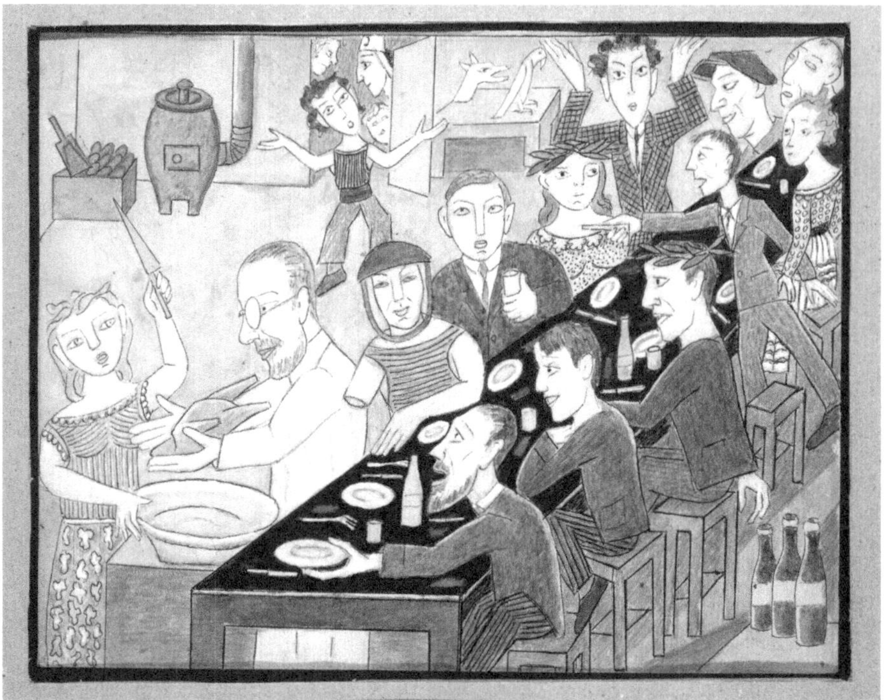

Figure 1.4 Marie Vassilieff, *Banquet Braque, January 14, 1917*

and Modigliani stands at the door, his arms outstretched in surprise. Executing in monochrome black and white with touches of red, Vassilieff captures the animated evening in a simplified style resembling a woodblock print. The distorted perspective, rudimentary form and limited shading recalls folk art, in particular, the Russian Lubok (a popular Russian print).

Vassilieff's canteen also became a popular meeting ground for Russian politicians. She recounts how Leon Trotsky and a dozen of his friends stopped by one day. She fed them, but as soon as they began discussing politics, she interrupted, "Trotsky, to make your speeches, go to the courtyard; here, we sing, we do not discuss politics."[66] She knew Lenin and attended his conferences at Place d'Italie on the Left Bank. She was also acquainted with Lev Kamenev and his wife. She acknowledges, "It is certain that my friendly relations with all these leaders of the Revolution must have given me the reputation of a revolutionary myself, of a Bolshevik, for which I suffered greatly later, despite my innocence."[67] Vassilieff held socialist ideals, but she was not a spy.

Starting in 1917, a series of turbulent events shook and threatened Vassilieff's career and livelihood. After a short affair with a French-Moroccan lieutenant, Amar Chrouat, she realized that she was pregnant. No longer able to direct her canteen, she closed it down. She had a son, Pierre, in June 1917 and chose Goncharova as his godmother. The lieutenant abandoned Vassilieff, who was left to raise the child on her own. Later that year following the October Revolution, Vassilieff fled to Nice, a point of embarkation for Russians returning home. In the end, she chose to stay in France, accepting Jeanne Léger's invitation to come to Bizy-par-Vernon with her son. Léger and his wife were vital in helping Vassilieff survive the difficult war years (figure 1.5).

The following spring, her studio was partially destroyed by German artillery, "Dicke Bertha" (Big Bertha), during a bombardment between March and August, 1918. Then, in December, 1918, an anonymous letter denounced her as a Bolshevik spy to French authorities. The accuser noted that Trotsky was a regular at her canteen.[68] In February, 1919, she was placed in an internment camp (*résidence surveillée*) in Melun near Fontainebleau where she stayed until April of that year. It must have been a horrific experience, as she refers to the residence as a prison and concentration camp. She recounts the terrible episode in detail and documents the events through a series of illustrations in her memoir. One sketch depicts the artist in her studio with her infant son, Pierre, praying before an image of the Virgin (figure 1.6). Another captures her arrest (figure 1.7). Pierre has been lifted out of his cradle and appears in the arms of a nurse. Vassilieff lies unconscious on the floor as a nurse and soldier attempt to wake her; sculptures and dolls are strewn everywhere. She insisted in her memoir that she was not a collaborator.

In an interview with the *New York Tribune* in 1922, Vassilieff stated that when she was released and allowed to return to Paris several months later, she was aghast to find her studio entirely empty. Her artwork had been pillaged.[69] With her studio bombed and ransacked during the war, it is a miracle that any of her pre-war works have survived. Without the income from her former academy and canteen, Vassilieff struggled financially for the remainder of her career. She could not receive government aid because she was not a French citizen. Since she did not return to her homeland after the Russian Revolution to reclaim her Soviet citizenship, she was left stateless. Seeking French citizenship was an unsuccessful lifelong mission.

The nude made androgynous

Situated at the crossroads of myriad styles and discourses, Vassilieff's nudes engage in the avant-garde preoccupation with the representation of the figure across multiple temporalities and spatial planes within a single image. In the ensuing paragraphs, I demonstrate how her art resonates with the plurality of aesthetics and concerns within Cubism, yet resists the movement's masculinist ideologies.

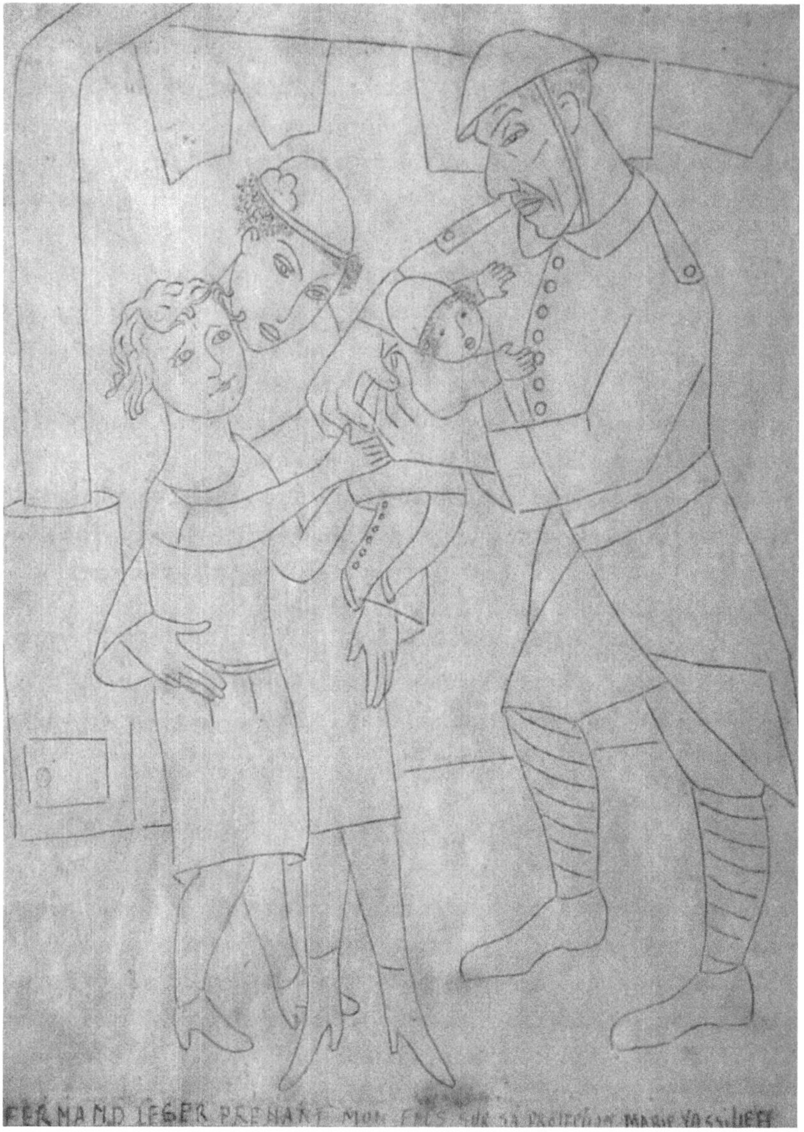

Figure 1.5 Marie Vassilieff, *Fernand Léger prenant mon fils sous sa protection*, 1929

From her arrival in Paris, Vassilieff set out to paint a modern nude:

> I began visiting all the art schools in the Montparnasse district: Colarossi, la Grande Chaumière, l'École Moderne, rue Notre Dame des Champs, and also Julien, and I went to see the École des Beaux-Arts. I saw it all, and, taking a very clear look at it, decided that all I had seen – almost all nudes – was of little value to my very modern taste.[70]

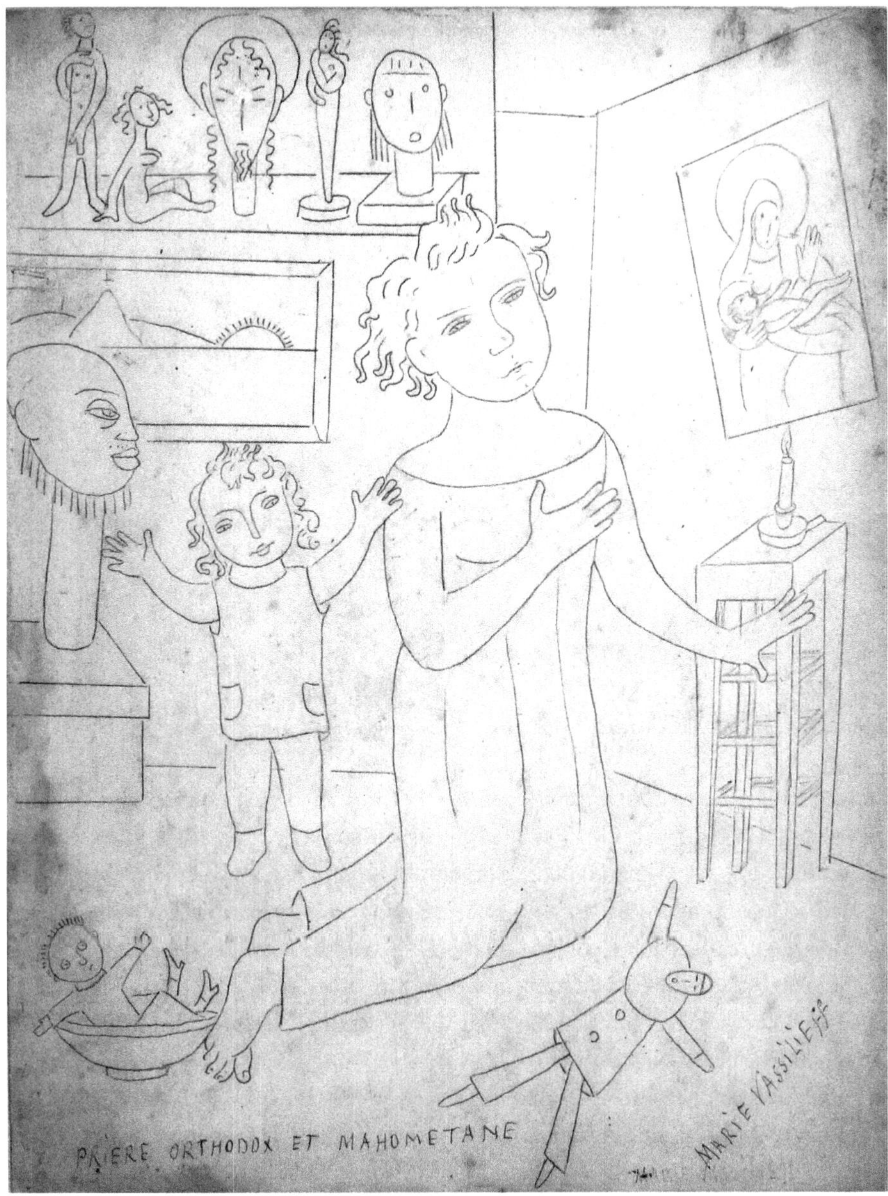

Figure 1.6 Marie Vassilieff, *Prière orthodoxe et mahométane*, 1929

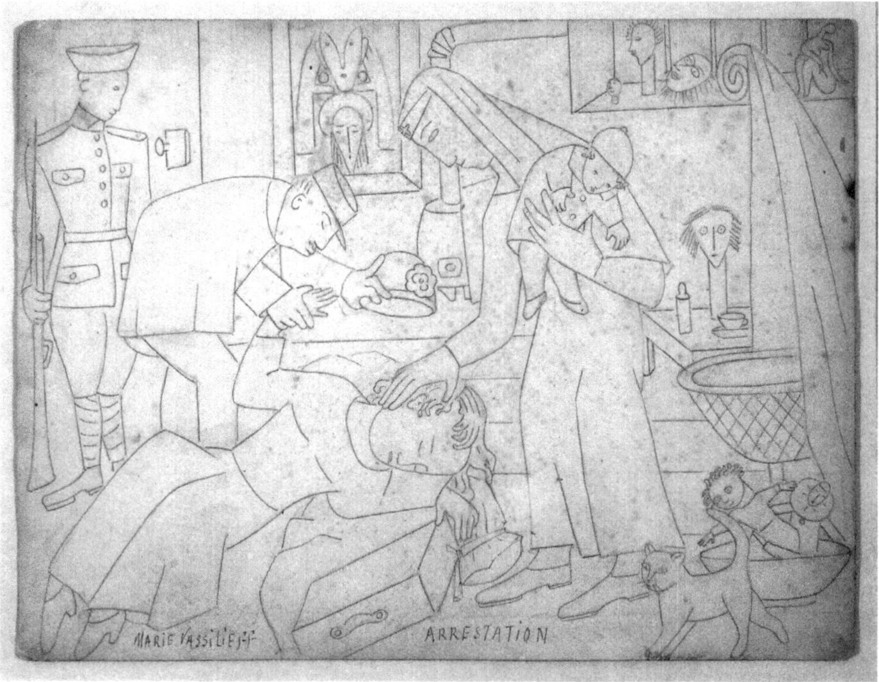

Figure 1.7 Marie Vassilieff, *Arrestation de Marie et Pierre Vassilieff*, 1929

One of her earliest surviving nudes shows her desire to defy conventions – *Jeune adolescent* (1911) (figure 1.8). Vassilieff likely saw some of Matisse's academic studies, including *Nude Male* (1900).[71] She employs a Matissian palette of vivid hues and encircles the figure with a thin and dark line. However, unlike Matisse's large muscular figure, the adolescent boy's body is lithe and sinuous. He lays his arm across his lap, concealing the midriff area, and, with the other arm, reaches toward a large vase. This curvaceous object, along with the background colored in amaranth and violet, underscores an aura of sensuality.

Vassilieff androgenizes the female figure in *Femme aux bas noirs* (Plate 1). Curators have dated the painting to 1913–14, but it was likely executed a year or two earlier.[72] Painted on a bed sheet measuring three feet high, Vassilieff probably lacked the funds to buy a large canvas. Bedding materials could serve as an inexpensive and plentiful substitute for a starving artist. Sonia Delaunay's *Bal Bullier* (1913) of the same period was painted on mattress ticking.[73] Vassilieff's rigid nude, clad in black stockings and angled upward, assumes a dominating presence. A bold, chromatic range of colors from fuchsia on the elbow to pink lavender on the face and violet blue on the breasts animates the painting. The thighs are modeled in green with yellow highlights. The left hip, accentuated in teal, forms a jagged triangle that pierces

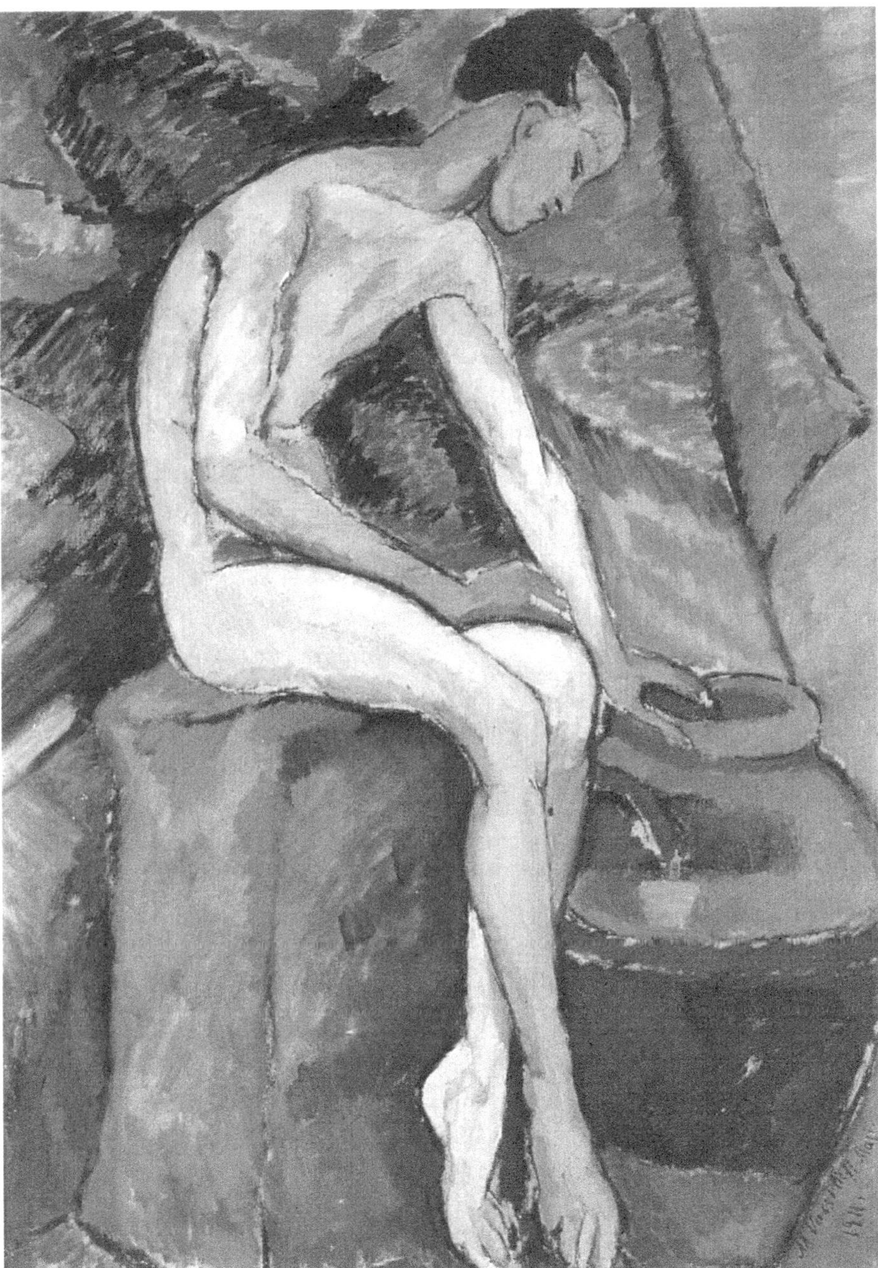

Figure 1.8 Marie Vassilieff, *Jeune adolescent* (*Young Adolescent*), 1911

outward. Touches of alizarin red are interspersed throughout paired with Prussian blue drapery. A splash of lime green on the bottom left draws attention to the black stockings. The canvas is thinly painted, and with exposed, unprimed patches it almost resembles a watercolor.

Femme aux bas noirs conveys Vassilieff's debt to Cézanne in the dominance of blue and green hues, the use of constructive, parallel brushwork, and flat planes of color that converge in the manner of Cézannesque *passage,* a technique that the Cubists frequently utilized. In Vassilieff's painting, *passage* creates an oscillation between a sense of volume and flatness. For the majority of the French and Russian avant-garde artists, from Braque and Matisse to Larionov and Goncharova, Cézanne's oeuvre was regarded as the cornerstone of modern painting, and his innovations served as an important launching point for the development of novel painting techniques. In 1912, Albert Gleizes and Jean Metzinger praised Cézanne in *Du Cubisme* as "reminiscent of Rembrandt," and wrote, "Anyone who understands Cézanne has an inkling of Cubism."[74] Vassilieff presumably saw Cézanne's retrospective at the Salon d'Automne in 1907 and certainly studied his work with Matisse, who emphasized his importance to his students.[75]

Along with Cézanne's *passage*, Vassilieff employs "simultaneity," or multiple viewpoints, a technique all Cubists employed to varying degrees. Simultaneity was most extensively theorized by the Salon Cubists. Also referred to as the "Public Cubists," the "Section d'Or Cubists," and the "Puteaux Group," they were a loose group of artists who promulgated Cubism through exhibitions and publications.[76] They included Léger, Gleizes, Metzinger, Robert Delaunay, the Duchamp siblings, Henri Le Fauconnier and others.[77] The group formed during 1909 and 1910 and made its public debut in "salle 41" of the 1911 Salon des Indépendants, exhibiting frequently thereafter. The distinctions between the so-called "Salon Cubists" and the "Gallery Cubists"[78] (Picasso, Braque, Derain and later Gris and Léger) and their theories, or lack thereof, have been discussed extensively.[79] Overall, the multitude of styles, heterogeneous approaches and distinct priorities denote the diversity inherent in the Cubist idiom.[80] What remained consistent among all Cubist groups was the exclusion of women. Marie Laurencin was the only female artist to exhibit regularly alongside male Cubists, thanks largely to her partner, Apollinaire. Her work was shown in salle 41 likely due to his request, and she was the only woman artist mentioned in Apollinaire's *Peintres cubistes* (1913).[81] Around 1910, Laurencin had conceived an aesthetic that was deemed thoroughly feminine and therefore unthreatening to her male peers. With a palette of pastel creams and pinks, she painted slender female figures draped in loose, ethereal fabrics and adorned in ribbons and pearls. During the interwar period, Laurencin came to prominence as one of France's leading artists.[82] She later expressed feelings of inadequacy: "If I have not become a Cubist painter, it is because I cannot. I did not have the ability, but I was passionate about their inquiries."[83]

Of the Salon Cubists, Vassilieff was closest with Léger, whom she met some time between 1907 and 1910 while he was living at La Ruche.[84] Vassilieff's esteem for the artist is reiterated throughout her memoir. She promoted his work in Russia and facilitated the exhibition of five of his paintings at the second Salon du Valet de Carreau / Jack of Diamonds (Bubnovyi valet) in Moscow in 1912.[85] There, his *Essai pour trois portraits* (1910–11) made a strong impression on Kazimir Malevich, Alexandra Exter and Pavel Filonov.[86] Vassilieff invited Léger to speak at her academy in 1913 and 1914. She explains, "My school became more and more famous. To give it even more importance, I invited an extremely modern painter, Léger ... He gave a whole series of conferences on modern art."[87] Two of these lectures are often cited by scholars and have been studied at length in relation to his art.[88] Vassilieff's Cubist work testifies to her dialogue with Léger, in particular, his treatment of form. For example, in *Femme aux bas noirs*, her deconstruction of the body into an ovoid torso with tubular limbs, as well as the drapery and foliage broken into a multitude of rounded and pointed units, bears an unmistakable resemblance to the cones and prisms in his work.

Femme assise (c. 1913) (Plate 2) surely postdates *Femme aux bas noirs.* An evolution has taken place in Vassilieff's oeuvre – her variation of Cubism is now in full swing. While the figure is still visible as a female nude, the environment is elusive. Removed are the studio props, the potted plants, drapery and, most noticeably, the stockings. While in *Femme aux bas noirs* shading was applied in a relatively naturalistic manner, here it contradicts the laws of light and shadow. The face, composed of straight edges and arched lines, appears mask-like. Constructive strokes applied throughout convey volume. Sharp angles contrast with rounded arcs, and *passage* has been amplified into flat planes of color that abruptly intersect. Vassilieff condenses the figure into irregular, geometric shapes – cylinders, cones, and spheres. The torso is an amalgam of jagged and asymmetrical pieces. The limbs appear sharp and robotic, except for the left arm which swells like a balloon. The background is likewise composed of layered, angular forms. The interpenetrating planes and volumes lend the work a sense of movement, antithetical to static single-point perspective.

Through simultaneity and *passage*, Vassilieff reduces the nude to a complex array of planes that tilt forward and back. The organic form of a human is evoked through rounded shapes, while the grid of rectilinear structures surrounding the figure hint at the space of an interior. Reversing the naturalistic order of things, the strident, unmodulated teal, turquoise, violet and magenta highlight the body against a neutral, skin-toned background. These tertiary hues appear all the more striking against the burlap colored surface, which in areas is interrupted with triangular patches of solid black. The lightly primed canvas is visible in crevices between merging planes, where it assumes the role of line. *Femme assise* reflects Léger's predilection for dissonance. In his second lecture at Vassilieff's academy he stated, "Contrast = dissonance and, as a result, the maximum expressive effect."[89] He used the term "multiplication painting" for his technique. By contrasting form and color, Léger believed that artists could more aptly describe dynamic movement, which for him was a key characteristic of the modern age.[90] For him, contrasts and dissonance were means of expressing this modern way of seeing. He maintained that even traditional subject matter, such as the nude, should be rendered in accordance with the fragmentary intensity that he identified with modernity. Rather than strive for a harmonious relation of pictorial elements present in academic painting, Vassilieff creates discord through a maximum contrast of volumes, angles, curves, lines and planes. The image appears as a cacophony of exploding colors and a confusion of rigid and curved edges. Her work achieves a distinctive boldness due to the mingling of rounded and straight lines and colors, both bright and subdued, along with a heterogeneous range of plastic forms.

The Cubists sought to capture the pulse of modern life in their art. They rebelled against quantitatively measured space and its application in art as single-point perspective, artistic tenets held in place since the Renaissance. They considered their art to be an anti-rationalist and intellectual endeavor, distinct from Impressionism and its association with the rendering of sensations. Akin to Léger's method of "multiplication painting," artists used simultaneity as a means for capturing the flux and dynamism of modernity. Through simultaneity, an artist depicts objects not from a fixed angle with one-point perspective, but from various perspectives within a single image. In Vassilieff's *Femme assise*, the body is broken like shards of glass into a multitude of facets, lending the impression of a figure seen from numerous angles at once and across multiple temporalities. The robotic nude, composed of sharp and cylindrical shapes, seems to be rotating in myriad directions at a jarring cadence. Dark-colored planes of amethyst, indigo and ultramarine are placed adjacent to the figure so that the nude seems to project outward. Certain body parts appear distended and others concaved, as if the body swells and deflates at once. This energized composition engages the viewer in a nearly physical manner. Vassilieff obliterates any rational sense of the figure's three-dimensional volume. In some areas, the disaggregated body parts fuse with the background, while in others they protrude, creating a sense of space which is as ambiguous as it is dynamic. Vassilieff captures an idiosyncratic experience of space and time – precisely what the Salon Cubists aimed to represent.

Responding to Bergson

The Salon Cubists justified their use of "simultaneity" with the anti-rationalist theories of Henri Bergson, the most prominent and influential French philosopher of the late nineteenth and early twentieth centuries.[91] In *Time and Free Will* (1898), Bergson contested the idea of measurable time and argued that time as we experience it, *la durée réelle* (real duration), cannot be quantified through mechanistic means. Any attempt to measure time leads to a distortion of the real thing. He laid emphasis on intuition, a kind of empathetic perception, as the only way to discern duration. The Salon Cubists believed that through mobile perspective they could convey the psychological idea of time and space about which Bergson had theorized.[92] The Cubists were not alone in gravitating towards Bergson. Beginning about 1905 until the start of World War One, Bergson's popularity soared. His ideas pervaded French society as well as the Parisian avant-garde in a manner so profound that the period has been called a "Bergsonian moment."[93] By 1914, his books were translated into all the major European languages, including English and Russian.[94] As one scholar wrote, he became "the most controversial philosopher in the world and the first in the twentieth century to become an international celebrity."[95]

Indeed, Paris was abuzz with Bergson's ideas. By 1911, his concepts, often simplified. "[were] the common property of the avant-garde."[96] He was a regular topic of conversation among artists in Montparnasse, especially at the Salon Cubists' weekly meetings at Closerie des Lilas, a café Vassilieff frequented.[97] As noted previously, Vassilieff learned about Bergson's theories as early as 1909 when she translated Matisse's "Notes of a Painter." Moreover, as the founder of a modern art academy, Vassilieff was abreast of the manifold vanguard artistic investigations and approaches within Cubism as well as the intellectual discourses circulating Paris's Left Bank. Advocating cutting-edge styles, she likely mediated discussions on Cubist techniques as well as Bergson's theories.

The Salon Cubists employed Bergson's theories to substantiate their dismissal of the artistic conventions of the past and to validate their revolutionary methods. This is expressed in *Du cubisme*, a quasi-manifesto on Cubism.[98] Written by Gleizes and Metzinger, it was meant to articulate the techniques of all of the Salon Cubists who had exhibited together earlier in 1911 in the salle 8 (room 8) of the Salon d'Automne: Léger, Gleizes, Metzinger, Le Fauconnier, Roger de La Fresnaye, Jacques Villon and Duchamp.[99] Its publication coincided with the first Salon de la Section d'Or in October 1912.[100] Vassilieff later participated in the second Section d'Or exhibition in 1920 alongside Goncharova, Larionov and other Russian artists.[101] In *Du cubisme*, Gleizes and Metzinger explain how they render an object in space: "The fact of moving around an object to seize from it several successive appearances which, fused into a single image, reconstitutes it in time."[102] This process, represented through multiple viewpoints or "simultaneity," was a means of conveying Bergson's duration. They use Bergson's terminology, stating, "Oil painting allows the expression of notions of depth, density and duration [*la durée*], thought inexpressible, and encourages us to present within a limited space, governed by a complex rhythm, a true fusion of objects."[103] The Bergsonian inferences were made obvious, and, for their contemporaries, clearly understood. Bergson, who became aware of his influence on Cubism, was actually quite critical of their theories. He believed that art should be the product of intuition and creativity, not theorizing. Even without his endorsement, however, the Cubists continued to make use of his ideas to justify their own novel approaches to art making.[104]

In addition to their Bergsonian dismissal of rational systems of measurement and logic, the Salon Cubists turned to geometry and mathematics. They were especially interested in the *section d'or*, or golden section (also known as the golden ratio) which they referred to in the title of their exhibition in 1912. Used by the Egyptians, further developed by Fibonacci, rediscovered by Leonardo da Vinci and revived in the early twentieth century, it served as a practical way for artists to measure the proportions of a composition.[105] The idea was that if an artist constructed a work following the golden section, the proportions would appear harmonious. Leonardo wrote about the concept in *Trattato della pittura*, which was translated into French in 1910.[106] Jacques Villon, Juan Gris, Metzinger, Gleizes and others began studying the text by 1912.[107] Gris and Metzinger employed this approach in some of their work.[108] The title of the exhibition, *La section d'or*, bears testament to the Cubists' fascination with the concept. Metzinger and Duchamp chose the title to underscore the academic rigor of their pursuits, and the importance of philosophical and scientific thought for the exhibiting group as a whole.[109]

Portrait de femme (Plate 3) confirms that Vassilieff was engaging with techniques and theories central to the Salon Cubists. She shatters the body into an assemblage of jagged geometric forms. The figure is fragmented to such a degree that the body parts resemble jigsaw puzzle pieces. The torso appears rotated in various directions, severed by straight angles on the left and black rectangular shards running vertically on the right. The breast seems to be removed entirely from the chest. There is a gaping hole where the neck meets the torso, so that the head appears dislocated. The neck itself made up of planes of color – mustard and turquoise – seamlessly blends with the background, which is an incoherent jumble of partially painted planes. Sections appear unfinished, with unprimed canvas visible. Vassilieff's singular, vivid palette of blues, purples, greens and citrus yellow is contrasted with white and black along with the neutral color of the exposed canvas. Splashes of fuchsia and royal blue intensify the image. Through simultaneity, Vassilieff captures the body from compound spatial and temporal positions. Splintered in every possible direction, the torso appears to gyrate; the breast juts out to one side, the shoulder dislocates, and the upper portion of the spine seems to spin forward in a manner which defies human anatomy.

On close inspection, it is evident that Vassilieff planned *Portrait de femme* in accordance with the golden section. The golden section consists of the division of segments in relation to the golden ratio—approximately 1.618, or the inverse of 0.618. An analysis of Vassilieff's composition shows that it follows these proportions.[110] The canvas is shaped differently from Vassilieff's other works: it is in the form of a perfect square, facilitating easy measurement of proportions. Indeed, the work is divided in accordance with the golden ratio, 0.382 on the right and 0.618 on the left. To the naked eye, the proportions in the composition appear harmonious as a result. Vassilieff not only bifurcates the canvas according to the golden section, but she also makes reference to it within the composition. The silhouette of the woman forms a perfect triangle, while her body is segmented into rectangular and triangular forms. The triangles are related in size by the golden ratio; most notably, the dimensions of the small triangle on the left side of the painting are 0.618 of the dimensions of the large triangle on the right side. Furthermore, the triangles form a windmill-like shape on the lower left portion of the composition, calling to mind the spiraling pattern inside a Nautilus shell. This pattern suggests the Fibonacci ratio, which is how the golden section is described mathematically. The placement of the woman's arms, one dangling over her head and the other outstretched and fragmented, creates a sense of whirling movement, further evoking a Nautilus shell.[111] Rather than achieve harmony overall, Vassilieff's employment of the ratio augments a sense of dynamism and discord.

Apollinaire noted of Vassilieff's work from this period, "Miss Vassilieff composes with a voluptuous science portraits of young women with subtle eyes, feline gestures where the acidity of modern colors imbues a charm that sometimes redeems the brutality of the forms."[112] The precise paintings that he was discussing are not known, and the review could predate Vassilieff's *Portrait de femme*. Nevertheless, the phrase "voluptuous science" resonates markedly with the composition in its use of the golden section. He also noted a "brutality of forms," which accords with the fractured nude. Such "masculine" descriptors were seen as complimentary when applied to a male artist at a time when innovation was aligned with virile aggression.

Conversely, "brutality of forms" is not an apt description of female nudes by Le Fauconnier, Gleizes or Metzinger. Le Fauconnier's monumental *L'abondance* (1910–11) is characteristic of the Salon Cubists' nudes, which evoke woman's undeniable regenerative capacity. The work made its debut in the 1911 Salon des Indépendants, where Vassilieff also showed her work, and it was subsequently displayed in modern art exhibitions around Europe. Art historian David Cottington asserts that the painting was so popular that it came to represent Cubism before 1914.[113] Its success led Le Fauconnier to be considered one of the most daring artists of his time and an innovator of a new artistic movement.[114] It depicts a larger-than-life-sized female nude and her male progeny immersed in nature. A basket copiously laden with ripe apples balances on her head as her arms stretch upwards like the branches of a tree. The nude mirrors her environment in form and color. Her round breasts and swollen womb are centralized in the composition. The figure and her surroundings are made up of smoothly rounded shapes, mirroring the apples she harvests. The subdued earth-toned palette of her flesh is reflected in the background, evocative of an autumnal forest. Together, these elements reinforce the nude's "abundance." As the title implies, the nude represents fertility and regeneration.[115] Although the painting would have appeared aesthetically progressive with its Cubist facture, this image of womanhood conforms to the long-held dichotomy: woman-as-nature / man-as-culture.

For the Salon Cubists, the nude's fecundity in *L'Abondance* symbolized *élan vital* as encapsulated by their reading of Bergson. In *Creative Evolution* (1907), Bergson presented this concept, also called "vital force," to denote the impulse that propels the creation of all living species. He contends that *élan vital* accounts for the making of life and the diversity that arises from evolution. The theory had vast implications and resonated widely with progressives and conservatives alike, as well as among non-academics.[116] It struck a deep chord with the Salon Cubists and led them to form their own gendered theories of creativity. As men, they possessed innate intuitive powers and were creators of *élan vital*. By contast, women were solely the product of this *élan*. The Salon Cubists interpreted *élan vital* as synonymous with female reproduction, considering woman's creative ability as limited to natural processes.[117] Men lacked women's natural creative functions, and therefore had to exert their creativity elsewhere – by making works of art, for example. Only men had the creative potential within the realm of culture. The female-as-nature / male-as-culture division was maintained as a truism, except that in the Cubist idiom it was updated with a new aesthetic and reinforced with a novel, philosophical concept.

In accordance with their reactionary gender views, the Salon Cubists' work is teeming with fecund female nudes situated in natural environments, as in Gleizes's *Les Baigneuses*, 1912, or in domestic settings like Metzinger's *La Femme au cheval*, 1911–12.[118] Male nudes are scarce. To develop a male counterpart to the fertile female body, the Salon Cubists turned to competitive sports, including rugby, boxing and even aviation.[119] Gleizes's *Football Players* (1912–13), Delaunay's *Cardiff Team* (1913) and Metzinger's *The Cyclist* (1913) are a few examples.[120] To underscore a sense of vigor in their renderings of clothed, athletic male bodies, they used a style considered masculine: lucid colors, blazing contrasts and razor-edged forms. Through their art, they obstinately aligned women with procreation, nature and domesticity and men with physical exertion.

Bergson's ideas circulated at a time when the burgeoning feminist movement was gaining momentum and threatening the status quo. Conservatives advanced Bergson's ideas as they advocated the unceasing subordination of women. Cottington explains, "Scientists, sociologists and writers were engaged in the pre-war years in forging modern theories to support prevailing sexual inequalities – more severe in France than in most other European countries."[121] In France, the début of the *femme nouvelle*, or the New Woman, threatened established gender roles and was seen by many to have a detrimental impact on population growth. Women were spending less time at home as they began to seek opportunities in professional and academic arenas. An increasing number of women were graduating with their *baccalauréat* and pursuing higher education, which enabled them to obtain careers in the traditionally masculine domains of medicine and law.[122] With industrial and commercial development, more women entered the workforce. Conservative politicians, writers and journalists linked these developments with the declining birthrate in France. In comparison with other countries, France's population growth was diminutive: the French population increased by only 8 per cent from 1871 to 1911, while Germany's rose by 42 per cent and England and Wales's by 59 per cent.[123] For conservatives, the waning birthrate was an alarming indication of shifting gender roles. The *femme nouvelle* and her embodiment of woman's emancipation, both professionally and sexually, were seen as highly threatening by a large part of society, and further aggravated a crisis of masculinity.[124]

While Vassilieff engaged with Bergson's theory of duration, she simultaneously rejected the regressive gender implications of *élan vital.* Employing a Cubist grammar, Vassilieff presents nudes of ambiguous sex that resist gendered stereotypes. In *Femme aux bas noirs*, for example, the figure is not soft or supple but taut and angular. Lines incise, dislocate and sharpen the body parts into jagged extremities. A thick contour divides the upper half of the abdomen, lending the nude a robust appearance. Far from being an ingratiating object of male desire, she sits erectly, with hands on hips, indubitably in control of her own sexuality. Pushed to the foreground with reddish fingers delineated in black, her left hand is claw-like. The nude's genital region is indicated by a black triangle. Rather than conceal it, the hand draws attention to this element, which along with the stockings, stand out as prominent features in the composition. While the triangle is intended to convey a patch of pubic hair, its dark phallic shape serves as both a marker of sex and its lack.

Pubic hair is largely absent in Cubist nudes of this period. Gleizes, Metzinger, Léger, Robert Delaunay and Le Fauconnier avoided it altogether. Modigliani, a friend of Vassilieff's, caused a scandal when he exhibited fully bare female nudes in December of 1917. During a solo show at Berthe Weill's gallery, his nudes were displayed in the window, attracting such a large crowd that the police intervened. In her memoir, Weill recounts being called into the prefecture where she was ordered to remove the offensive paintings. According to Weill, the display of pubic hair was the main issue for the police, as it was considered indecent:

> Sunday we hung and Monday December 3rd 1917 was the opening. Sumptuous nudes, angular faces, tasty portraits, select gathering … The owner of the gallery is asked to go and see the police chief. I went up. Packed office … I asked "Have you asked me to come up?" – "Yes! And I order you to take all this filth down." "What is wrong with these nudes?" – "These nudes … these nudes have h-h-h-air!"[125]

She was forced to cancel the opening and dismantle the window display, but the exhibition still ran.[126] Given the possible repercussions for the blatant depiction of body hair, Vassilieff's handling of the nude was extremely daring.

Vassilieff resolutely counters the staunch reinforcement of gender difference conspicuous in the works of her contemporaries. Her nudes do not recline. Rather than pose submissively, their bodies are confidently erect. They are not passive, graceful or curvaceous, and they are not reduced to flesh. In fact, flesh colors are minimized in favor of pulsating hues. Composed of unflinching forms, the figures are not supple but jagged and blazing; flashes of acidic colors instill the nudes with energy and force. While the Salon Cubists situate their nudes in nature or in domestic interiors with fruit, flowers and birds, Vassilieff resists outmoded stereotypes. Instead, she probes the visual markers of gender ambiguity, rendering the human form as an amalgam of angular lines, planes and geometric shapes. The harsh contours of her figures bring to mind Picasso's early Cubist works circa 1907 – in particular, *Demoiselles d'Avignon*, wherein the nudes are likewise upright and sexually assertive.[127] One of the most widely discussed and thoroughly analyzed paintings in the Cubist canon, it is generally agreed to be a visual manifestation of male sexuality.[128] Emily Braun succinctly surmises that Picasso, "Unleashed his sexual drive as the primary source and subject of his art."[129] Displayed in a brothel, Picasso's nudes nevertheless reflect gendered codes as objects of masculine erotic desire, fantasy and fear. Unlike Picasso's demoiselles, Vassilieff's nudes do not entertain male illusions or perpetuate culturally determined stereotypes. Her painterly project is an assault on the masculinist ideologies inherent within Cubism.

Gender parity

Vassilieff was not the only artist to paint androgynous nudes. They surface in certain Cubist works, such as in the hermetic Cubist paintings of Picasso and Braque from

1910 to 1912 and in Léger's so-called "pure painting" from 1912 to 1914. But it was the female body that served as the subject of these aesthetic exploits and most of them were short-lived. Picasso's *Woman in a Chemise in an Armchair* (1913–14) "marks an aggressive return to the representation of sexual difference in Picasso's art."[130] Here, Picasso goes further than in *Demoiselles d'Avignon*, entirely deforming the female body: the head is misshapen and the torso is amputated. He then adds crude details: armpit hair, a belly button and two pointy breasts that appear like weapons nailed to the torso. To the viewer's horror, the crumpled underwear and rumpled fabric of the purple armchair simulate the nude's internal organs. This nightmarish image reveals too much; it appears as if the woman's intestines are oozing out of the body like a mutilated corpse. Maimed and deformed, Picasso's nude is ripped violently apart, yet her sex remains visible. It all becomes even more disturbing once the viewer learns that the sitter, likely Picasso's mistress, Eva Gouel, died prematurely from cancer three years after the painting was made.[131] The work has been lauded as a masterpiece by some, and criticized as sadistic by others. Nonetheless, for most viewers, it arouses discomfort.[132] In her seminal essay "Virility and Domination in Early Twentieth-century Vanguard Painting" (1973), Carol Duncan specifically cited *Woman in a Chemise* as an example of a painting that denies woman's humanity.[133] She argues that Picasso aggressively asserts sexual difference, reducing the woman's identity to her private parts. Picasso represents the female body as hostile territory. Vassilieff deconstructs the female nude into interlocking planes in works such as *Portrait de femme*, but these bodily distortions do not insinuate disease, decay or death. There is no sense of the body brutally mutilated or dehumanized. Rather, Vassilieff's painterly manipulations work to erode the distinctions between female and male bodies. Gender parity is the heart of her project.

Numerous life-drawing studies by Vassilieff survive which reveal fervent experimentation with the gender-neutral body. None of the sketches is dated, but, given the strong resemblance with her Cubist paintings, they were likely executed between 1910 and 1914. There is a tremendous sense of energy in these images. The figures are composed of an interplay of lines, curved and straight, which render the body as a compilation of mobile spherical and geometric parts. *Standing Female Nude* (figure 1.9) is a molten assemblage of rhythmic lines as the figure swivels a circular object above its head. Body hair both conceals and highlights the figure's sex. In *Standing Male Nude* (figure 1.10), an upright male holds a large doughnut-shaped form, which he appears to swing back and forth. The doubling of contours lends a sense of movement. In *Standing Male Nude with Arm Akimbo* (figure 1.11), a muscular model poses with one hand on his hip, the other behind his tilted head. The effeminate pose is at odds with the nude's sinewy form. Gender indeterminacy is exacerbated in *Reclining Nude* (figure 1.12). The model's arms are folded across the chest and the legs are splayed open revealing a web of crisscrossing strokes. The nude is devoid of any distinctive

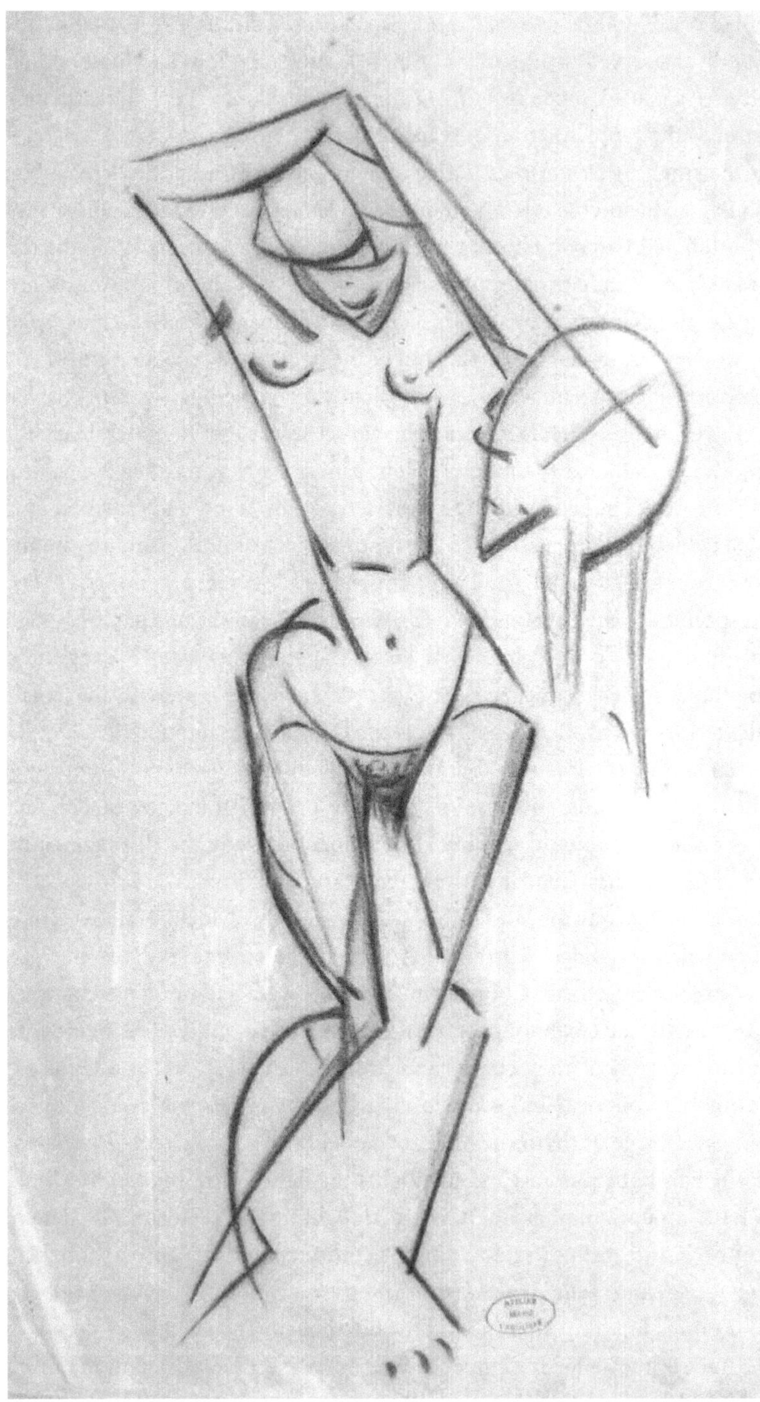

Figure 1.9 Marie Vassilieff, *Standing Female Nude*, c. 1910–14

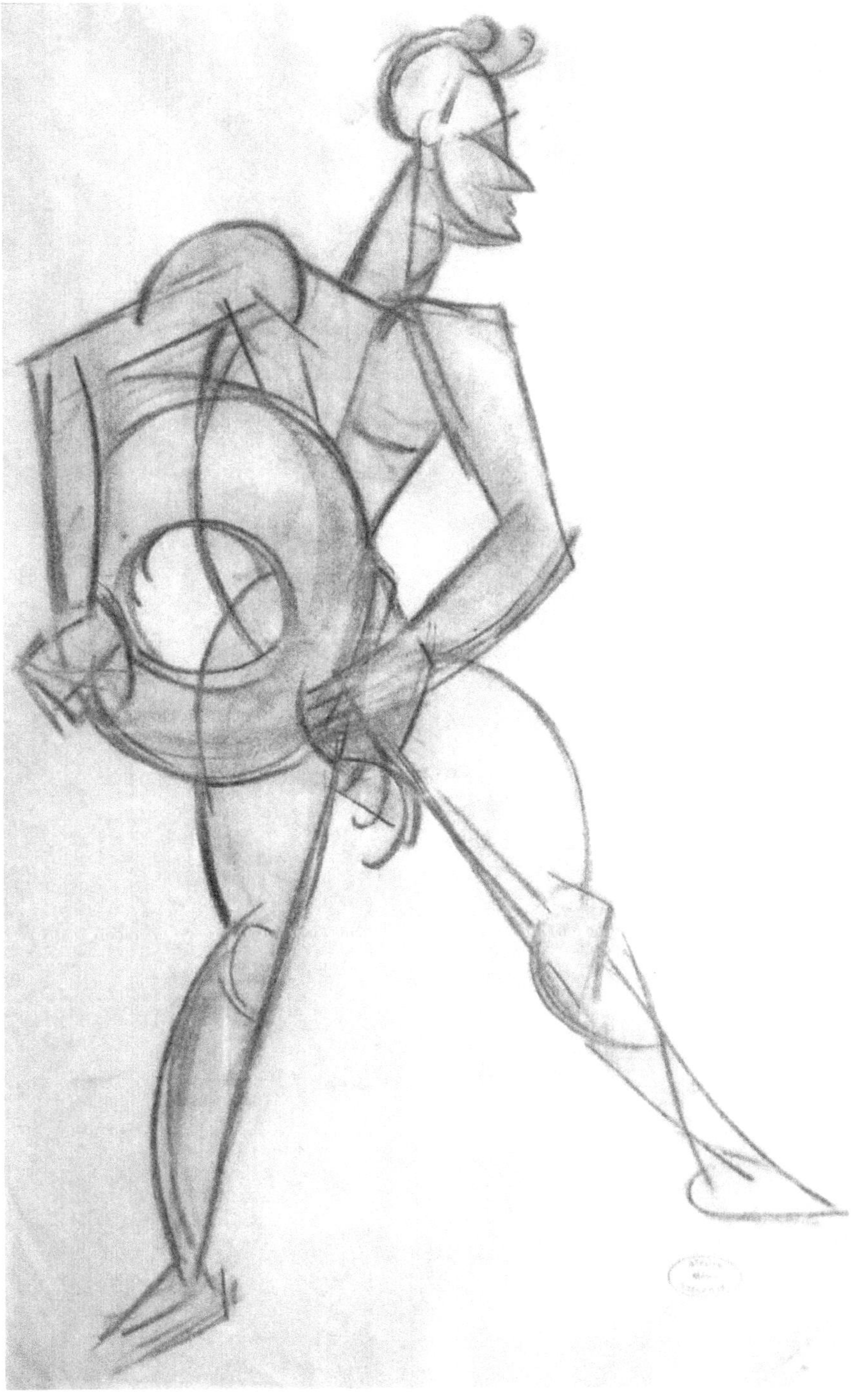

Figure 1.10 Marie Vassilieff, *Standing Male Nude*, c. 1910–14

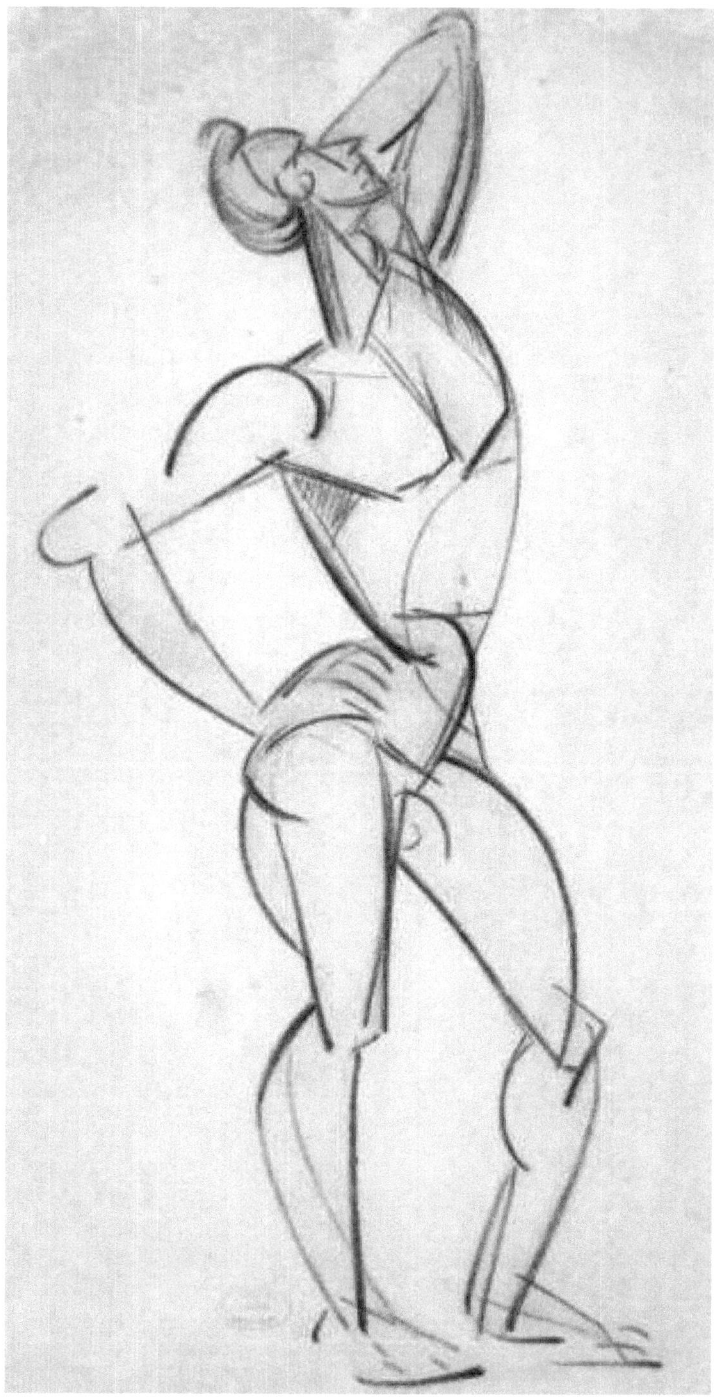

Figure 1.11 Marie Vassilieff, *Standing Male Nude with Arm Akimbo*, c. 1910–14

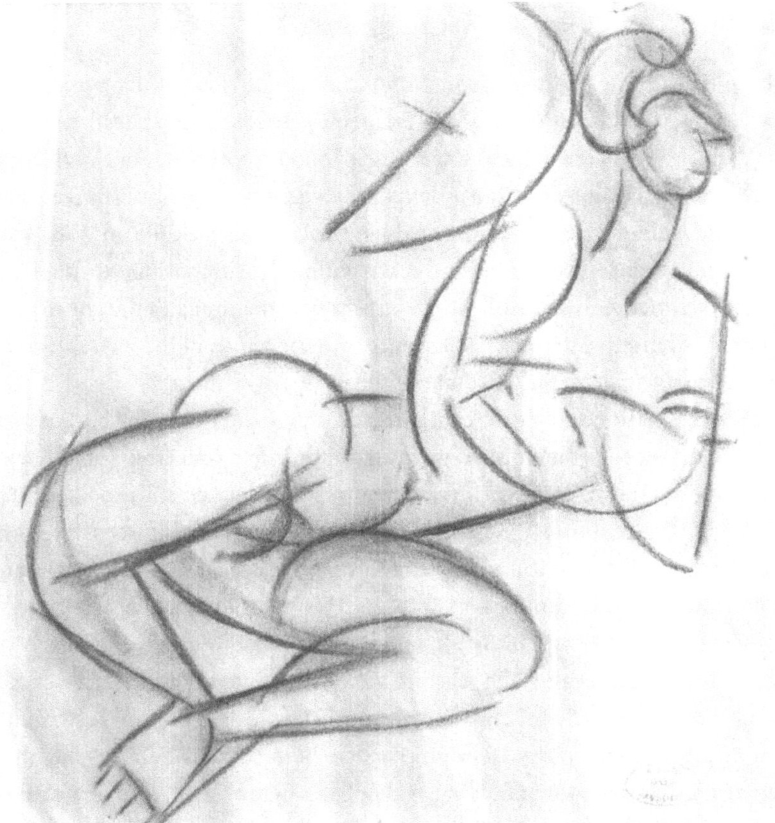

Figure 1.12 Marie Vassilieff, *Nu couché* (*Reclining Nude*), c. 1910–14

female or male physical traits. Perched on the figure's shoulder is a circular entity, like the one in *Standing Female Nude*. Objects and body parts commingle in these drawings in odd ways. Vassilieff underscores sexual hybridity by reducing the body to a series of moving, mechanical parts.

Regardless of the model's gender, Vassilieff adapts and applies aspects from her drawings in her paintings of female nudes. The dynamic interplay of jagged and smooth forms along with the rhythmic, flowing lines which characterize her sketches are also apparent in *Femme aux bas noirs*. In *Femme assise*, the limbs resemble those in *Standing Male Nude*. The nude's chiseled shoulder approximates the man's arm, while the legs appear to echo the male model's rigid thighs and bulbous calves. The peculiar spherical object in the drawing becomes part of the nude in *Femme assise* in the form of an engorged arm. Her drawings serve as preparation for her paintings, as she mines the shifting interaction between the body and space as well as between male and female anatomy through a kinesthetic treatment of corporeal form.

Homme et femme

Gender fluidity comes to the fore in *Homme et femme* (Plate 4, Plate 5). This work reflects an intersection of avant-garde theoretical discourses and aesthetic concerns through which Vassilieff mediates a new kind of bodily representation. With Bergson's duration and intuition as conduit, she reverses the intransigent narrative of gender difference in Cubist art, and does so through the language of Cubism. Vassilieff renders a dynamic experience of time and space within the composition through *passage* and other pictorial tools at her disposal, but she also manipulates the construction of the work to extend this dynamic experience into the hands of the viewer. In *Homme et femme*, Vassilieff alters the customary process of viewership.

Normally, a painting is seen from one side only – the front. The back is typically hidden from view once the finished painting is hung on a wall. The Cubists, who discarded traditional art rules and contrived new pictorial devices, still executed oil paintings following this centuries-old standard.[134] However, certain Cubists painted on both sides of the canvas for practical and economic reasons. Léger and Gris often treated the front and back of their paintings.[135] For Gris, this was a financial necessitude.[136] For Léger, when unsatisfied with his work, rather than discard the piece, he simply turned it over and started afresh.[137] The reasons Vassilieff painted both surfaces of *Homme et femme* were not merely for convenience or thrift. Designations of recto and verso are not helpful as neither side takes precedence. Both compositions display the same degree of finish. Given the matching scale of the figures, their proportionality and the stylistic similarities in their treatment, it seems as if the two images were planned and painted together. Shortly after the paint dried, Vassilieff turned the canvas over, presumably still unstretched, to tackle the other nude, or perhaps she worked on the two sides concurrently, flipping the canvas back and forth. She executed numerous double-sided works, but, in all other instances, each side stems from a different period in her career. *Homme et femme* is the only surviving example in her oeuvre in which she presents two contemporaneous images back to back.

Not only is this painting double-sided, but the figures are painted in reverse.[138] The work is inverted so that the head of *Homme* is on the same plane with the feet in *Femme* on the other side. One must turn the canvas *longitudinally*, like a cheval mirror, in order to view both images. In this manner, the work requires the direct involvement of the spectator – he or she must literally flip the piece in order to view it in its entirety. How exactly she intended the viewer to physically rotate a large painting within an exhibition space, and whether or not it was even shown publicly, remains a mystery. The necessitude of this inversion is baffling to its owners today. In an interview, the collectors explained that, for a recent exhibition, they were unsure of how to display *Homme et femme*, and simply decided to show one side.[139]

Lacking a fixed orientation, the work entices the viewer to turn the piece back and forth. This process results in a unique phenomenon. When rotating the painting, one visualizes a splintering, a transformation of one body into two.

Homme et femme was likely conceived at her academy where, as she explains in her memoir, two models, often a white woman and a Black man, would pose side by side. In both works, the nudes appear in a studio setting. In *Femme*, an assorted collection of pots and vases is set on shelves in the background which dissolve into a complex web of intersecting lines and planes. Vassilieff ruptures the surface with a medley of sharp, jagged shapes. Like the nude sketches, the body is deconstructed into cylindrical and rectilinear forms that mirror the objects around it. The circle on the nude's abdomen rhymes with the adjacent black sphere. An odd cluster of pyramids and circles, vibrantly colored, floats illogically in space to the left of the nude. The figure's triangular-shaped pubis echoes this strange mass of hovering objects. *Homme* is set before a backdrop of green-striped and bronze-colored drapery with vases on either side. Highlighted with colorful areas of *passage* in chromatic shades of turquoise, jade, sienna, pink and lilac, the body is given plasticity and volume. Circular lines around the shoulder and neck lend the figure a sense of movement. Anatomical inconsistencies abound: part of the left shoulder is missing, one pectoral muscle is smaller than the other, and the legs are misshapen. This inconsistency is the result of the fragmentation of the figure into facets through simultaneity. Such distortions appear in the background as well; the wrinkles in the drapery are implied by jagged segments incised by black lines which flatten form and suggest three-dimensionality at the same time. The ochre and greenish skin tone of the male nude are darker than that of *Femme*. The face is geometrized; slanted triangles for eyes, a line for the nose and a narrow gap for the mouth approximate the features of a Fang mask.[140] The black hair is piled into a wedge-shaped mass. The model may have been African. If this tentative hypothesis is true, *Homme* is a rare Black male Cubist nude.

Vassilieff seems to be the only Cubist who engaged consistently with the male body. Scouring catalogues raisonnés for Cubist male nudes uncovers a few examples, but nothing matching the audacious candor of Vassilieff's *Homme*. Léger executed a couple of sketches of male nudes, but they appear hesitant and self-conscious in comparison with his contemporaneous drawings of female figures. Gleizes exhibited a male nude in the 1911 Salon des Indépendants, which Apollinaire described: "Gleizes made a great effort that resulted in his figures: 'Homme nu,' 'Femme aux phlox,' where there is personality, vigor."[141] *Homme nu*, now lost, is documented in a black and white photograph.[142] The nude poses awkwardly and appears robotic, with a hulking torso and unmalleable limbs. In the same journal, Roger Allard wrote of the painting, "I perceive strange intentions of making an academic study."[143] To Allard, the image appeared like an *académie*, not a finished painting. The critic was probably bewildered by the appearance of a bulky, muscular body that seemed at odds with its domestic setting. In Léger's *Nudes in the Forest* (1909–11), the female nudes were mistaken for male bodies when the painting was shown at the Salon des Indépendants of 1911.[144] Resembling mechanical parts, the nudes lack identifiable sexual attributes. Apollinaire described the figures as "woodcutters."[145] For the critic, the image represented a brutal confrontation between naked lumberjacks and nature, set in the depths of a nondescript forest. Christopher Green argues that the nudes were in all likelihood female, and points to several visual clues: the rounded pelvic area of the leftmost figure and the long hair.[146] Although androgynous, Vassilieff's *Homme* still reads as male.

For a male artist in early twentieth-century France, painting and exhibiting a male nude was unusual and often led to critical disapproval. For a female artist, this was a transgressive act. Vassilieff's *Homme* is a gross aberration from the meek male nudes of her contemporaries. She does not shy away from rendering the genitalia. The male organ is placed at the center of the vertical axis and just below the horizontal, at eye level. Tackling the male nude in a brazen way could pose serious risks for women. As Tamar Garb states, "Any deviation from normative gender roles or blurring of difference was a threat to the social order, a form of racial and cultural regression and a perversion of the natural."[147] Just before Vassilieff painted *Homme*, Goncharova caused controversy in Moscow in 1910 for exhibiting male nudes.

On the evening of March 24, 1910, Goncharova held a solo exhibition in Moscow featuring twenty-two of her paintings.[148] Only members of the erudite Society of Free Aesthetics were invited. A critic managed to infiltrate the opening and wrote an incendiary review denouncing the show, which appeared the next day in *Golos Moskvy*, a daily Moscow newspaper.[149] The critic described Goncharova's work as disturbing and perverse. He wrote that certain nudes, in particular the male ones, "surpassed the pornography of secret postcards."[150] The fact that Goncharova's nudes were not idealized led him to associate them with pornography. Also at issue was Goncharova's gender. He wrote, "it is most disturbing that the painter is a woman, who under the influence of half-sick, overblown decadent types, has stepped beyond the boundary of morally correct behavior."[151] The article was disseminated widely. The next day the police seized the paintings, and Goncharova was arrested "for the public display of blatantly corrupting pictures."[152] Taken to trial on charges of pornography, she was eventually acquitted on the grounds that the exhibition had been closed to the public. Goncharova scholar Jane Sharp contends that "Goncharova's problems arose with her increasing visibility as a woman who painted subjects associated with masculine creative identities, especially the nude life study."[153] For a woman to paint and exhibit nudes that did not follow time-honored artistic standards was radical – in Russia and in France. Vassilieff was not present, but she would have heard about the incident later, as she kept abreast of artistic currents in Russia. Like Goncharova, Vassilieff dared to risk her career and reputation when she treated the male body. She did so without hesitation or discretion – Vassilieff signed her name prominently in capital letters on the lower right of *Homme.*

After the 1910 trial, Goncharova would forsake the nude for other genres and founded Rayonism with her partner, Larionov.[154] She met Vassilieff in Paris sometime between 1914 and 1917.[155] The two women worked together as members of the Union des Artistes Russes and they participated in the same group exhibitions including the Section d'Or in 1920 and the Russian Arts and Crafts show at Whitechapel Gallery in London in 1921. Vassilieff's admiration for the artist was manifest when she designated Goncharova as her son's godmother. It is plausible that Vassilieff heard stories about her arrest.

Although none of Goncharova's male nudes survives, there is an extant female nude that provides insight into her early nude practice.[156] In palette and facture, Goncharova's *Female Nude (Life Study)* (1908–9) demonstrates an awareness of modern French styles. In Moscow, she had access to paintings by Matisse, Cézanne and Picasso, among other artists in private collections.[157] Pressed closely to the foreground, the nude's head and legs breach the limits of the picture plane. The arms are raised so that the full torso is exposed. The figure's sexuality is foregrounded within the composition; a marked vertical axis draws our eyes downward to the shadowed pubis.

In *Femme*, Vassilieff likewise employs visible brushwork, bold contours and Cézannesque *passage*, but she departs from nature to a greater degree. The flesh is colored flaxen and cream with flecks of teal, rose and lavender. The background is a vast chromatic spectrum as well. Areas of exposed, unprimed canvas interspersed throughout lend an unfinished appearance. Through simultaneity, Vassilieff breaks the body into geometricized segments, imbuing the sensation of multiple views. Just as with *Homme*, the body exhibits numerous anatomical disparities: the hands and feet are disproportionately large, the shoulders too wide and the arms too thin. The face, reduced to an assemblage of small triangles painted in variegated pinks, plainly shows the combined influence of Fauvist portraits and African masks.

The most striking aspect that distinguishes Vassilieff's nude from Goncharova's is its gender ambiguity. Sexual attributes are limited to a pair of diminutive breasts, a narrow waist and a highly perched chignon incongruously affixed to a strapping, athletic body with broad shoulders and vigorously muscular legs. A mixture of male and female traits, the figure's sex is almost indeterminate. The breasts, incised by diagonal lines, resemble male pectoral muscles. The abdomen, bisected by a straight line, appears muscular. Rather than curvesome, this nude is stiff and angular. The legs are just as brawny as those of the male nude on the other side. The rigid lines defining the quadriceps and the tibia resemble chiseled muscles. Vassilieff, who studied anatomy as a young medical student in Russia, eschews the laws of science as she pronounces anatomical abnormalities. But the most perplexing element is the triangular pubis. As we have seen, pubic hair in art was considered explicit, but this hardly seems like a patch of hair. Instead, the narrow, jagged triangle pierces downward and extends past the thigh in the manner of a phallus. The oversized paw-like hands that hover above it do not conceal this element, but accentuate it. When comparing this feature with the male organ on the reverse, they are approximately the same size and shape and are placed in roughly the same spot on each side of the canvas.

Like *Femme*, *Homme* hardly stands up to its title. The positioning of the body from the head, cocked slightly to one side, pointed shoulders, slender waist, laterally tilted hips to the knees, angled inward, forms a sensual S-curve. The pelvic muscles, normally emphasized in representations of the male body, are not convincing. Instead, they highlight the curvature of the oversized hips, which are thrusted sideways. The kind of engaged, confident stance that contrapposto normally conveys is transformed into an effeminate, idle posture. The background, distinct from the studio space in *Femme*, is draped in richly colored fabric and decorated with vases and vibrant floor tiles, evoking an Orientalist scene – a space normally coded as feminine. In assimilating African masks for the figure's visage and filling the space with Orientalist accoutrements, Vassilieff exoticizes this male nude in a manner typically reserved for the female body. At the same time, she blurs race. Due to the Cubist and Primitivizing distortions, it is impossible to determine with certitude the race of the figure, although the complexion does not seem to be that of a white male. With its mask-like visage, zigzag lines that incise the body and the ochre-colored, serrated drapery in the background, *Homme* faintly recalls *Demoiselles d'Avignon*, save for the complete absence of male nudes in Picasso's painting. In her double-sided canvas, Vassilieff rejects oppositional dichotomies of gender, amalgamates male and female bodies and conceives a radically new image of the nude.

The gender indeterminacy of *Homme et femme* and the visual parallels Vassilieff draws between male and female bodies is entirely at odds with the insistence on gender difference in the works of her male contemporaries. Through Cubist means, Vassilieff overturns regressive gender views and revokes evocations of *élan vital*. Yet, while challenging one concept, Vassilieff engages with another – Bergson's theory of duration – not just through simultaneity, but on an integral level. It is implicit in the painting's very construction. Composed of two images, it is likely that *Homme et femme* was meant to be viewed in sequence. This unusual presentation relates to Bergson's theories on psychological time in multiple ways. As we have seen, the painting represents the combined assemblage of viewpoints – the artist's collected encounters with the nude over a stretch of time through simultaneity. The work captures the mobile and ever-changing process of life drawing, revealing how Vassilieff perceived the body, male and female, over a certain interval of time. Of course, in painting, the factor of time is not so easily implied, as the effect of an image normally occurs in a single moment. However, in Vassilieff's work, viewing is no longer limited to a static, one-sided experience. Instead, the painting necessitates the viewer's mobility. Time is incorporated into the viewing process itself; one must flip the canvas lengthwise in order to view it in its entirety. The process which Gleizes and Metzinger describe "of moving around an object to seize from it several successive appearances" which permits the artist to "reconstitute it in time," is then reenacted by the viewer when beholding the work through the physical act of rotation.[158] Multiple viewpoints and different temporal and spatial settings are doubly implied as one flips the canvas vertically, at which point the spectator is faced with two bodies of different, but ambiguous, gender.

The work echoes Bergson's theory of intuition as well. Intuition is the alternative to a codified, rational representation of time. Bergson argued that intuition can never actually be represented through a work of art, but it can be *suggested* by a treatment of space which is not mathematical but guided by the artist's own feelings.[159] Discarding rational or measurable approaches to conceive form and space, the Salon Cubists held their work to be a product of personal expression, consciousness and feeling.[160] They believed that when a work of art was the result of an intuitive act, it would reflect the whole self of the artist.[161] Moreover, Bergson maintained that, "if an [artist's] intuition is to be suggested [to the spectator], the art work itself must induce an *illogical* state of mind in the beholder."[162] In their interpretation of Bergson, the Cubists considered their novel artistic devices, such as *passage,* simultaneity, arbitrary scale and spatial disjunctions as evocations of intuition. Vassilieff incorporates these techniques in *Homme et femme,* portraying dynamic, shifting figures on each picture plane. Additionally, the construction of the work defies logic. With two compositions joined, the figures reversed and separated bilaterally front and back, the work's orientation breaks with any logical picture viewing process. Directed by her own accumulated experience of male and female bodies of diverse ethnicities, Vassilieff reveals her unique perception of gender, sexuality and race.

The Cubists believed that, if an artist's intuition were to become evident, it would elicit a reaction *from the viewer.* Gleizes and Metzinger state,

> It is our whole personality which … transforms the plane of the picture. As it reacts, this plane reflects the personality back upon the understanding of the spectator, and thus pictorial space is defined: a sensitive passage between two subjective spaces.[163]

Through a qualitative handling of space, a work of art could express intuition, and it could also excite a perceptive spectator's emotions. *Passage* was considered to be a powerful technique for granting the spectator a sense of the dynamism of form and could in turn provoke a psychological response.[164] Might the simple act of rotating the canvas vertically encourage an intuitive reaction from viewers as well? It would allow them to perceive not only space, but also sex and race, dynamically. It would enable them to discern these elements, not as mutually exclusive, but analogous and interconnected. The painting in its construction reinforces the analogies between genders already apparent on each picture plane. *Homme et femme* at first evokes a kind of coexistence of genders, since they are not side by side. Once the canvas is flipped, a strange doubling or fusion of genders occurs across two contiguous planes. The flexibility of gender traits is reinforced through an engagement with the work itself; the beholder, when viewing each side, is encouraged to draw parallels between the female and male sex. Finally, the option to reverse the painting gives the viewer the choice either to decide with which nude he or she identifies, or to ascertain fluidity across gender lines. Not only is the body dynamic and shifting in *Homme et femme*, gender and race are in a state of flux. Vassilieff disavows sexual difference and strict gender binaries manifest in Cubism, while allowing the viewer to perceive the body in entirely new ways.

Vassilieff's *Poupée-autoportrait* and the avant-garde doll

"Ni homme, ni femme," wrote Marie Vassilieff in her memoir as she described her appearance and character as neither male nor female. Through dress, comportment and lifestyle, she divorced herself from the expectations of middle-class femininity and asserted her independence and agency. She was extremely self-aware of her self-enacted gender disruption, and this extended into all aspects of her life and artistic practice. While in her Cubist paintings she defied sexist ideologies as well as masculine erotic desire conceiving gender-blending nudes, in her self-portraits she would apply a similar tactic. Around 1915, her non-conformist approach to the body intensified and extended past the easel. She designed costumes and cross-dressed in theater performances and artist balls, an important aspect of life in Montparnasse. She also launched a new art form – her signature *poupée-portrait* – and navigated a new subject – the nude self-portrait (figure 1.13).

Although these works are distinct from her Cubist paintings in medium and aesthetic, I wish to highlight a continuum in Vassilieff's oeuvre. As she pivoted from Cubism to her own kind of Dadaist doll production, she exacerbated the gender *indistinction* she herself embodied. In what follows, I consider the ways in which Vassilieff pushed the bounds of gender in representation through her own self-image. In her nude self-portrait doll, she moved beyond binaries as she negotiated her own hybrid identities.

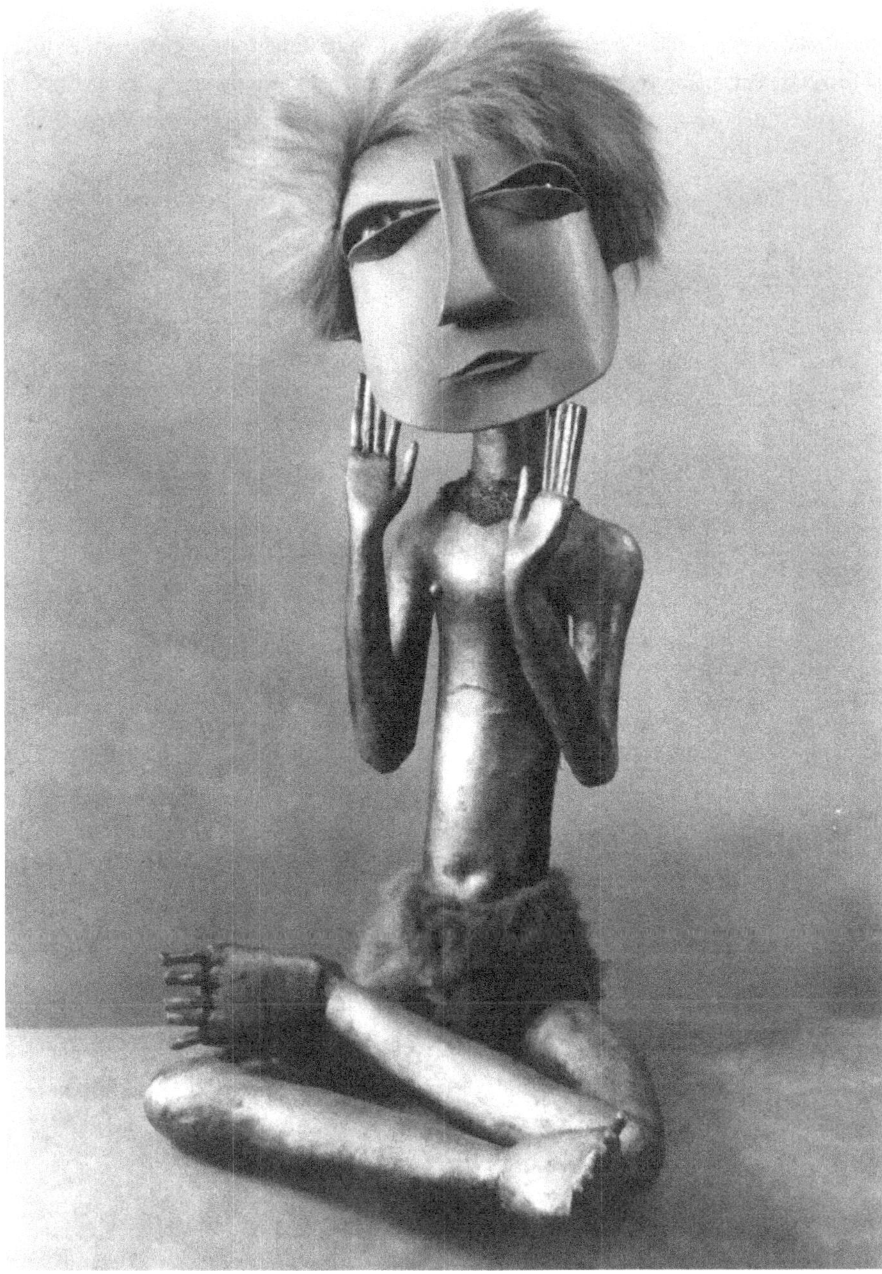

Figure 1.13 Marie Vassilieff, *Poupée-autoportrait* (*Doll Self-Portrait*), 1929

Vassilieff pioneered a new kind of modernist doll – the *poupée-portrait.* Effigies in one sense, avant-garde sculpture in another, they represented various personalities of interwar Paris. The style varied from caricatures, to a loose resemblance of African sculpture, to pure fantasy (figure 1.14). Reducing her sitters' characteristics to the

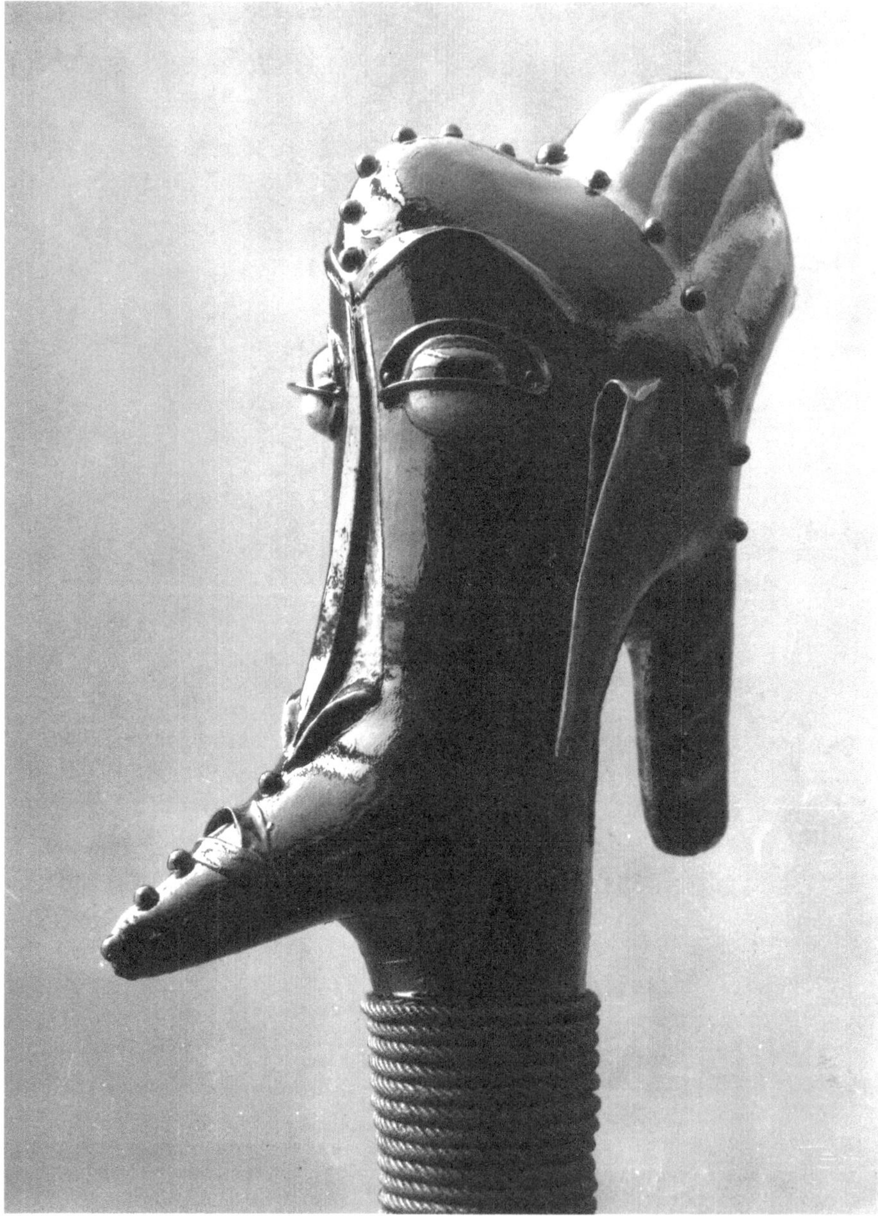

Figure 1.14 Marie Vassilieff, *Soulier primitif (Tête ou pomme de canne)* (*Primitive Shoe*), 1925

most essential traits, Vassilieff captured their personality with succinct and particular visual clues. She made no distinction between her *poupées-portraits* and her creations in other art forms. She considered her dolls serious artistic innovations rather than mere craft, and critics agreed. One noted, "as for Marie Vassilieff, her dolls are true works of art. No one can be deceived; they have such a character that we can recognize them among a thousand."[165] Vassilieff broke down artistic hierarchies that separated craft from the fine arts as she elevated ordinary doll-making into vanguard sculpture practice.

Vassilieff's idiosyncratic doll-making technique required ingenuity and dexterity and reaped unexpected results. In an article she published in 1925 in the journal *Montparnasse*, Vassilieff articulated what she was striving for in her *poupées-portraits*. She wrote, "My doll portraits are not mere surfaces; they are in fact demonstrations against the severe banality of modern and classical sculpture, which have at their disposal all the richness of materials which they do not know how to exploit."[166] In contrast with modern sculpture which she considered "banal," Vassilieff employed a rich diversity of unconventional materials. "Satin, leather and enamels are instruments of my orchestra," she stated as she crumbled the hierarchies that had separated fine art from craft.[167] The exact makeup of each doll was unique. Unfortunately, the majority of them no longer exist and were never catalogued. By assessing extant dolls, photographs of those now lost, and descriptions in journals and newspapers, it is possible to determine which materials she favored.[168] As explained in another article, "the confection of her dolls" varies from "papier-mâché painted in red, black or gold … fabric, wool, goat leather or metal … [The] eyes are glass beads and the eyebrows tapered velvet."[169] Most often, the dolls' bodies were made with leather and filled with sawdust.[170] In those instances, each part of the doll was made separately and sewn together, making the body semi-mobile.[171] Certain features were painted on pieces of silk or chiffon and applied to the doll. When she could not afford these materials, she utilized objects found in the trash. She even made dolls out of vegetables when funds were extremely low.[172]

Vassilieff began creating dolls during her last trip to Russia from 1915 to 1916. She displayed her first *poupées*, which she described as "*types parisiens*," in the notable exhibition *Magazin*, organized by Vladimir Tatlin in Moscow.[173] She also exhibited in the legendary "0.10" alongside Kazimir Malevich in Petrograd.[174] Upon her return to Paris, she expanded into a steady production of *poupée portraits*, representing prominent personalities. She created dolls of the writers Apollinaire, Blaise Cendrars, the artists Matisse, Picasso, Léger, Orloff, Othon Friesz, the couturier Poiret, theorist Henri Poincaré and politicians such as Trotsky, foreign diplomats, and famous performers including Josephine Baker. She confounded race, sometimes representing white men or women with dark skin, as is the case with her portrait of Poiret. In her memoir, Vassilieff noted the popularity of her *poupées*. Even Valadon owned one.[175] Her doll portraits caught the attention of Léger, who noted his desire to promote them in a letter to Louis Poughon in 1917.[176] Unfortunately, this project never came to fruition. Still, by the 1920s Vassilieff had established herself in the avant-garde community as a creator of portrait dolls. Poiret was an ardent supporter of her anthropomorphic figures. He promoted them in a number of exhibitions, including a solo show at the Chez Martine gallery in 1922. One year later, Man Ray photographed Vassilieff as an avant-garde doll-maker. Dressed up as a man in a collared shirt and wide-brimmed hat, she holds an African-inspired doll and gazes wistfully at the viewer.

Vassilieff's *poupée-portraits* reveal her sustained engagement with African art.[177] Her introduction to African art began while under Matisse's tutelage. Primitivism, or the cultural appropriation of non-Western cultures, was pervasive during the early twentieth century, and by the interwar period an influx of literature appeared on the topic. Perhaps Vassilieff owned a copy of Carl Einstein's book *Negerplastik*, published in German in 1915 and in French in 1922. *La Sculpture nègre primitive* by Paul-Guillaume and Thomas Munro (1929) was another key source. Even earlier, she likely read Apollinaire and Paul Guillaume's *Sculptures nègres* (1917) as well as Henri Clouzot and André Level's *L'Art nègre et l'art océanien* (1919).[178] Moreover, she had access to displays of African sculptures in the collections of Picasso and other artists she knew, as well as at the Musée d'Ethnographie du Trocadéro, at flea markets, and in African art exhibitions in Paris. One such exhibition was held in Montparnasse in 1916 and consisted of modern paintings positioned alongside "sculptures nègres." It was organized by Guillaume with support from the arts association Lyre et Palette. Another example was the *Première exposition d'art nègre et d'art océanien*, organized by Level and Guillaume in May of 1919.[179]

Artists flocked to the *marché aux puces* in search of "*objets sauvages*," amassing large numbers of ethnographic objects. James Clifford states, "Such objects – stripped of their functional context – were necessary furnishings of the avant-garde studio."[180] The allure was their supposed exotic or wild nature. As Jean Laude noted in an early and important book on primitive art, "*L'Art nègre* is taken as an exotic source. In this sense, it reflects a great deal less the specific characteristics and serves instead as an example of wild art, of primitive art."[181] For the vanguard, "The exotic was a prime court of appeal against the rational, the beautiful, the normal of the West."[182] Of course, cultural appropriation is inherently problematic. In drawing from so-called "primitive" sources, Vassilieff failed to critique Europeans' racist views. Alas, she was a figure of her time and was not immune to the ubiquitous colonialist and racial prejudice of the interwar moment.[183] What interested Vassilieff was not ethnographic study in the actual tribal cultures themselves, nor in perpetuating troubling stereotypes, but rather how the essence of difference that she saw in those objects could serve as a metaphor for the Otherness which she herself embodied.

Vassilieff incarnated herself as a doll in *Poupée-autoportrait* (c. 1920–29) (Plate 6) and constructed an identity outside European cultural norms. She abbreviates her facial features to a long, tubular nose flared at the bottom and bulging eyes. Her eyebrows are composed of a thin black line and her pink lips are straight and narrow. She sports a blonde, shaggy wig composed of real hair. Her eyes are made of glass beads encased within protruding leather flaps, resembling eyelids.[184] These lifelike, protuberant eyeballs lend the *poupée* the appearance of an effigy.[185] While the cropped hair and translucent eyes recall the artist's own, the rest of the mask's features approximate those of a Pende Mask (figure 1.15). In particular, the encasement of the eyes between narrow slits, the semi-circular eyebrows, thin nose and minuscule mouth echo the Pende mask that appears on the cover of Einstein's *Negerplastik*. Even if she had not seen this illustration, she undoubtedly saw the two Pende masks in Matisse's collection.[186] In the majority of her *poupée portraits*, Vassilieff translates the African masks into simple geometric forms, breaking any recognizable tie with the original ethnographic source. Her self-portrait, however, retains a noticeable resemblance with its source material.

Contrary to the traditional self-portrait which offers a lifelike impression of the artist's external appearance, Vassilieff's *Poupée-autoportrait* is not a true likeness at all. In blending her own image with the mask's, Vassilieff associates herself with Otherness. Through self-portraiture, she examined the complexity and ambiguity of her own position in society. Paris was fraught with misogyny and xenophobia during Vassilieff's lifetime, which surely augmented her sense of marginality. She transcribed her feelings of dislocation as a nationless, foreign woman into an obscured self-image of irresolute gender and ethnicity. In this manner, Vassilieff engaged in a process that may be called "self-othering."[187] Through an inextricable merging of Self and Other, she constructed a new identity outside accepted social norms and expectations. In *Negerplastik*, Einstein wrote of the metamorphic powers of the mask which was said to annihilate the wearer's character.[188] For Vassilieff the mask is not simply a form of effacement, but an apparatus of transformation. Through it she constructed a self that was divergent from normative, French womanhood. Vassilieff refashioned a liminal and fluctuating identity, suspended between the familiar and exotic, Self and Other, male and female.

An analogous process has been identified in the work of Modigliani, with whom Vassilieff was close. Mason Klein contends that "through portraiture, the artist examined the nature and ambiguity of identity against an array of cultural types, a meditation that addressed his own dislocation within the Diaspora, his own secular Italian/Jewish identity."[189] As a Sephardic Jew from Italy, Modigliani occupied a marginal

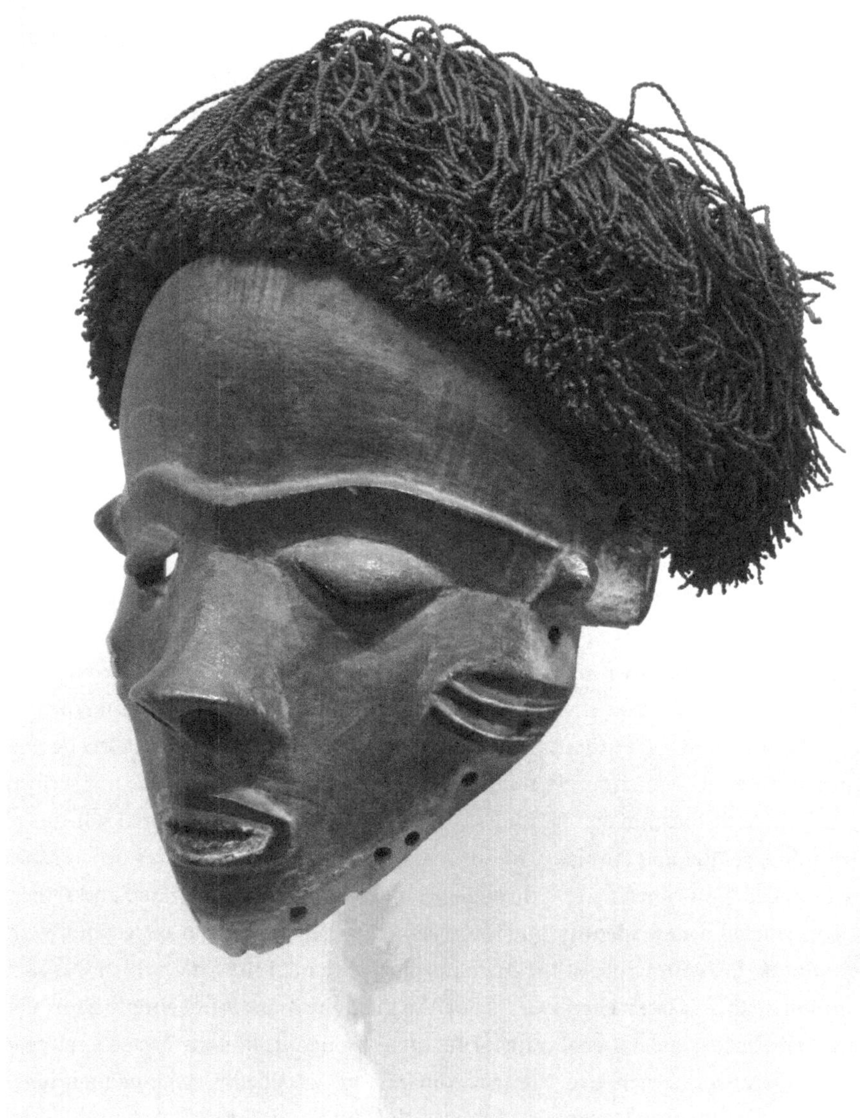

Figure 1.15 Pende people, *Female Face Mask (Gambanda)*, Central Africa, Democratic Republic of the Congo, early 1900s

status in the anti-Semitic Parisian milieu. Like Vassilieff, his sense of self was highly complex, and his outsider status led him to seek out culturally diverse forms in art. Nevertheless, Vassilieff's oeuvre is distinct from Modigliani's in style, in concern, and in the continuous rendering of herself as androgyne. Furthermore, she never created anything like the overtly erotic nudes for which Modigliani is known. Vassilieff's memoir recounts how he frequented her canteen, often in a drunken state, causing trouble, such as at the Banquet Braque. She notes that she looked after him and at times served as a mother figure. Modigliani painted Vassilieff around 1916. The geometric simplification of her features is characteristic of his portraits from this period. He fuses his sitter's qualities with those of ancient ethnographic art into a kind of masked portrait.

In her *Poupée-autoportrait*, Vassilieff equivocates boundaries of gender as well as race. In opposition to white porcelain dolls, highly coveted in France at the turn of the twentieth century, the body's skin tone is a light chestnut color comparable to *Poupée Josephine Baker* (1925–27, uncertain attribution). The Baker doll is embellished with a fuchsia feather tutu, pearl necklace, large gold chest plate and a boa that frames the torso and face. The American dancer is made recognizable with her signature bobbed haircut and enormous smile. Besides a simple beaded necklace, Vassilieff's *Poupée-Autoportrait* lacks the glittery accessories adorning the Baker doll. Naked except for a fur loincloth, the body is darkened and reduced to a cylindrical form with long, slender limbs, not unlike many African reliquary figures illustrated in Carl Einstein's *Negerplastik*, Apollinaire and Guillaume's *Sculptures nègres* and Clouzot and Level's *L'Art nègre et l'art océanien*. These publications, in particular the latter two in French, likely served as important resources for Vassilieff. Visual parallels abound between her portrait dolls and the sculptures illustrated in these early books on African and Oceanic art. For example, a male Fang figure from a reliquary ensemble illustrated in *Negerplastik* also exhibits a narrow, cylinder-shaped body.[190] Appearing in *L'Art nègre et l'art océanien*, a Bamana female statue from Mali has long, slender arms as well as a disproportionately protracted torso.[191] From *Sculptures nègres*, a Sudanese reliquary figure from Matisse's collection displays similar characteristics of a tubular core with lengthy and narrow limbs.[192] Limited to an assemblage of geometric forms, all three figures are nevertheless identifiable as either male or female. In certain cases, they have pronounced sexual attributes, such as cone-shaped, protruding breasts. By contrast, the lithe body of Vassilieff's self-portrait doll does not exhibit any specifically masculine or feminine characteristics.

On occasion, Vassilieff would reuse the body of the doll for different portraits. This appears to be the case with her own self-portrait. Vassilieff employed the same or near-identical doll body for her *poupée* of the male Hungarian painter, István Farkas (figure 1.16). Besides economic practicality, recycling of the doll's form

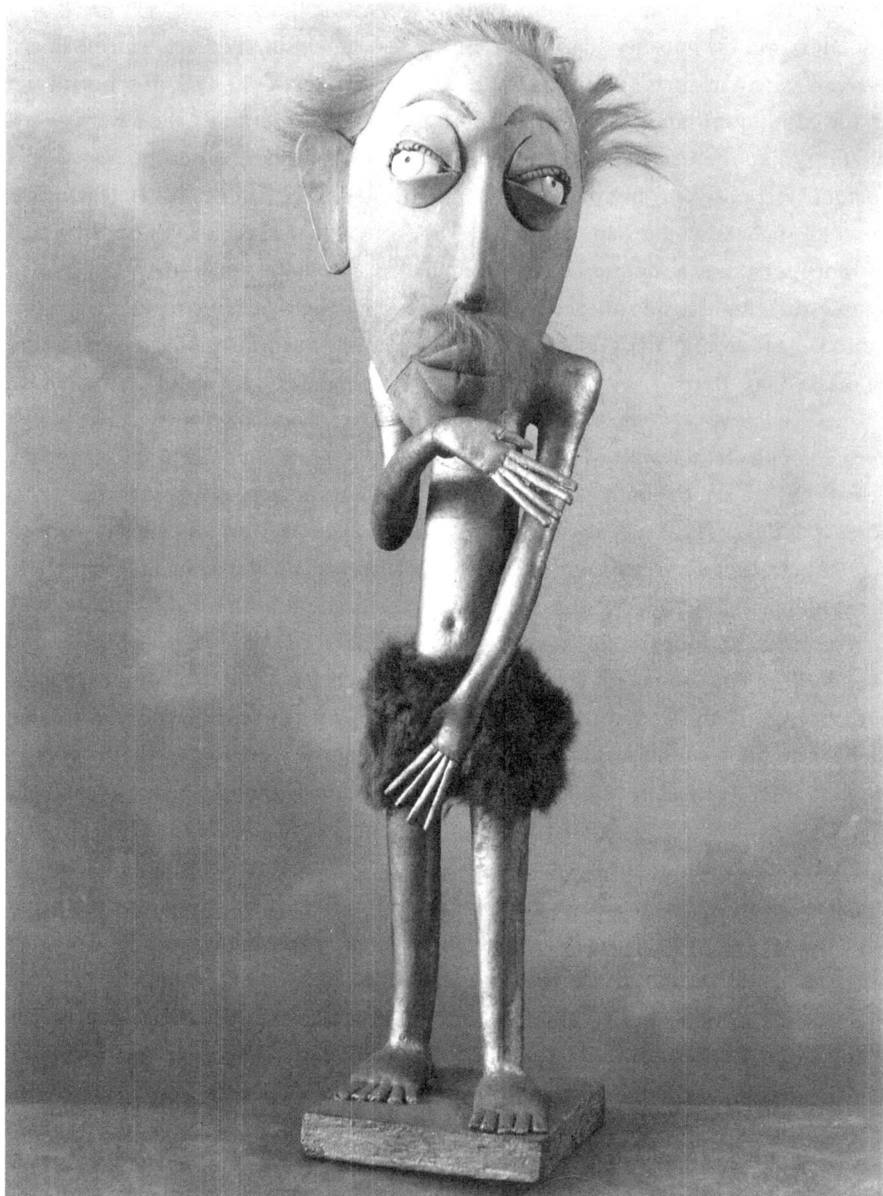

Figure 1.16 Marie Vassilieff, *Poupée István Farkas* (*István Farkas Doll*), 1929

has greater implications. The interchangeability of its corporeal parts negates the assumed link of the doll with the white female body. Male and female, white and Black, Self and Other are no longer opposites. Vassilieff overturns the doll's ideological morphology and its embedded, traditional gendered associations. Through her

Poupée-autoportrait, she reconsiders her own multifarious identity as she moves beyond binaries of race and gender to their reconciliation.

Vassilieff repeatedly deemphasizes gender in her self-portraits. Whether as a *poupée* or in a painting, she hides or obscures the groin and takes on the form of the sexless body of a toy doll. Rather than positioning gender as dominant, she diminishes its role in identity construction. Her work suggests that the play of gender is only one minor aspect of identity. Vassilieff produced a clothed version of her *Poupée-autoportrait*. Now lost, it appears in a photograph from the journal *Paris-Montparnasse* from 1929 (figure 1.17). She made an illustration of that doll for the cover of her memoir, *La Bohème du XXe siècle* (figure 1.18). The face is a clone of the nude self-portrait, with its almond-shaped eyes, stenciled eyebrows and small, flared nose. The mask-like visage is affixed to a puppet-like body. Rather than a loincloth, she sports contemporary, masculine attire: a collared jacket and necktie. She poses rigidly with straight and bent arms, her head slanted, and she emits a blank stare through gaping, inhuman eyes. With her legs jutting outward in the stiff manner of an inert puppet, she splays her hand out flat between her legs – a gesture which, rather than displaying modesty, defiantly asserts a self-possessed sexuality. Confidently cross-dressing in a jacket and tie, Vassilieff's self-portrayal lacks a fixed gender. She wore similar clothing in everyday life, as captured in numerous photographs. Parading an androgynous appearance, Vassilieff molded a self unhindered by social mores or stringent definitions of gender.

Vassilieff unites dichotomous artforms – the common doll with the "high" art of sculpture as she simultaneously discards the traditional implications and meanings that the doll carries. Vassilieff's clothed *Poupée-autoportrait* belonged to Valadon, and the subject of the doll fascinated both artists.[193] Valadon's *La Poupée délaissée* (*Abandoned Doll*) (1921) depicts a nude adolescent girl. Affixed to the crown of her head is a large, pink bow, matching the one on the discarded doll. The girl pays no attention to her toy. She turns to her reflection in a hand mirror instead, "abandoning" the doll as a symbol of her childhood. With her budding curves, the girl's naked form is caught somewhere between youth and womanhood. Unlike Valadon, Vassilieff extricates the doll from its usual associations. In Western culture, the doll in its myriad manifestations is conventionally linked with girlhood. Playing with dolls was advocated, as it was believed to be an edifying method of instilling a desire for womanly dress and inculcating ladylike demeanor. Sharon Marcus explains that "dolls exemplified ideals of genteel female appearance," and they were "designed to inspire a passion for femininity in girls."[194] Dressing up the doll was an important part of this process, as it promoted identification with the doll. Doll manufacture proliferated in the nineteenth and early twentieth centuries, with France as the dominant producer.[195] The materials varied from cheaper versions in rag, wood and leather,

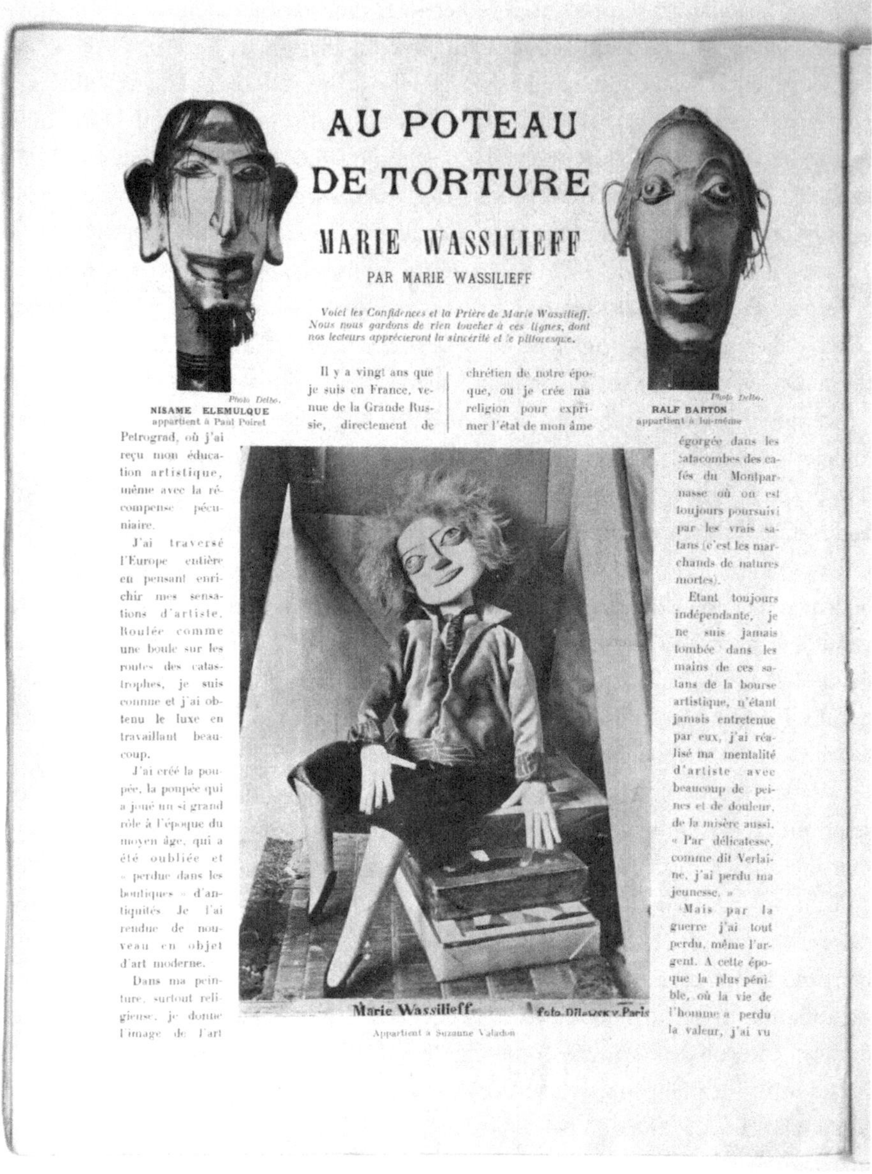

AU POTEAU DE TORTURE

MARIE WASSILIEFF

PAR MARIE WASSILIEFF

Voici les Confidences et la Prière de Marie Wassilieff. Nous nous gardons de rien toucher à ces lignes, dont nos lecteurs apprécieront la sincérité et le pittoresque.

Photo Delbo.
NISAME ELEMULQUE
appartient à Paul Poiret

Photo Delbo.
RALF BARTON
appartient à lui-même

Il y a vingt ans que je suis en France, venue de la Grande Russie, directement de Petrograd, où j'ai reçu mon éducation artistique, même avec la récompense pécuniaire.

J'ai traversé l'Europe entière en pensant enrichir mes sensations d'artiste. Roulée comme une boule sur les routes des catastrophes, je suis connue et j'ai obtenu le luxe en travaillant beaucoup.

J'ai créé la poupée, la poupée qui a joué un si grand rôle à l'époque du moyen âge, qui a été oubliée et « perdue dans les boutiques » d'antiquités. Je l'ai rendue de nouveau en objet d'art moderne.

Dans ma peinture, surtout religieuse, je donne l'image de l'art chrétien de notre époque, où je crée ma religion pour exprimer l'état de mon âme égorgée dans les catacombes des cafés du Montparnasse où on est toujours poursuivi par les vrais satans (c'est les marchands de natures mortes).

Etant toujours indépendante, je ne suis jamais tombée dans les mains de ces satans de la bourse artistique, n'étant jamais entretenue par eux, j'ai réalisé ma mentalité d'artiste avec beaucoup de peines et de douleur, de la misère aussi. « Par délicatesse, comme dit Verlaine, j'ai perdu ma jeunesse. »

Mais par la guerre j'ai tout perdu, même l'argent. A cette époque la plus pénible, où la vie de l'homme a perdu la valeur, j'ai vu

Marie Wassilieff

Appartient à Suzanne Valadon

Figure 1.17 Marie Vassilieff, Photograph of Marie Vassilieff's *Poupée autoportrait*, reproduced in "Au poteau de torture" in *Paris-Montparnasse*, March 15, 1929

to more expensive versions in wax and porcelain, with a copious selection of lavish outfits. Meanwhile, in Russia, the Matryoshka, or nesting doll, first appeared at the end of the nineteenth century and reinforced similar tropes about effeminateness and fertility. These dolls were produced in the artist colony Talashkino, the site of a

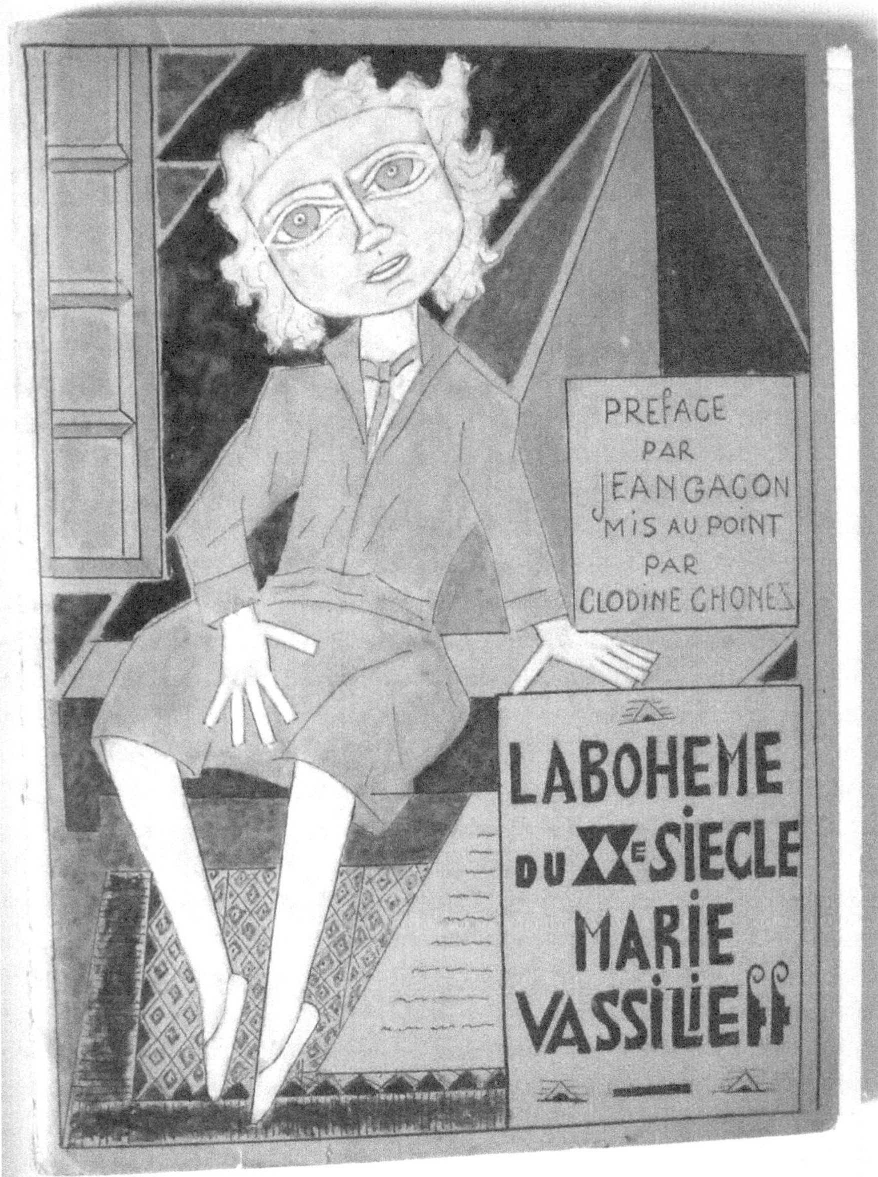

Figure 1.18 Marie Vassilieff, *La Bohème du XXe siècle*, cover illustration, c. 1930

Russian folk art revival near Vassilieff's hometown of Smolensk.[196] But Vassilieff's dolls bear no visual or symbolic link with either of these customs. Furthermore, she ventured into new territory by choosing to represent race in her *poupées*. Black dolls were exceedingly scarce in the early twentieth century, especially in Europe.

When they did appear, more often than not they conformed to worn-out stereotypes.[197] In her *Poupée-Autoportrait*, Vassilieff overthrows the doll's archetypal function as an exemplary model of white, heteronormative womanhood and passivity. She downplays the role of gender, confounds race, denaturalizes social identity and provides a taxonomy which is fluctuating and unstable.

Vassilieff's interdisciplinary approach to art, including her employment of sundry materials and enquiry into doll-making as an art form, resonates profoundly with Dada. In particular, her *poupée-portraits* strike a chord with Dadaist doll and puppet creations. Marionette performances occurred regularly at the Dadaist Zurich nightclub, Cabaret Voltaire, co-founded by Emmy Hennings and Hugo Ball. Hennings performed in radical left-wing theater and, like Vassilieff, created innovative dolls and puppets.[198] A photograph from 1917 shows her with a hand puppet of her own creation.[199] Also based in Zurich, the Dadaist Sophie Taeuber-Arp made avant-garde dolls and puppets. Hers were composed of an assemblage of recycled materials, as seen in Vassilieff's myriad creations. Taeuber-Arp's marionettes became well known, especially those made for the 1918 performance *King Stag*.[200] Rather than modeling her figures after human forms, she composed them purely out of geometric shapes. With her innovative puppets, Taeuber-Arp made significant contributions to avant-garde theater. Hannah Höch, the German artist associated with Berlin Dada and most widely recognized for her work in photomontage, made dolls as well; she appears with them in several photographs.[201] And Alexandra Exter, the Russian Cubist painter, created a series of marionettes in the 1920s using heterogeneous recycled materials.[202] Later, for the Surrealists such as Hans Bellmer, dolls and mannequins would take on new meaning.[203] They were associated with the unconscious, primal drives, male erotic fantasies and fears. At odds with Vassilieff's work are the exposed female sexual organs and the violence inherent in Bellmer's mutilated dolls.

Vassilieff did not have any direct ties with Zurich or Berlin Dada and, other than Exter, she may not have known about these other artists. Nonetheless, like the Dadaists, for Vassilieff the doll was a radical *objet d'art*. In its various forms, the use of the doll by avant-garde female artists was a highly dissident practice. As David Hopkins argues, "The exploitation of a trope like the doll by women artists is always already political. It transforms the doll's significance, wresting it away from the 'major' (patriarchal) meanings it has historically accrued."[204] Vassilieff effectively dislodges the doll's associations with femininity and docility while also contesting conventional artistic practices. Among her female contemporaries, she appears to be the sole artist creating nude dolls as well as self-portraits in doll form.

Indeed, the political possibilities of the doll are manifold. A familiar object that carries with it the nostalgia of girlhood and socially constructed feminine ideals, it offers endless possibilities for rescinding those very ideologies. Typically, the doll is attired to reflect its owner's whims and desires. Rather than dress up the doll, in *Poupée-autoportrait* Vassilieff leaves the doll bare. Even while nude, she refuses to the audience any sight of her actual body. The pre-pubescent, nondescript form declines any cohesive reading of gender and escapes the limited designations of race as well. Her doll bespeaks a multifaceted and unfixed identity. In addition to the process of Othering, disidentification as theorized by José Esteban Muñoz sheds greater light on Vassilieff's practice. He states, "Disidentification for the minority subject is a mode of *recycling* or re-forming an object that has already been invested with powerful energy."[205] Disidentification was developed as a concept to theorize postmodern and contemporary work by queer artists as well as those of color. Without aiming to minimize or compare marginalized groups or individuals, the theory alone is also apt for analyzing the work of a foreign woman artist who endured the misogyny and xenophobia that reigned in France and in the art world at the beginning of the twentieth century. Through the self-portrait doll, Vassilieff works within and against hegemonic practices and transfigures cultural patterns and stereotypes. Through the arcane form of the doll, she enacts compound identities that both respond to and resist the standard assumptions about gender, race and sexuality.

Vassilieff embodies her particular plight as foreign female artist in the doll – a quotidian object which harks back to the primitivity of childhood, and reforms it into one which connotes disidentification. As Muñoz argues, "Disidentification is meant to be descriptive of the survival strategies the minority subject practices in order to negotiate a phobic majoritarian public sphere that continuously elides or punishes the existence of subjects who do not conform to the phantasm of normative citizenship."[206] Vassilieff's very identity was at odds with the world in which she lived. The tribulations she encountered as a woman artist, compounded with her sense of estrangement as a Russian immigrant in France, surely led her to question her role in society. Her art was formed in part as a response to what Muñoz terms the "cultural logics of heteronormativity."[207] Vassilieff devised the *poupée-portrait* around the time of the Russian Revolution, when she suffered a loss of nationhood. She also faced increasing economic misfortune and struggled as a single mother. Her earlier imprisonment, the destruction of the art in her studio, failed attempts to sell her work and gain recognition were all sources of trauma. Working on and against cultural patterns unfavorable to her success, Vassilieff enacts a disidentificatory process. Hers is a strategy that subverts the commonplace object of the doll into an entity which offers new lines of identification. Significantly, Muñoz insists that identity is not a binary choice, not merely a choice between identification or counter-identification. It is a process neither of heteronormative identification nor of outright rejection and marginalization. Likewise, Vassilieff's self-portrait practice is an intricate process of negotiation, elimination and reshaping. In her

Poupée-autoportrait and its myriad transfigurations, Vassilieff asserts identity as a category that is self-made and malleable.

Self as Other

Vassilieff reinvented herself through her self-portrait doll, which becomes an alter ego surfacing later in her paintings. In *Autoportrait avec sa poupée-portrait* (1929) (Plate 7), the doll appears together with the artist. A self-portrait within a self-portrait, the painting is in a sense a *mise en abyme.* With her hands raised and palms visible, Vassilieff poses in the same stiff manner as the doll on her lap. The painting is based on a contemporaneous photograph by Cami Stone (figure 1.19), a Belgian female photographer active during the interwar period. In both images, woman and puppet bond in a playful enactment of artifice and disguise. In the painting, Vassilieff consciously constructs the personal narrative she wishes to convey. She makes slight changes to conceal the doll's identity and gender. She paints the doll's hair brown and covers the doll's naked torso with a long-sleeved and high-collared black top. Repeatedly, Vassilieff minimizes the role of gender in her self-formation.

In 1930, Vassilieff inconspicuously incorporated her *Poupée-autoportrait* into another painting: *Nude with Two Masks* (Plate 8). Recently, scholars have proposed that the model was Juliette Germain, but I argue that this is an intentionally obscure nude self-portrait.[208] Vassilieff appears in the form of her alter ego – her *Poupée-autoportrait.* Stylistically, the work bespeaks the influence of Surrealism. Rachel Grew writes about alter egos in the works of the Surrealist artists Duchamp, Max Ernst and Bellmer. She contends that these artists obsessively "re-invented their selves through … alter-egos, changing their age, gender and even their species."[209] In *Nude with Two Masks*, Vassilieff leverages a similar strategy. Although not identical, there is a striking resemblance between the nude in the painting and the *Poupée-autoportrait.* As in the *poupée*, the hair is cropped short, the face is mask-like and expressionless, and the body is androgynous. Except for two small breasts perched high on the crest of the torso, there is little vestige of the female sex. The pubic area is elided. The tubular, elongated torso, attenuated limbs and enlarged hands and feet are puppet-like. Vassilieff morphs male and female traits into a nude which refuses standard gender classifications; it resembles a genderless doll. The nude is flanked by strange objects – a horned mask, an animal-like sculpture, a heart and a truncated hand displayed palm up. The horned mask and animal statue faintly recall Baul Helmet masks from Côte d'Ivoire illustrated in Elie Faure, *Histoire de l'art: l'art medieval* (1921)[210] and in *L'Art nègre et l'art océanien.*[211] The empty space and shadow cast by the nude create a sense of dislocation. Together, the lone nude and assorted objects create a cryptic image which may be read as a collision of various types of primitivisms, European and

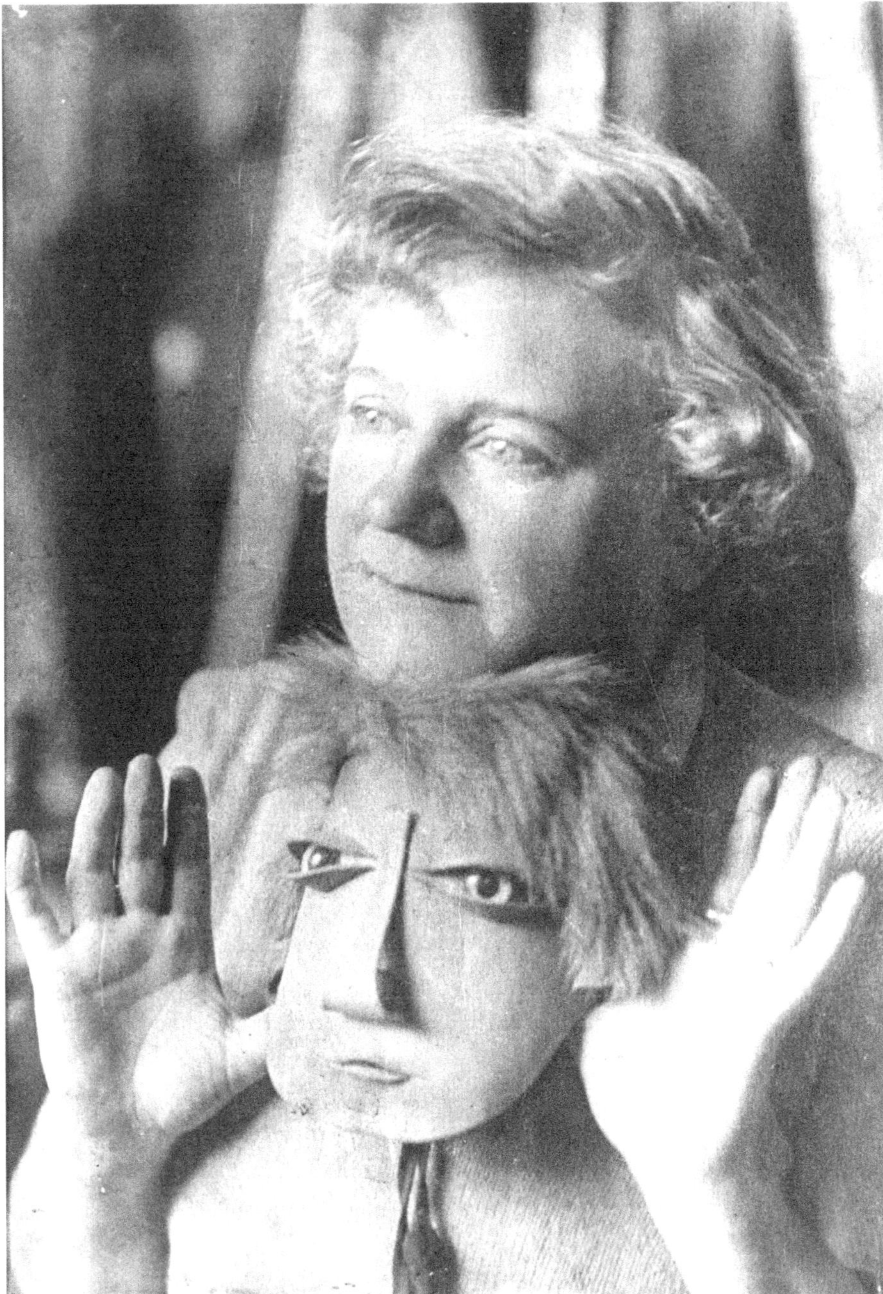

Figure 1.19 Cami Stone, *Marie Vassilieff et son effigie*, 1929

non-European, that Vassilieff maps onto her own body. Through her alter ego – the doll – Vassilieff becomes anonymous, yet still reveals her inner essence. She unites opposite poles – male and female, Self and Other – and transcends her marginalized social status.

Two years afterwards, Vassilieff experienced total financial ruin. She suspended her activity and attempted to sell all of the work in her studio. A letter that she wrote to Constantin Brancusi asking for his help to fund her teenage son's schooling is conserved in the Brancusi archives in Paris.[212] She announced the liquidation of her work to the Paris art world with effervescence. Dubbing herself as a "bonne à tout faire" (all-purpose maid), she invited all of Paris to her studio where "Here, we eat, we laugh, we talk and we are at home. All are welcome."[213] A video filmed in her studio at this time shows her as a welcoming host despite misfortune, serving her guests a hearty and simple meal.[214]

Vassilieff later resumed her artistic practice but was plagued by financial constraints. She made dolls as well as paintings, posters, ceramics, furniture and other works, but she never received the financial rewards that she merited, and she suffered considerably. In face of hardship, Vassilieff nevertheless continued to work against the grain and exert a liberated self. She wrote toward the end of her life, "I am a free woman. Free in the manner of Diogenes."[215] She died penniless in a retirement home outside Paris in 1957.[216]

Neither man, nor woman – Vassilieff viewed herself apart. She occupied the roles of woman artist, single mother, breadwinner, foreigner and accused spy, all of which were difficult to reconcile in the early decades of the twentieth century. From her unique, tenuous and shifting position, Vassilieff transposed her sense of alienation into imagery which probes and blurs gender identification. In Vassilieff's oeuvre, we see bodies in states of transformation. Earlier, in *Homme et femme*, she overturned reactionary gender views and blurred the boundaries between the sexes in her representations of male and female nudes. Later, in her self-portraits, she portrayed herself as a liminal being beyond standard dichotomies of gender or race. Gender as represented in Vassilieff's oeuvre is not static, and the equivocal sexual orientations of her nudes and self-portraits reflect her nebulous role as Other. Nevertheless, as a white woman, she veered into problematic territory when she assumed various cultural forms as dolls, masks and costumes. But imagining herself in different guises – as an African figure wearing a loincloth, or as a dandy in a suit and tie – enabled her to push past binaries. Through a complex process of Othering and disidentification, Vassilieff rejected the image of the sexualized female body and represented hybrid identities. At the same time, she pioneered a novel art form, altering the doll from craft to high art, along with a new language within self-portraiture. Ultimately, for this artist the doll offered limitless opportunities to defy monolithic categorizations of gender, sexuality and race.

Wresting the doll from its associations with girlhood and femininity, she exploited it as a device to undermine hegemonic discourses. In taking on the mantle of the doll, Vassilieff established an identity that was complex, mutable and transcendent.

Notes

1 *"Neither man nor woman."* Marie Vassilieff, *La Bohème du XXe siècle* (unpublished memoir), 1929, n.p., Marie Vassilieff archives, Claude Bernès, Paris. All translations by author.

2 Billy Klüver, *A Day with Picasso: Twenty-four Photographs by Jean Cocteau* (Cambridge, MA: MIT Press, 1997), 22.

3 Unless indicated otherwise, biographical information is drawn from Marie Vassilieff's unpublished memoir, *La Bohème du XXe siècle*, written in 1929, Marie Vassilieff archives; Claude Bernès and Benoît Noël, *Marie Vassilieff (1884–1957): L'Oeuvre artistique, l'académie de peinture, la cantine de Montparnasse* (Livarot-Pays-d'Auge: Éditions BVR, 2017); "Dossier Vassilieff," Kandinsky Library, Centre Pompidou; Hilary Spurling, *Matisse, le maître. II, 1909–1954*, translated by Paule Guivarch (Paris: Éditions du Seuil, 2009).

4 She changed her last name to Vassilieff when she arrived in France. Her parents were Anna Gontcharova and Ivan Vassiliev.

5 Women artists and artisans played an integral role in the colony. Wendy R. Salmond, *Arts and Crafts in Late Imperial Russia* (New York: Cambridge University Press, 1996), 115–43.

6 More upper-middle-class women began studying medicine in Russia at the end of the nineteenth century. The new institute helped accelerate the ever-growing number of female doctors joining the profession. Elianne Riska, *Medical Careers and Feminist Agendas: American, Scandinavian and Russian Women Physicians* (New York: A. de Gruyter, 2001), 76; Marcelline J. Hutton, *Remarkable Russian Women in Pictures, Prose and Poetry* (Lincoln, NE: Zea Books, 2013), 194.

7 Jean-Claude and Valentine Marcadé, *L'Avant-garde au féminin, Moscou, Saint-Petersbourg, Paris: 1907–1930* (Paris: Artcurial, 1983), 5.

8 Marianna Wladimirowna Werewkina (1860–1938), another Russian artist from this period who moved to Europe (Munich, and later Switzerland) to pursue an artistic career, studied with Ilya Repin. See Tanâ Malyševa, and Isabel Wünsche, *Marianne Werefkin and the Women Artists in Her Circle* (London: Brill/Rodopi, 2017).

9 Although her exact whereabouts between 1905 and 1907 remain unclear, scholars agree that she settled in Paris permanently in 1907.

10 Marie Vassilieff's memoir, *La Bohème du XXe siècle*, first written in 1929, completed in 1946 and 1950, was never published. A single typewritten copy is found in the Vassilieff archives.

11 Marie Vassilieff, *La Bohème du XXe siècle.*

12 In her memoir she states that she rented a room on rue d'Ulm in the fifth arrondissement. This may have been her second address. Bernès and Noël believe that she first resided at 64 boulevard de Port-Royal, a boarding house which lodged Russian artists, including Sonia

Terk (Delaunay) and Elizaveta Kruglikova. Delaunay states that she lived in the Latin quarter with four other Russian girls, without mentioning names. Sonia Delaunay, *Nous irons jusqu'au soleil* (Paris: Éditions Robert Laffont, 1978), 19.

13 Bernès and Noël, *Marie Vassilieff*, 19; Klüver, *A Day with Picasso*, 49.

14 According to Bernès, Vassilieff did not have any direct connections with either Popova or Udaltsova in Paris. They did exhibit together in the 0.10 exhibition in Petrograd, 1915. Interview with Bernès, April 9, 2018.

15 Vassilieff, *La Bohème du XXe siècle.*

16 Matisse's academy was located at 33 boulevard des Invalides.

17 Illustrated in Billy Klüver, Julie Martin and Édith Ochs, *Kiki et Montparnasse: 1900–1930* (Paris: Flammarion, 1998), 38.

18 Marie Vassilieff, *La Statue et le comptier bleu* (verso, *Vase de fleurs*), 1910–12, oil on canvas, private collection; Vassilieff, *Nature morte à la cruche*, c. 1909, oil on canvas, private collection; Vassilieff, *Portrait d'une femme au chapeau*, c. 1908 (verso, *Vierge*), oil on canvas, private collection.

19 *La Toison d'Or*, no. 6, June, 1909.

20 Mark Antliff, "The Rhythms of Duration: Bergson and the Art of Matisse," in *The New Bergson*, edited by John Mullarkey (Manchester: Manchester University Press, 1999), 185.

21 Ibid., 184–208; Eric Alliez, "Matisse, Bergson, Oiticica, etc," translated by Hager Weslati, in *Bergson and the Art of Immanence: Painting, Photography, Film*, edited by John Mullarkey and Charlotte de Mille (Edinburgh: Edinburgh University Press, 2013), 63–79; Pierre Schneider, *Matisse* (Paris: Flammarion, 2002), 78, 222, 234.

22 Antliff, "The Rhythms of Duration," 203.

23 Pierre Schneider notes that Matisse owned Bergson's books (without specifying which ones). Schneider, *Matisse*, 360.

24 Amedeo Modigliani, *Marie Vassilieff* (c. 1916), oil on canvas, private collection; Tsugouharu Foujita, *Avant le bal* (1925), oil on canvas, Ohara Museum of Art, Kurashiki, Japan.

25 Letters from Vassilieff to Picasso are housed in the Picasso archives. The earliest letter dates to 1912. She wrote to him regularly until a year before her death. Fonds Picasso, Centre historique des Archives nationales, Paris.

26 André Salmon, "Marie Vassilieff vue par André Salmon," in *Un peintre cubiste méconnu: Marie Vassilieff, toiles 1908–1915* (Paris: Galerie Hupel, 1969), n.p.

27 Her painting was displayed in salle 44. Guillaume Apollinaire, *Chroniques d'art, 1902–1918*, edited by Leroy C. Breunig (Paris: Gallimard, 2002), 215.

28 Vassilieff exhibited six paintings (now lost), *Portrait de Mme N., La Mère et l'enfant, Portrait, Fillette, Nature morte, Récifs bretons.*

29 Apollinaire, *Chroniques d'art*, 215.

30 The house was located on impasse Ronsin and was previously owned by Marguerite Steinheil (1869–1954). She became known for her affair with the president, Félix Faure. He died of a seizure while they were having intercourse.

31 Vassilieff, *La Bohème du XXe siècle.*

32 Apollinaire's exhibition review mentions Vassilieff's work favorably and gives insights into the attendees: Matisse, Friesz, Laurencin, Van Dongen among others, and a number of now obscure Russian artists. Apollinaire, "Les Peintres russes Impasse Ronsin. La vérité sur l'affaire Steinheil," *L'Intransigeant*, October 31, 1910, in Apollinaire, *Chroniques d'art*, 162.

33 Pragmatic, Vassilieff organized a performance, *La Religion de la beauté*, and, in tandem, made use of Matisse's support, convincing him to collaborate in a lottery to help fund the new academy. Unfortunately, a misunderstanding occurred and Vassilieff was accused of embezzlement. Although the academy's jury exonerated her of these charges, she was nevertheless forced to cede her post the following year in February 1912 (the sculptor Serguëi Bulakovsky took over as director). Bernès and Noël, *Marie Vassilieff*, 51, 53; Spurling, *Matisse, le maître*, 32.

34 Now the site of a contemporary art and research center: Villa Vassilieff, Bétonsalon – Centre d'Art et de Recherche et la Cité Internationale des Arts.

35 Felix Marcilhac, *Chana Orloff, catalogue raisonné* (Paris: Éditions de el'Amateur, 1992), 19.

36 Some scholars argue that Vassilieff's academy followed a similar model as that employed at the Artel des Artistes de Saint-Pétersbourg, an independent art organization created by Ivan Kramskoï in 1863. However, the Peredvizhniki had a very different purpose (social and political). See Elizabeth K. Valkenier, *Russian Realist Art: The State and Society: the Peredvizhniki and Their Tradition* (New York: Columbia University Press, 1989).

37 Marcilhac, *Chana Orloff, catalogue raisonné*, 19.

38 Vassilieff, *La Bohème du XXe siècle.*

39 Ibid.

40 Ibid.

41 One example is the studio of Ilya Mashkov and A.N. Mikhailovsky in Moscow where Goncharova and Laionov taught around 1908 and 1910. Like Vassilieff's academy, emphasis was on nude study. Jane A. Sharp, "Redrawing the Margins of Russian Vanguard Art: Natalia Goncharova's Trial for Pornography in 1910," in *Sexuality and the Body in Russian Culture*, edited by Jane T. Costlow, Stephanie Sandler and Judith Vowles (Stanford: Stanford University Press, 1993), 105.

42 Anthea Callen, "The Body and Difference: Anatomy Training at the Ecole des Beaux-Arts in Paris in the Later Nineteenth Century," *Art History* 20, no. 1 (1997), 23–60.

43 See Jane R. Becker and Gabriel P. Weisberg, *Overcoming All Obstacles: The Women of the Académie Julian* (New York: The Dahesh Museum, 2004).

44 Ibid., 124.

45 Tamar Garb, *Sisters of the Brush: Women's Artistic Culture in Late Nineteenth Century Paris* (New Haven: Yale University Press, 1994), 104.

46 "16 francs a month or 4 francs a week; and for two hours of sketching, 30 centimes." Vassilieff, *La Bohème du XXe siècle.*

47 Klüver, *A Day with Picasso*, 49.

48 Nina Hamnett, *Laughing Torso: Reminiscences of Nina Hamnett* (London: Constable and Co., 1932), 50.

49 Ibid., 57.

50 Ibid., 58.

51 Vassilieff, *La Bohème du XXe siècle.*

52 Ibid.

53 Ibid.

54 See Michel Fabre, "Rediscovering Aïcha, Lucy and D'al-Al, Colored French Stage Artists," *S&F Online* 6, nos 1–2 (2007–8): 1, http://sfonline.barnard.edu/baker/mfabre_01.htm;

Wendy Grossman, "Unmasking Adrienne Fidelin: Picasso, Man Ray, and the (In) Visibility of Racial Difference," 5 (2020), https://doi.org/10.26597/mod.0142; Denise Murrell, *Posing Modernity: The Black Model from Manet and Matisse to Today* (New Haven: Yale University Press, 2018).

55 One notable Black male model in early nineteenth-century France was Joseph (c. 1793–1870, last name unknown). Originally from Saint-Domingue, he became a famous artist's model in Paris and posed for artists at the École des Beaux-Arts as well as in private studios. He appears in works by Théodore Géricault and Théodore Chassériau. See Cécile Debray, Isabelle Bardon, Estelle Bégué, David Bindman et al., *Le Modèle noir de Géricault à Matisse* (Paris : Musée d'Orsay, 2019).

56 Hamnett, *Laughing Torso*, 54.

57 "La Croix Rouge," Vassilieff, *La Bohème du XXe siècle*, n.p.

58 Spurling, *Matisse, le maître*, 24.

59 Klüver et al., *Kiki et Montparnasse*, 71.

60 Klüver, *A Day with Picasso*, 50.

61 Klüver et al., *Kiki et Montparnasse*, 71.

62 Hamnett, *Laughing Torso*, 72.

63 Bernès and Noël, *Marie Vassilieff*, 76.

64 Ibid.

65 Ibid., 78.

66 Vassilieff, *La Bohème du XXe siècle*; Hamnett writes that "[Trotsky] ate every evening at the canteen, free of charge, as Wassileiff [*sic*] was extremely kind and hospitable, especially towards her own countrymen." Hamnett, *Laughing Torso*, 122.

67 Vassilieff, *La Bohème du XXe siècle.*

68 Her trip to Russia in 1915–16 also raised suspicion. The Treaty of Brest-Litovsk, signed between Soviet Russia and the Central Powers, further worsened her case.

69 Clara Wold interview with Marie Vassilieff, *New York Tribune*, 1922. Newspaper clipping, Vassilieff archives.

70 Vassilieff, *La Bohème du XXe siècle.*

71 Henri Matisse, *Nude Male* (1900), oil on canvas, Museum of Modern Art, New York.

72 Suzanne Pagé, Jean-Louis Andral, Sophie Krebs, Gladys Fabre et al., *L'École de Paris 1904–1929, la part de l'autre* (Paris: Museé d'Art Moderne de la Ville de Paris, 2001).

73 Sonia Delaunay, *Bal Bullier* (1913), oil on mattress ticking, Musée National d'Art Moderne, Centre Pompidou, Paris.

74 Albert Gleizes and Jean Metzinger, *Du cubisme*, in Robert Herbert, *Modern Artists on Art* (Mineola, NY: Dover Publications, 2000).

75 Spurling, *Matisse, le maître*, 32.

76 Christopher Green, *Art in France, 1900–1940* (New Haven: Yale University Press, 2003), 25.

77 Other painters associated with the group included Juan Gris (1887–1927), Marcel Duchamp (1887–1968), Raymond Duchamp-Villon (1876–1918), Jacques Villon (1875–1963) and Robert de la Fresnaye (1885–1925).

78 The Gallery Cubists had an exclusive contract with the art dealer Daniel-Henry Kahnweiler in the years leading up to World War One, and exhibited privately only at his gallery.

79 See: Green, *Art in France*; David Cottington, *Cubism and Its Histories* (Manchester: Manchester University Press, 2004); Mark Antliff, *Inventing Bergson: Cultural Politics and the Parisian Avant-Garde* (Princeton: Princeton University Press, 1993).

80 Green, *Art in France*, 26.

81 Guillaume Apollinaire, *Les Peintres cubistes: meditations esthetiques*, edited by L.C. Breunig, and J.-Cl. Chevalier (Paris: Hermann, 1965) (originally published 1913).

82 Perry demonstrates some of the reasons behind Laurencin's success, citing dealers (she had contracts with Paul Rosenberg and Jos Hessel), critical reception of her work, as well as "the ease with which her work was appropriated into a critical language of difference." Gill Perry, *Women Artists and the Parisian Avant-Garde* (Manchester: Manchester University Press, 1995), 88, 144–5.

83 Laurencin quoted in Marsha Meskimmon, *The Art of Reflection: Women Artists' Self-Portraiture in the Twentieth Century* (New York: Columbia University Press, 1996), 44.

84 Patricia Leighten and Mark Antliff (eds), *A Cubism Reader: Documents and Criticism, 1906–1914* (Chicago: University of Chicago Press, 2008), 543.

85 Jean-Claude Marcadé, "Léger et la Russie," *Europe; Revue Littéraire Mensuelle* 75 (1997), 58–72.

86 Fernand Léger, *Essai pour trois portraits* (*Study for Three Portraits*) (1910–11), oil on canvas, Milwaukee Art Museum, Milwaukee, WI.

87 Vassilieff, *La Bohème du XXe siècle*.

88 Léger's first lecture at Académie Vassilieff, Paris, 1913: "Les Origines de la peinture et sa valeur representative," *Montjoie!* 8 (1913), 9–10. Second lecture Paris, 1914 "Les Realisations picturales actuelles," *Soirées de Paris* 25 (June 15, 1914), 349–56. Christopher Green, *Léger and the Avant-Garde* (New Haven: Yale University Press, 1976), 56; Matthew Affron, "Line, Form, Color, Luster: Léger's Contrasts of Forms," in *Cubism: The Leonard A. Lauder Collection*, edited by Emily Braun and Rebecca Rabinow (New York and New Haven: The Metropolitan Museum of Art and Yale University Press, 2014), 91.

89 Léger quoted in Leighten and Antliff, *A Cubism Reader*, 639.

90 Elma Adamowicz, "Fernand Léger's *La Noce*: The Bride Stripped Bare?" in *Back to the Futurists: The Avant-Garde and Its Legacy*, edited by Elma Adamowicz and Simona Storchi (Manchester: Manchester University Press, 2017), 134.

91 Although it had different implications for each of the various avant-garde factions that employed it, the notion of simultaneity can be traced back to the anti-rationalist theories of Henri Bergson. Delphine Bière, "The Dispute over Simultaneity: Boccioni – Delaunay, Interpretational Error or Bergsonian Practice?" in *Back to the Futurists: The Avant-Garde and Its Legacy*, edited by Elma Adamowicz and Simona Storchi (Manchester: Manchester University Press, 2017), 117.

92 Bergson, who became aware of his influence on Cubism, was actually quite critical of their theories. He believed that art should be the product of intuition and creativity, not theorizing. Even without his endorsement, however, the Cubists continued to make use of his ideas to justify their own novel approaches to art making. Antliff, *Inventing Bergson*, 3.

93 Frédéric Worms, *La Philosophie en France au XXe siècle: moments* (Paris: Gallimard, 2010), 33.

94 Bière, "The Dispute over Simultaneity," 114.

95 Robert C. Grogin, *The Bergsonian Controversy in France, 1900–1914* (Calgary: The University of Calgary Press, 1988), ix.
96 Green, *Léger and the Avant-Garde*, 25.
97 Antliff, *Inventing Bergson*, 71.
98 Acknowledging that multiple themes pervade *Du "cubisme"*, including Nietzschean ideas and Henri Poincaré's theories of space, Antliff argues that it was written "with Bergson in mind." Antliff, *Inventing Bergson*, 39, 40.
99 Green, *Léger and the Avant-garde*, 19.
100 Galerie de la Boétie, October, 1912.
101 There were three Section d'Or exhibitions, in 1912, 1920 and 1925; Vassilieff exhibited in the 1920 exhibition, alongside fellow Russians: Archipenko, Léopold Survage, François Angiboult, Goncharova and Larionov. The second Section d'Or, organized by Archipenko, Survage and Gleizes, offered greater opportunity for foreign artists to exhibit. Cécile Debray and Françoise Lucbert, *La Section d'Or 1912, 1920, 1925* (Paris: Cercle d'Art, 2000), 21; Françoise Lucbert. "L'amité artistique franco-russe, le cas exemplaire de la Section d'Or," in *Paris Russe, 1910–1960*, edited by Joseph Kiblitsky, E.A. Petrova, and Juan Allende-Blin (Saint-Pétersbourg: Palace Editions, 2003), 25.
102 Gleizes and Metzinger, *Du cubisme*, 36, 19. Also see: Antliff, *Inventing Bergson*; Green, *Art in France*, 40.
103 Gleizes and Metzinger, *Du cubisme,* 36.
104 Antliff, *Inventing Bergson*, 3.
105 Debray and Lucbert, *La Section d'Or 1912, 1920, 1925*, 24.
106 Stanley R. Johnson, *Cubism & La Section d'Or: Reflections on the Development of the Cubist Epoch: 1907–1922* (Chicago: Klees-Gustorf Publishers, 1991), 21–2.
107 Ibid.
108 Cottington, *Cubism and Its Histories*, 112. For an analysis of Gris's employment of the golden section, see William A. Camfield, "Juan Gris and the Golden Section," *The Art Bulletin* 47, no. 1 (1965), 128–34.
109 Debray, *La Section d'Or*, 22.
110 I am grateful to Douglas Jimerson for his input on the golden section.
111 For more information on the golden section see: Eli Maor and Eugen Jost, *Beautiful Geometry* (Princeton: Princeton University Press, 2017), 66–8; Hans Walser, *The Golden Section*, translated by Peter Hilton and Jean Pedersen (Washington DC: The Mathematical Association of America, 2001); Scott A. Olsen, *The Golden Section: Nature's Greatest Secret* (Glastonbury: Wooden Books, 2009).
112 Apollinaire, "Les Peintres russes Impasse Ronsin. La vérité sur l'affaire Steinheil," 162.
113 Cottington, *Cubism and Its Histories*, 88.
114 Le Fauconnier made an impression on Russian artists when an oil study for *L'Abondance* was exhibited at the second Jack of Diamonds exhibition, Moscow, 1912. Neither the renowned status of the painting nor that of the artist has endured. Today, the painting is stored in the reserves of the Gemeentemuseum in The Hague. David Cottington, *Cubism in the Shadow of War: The Avant-Garde and Politics in Paris: 1905–1914* (New Haven: Yale University Press, 1998), 32, 87–99.
115 Green, *Léger and the Avant-Garde*, 32.

116 G. William Barnard, *Living Consciouness: The Metaphysical Vision of Henri Bergson* (Albany: SUNY Press, 2011), xviii.

117 Antliff, *Inventing Bergson*, 70.

118 Albert Gleizes, *Les Baigneuses* (1912), oil on canvas, Musée d'Art Moderne de la Ville de Paris; Jean Metzinger, *La Femme au Cheval* (1911–12), oil on canvas, Statens Museum for Kunst, Copenhagen.

119 Antliff, *Inventing Bergson*, 70.

120 Albert Gleizes, *Football Players* (1912–13), oil on canvas, National Gallery of Art, Washington, DC; Robert Delaunay, *Cardiff Team* (1913), oil and tempera on canvas, National Galleries Scotland; Jean Metzinger, *The Cyclist* (1913), oil on canvas, Peggy Guggenheim Collection, Venice.

121 Cottington, *Cubism in the Shadow of War*, 95.

122 Ibid., 16.

123 Ibid.

124 James F. McMillan, *France and Women 1789–1914: Gender, Society and Politics* (London: Routledge, 2002), 140–155; Mary L. Roberts, *Disruptive Acts: The New Woman in Fin-de-Siècle France* (Chicago: University of Chicago Press, 2005), 3.

125 Berthe Weill and François Roussier, *Pan! Dans L'oeil!: Ou trente ans dans les coulisses de la peinture contemporaine, 1900–1930* (Dijon: L'Échelle de Jacob, 2009), 227–9.

126 Griselda Pollock, "Modigliani and the Bodies of Art," in *Modigliani beyond the Myth*, edited by Mason Klein and Maurice Berger (New Haven: Yale University Press, 2004), 56.

127 Picasso, *Les Demoiselles d'Avignon* (1907), oil on canvas, Museum of Modern Art, New York.

128 A few key sources include Anna Chave, "New Encounters with *Les Demoiselles d'Avignon*: Gender, Race, and the Origins of Cubism," *The Art Bulletin* 76, no. 4 (1994), 606; Christopher Green, *Picasso's Les Demoiselles d'Avignon* (Cambridge: Cambridge University Press, 2002); Patricia Leighten, "The White Peril and l'Art Nègre: Picasso, Primitivism, and Anticolonialism," *The Art Bulletin* 72, no. 4 (1990), 609–30; William Rubin, Hélène Seckel-Klein and Judith Cousins, *Les Demoiselles d'Avignon* (New York: Abrams, 1994) and, most recently, Suzanne P. Blier, *Picasso's Demoiselles: The Untold Origins of a Modern Masterpiece* (Durham, NC: Duke University Press, 2019).

129 Braun, "Picasso's Female Anatomies," 147.

130 Ibid., 150.

131 Ibid., 149.

132 Ibid.

133 Duncan, "Virility and Domination in Early Twentieth-Century Vanguard Painting," 298.

134 Emily Braun and Rebecca Rabinow, "The Backs of Things," in *Cubism: The Leonard A. Lauder Collection*, edited by Emily Braun and Rebecca Rabinow (New York and New Haven: The Metropolitan Museum of Art and Yale University Press, 2014), 225.

135 Ibid., 226.

136 Ibid.

137 This is the case with Léger's *Houses under the Trees* (1913). An untitled work appears on the back, which he painted over in black, hiding it from the public eye. Ibid.

138 Interview with Tatiana Khatsenkov, May, 2016.

139 Ibid.
140 For illustrations of Fang masks see John Warne Monroe, *Metropolitan Fetish: African Sculpture and the Imperial French Invention of Primitive Art* (Ithaca: Cornell University Press, 2019).
141 Apollinaire, *Chroniques d'art*, 211.
142 Gleizes, *Homme nu*, 1911, location unknown. Image reproduced in Gladys Fabre, "Albert Gleizes et l'Abbaye de Créteil," in *Albert Gleizes: le cubisme en majesté*, edited by María T. Ocaña and Vincent Pomarède (Paris: Éditions de la Réunion des Musées Nationaux, 2001), 140.
143 Roger Allard, "Sur quelques peintres," *Les Marches du Sud-Ouest*, June 2, 1911, 60.
144 Fernand Léger, *Nudes in the Forest* (1909–11), oil on canvas, Kröller-Müller Museum, Otterlo.
145 Apollinaire quoted in Green, *Léger and the Avant-Garde*, 318.
146 Ibid., 318.
147 Garb, *Sisters of the Brush*, 112.
148 Jane Sharp, *Russian Modernism between East and West: Natal'ia Goncharova and the Moscow Avant-Garde* (Cambridge: Cambridge University Press, 2006), 103.
149 Ibid., 104.
150 Critic quoted in ibid.
151 Ibid.
152 Ibid., 105.
153 Ibid., 113.
154 Ibid., 305.
155 Goncharova first visited Paris in 1914 to design for Diaghilev's Les Ballets Russes, returned in 1917, and settled permanently in 1919. Beate Kemfert. "The Life of Natalia Goncharova," in *Natalia Goncharova: Between Russian Tradition and European Modernity* (Ostfildern: Hatje Cantz, 2010), 16–18.
156 Ibid., 107.
157 Sergei Shchukin was one prominent collector who enabled exposure for Russian artists, including Goncharova, to the latest currents in French modern art in his own private home in Moscow. See Natalya Semenova, *The Collector: The Story of Sergei Shchukin and His Lost Masterpieces* (New Haven: Yale University Press, 2020). Cécile Debray, Isabelle Bardon, Estelle Bégué, David Bindman et al., *Le Modèle noir de Géricault à Matisse* (Paris: Musée d'Orsay, 2019).
158 Gleizes and Metzinger, *Du cubisme*, 36.
159 Antliff, *Inventing Bergson*, 47.
160 Ibid., 43.
161 Ibid., 46.
162 Antliff summarizing Bergson's "The Introduction to Metaphysics," 1903, in Antliff, *Inventing Bergson*, 49. Italics mine.
163 Gleizes and Metzinger, *Du cubisme*, 23.
164 Antliff, *Inventing Bergson*, 52.
165 Marie Dormoy, "Poupées nouvelles," *Art et Décoration*, 1920, Vassilieff archives.
166 Marie Vassilieff, "Mes poupées," *Montparnasse* 42, December, 1925.
167 Ibid.

168 Little is known about who Pierre Delbo who photographed many of Vassilieff's dolls in the 1920s. Vassilieff sold a number of these photographs as limited edition sets, or "Albums de Luxe," in 1929. Bernès and Noël, *Marie Vassilieff*, 170, 172.
169 Michelle Deroyer, "Marie Vassilieff parle des poupées," *La Semaine à Paris*, December 30, 1932, Vassilieff archives.
170 Untitled article in London newspaper *The Queen*, Vassilieff archives.
171 Julie Richard, "Les Poupées de Marie Vassilieff (1884–1957): entre utopie et dystopie, les déploiements de l'effegie dans l'arts expérimental des avant-gardes historiques," Master's Thesis, Université du Québec à Montréal, 2016.
172 Ibid.
173 Bernès and Noël, *Marie Vassilieff*, 20.
174 Vassilieff exhibited *Portrait d'un jeune homme*, *Usine*, *Paquebot et usine*, *Paysage d'Espagne*, *Portrait de Mme M.* and *Recherche I.* Kazimir Malevich exhibited *Black Square* (1915).
175 Vassilieff notes that Valadon purchased a doll portrait. *La Bohème du XXe siècle.*
176 In a letter dated December 9, 1917, Léger wrote to his friend Louis Poughon about promoting Vassilieff's dolls. Fernand Léger, *Fernand Léger: une correspondance de guerre à Louis Poughon, 1914–1918*, edited by Christian Derouet (Paris: Éditions du Centre Georges Pompidou, 1997), 85–6. Klüver et al., *Kiki et Montparnasse*, 71.
177 Ellen McBreen, *Matisse's Sculpture: The Pinup and the Primitive* (New Haven: Yale University Press, 2014), 84.
178 Carl Einstein, *Negerplastik* (Munich: K. Wolff, 1915); Guillaume Apollinaire and Paul Guillaume, *Sculptures nègres* (Paris: Chez P. Guillaume, 1917); Henri Clouzot and André Level, *L'Art nègre et l'art océanien* (Paris : Devambez, 1919); Paul Guillaume and Thomas Munro, *La Sculpture nègre primitive* (Paris: G. Crès, 1929).
179 For information on early twentieth-century exhibitions and publications on African art by Paul Guillaume, Henri Clouzot and André Level, see John Warne Monroe, *Metropolitan Fetish: African Sculpture and the Imperial French Invention of Primitive Art* (Ithaca: Cornell University Press, 2019), 87–165.
180 James Clifford, *The Predicament of Culture: Twentieth-century Ethnography, Literature, and Art* (Cambridge, MA: Harvard University Press, 2002), 543.
181 Jean Laude, *La Peinture française (1905–1914) et "l'art Nègre" (contribution à l'étude des sources du fauvisme et du cubisme)* (Paris: Editions Klincksieck, 1968), 23.
182 Clifford, *The Predicament of Culture*, 546.
183 See discussion in Chapter 3 below.
184 Richard, "Les Poupées de Marie Vassilieff," 81.
185 Ibid.
186 Pende masks come in various forms and styles. The illustration on the cover of *Negerplastik* is slightly different from the one illustrated in this book. However, both exhibit prominent eyebrows and protruding eye sockets. Einstein, *Negerplastik*, 1915. McBreen mentions that Matisse owned two Pende masks. McBreen, *Matisse's Sculpture*, 43.
187 This term has been used in numerous ways. See: Kobena Mercer, "1968: Periodizing Postmodern Politics and Identity," in *Cultural Studies*, edited by Lawrence Grossberg, Cary Nelson and Paula A. Treichler (New York: Routledge, 1992), 432; Hal Foster,

"The Artist as Ethnographer," in *The Return of the Real* (Cambridge: MIT Press, 2009), 180.

188 McBreen, *Matisse's Sculpture*, 195–6.

189 Mason Klein, "Modigliani against the Grain," in *Modigliani beyond the Myth,* edited by Mason Klein and Maurice Berger (New Haven: Yale University Press, 2004), 8.

190 Einstein, *Negerplastik*, 40.

191 Clouzot and Level, *L'Art nègre et l'art océanien*, plate XL.

192 Apollinaire and Guillaume, *Sculptures nègres*, plate V.

193 An image of the doll with the caption "appartient à Suzanne Valadon" appears in the journal article Marie Vassilieff, "Au poteau de torture: Marie Wassilieff par Marie Wassilieff," in *Paris-Montparnasse*, March 15, 1929, 12. I am grateful to Claude Bernès for this discovery.

194 Sharon Marcus, *Between Women: Friendship, Desire, and Marriage in Victorian England.* (Princeton: Princeton University Press, 2009), 265, 266.

195 Ibid., 263.

196 Wendy Salmond, "A Matter of Give and Take: Peasant Crafts and Their Revival in Late Imperial Russia," *Design Issues* 13, no. 1 (1997), 11.

197 Black dolls begin to appear in the United States at the end of the nineteenth century. A recent exhibition devoted to the history of black dolls entitled *I See Me: Reflections in Black Dolls* took place at the Charles H. Wright Museum of African American History in Detroit in 2017.

198 Ruth Hemus, *Dada's Women* (New Haven: Yale University Press, 2009), 50.

199 Ibid., 50.

200 Ibid., 59.

201 Ibid., 123.

202 Richard, "Les Poupées de Marie Vassilieff," 50.

203 See: Malcolm Green, *The Doll* (London: Atlas Press, 2005); Michael Semff and Anthony Spira, *Hans Bellmer* (Paris: Centre Pompidou, 2006); Sue Taylor, *Hans Bellmer: The Anatomy of Anxiety* (Cambridge, MA: MIT Press, 2000).

204 David Hopkins, *A Companion to Dada and Surrealism* (Malden: Wiley Blackwell, 2016), 377.

205 José Esteban Muñoz, *Disidentifications: Queers of Color and the Performance of Politics* (Minneapolis: University of Minnesota Press, 1999), 39.

206 Ibid., 4.

207 Ibid., 5.

208 Juliette Germain was the wife of Dr. Germain with whom Vassilieff was close. Bernès and Noël, *Marie Vassilieff*, 124.

209 Rachel Grew, "The Immortal Self: Surrealist Alter Egos." Queen's University Belfast, 2007, https://repository.lboro.ac.uk/articles/The_immortal_self_surrealist_alter_egos/9335282. Accessed January 20, 2020.

210 Elie Faure, *Histoire de l'art: l'art medieval* (Paris: G. Crès et Cie, 1921), 158.

211 Clouzot and Level, *L'Art nègre et l'art océanien*, plate XXII.

212 Letter from Vassilieff to Brancusi, dated February 3, 1932. Fonds Constantin Brancusi, Kandinsky Library, Centre Pompidou.

213 Carte de visite. Marie Vassilieff archives, Claude Bernès, Paris.

214 On view in the exhibition *Pionnières: artistes dans le Paris des années folles,* edited by Camille Morineau and Lucia Pesapane (Paris: Editions de la Réunion des Musées Nationaux – Grand Palais, 2022).

215 Vassilieff quoted in Noël, *Marie Vassilieff*, 42.

216 The retirement home was in Nogent-sur-Marne.

2 Painting pleasure: Émilie Charmy and *aesthetics of female jouissance*

A flurry of brushwork bares and blurs the body, as variegated pigments shimmer on the surface. Impasto layers applied *alla prima* generate a surplus of material residue, juxtaposed with areas of thinly painted or exposed canvas. Charmy's haptic use of paint was noted by critics: "Émilie Charmy … sees like a woman and paints like a man," wrote Roland Dorgelès in 1921.[1] Roughness, bravura brushwork and bold color connoted maleness to the early twentieth-century mind, and Charmy's robust execution ran counter to this prevailing current. Dorgelès's description reflects the gendered reception of her work.[2] As with the paintings by other women in this book, Charmy's work was characterized as "masculine" in nature by critics. To paint boldly was considered unwomanly.

Although Charmy "paints like a man," her most sensual nudes are contrarily oriented toward a woman's desire. In the 1910s and 1920s, Charmy painted eroticized female nudes with the same emphatic approach. Concealed in her studio, they were not exhibited during her lifetime. In these intimate works, Charmy communicates pleasure through her distinctive painterly practice. They feature what I have termed the *aesthetics of female jouissance*, a sensorial handling of paint, which invokes pleasure through the sensation of touch. Eroticism is manifest in these paintings, but it is not prurient, nor is it designed for male gratification. Instead, Charmy's painting resonates with the unfettered exploration of female sexuality in the writings of her contemporary, Sidonie-Gabrielle Colette. In addition, Charmy's facture is illuminated by theories about the tactile nature of women's sexual satisfaction by the feminist philosopher Luce Irigaray. Capturing the human form with a fluid and loaded stroke, Charmy renders female sexuality outside the norms of male heterosexual experience and gives voice to her own idiosyncratic *jouissance*.

Throughout this chapter, I emphasize the effects of Charmy's facture and palette not simply to confirm the sheer mass of its presence or its optical impact, but to decipher its implicit meaning. My approach is based on the premise that, in addition to symbolic or socio-historical meaning, painting technique and coloring serve as indication of an artistic intent. Of course, we can never fully ascertain Charmy's intention. Any attempt to do so is hampered by scant archival material – Charmy left few written accounts and correspondence, and her letters offer limited insights into her character and artistic practice. Through detailed visual analyses, combined with a close examination of the historical and gendered context, I elucidate the semantic function of the pictorial phenomena in Charmy's oeuvre. In this manner, I follow the approach set forth by Nicola Suthor in her book *Rembrandt's Roughness*, a ground-breaking study that emphasizes how paint texture generates meaning.[3] Although, unlike Rembrandt, Charmy devoted her career almost entirely to the representation of the female body, exploring female sexuality in paint. This chapter demonstrates how Charmy revealed female *jouissance* through her individual, weighty facture and vibrant palette. Portraying the figure in a sensual manner with opulent brushwork and vivid color, she captured both a visual and tactile representation of the body. Pushed to the foreground with accents of iridescent pigment, her nudes command our attention. Shown in provocative poses, they reveal unbridled pleasure. Often, Charmy used her own body in lieu of a model's, creating brazen self-portraits. She thus pioneered a conception of the body informed by a liberated, sexually conscious self. For Charmy, painting itself was a form of self-pleasuring inseparable from her own desires. Long before feminist studies theorized about the subject, she manifested erotic female pleasure in art oriented toward a female viewership.

Early life and work

During an artistic career spanning over fifty years, Charmy painted alongside the Fauves at the beginning of the twentieth century. She exhibited regularly in France and internationally, including at the New York Armory Show in 1913, and was awarded the Legion of Honor in 1926.[4] Nevertheless, she has been largely forgotten. Beyond the academic circles of French modern art and a handful of collectors, Charmy's name has fallen into obscurity. There are only a handful of regional and university museums in France and the US which exhibit her paintings. Her most striking pieces, including many discussed in this book, are in the hands of private collectors and the artist's descendants.

Émilie Espérance Barret, later known as Émilie Charmy, in Saint-Étienne on April 2, 1878, into a bourgeois family.[5] Her father was a mill operator at a steelworks factory in Saint-Étienne. Despite growing up in an industrial setting with little exposure to art, Charmy developed a passion for painting from a young age.[6] Orphaned as a teenager, Charmy relied on her elder brother, Jean, who became a significant influence during her formative years and the beginning of her career.[7] After selling the family's mining commissions, they moved together from Saint-Étienne to Lyon in 1898. There, Charmy met Jacques Martin, who was well known locally for his portraits and still lifes, as well as his wall paintings in public buildings. He served as her mentor from around 1898 to 1902, when formal art education was not yet accessible for women in this region. The École des Beaux-Arts in Lyon did not open its doors to women until 1906.[8] But the instruction she received from Martin provided her with a solid background. Under his tutelage, she studied the genres of still life, portraiture and the nude. Martin's characteristic bright palette and sumptuous impasto, evident in *Bouquets of Flowers with Two Vases* (c. 1900), would have a lasting impact on Charmy. In addition, she had direct access to works of important nineteenth-century painters in his collection, including Eugène Delacroix, Berthe Morisot, Pierre Puvis de Chavannes and Auguste Renoir. Martin personally knew the latter three.[9] Outside Martin's studio, Charmy benefitted from the growing cultural initiatives in Lyon.[10] Though the city was recognized as an important center for industry and commerce, it also boasted an important museum, the Musée des Beaux-Arts de Lyon, and a burgeoning art market.[11] Although far from the capital, Charmy was nevertheless exposed to the art currents of the preceding decades, including Impressionism.

Charmy's *Interior in Saint-Étienne* (c. 1897–1900) dates from this period and bespeaks the influence of Morisot. The painting features two women in a *grand salon* surrounded by objects of feminine refinement: a crystal chandelier, candelabra, vases, gilt-framed mirrors, a mantelpiece, eighteenth-century-style décor and a piano.[12] These parlor pieces, typically found in Morisot's interiors, serve as "constituent signs of feminine place."[13] The women take part in respectable feminine pastimes; one is reading while the other plays the piano. Charmy treats oil paint as if it were a synthesis of pastel and watercolor, capturing the soft curves of the baroque-style furnishings and the women's bustle dresses with a highly gestural brushstroke in soft hues of pink and blue. Charmy's feather-like touch is reminiscent of Morisot's facture in which "altogether the impression is of dash."[14] As a result, Charmy's *Interior in Saint-Étienne* appears swiftly executed, the figures' forms are abbreviated to silhouettes and their faces are faintly visible. Charmy saw works by Morisot in Martin's private collection; the Impressionist had personally gifted him several watercolors with dedications inscribed. These were recorded in an estate sale after Martin's death.[15]

Even under the mentorship of a relatively traditional painter, Charmy increasingly broke with convention. *Woman in an Armchair* or *La Morphinomane* (c. 1897–1900) (Plate 9) features a young woman in a burgundy gown, idly posed in an armchair.[16] Closer inspection discloses the reason for the woman's vacant stare and lethargic pose. Adjacent to her on an occasional table are a glass jar and vial. In her hands she holds a white handkerchief and syringe. All appears still, except for the blackbirds in the wallpaper that seem to take flight, conjuring up the swirling imagery of a morphine-induced hallucination. Here, Charmy transposes a dark childhood memory into a haunting image of an anonymous woman; her father suffered from severe liver problems toward the end of his life and became addicted to morphine.[17]

Morphine was commonly used by women of the upper middle class during the last quarter of the nineteenth century, and vials and syringes were readily accessible at jewelry stores in France.[18] It was a popular cure for hysteria, serving as a key component in the cocktail of drugs that the neurologist Jean-Martin Charcot prescribed to treat this distinctly "feminine" disorder.[19] Morphine and other narcotics became prevalent subjects in art, especially in lithography, yet, this subject rarely surfaces in art by women at this time.[20] Charmy's *La Morphinomane* tests the boundaries of acceptable subject matter for women. Art historian Gill Perry notes that the painting "reveals an engagement with a 'modern life' theme, a post-Baudelairian preoccupation with the seedier aspects of a woman's life more often associated with the late nineteenth-century work of male painters such as Degas, Manet or Toulouse-Lautrec."[21] In particular, the woman's vacant stare, hunched posture and lethargic stupor recall Degas's melancholic *Absinthe* (1875–76). Both depict the use of drugs and hallucinogens frankly and without forthright moral judgment. Yet Charmy's subject is not an urban worker, but an upper-middle-class woman in a domestic interior. The painting makes the private public, revealing an intimate aspect of a bourgeois woman's world.

La Loge (c. 1900) (Plate 10) is an unprecedented image of a brothel.[22] The title translates to "artist's dressing room," a malapropos. Discreetly chosen by her descendants later, the title does not accurately describe the scene.[23] In this work, Charmy unites two dichotomous themes – that of the interior, a predominant subject in her earliest extant works, with a new interest, the nude. With its terracotta walls and carpet in variegated shades of turquoise and coral, the space resembles that in *Interior in Lyon* (c. 1900). Similar furnishings are also found in *Lyon Interior: The Artist's Bedroom* (c. 1900), suggesting that all three works were painted contemporaneously, perhaps in Charmy's residence in Lyon. Her descendants have proposed that this painting was inspired by the life-drawing sessions she witnessed in Martin's studio, but the scheme and layout of his atelier in a contemporaneous photograph do not support this hypothesis.[24] It was also rare for Martin to paint multi-figure compositions. Moreover, unlike a painting of working models such as Georges Seurat's *The Models* (1888), there are no studio props, paintbrushes, easels or paintings in progress to indicate an artist's workshop.[25] Several nudes scatter around the room, certain ones are clustered together, others isolated; few show signs of interaction. The awkward placement of the figures, some seated on the floor, others standing, defies any clear-cut narrative. Each is clad in black stockings, familiar accessories of the demi-monde.[26] The women do not appear to be mere studio models – rather, prostitutes idly waiting for a customer.

Brothel scenes were common subjects for male artists at the turn of the twentieth century but this was uncharted territory for female painters.

Obviously, as a bourgeois woman, Charmy would never have entered a brothel to observe such an environment firsthand. Nonetheless, she had many sources from which to borrow, including photographs. The stately interior in *La Loge* reflects certain sumptuous bordellos in Paris and major cities in France. With "a profusion of rugs, curtains, and wall hangings" the *maison closes* (brothels) were decorated "to make the premises [appear] as respectable as a bourgeois salon."[27] Without a trace of vulgarity, these embellishments created an illusion of decorum for bourgeois male clients. In addition, Charmy culled from the latest art currents, including Impressionism, as her loose brushwork attests. In addition to Martin's personal collection, she would have seen Impressionist works in major salons and exhibitions in Lyon, as well as in reproductions in art journals. Certain scholars have proposed that Charmy traveled to Paris to view modern art at the *Exposition universelle* in 1900.[28] There, she could have seen paintings featuring prostitutes by Édouard Manet.[29] At the Musée du Luxembourg, she perhaps saw his *Olympia*.[30] Even more than with Manet, *La Loge* resonates uncannily with Degas's brothel images, such as *The Name Day of the Madam*, though this monotype was not exhibited. Still, Charmy handles the theme of *maison close* less candidly than either Degas or Manet. She captures a liminal space between a respectable bourgeois salon and a brothel and effaces any details with which to identify the scene or the women. Naked bodies are juxtaposed with their polished surroundings – a clash that, with all its ambivalence, is strongly imbued with a sense of artistic individualism that defies artistic categories and confounds expectations. Perhaps *La Loge* is Charmy's imagining of *her* studio and *her* models. In this manner, *La Loge* could function as a displaced self-portrait – an expression of Charmy's artistic identity and originality. Charmy lays out her artistic vision while trespassing on a "masculine" subject. The idle models anticipate her future work in the nude genre.

Charmy's nascent, singular facture and treatment of form are evident in this early work. The brushwork is so fluid that the nudes are barely discernible. The gossamer bodies are offered not as a sensual or grotesque display; Charmy obscures their forms so that any salacious undertones are buried. An amorphous woman seated on the lower right has semi-translucent limbs. A third arm mysteriously rests on the table next to her, detached from its body. The cluster of nudes in the background is rendered by a blur of sienna hues. With its lack of polish, the painting appears like a preparatory sketch, but its not-so-modest size negates such a possibility. Close inspection reveals rough cuts and fine scratches throughout where Charmy inflicted damage to the surface, grazing it with a coarse brush. Charmy's unusual process draws attention to surface, form and texture. Through her anomalous particularities, she manifests her mark as creator.

Charmy chez les Fauves

Optimistic about a future career in the capital, Charmy and her brother left Lyon for Paris in 1903. She made her debut that same year in the Salon des Indépendants. She would participate annually in that salon until 1914 (except for 1910).[31] Initially residing in the sixteenth arrondissement and then Saint-Cloud, by 1908 she had a studio at Place de Clichy at the foot of Montmartre where many contemporary artists lived and worked.[32] Around 1910, she moved with her brother to the seventh arrondissement where she also had her studio.[33] For the remainder of her life, Charmy would call this address home. Exhibiting regularly at the Salon des Indépendants and Salon d'Automne, Charmy's work began to be noticed. She is mentioned along with numerous other artists in sweeping résumés of the Salon. The well-known critic Louis Vauxcelles called attention to her paintings in the 1905 Salon d'Automne, stating, "Mlle Charmy is an interesting student of the Lyonnais school of flower [painting]; she takes her place in the line of [Jean] Seigne-martin and [François] Vernay."[34] Whereas Vauxcelles situates Charmy within the nineteenth-century Lyonnais still-life tradition, Charmy was actually forging her own path, employing techniques of the burgeoning Fauve style, including crude brushwork and exuberant, non-naturalistic colors. Two early still lifes from around 1904 demonstrate a shift in her oeuvre. In the 1905 Indépendants, Charmy exhibited a painting entitled *Grenades*, likely the same painting as what is now titled *Still Life with Pomegranates*.[35] Rendered with a molten stroke and loaded brush, the fruit appears ripe and moist. Charmy juxtaposes the orange and vermillion pomegranates against a background mottled in green and ochre, creating a vibrant play of color. The impasto-laden brushwork recalls the work of Martin, but the degree to which Charmy amplifies color contrasts and loosens the paint handling demonstrates her adoption of vanguard artistic methods.

The palette in *Still Life* (c. 1904), is even more intense. Perhaps this painting corresponds with "Fruits" listed in the Salon d'Automne catalogue of 1905.[36] Four brightly colored melons are haphazardly set on a variegated tablecloth. Their vines extend upward, unfurling heart-shaped leaves. The fruit is encased in a shell of turquoise and yellow green. Two are cracked open, spewing multihued juices and seeds. Such a work is far removed from the still lifes of Martin or other Lyonnais artists Vauxcelles cites. Gone is the muted ochre background seen in the pomegranate arrangement; flamboyant red dominates. The white of the tablecloth and the robin's egg blue of the melons appear to be scumbled on top of the red ground, creating a backlit glow. She applies the paint in thin layers so that the texture of the canvas weave is exposed in certain areas. Color contrasts of red and green, orange and turquoise, along with flecks of white animate the still life. The ferocious tones and untamed brushwork imbue the work with a sense of immediacy and vitality. The work appears spontaneous, as if executed rapidly to capture the fruit at the peak of its ripeness.

In the very same Salon d'Automne in which Charmy exhibited her still lifes, Henri Matisse, Albert Marquet, Henri Manguin, Charles Camoin, Pierre Girieud and André Derain provoked a *succès de scandale* in salle VII (room VII). Their blazing colors, unmodulated forms and utter disregard for artistic convention earned them the title of "Fauves," or wild beasts, by the same critic who described Charmy's still-life paintings as meek. Vauxcelles writes, "The candor of these busts surprises in the midst of the orgy of pure tones: Donatello chez les fauves …"[37] While the term has been frequently misinterpreted as derision or mockery, he was in fact celebrating the virile boldness of these artists whose paintings appeared fierce in comparison with the Donatello sculpture in the room.[38] Thus, from its inception, the "wild" style of the Fauves came to be associated with virile expression to the exclusion of women artists.[39] Moreover, Matisse took initiative in forming the group and promoting an image of a camaraderie of artist rebels.[40] As a member of the hanging committee of both the Salon des Indépendants and the Salon d'Automne in 1905, Matisse would have had a voice in the arrangement of his coterie's paintings.[41] By showing their work together, he and the soon-to-be-named Fauves wanted to promote themselves as pioneers who were radicalizing painting.[42] As Camoin scholar Claudine Grammont explains, "here reigns a true group spirit, declared by the artists themselves" with Matisse as ringleader.[43] A tight-knit circle of male artists was no place for a woman.

Fauvism was never a cohesive group with a definitive list of members nor was it a coherent movement defined by a specific set of techniques.[44] Critics, and later art historians, were responsible for creating a veneer of solidarity for the Fauves. In fact, Vauxcelles, who appeared to have discovered the Fauves, regularly frequented Berthe Weill's gallery and was already familiar with Matisse and others aligned with the group before their salon debut.[45] In the 1906 Indépendants, their paintings were hung together once again, reinforcing their unity. The artists and their proponents were invested in maintaining an image of a unified, masculine cadre. Women who were engaging with Fauve techniques, including Charmy and Sonia Delaunay, were not accorded the status of Fauve. The role of modern artist was to be played by men.[46]

In 1905, Charmy's work caught Weill's attention. With a keen eye and zealous spirit, Weill was a trailblazing art dealer who exhibited works by Picasso, Matisse and other innovative painters as early as 1902 before they gained prominence.[47] She opened her gallery at the foot of Montmartre in December 1901 and committed to showing young, up-and-coming artists of both sexes.[48] Weill claimed to be the first dealer to sell a work by Picasso in Paris.[49] Beginning in 1905, she regularly exhibited Charmy's work.[50] In her memoir, *Pan! … dans l'oeil* (Bang! … Right in the Eye), she recounts her first encounter with Charmy's paintings at the Indépendants:

> I notice paintings by a young woman who has not yet presented her work to me, whom I do not know, in whom I sense a true personality. I write to her asking her to bring me a painting or two, which she does. I sell one in a subsequent exhibition. After that, Mademoiselle Charmy became my best friend.[51]

Weill's memoir, along with their correspondence, which details everything from quotidian matters and personal anecdotes to more serious troubles they faced, reveals a lifelong bond between these two women. In *Portrait of Berthe Weill* (c. 1910–20) (Plate 11), Charmy pays homage to her dealer and confidante. Weill appears erudite and enterprising in her smart frock coat, scarf, gold-rimmed spectacles and a modern wristwatch. Her body, swathed in black fabric, accords her a looming presence that faintly recalls Auguste Rodin's *Monument to Balzac* (1898).[52] Charmy emphasizes Weill's discerning gaze with her pursed lips and a single raised eyebrow.[53] One filament of vanilla-hued paint bisects the eye. The portrait captures her persona as a shrewd and intellectual businesswoman, matching journalist Jean-Paul Crespelle's description:

> The merchant was one of the most original figures in the arts business; we consider her today with Vollard, Kahnweiler and Paul Guillaume as one of the main promoters of the art of the 20th century … With her pale complexion, her pursed mouth, her shapeless smock, she was both the chairwoman of the church and the teacher who has just tamed her class.[54]

Painted around the same time, Charmy's *Self-Portrait* (c. 1910–20) evinces a similar restrained palette and robust brushwork. Charmy strikes an equally confident pose and bears a professional countenance with a discreet, yellow-trimmed cravat. Like Weill's, her silhouette is enshrouded in healthy swabs of midnight blue and black. Their visages are endowed with a sense of vitality with thickly layered coral flesh tones, and their stern, but widening mouths are accented with meandering strokes of blush and magenta. Together, these works read like a pair of portraits.[55]

From 1905 until World War One, Charmy's career accelerated as she painted prolifically and exhibited regularly at Weill's and at the galleries of Eugène Druet and Clovis Sagot. She also expanded her network, establishing contacts with other progressive artists. Some time between 1906 and 1908, she met Charles Camoin, a recognized "Fauve" and friend of Matisse. With him, she cultivated both a professional and romantic rapport.[56] It is probable that Weill introduced them. Weill's memoirs do not discuss their relationship in detail,[57] but Camoin and Matisse mention Charmy in letters in early 1912.[58] Her artistic output from this period with Camoin is predominantly devoted to portraits and landscapes.[59] The two worked together in her studio at 88 rue de Clichy, pictured in Camoin's *Émilie at Her Easel* (c. 1908). Here, Charmy appears with a paintbrush in hand, her long, slender form mimicking the shape of the wine bottle posed on the table beside her. The image bespeaks Charmy's immersion in the avant-garde.

During the summer of 1910, and possibly earlier in 1906, Charmy and Camoin left the studio and traveled to Corsica and the South of France, seeking inspiration from the brilliant Mediterranean light.[60] Scholars have yet to agree on a precise chronology of their sojourns.[61] In an unpublished essay, Patrick Seale recounts:

> That was the year [1906] in which she went to Corsica with Camoin – itself a sign of her new independence. This was long a secret, or at least disavowed, phase of her life. In later years she told her son Edmond that she had gone to Corsica on a bicycle to explore the island on her own – and this was the version he believed for many years. In fact she did not go alone, nor was she a cyclist. There was always something improbable about the idea of this delicate figure on a bike laden with canvases and painting materials.[62]

Traveling as a young single woman with a male companion would have raised eyebrows. Unfortunately, correspondence from this early period has vanished. As Seale's account demonstrates, Charmy was surreptitious about her early explorations and relationship with Camoin. Nonetheless, a visual record remains. The landscapes which they produced bespeak a close artistic dialogue. One can imagine the two painters side by side, just like Matisse and Derain in Collioure in 1905. Bold contours, areas of unprimed canvas and vibrant hues situate their work firmly within the Fauve idiom.

Camoin's *The Calanques of Piana* (c. 1910) and Charmy's *Corsican Landscape* (c. 1910) depict dramatic cliffs along the coast of the island. Camoin, preoccupied with light, captures the scintillating rays peeking through the evergreen branches. The foliage becomes translucent against the luminous sky and blue cliffs. Although Charmy treats the same motif, she is less focused on the effects of light and atmosphere. Her trees are hardly recognizable as evergreens, her brushstroke looser and her contours denser. Her palette is less naturalistic still, with touches of lime green and pink and a bold orange stroke in the middle. In Charmy's *Rocky Landscape* (c. 1910), the rocks are defined by thick silhouettes, highlighted with touches of emerald, and juxtaposed against cobalt-blue water, while the exposed white canvas on the upper right denotes a lingering cloud. Charmy's landscapes appear further removed from nature than Camoin's, while her intense, vibrating palette evokes the hot Mediterranean sun in a manner which recalls Matisse's Collioure landscapes circa 1905–7.[63]

As Charmy departed from the artistic techniques of the past, ridding her work of naturalistic light and shadow, Camoin, concerned with light, maintained a dialogue with Impressionism.[64] This is evident when comparing Camoin's *The Pines at the*

Water's Edge at Trayas (1905 or 1910) with Charmy's *Piana, Corsica* (c. 1906–10) and *L'Estaque* (c. 1906–10). Camoin highlights the effects of sunlight with dabs of yellow and light blue before a white sky, as the trees cast shadows on the ground, rendered in swabs of blue and violet. In Charmy's landscape, the dark contours of the spindly trees in the foreground contrast with the ochre rooftops in the background. Areas of unprimed canvas peek through the foliage and branches to resemble the sky itself. The combination of flat areas of color and the curving arabesques of sinuous tree trunks creates an undulating pattern, while also reinforcing the flatness of the picture plane. As with Matisse, Charmy explored the decorative play of line, the relation between negative and positive space and the construction of form with color. Charmy's *Piana Corsica* and *L'Estaque* both recall Matisse's *View of Collioure* (1907). These landscapes demonstrate her experimentation with innovative approaches that the Fauves pioneered. Scholars have identified similarities between Charmy's *Femme au lac* (1907) and *Personnage assis – Corse* (c. 1907) and Matisse's *La Rive* (1907).[65] Like Matisse, Charmy reduces the landscape to flat areas of color and delineates the trees with dark, bold and sinuous lines. Although of the pair only Camoin was considered a "Fauve" by French critics and contemporaries, Charmy's landscapes are just as "wild."[66]

Charmy showcased her paintings of Corsica in her first solo exhibition, held at Galerie Druet in 1911. Two years later at the Armory Show in New York, Charmy exhibited four paintings, two of which were landscapes – one of Ajaccio and another of L'Estaque.[67] For the first time her work was grouped with the Fauves, specifically Camoin, Marquet, Manguin, Friesz, Rouault and Matisse. Displayed in Gallery H, the last room and culmination of the exhibition, the placement fortified her status as a pioneering painter.[68] Arthur Jerome Eddy, a collector and writer from Chicago, purchased Charmy's *L'Estaque* and later donated it to the Art Institute of Chicago.[69] He wrote about the painting in his book *Cubists and Post-Impressionism* (1914), notably employing the adjective "virile" when discussing Charmy's work, simultaneously aligning her with a male artist, Maurice de Vlaminck.[70] As we have seen, French critics later would use descriptors such as "masculine" to characterize her painting style; however, according to Eddy, Charmy was on par with her "wild" contemporaries.

In *Woman in a Japanese Dressing Gown* (c. 1907), Charmy treats a popular Fauve motif. Camoin, Derain, and Marquet had each painted Matisse's wife dressed in a kimono earlier, around 1904.[71] An exercise in form, pattern and color, the decorative design of the dressing robe becomes the main force, reinforcing the flat surface of the picture plane. Likewise, Charmy draws attention to surface pattern. The light blue robe is decorated with a large floral design and stands out against a complementary yellow background. In contrast, her figure is not entirely engulfed by color and arabesque. The frontality of her pose and the bold outlines encasing her form bring attention back to the woman, who may represent the artist herself.[72] *Young Pregnant*

Woman (1906–7) (Plate 12) is another Fauve portrait. Here, Charmy ventured into new territory. Rendered in pulsating colors, the woman's swollen womb dominates the composition. Charmy encircles the woman's wide girth with a thick black line and paints the dress in gamboge. With her flaming orange attire, she resembles a Buddhist monk. Typically, pregnancy was camouflaged in portraiture, as seen in Morisot's *The Mother and Sister of the Artist* (1869–70), where the sister's pregnancy is discreetly disguised with a loose white morning robe. The closest parallel to Charmy's remarkably bold portrayal may be found in the work of Paula Modersohn-Becker, an artist whom Charmy presumably never met.

From self-portraiture to the nude

Also distinct from her Fauve peers is Charmy's predilection for self-portraiture. In *Self-Portrait* (c. 1909–12) she applies broad strokes of Castilian red, tangerine and maise with darker swatches of caramel around the eyes and minutiae of empire green on the right eye. White over-painting highlights the upper lip and crown of the forehead and grazes the brim of her slender nose. The striking use of color is not unlike Matisse's portraits of the same period, for example, *Femme au chapeau*.[73] Similarly, there is little spatial modeling; color assumes a primary role. She likewise models the face with blocks of pulsating hues and generates pictorial contrast through complementary colors. *Self-Portrait with an Album* (1907–12) (Plate 13) is close to life-sized. Wearing a blue, polka-dotted dress set against a solid red background, Charmy faces the viewer confidently with her arms outstretched. Her facial traits are composed of haphazard strokes, with thick dabs pronouncing her eyes and lips. The impasto is most heavily built up on the face, creating an overall sense of three-dimensionality. Charmy employs various shades of creamy pigment stained with rose and mauve except for on the forehead, which is spotlighted with pure white paint. In lieu of a paintbrush, she holds an album with samples of her work, demonstrating her profession as artist.

Although the influence of Fauvism is apparent in these early self-portraits, Charmy concurrently interweaves her own painterly practice. The colors she employs are not as cacophonous as Matisse's, and her markedly heavy impasto is a departure from the Fauve's thinly painted canvases. With few exceptions, Chaïm Soutine among them, thick paint was generally not in vogue in French vanguard circles at this time. Rather than a short-lived experiment, her bold, meandering brushwork and accented color persist as consistent elements in Charmy's oeuvre. Her facture and palette do not accost the eye but draw the viewer in and stimulate the imagination. In *Self-Portrait* (c. 1910) (Plate 14), messy strokes encapsulate her visage; the left eye is composed of a mere dot and lips of two swabs of fuchsia, while a dense, wavering line delineates the contours of the face. Powder pink and cream coalesce on the surface like makeup heavily applied and unblended. Even though detail is restrained and shading is absent, the portrait nevertheless reads as Charmy's likeness while capturing a fleeting moment of introspection. A similar contemplative disposition is evident in Charmy's portrait of Camoin (c. 1906–9). She depicts him brooding with his head propped on his hand. Marked by dark swatches of blue, violet-black and green, the somber palette combined with his meditative posture conveys melancholy. Theirs was not an easy relationship and many details remain unclear. When they separated in 1912, Camoin was deeply affected and troubled; he destroyed all his paintings in his studio.[74] He burned some canvases and cut up others into many small pieces, and then threw them in a trashcan on rue Lepic. These pieces were later found, reassembled and sold at a flea market.[75]

Charmy painted *Large Nude* (c. 1912) around the time she separated from Camoin. Elevations of impasto distinguish the nude from the thinly painted background. Vigorous and flowing brushwork imbues and animates the figure as an undulating line of peach accentuates the bend of the hips and waist. Applications of scintillating champagne pink highlight the thighs and breasts, contrasting with the heavy black outline which envelops the body. The arms, composed of a flash of crimson, soften at the edges and blend into the murky background. The facial features are rendered in nightingale-brown. Given its analogous composition, brushwork, palette and identical dimensions, *Large Standing Nude* likely dates to the same period (c. 1912). The narrow, vertical format of these paintings diverges from the traditional horizontal reclining nude. As in *Large Nude*, the figure stands and gazes outward, but, in this case, she meets the viewer's gaze. She is attired in a floor-length robe and heels which accentuate her uprightness. The colorful garment in blue-gray and rose hangs open revealing a narrow sliver of her body, bounded with a heavy black border. Highlights of pale yellow generate a pearly dermal surface. Increasingly, Charmy conveys sensuality through the intricacies in her handling of color and form, suggestive poses and gestures, shimmering pigments and idiosyncratic manipulations of the brush. Meanwhile, the genres of self-portraiture and the nude become interlaced in her oeuvre; Charmy's intense introspective regard is compounded with an intimate study of the female body.

Charmy presumably saw Camoin's *Saltimbanque at Rest* (1905). In a garishly decorated boudoir, vermillion dominates, accompanied by loud accents of orange and green. On a diminutive bed, a naked woman slumbers, wearing only a pair of heels and striped stockings. According to Grammont, this is a depiction of a prostitute Camoin saw at a brothel in St Tropez.[76] Most shocking is her pose: her legs are indecorously spread. Camoin angles the composition so that her entire body is crudely displayed at eye level. This position effectively reduces the figure to her sex.[77] In contrast with *Saltimbanque at Rest*, stripped of all dignity, Charmy's *Large Nude* and *Large*

Standing Nude exude an air of self-assurance. Each figure retains her poise and emits forthright confidence. Rather than tawdry scenes of recumbent, comatose prostitutes, Charmy's nudes appear both aware and unembarrassed. Moreover, her descendants have identified both works as self-portraits. Indeed, the blunt execution of the facial features in *Large Nude* is not unlike her self-portrait from c. 1910 (Plate 14). Dated c. 1912, *Self-Portrait* appears as a direct retort to Camoin's *Saltimbanque at Rest*. The supine pose and diagonally positioned body mirror the Saltimbanque's relaxing posture. With the elbows flared, the face and chest are exposed in an unbashful manner, the nipples accented with ruby-orange pigment. The woman appears carefree, but not clownish. As with Camoin's nude, she wears knee-high stockings, but a loosely painted blue-lilac skirt conceals the abdomen and hips. Rather than a brothel, the woman luxuriates in a nondescript setting. The Prussian blue background lends the work a nocturnal aura. Pushed to the foremost plane, the figure is aggrandized within the composition, placing emphasis on the nude's own corporeal pleasure. According to the artist's exhibition history, none of these early nude self-portraits was shown during her lifetime. Evidently, Charmy's nudes were not intended as commodified images of languorous female bodies to lure male audiences, but rather as intimate works in tune with a particular feminine perspective. Charmy increasingly contravened gender norms as she examined a spectrum of female sexuality in her work.

Women and sexuality in early twentieth-century France

Little is known about women's intimate lives in France at the turn of the twentieth century. Even less is known about what they did for pleasure.[78] To begin with, women's sex education was extremely limited. As Rachel Mesch states, "Most bourgeois women were sorely lacking as they entered into their marital vows."[79] Social mores discouraged women from gazing at their own naked bodies, let alone another woman's. The leading authorities on sexual matters were male scientists and doctors. These specialists stressed that female sexual desire should be contained as it was separate from procreativity.[80] Moreover, woman's sexual desire was "often associated with deviance, prostitution and hysteria."[81] This divorce of pleasure from procreation was a mechanism by which the male-dominated scientific and medical communities could control female sexuality.[82] Furthermore, men's fear of female sexuality was an underlying tension leading to strict control of women's private lives. Unrestrained female appetite was considered dangerous. Therefore, for a woman to openly acknowledge her libido would have been a bold infringement on the implicit societal rules governing women's lives, bodies and respectability.

In bourgeois marriages during the nineteenth century, sex "was merely a backdrop."[83] The husband was responsible for controlling his wife's sexual needs, although he paid little attention to her pleasure.[84] Physicians warned that, "Should a wife be introduced to sexual pleasure, she might become a voracious sexual predator, sapping her husband's energy and ignoring her duties as a mother," hence, the prevalent male custom for satiating sexual desire with a kept mistress or with a prostitute at a brothel.[85] This was permissible by law under most circumstances, while adultery, if committed by the wife, was always a crime and could result in imprisonment.[86] A gradual shift from the exclusive emphasis on procreation toward a more "sensual conception of sexuality" emerged with the discovery of ovulation and improvements in contraception.[87] Nevertheless, anxieties around female sexuality persisted through the early twentieth century. Moreover, since studies revealed that the female orgasm was not necessary for pregnancy, husbands could remain indifferent to their wives' sexual pleasure.

Charmy's provocative display of the body and bold handling of paint oppose her era's scientific beliefs and social mores. Concurrently, she pursued an independent lifestyle, rejecting marriage, and chose her career over family. Charmy had a son with the artist Georges Bouche in 1915 but elected not to marry him until 1931. She hired a wetnurse to care for her infant son.[88] While pregnant, she painted herself nude. Although depictions of women and children appear frequently in the history of art, pregnant imagery is rare. Pregnant nudes are rarer still. Some of the oldest extant examples are sculptures from the prehistoric era, including the so-called "Venus of Willendorf." Estimated to have been made over 25,000 years ago, the figurine's ample breasts and hips emphasize fertility. Among the limited examples of pregnant nudes from the early twentieth century are Gustav Klimt, *Hope I* (1903) and Modersohn-Becker's *Self-Portrait on the 6th Wedding Anniversary* (1906). The latter is a self-portrait, although the artist was not actually pregnant when she painted it. Like Modersohn-Becker, Charmy treats the novel subject of a pregnant nude self-portrait, but the result could not be more distinct. Moreover, she did not paint "Mother Nude" as Modersohn-Becker had in *Reclining Mother and Child II* (1906).[89] Each artist treated the theme of pregnancy incognizant of the other and with no precedent to follow. Charmy did not exhibit her pregnant nude self-portraits; they were presumably too scandalous for public eyes. Since her death, these paintings have been hidden in storage. Unexpectedly, Charmy's pregnant nudes are expressive of self-gratification and pleasure rather than motherly desire. Conceived long before the women's liberation movement of the 1960s, her work speaks to some of the theories and ideas that would later develop. Although she was never a declared feminist, Charmy draws attention to a basic fact of life – pregnancy – and a proscribed topic of her era – female autoeroticism – in a frank, unprejudiced way. Over a century later, these images retain their capacity to fascinate and shock. She disregarded the conventions of the nude and bourgeois morality, pioneering novel body imagery. Charmy flouted expectations of femininity and motherhood to express her own uninhibited pleasure.

Charmy experimented with the theme of the pregnant nude self-portrait at least twice. Two paintings, long buried in storage, were unveiled to the author by the artist's descendants in the final stages of writing this book. In both works, she paints her own bare body lounging supine in a vivid and nondescript interior. The naturalistically weighted bosom seems to indicate that the artist examined her own body closely. The facial features and body parts are rendered with a crude and loose brushwork, as if spontaneously executed in an experimental mode. The lack of detail conceals the nude's identity, and places emphasis on movement. Neither nude is still or asleep. One hugs her waist while balancing her leg in the air. She turns her head away so that only the nape is visible. The other wraps an arm around her swollen abdomen, extends her leg out horizontally, while draping the other past the edge of the sofa or bed. She cocks her head back in a pose that conveys sexual satisfaction. The gritty texture of coagulated paint is visible on the thighs, hips, breasts and stomach. Both nudes are submersed in color – Prussian blue with accents of pink in one painting, and luscious shades of red in the other. Contrary to what one might expect of a pregnant nude in art, these works have nothing to do with fecundity. Charmy effectively divorces the pregnant body from the theme of maternity. These are radical nudes: not only is the subject matter new to the history of art, but they also exude a woman's sexual voice. In defiance of the expectations of motherhood as fertile, nurturing and protective, Charmy shows her pregnant body in a state of ecstasy. These daring images are resolutely expressive of female pleasure.

Forbidden female eroticism

Charmy's oeuvre stands apart from her contemporaries within the realm of the visual arts. Few women painted sensually provocative nudes in France at the beginning of the twentieth century.[90] Rather, nudes by women often appear chaste; they are either compliant with academic conventions or reflect voguish styles of lithe and girlish femininity. Seldom did women paint sexually charged nude self-portraits. Instead, literature was the chief art form through which women began to treat both the subject of female eroticism and the self through autobiography in revealing and complex ways.[91] Like Charmy, Colette defied bourgeois morality repeatedly in her oeuvre, starting with her first book, in *Claudine à l'école* (1900), which was published under her husband's name.[92] Loosely based on the author's childhood, the work explores taboo subjects including lesbianism. Later, in *The Pure and the Impure* (originally published under the title *Ces plaisirs …* in 1932), Colette studied the dynamics and relationships between women, both observed and experienced firsthand. The novel is based on the gay and bisexual spheres in Paris during the interwar years. In a labyrinth of fiction and autobiography, the protagonist, Charlotte, emulates the author in poignant ways: they bear a similar name, are approximately the same age and resemble each other physically.[93] Scholars often refer to Colette's autobiographical style as "autofiction." This genre allowed her to openly discuss sexuality, all while preserving her personal privacy and avoiding the revelation of potentially sensitive details.[94] Colette constructed new types of personae in order to speak freely of female eroticism.[95] For artists like Charmy, depicting oneself could offer this same kind of freedom of self-exploration. Tirza True Latimer argues that artists such as Romaine Brooks "created frameworks" that allowed them to engage with and transform female identity in representation. Utilizing portraiture and self-portraiture, Brooks and other lesbian artists mythologized their histories and explored formerly unmentionable aspects of their experience.[96]

A woman's behavior can only be comprehended within the social context of her era, and at the beginning of the twentieth century, the repercussions for overt displays of female sexuality or alternative sexualities were severe.[97] Speaking out or acting openly on the matter of physical yearnings was hazardous in a world that aimed to preserve women's respectability.[98] Thus, for female authors and artists, when exploring sexual and subversive topics, certain forms of subterfuge were often necessary. Charmy, Colette and their contemporaries could resist but could not fully separate themselves from the cultural and gender mores of their epoch. In addition to the lack of social acceptance, the vocabulary to adequately designate female sexuality, relationships or experiences, whether heterosexual, homosexual, bisexual etc., did not exist at the beginning of the twentieth century.[99] Therefore, individuals were not fully equipped with apposite language to describe themselves, their desires or their sexual orientation.[100] Although Colette did not "out" herself as a lesbian or bisexual, she did not refrain from exploring the full spectrum of feminine eroticism in her work. Scholars have unveiled unstated subtexts of lesbianism in Colette's writing. She underlined the unspoken word, accentuating its insinuations and igniting readers' imaginations. While Colette's viewpoint regarding homosexuality was ambiguous, scholars have still found it productive to analyze her literature within this context of same-sex sexuality and subjectivity.[101] I apply a similar approach to Charmy. As with Colette's prose, in Charmy's art, the exact nature of her desire is evasive. She reveals a subjectivity and sexuality that resist any fixed classification. In opposition to turn-of-the-century scientific discourses and social stereotypes, her work is informed by a deep awareness of the dynamics of female pleasure. Though she did not identify with or immerse herself in sexually liberated communities in Paris as Colette did, such as Natalie Clifford Barney's salons, her work speaks to a broad female audience of diverse sexualities. Privately, Charmy partook in an artistic counterculture, creating a new visual discourse for the representation of women's sexual pleasure.

"Colette of painting"

Charmy and Colette collaborated on just one occasion. In 1921, Colette wrote the text for the catalogue of Charmy's solo exhibition, entitled, "Quelques Toiles de Charmy, Quelques Pages de Colette," held in the Galerie d'Art Ancien et Moderne. In a panegyric of the artist, Colette states:

> Ignore Charmy, then discover her suddenly in twenty canvases that scatter and stick to the wall, the colors, the magnificent substance of flowers, living flesh, moving water, one receives a shock, the anxious pleasure that accompanies a romantic encounter.[102]

The writer lucidly describes the viewer's first encounter with Charmy's work as one of nervous wonder. Color and materiality breathe life into images of flowers, flesh and water. According to Colette, this first impression is akin to the apprehensive delight prompted by a romantic rendezvous. Clearly the admiration was mutual, for Charmy paid tribute to the writer with a painting, *Portrait of Colette* (1921), exhibited and reproduced as the frontispiece of the catalogue. Using her signature loose brushwork, she depicts a petite doll-like mouth, cropped and wispy hair and penetrating blue eyes. The portrait captures Colette's aura as both thinker and dreamer – her head tilted and propped on her hands as she gazes outward with a thoughtful expression. Colette clearly valued this portrait; it hung prominently in the living room of her Palais-Royal apartment until her death.[103]

In the rest of the essay, Colette attempts to define the painter's individual style and its expressive power through laudatory prose. Recognizing a singularity in Charmy's style, Colette praises her for working outside and "against" dominant art methods, past and present: "'progress, process, [artistic] school ...' these words have no place here, under the name of an artist who was born so well-armed against them."[104] Rather than theory or collective ideology, "the brush, subtle, without artifice, is guided by a lucid passion."[105] According to Colette, Charmy is swayed by sensation instead of techniques or styles propagated by contemporaneous movements. Likewise, scholars have noted the difficulty of categorizing Colette's work within existing canons.[106] A self-reflective quality in the essay is apparent, as if Colette found resonance with her own work. With exceedingly rich prose, Colette describes how Charmy's paintbrush

> Suspends, over the sea, a creamy fold of wave, a foam of silver, a mist in which the changing colors of the iris play, elusive and visible, it is this brush which attaches, from an infallible lick, the drop of light to the varnished leaves of the camellia, the velvet fat to the petal of the rose, the sunny tuft to the branch of the corchorus.[107]

These words recall other writings by Colette, particularly in her lush descriptions of flora.[108] With poetic imagery, Colette continues, describing Charmy as a "masterful servant to female flesh." She brings the female form to life, so that "the cries of frenzied fecundity" can be heard. Like the fluctuations of the ocean tide, "the body swells and hollows out." Charmy's nudes are, for Colette, "eternal."[109] Her sumptuous prose is overwrought, but nevertheless reveals an attempt to limn the idiosyncratic traits of Charmy's style with its heightened sensorial impact, as well as the visual experience for the beholder. Furthermore, it demonstrates an enthusiastic and atypical effort on the part of the writer to align herself with a painter. Colette did not often write about art, and advancements in modern painting vexed her. She was especially critical of Cubism.[110] Colette likely identified a shared affinity with Charmy's approach to the world of corporeal delights.

A few years later, critics referred to Charmy as the "Colette of painting."[111] They recognized these two artists – one visual, one literary – as women who paid particular attention to sensuality in their work. Charmy was given the *chevalier* of the *Légion d'honneur* in 1926, an award that Colette had received six years prior. With this honor, they both became regarded as prominent women in the arts in France. Their association waned by the 1930s, at which point Charmy and Colette had assuredly parted ways. Scholars have conjectured that for a brief period the two were romantically involved.[112] It has been speculated that this relationship ended in a dispute so severe that they erased all traces of their liaison. Perhaps respect and admiration turned into competition and jealousy.[113] Mining both the Charmy and Colette archives, no correspondence between the two of them exists to validate this supposition.[114]

Still, Charmy did not discard all materials related to the writer. A few informal sketches of Colette are held in private hands and in the archives maintained by her descendants. In a preparatory sketch for the painted portrait, Colette is shown from a close vantage point, lending the image a sense of intimacy. Her disheveled tresses, heart-shaped face, and slanted, darkly rimmed eyes are rendered with a rapid and flickering line. In an unfinished drawing, the author slumbers in an armchair wearing only lingerie.[115] It appears swiftly executed, with lightly smudged lines. In a third sketch, Colette's visage is rendered with coarse, bold lines. The word "Chéri" is written across the bottom. Colette's *Chéri* was published in 1920, around the time the two met. Perhaps Charmy was devising book illustrations for Colette's novel.[116]

In *Portrait de Colette* (c. 1921), Colette is recumbent, resting her head on her arm. The paint application is loose and thick. A contemporaneous painting entitled *Colette Nude* is presumed to be a depiction of the author (c. 1919–21). Lying prone, her spine forms an undulant line as she gazes coyly at the viewer. The swirling green and russet-colored background create an illusory space. The short wavy hair, blue eyes and petite rouged mouth resemble Charmy's contemporaneous portraits of Colette, but her figure is elongated and stylized beyond recognition. Who posed for this work is uncertain. Meanwhile, the writer's profile is unmistakable in a frank pencil drawing, entitled *Sleeping Nude*. The angular, pointed chin, long thin nose, large eyes and tousled hair all closely resemble Colette's features in the preparatory sketch for the Saint-Sauveur-en-Puisaye portrait. Her form is not idealized as it is in *Colette Nude*. Certain areas, such as the forehead and the arm, are rendered with a coarse line; other sections, including the breasts, abdomen and navel, are lightly sketched. The close viewpoint suggests a body seen firsthand. In *Reclining Nude*, swirling pencil lines capture the mounds and crevices of a female form, who, like the previous drawing, has a pointed chin, although the rest of the facial features are obscured. Viewed at an angle, foreshortening places emphasis on the woman's lower body, with jagged lines intersecting at her sex.

While the painted image can never directly correspond to the written text, insightful correlations are found in the work of these two women. First, the term "autofiction" is pertinent to Charmy's oeuvre. Her self-portraits and nudes may be seen in relation to Colette's profusion of first-person figurations, as they both reflect and depart from their creator. Her grandson notes that she rarely hired models and estimates that ninety-five per cent of her nudes are self-portraits.[117] Many of Charmy's nudes bear some resemblance to herself, although they are not always identified as self-portraits. Charmy did not usually title or date her work. Often, it is impossible to pinpoint with certainty who posed for her nudes. Curators have had difficulty identifying her subjects, and consequently, discrepancies in the titling abound. The actual number of self-portraits Charmy created is uncertain. Twenty-five were included in the Musée Paul-Dini exhibition, but curator Sylvie Carlier states that this is in fact only a small quantity, estimating that there are over a hundred in total.[118]

Charmy's constant reworking of her self-image caught the attention of critics. In the preface to a catalogue from her 1919 exhibition at Galerie Pesson, E. Gómez Carrillo wrote: "She transforms her appearance according to her fantasy, giving an image of herself constantly renewed, a woman who, changing her look, smile, color, hair, mouth and body, was lyrically always the same."[119] Charmy renders herself as an unstable and evolving character, which Carrillo terms "transfigurations." Charmy's son, Edmond Bouche, in his essay entitled, "My Mother," similarly notes the mutable qualities of her persona, reflected in her self-portraits:

> On certain days, my mother appears with an altered visage: a face that is changed or different in both its expression as its features. This is Charmy confronting Charmy in the reflection of the mirror … Sometimes Mongol or Chinese; or entirely dissimilar, an Amazon of the seventeenth century, or a woman of the Touraine from the banks of the Loire. My mother has never revealed to me the secret of this self-transformation for which she requires neither makeup nor masks.[120]

Here, it is unclear whether Edmond is describing his own mother or her self-portraits – he seems to meld the two.[121] In her mutable self-portrayals, Charmy presents a mercurial identity. She turned to the self as well as the body as subject matter that allowed for endless transfigurations, as if negotiating her identity and sexuality simultaneously. Through her self-portraits and nudes, Charmy exhibited a latitude of sexual freedom while capturing a modern female subjectivity – one that is complex, fluid and emergent.

As Charmy rendered a metamorphosis of the self in paint, she simultaneously cultivated a façade and a patina of respectability. She was less unfettered than Colette in her public demeanor even among friends and relatives. Her social circle was distinct from Colette's – she did not mingle with the "women of the Left Bank," or the wealthy, lesbian and expatriate elite at Barney's salons.[122] Charmy was obligated to make a living from her art. To promote herself within a male-dominated realm, she seems to have placed a high value on her interactions with influential figures in the art world. She deftly navigated androcentric political and artistic realms to promote her career. Correspondence as well as portraits reveal an erudite social circle that included politicians, journalists and critics. She painted the journalist Joseph-Élie Bois twice, and the former Prime Ministers of France – Édouard Daladier and Aristide Briand. She also liaised with the Count de Jouvencelles and the art critic André Warnod, among others.[123] During the interwar period, she held intellectual gatherings in her home.[124] She appears to have thoughtfully cultivated a circle of friends and proponents who would advocate her work, a strategy which must have contributed to her recognition in France and the accolade of the Legion of Honor. She relinquished it all at the start of World War Two, when she retreated with her husband and son to Marnat, near Lyon. Returning to Paris in 1945, she retired from the public eye. She still maintained friendships with prominent figures, however, including Louise Weiss, an author, feminist and politician. Weiss was the director of the political journal *L'Europe nouvelle*, and she adamantly campaigned for women's rights and suffrage.[125] She mentioned Charmy fondly in her memoir.[126] And she owned a number of her paintings, which she later donated to the Musée Louise Weiss in Saverne.[127] In a preface to the catalogue of a Charmy exhibition in 1951, Weiss wrote, "Little Charmy is one of the most sensitive, strong, and well-rounded artists among the women in French painting. She is originality itself."[128]

In personality, Charmy was reticent and reserved. According to Weill, she was very guarded in nature, a trait which was often mistaken as pride:

> As she does not belong to any school, her reserve, of which to a great degree is shyness, was attributed to pride, disdain. If it is to be proud for not straying in order to follow fashion, from the line of conduct that one has traced in art to impose one's personality, then yes! She is very proud! And a pride that I consider strongly.[129]

Patrick Seale perceived an aura of "haughty" mystery about her:

> She rarely made known what she thought. It took a lot of effort to get her attention, even more to get her approval ... Sometimes she let a few words slip, but more often her sentences were left unfinished.[130]

Jeanine Warnod (daughter of André Warnod), who visited Charmy and Edmond during World War Two at her home in Marnat, described Charmy as someone who preferred solitude to companionship.[131]

Intimacy and secrecy pervade Charmy's oeuvre. She maintained a high level of privacy about her personal experiences, her sexuality and her art. The endeavor to illuminate the equivocal aspects of her work by searching for the identity of her models, interviewing her descendants, or reading between the lines of the trace correspondence that remains, reaps little sustaining evidence. Efforts to distill meaning through biographical and documentary evidence alone are insufficient – the extant documentation of Charmy's life is too meager to offer a clear picture. Such study will always remain speculative, thwarted by an artist who, in the face of the prejudices of her era, and in her own manner, was a very private woman. While I do not intend to go to the extreme of entirely divorcing the artist from the particular socio-historical factors that impacted her life and her art, I wish to acknowledge, as Suthor does with Rembrandt, that attention "to the making of [her] works may be a precondition to understanding the nature of their meaning."[132] Upholding the thesis that artist's intentionality is evident through painterly texture, "the realized image" may be regarded "as visual evidence of an achieved intention."[133] The significance of Charmy's work is to be revealed layer by layer, within her facture, wherein we find an intricate expression of *jouissance.*

Jouissance – in paint and ink

To better understand Charmy's representations of woman's sexual ardor, it is necessary to look to feminist theory developed after the artist's lifetime. In particular, the concept of *jouissance* sheds light on her work. A nuanced term with numerous connotations, it comes from the verb *jouir*, to enjoy, and translates to "pleasure" in the simplest sense, but more specifically means an orgasm. Since the early 1970s, the term has carried intricate feminist connotations. Ann Rosalind Jones explains that for French writers, such as Julia Kristeva, Irigaray and Hélène Cixous, "Resistance [takes] place in the form of *jouissance*, that is, in the direct reexperience of the physical pleasures of infancy and of later sexuality, repressed but not obliterated by the Law of the Father."[134] Irigaray and Cixous stress that women, restricted historically as sexual objects for men, have been stymied from articulating their sexuality "in itself or for themselves." If they can express this, and if they can articulate it through the novel and unique languages necessary, then they will establish a perspective "from which phallogocentric concepts and controls can be seen through and taken apart, not only in theory but also in practice."[135] Although *jouissance* was not applied during Charmy's lifetime in a theoretical way, engaging with this postmodern term offers new and critically gendered insights into her representation of the nude.

In *Nude on Red Sofa* (c. 1925) (Plate 16), Charmy depicts a woman in the throes of ecstasy. The nude thrusts her head back, her black hair cascading over the plush arm of the sofa, as she arches her chest upward. Her thighs breach the limits of the picture plane, and her legs extend beyond it. Red dominates the composition, capturing the growing sense of heat and restless movement. Rather than purely imitative, pigment autonomously produces meaning. It is granted an active role, serving to augment the sense of ardor. This color, after all, is "the color of seduction." It is "a color frequently associated with pleasure, especially with the pleasure of the senses" as well as "eroticism and femininity."[136] Myriad shades of it appear: a velvet chaise longue in crimson before a background in rosewood, highlights of peach blossom and arbutus on the skin, carnation-colored nipples and scarlet lips. The gleaming reds transmit warmth, igniting the image with unbound pleasure. Composed of swirling strokes of variegated pinks, the woman's face appears flushed. A dash of magenta highlights her flared nostril. In some sections, the body seems to dissolve into the plush fabric underneath it, particularly the left shoulder and thigh, uncontained by contours. A sinuous black line peeks through thinly scumbled layers on the outer edges of the arm, neck and abdomen. Charmy initially sketched the figure loosely in black before applying a top coat of cream-colored paint. In some sections, this added layer blends with the underlying black, to create a visual effect resembling chiaroscuro.

The work has the illusion of total spontaneity. Certain brushstrokes appear haphazard, even accidental, such as the noticeably large dash of yellow green just below the elbow, further augmenting a sense of instantaneity. Two hair-thin strokes of white paint accentuate the mouth with one line between the lips to separate them slightly. A dab of pink trails below the right nipple, as if Charmy's brush had mistakenly slipped. The body appears volumetric due to a strategically textured arrangement of impasto layers. The most generous swatches of paint are applied to the woman's body, with abundant touches on the woman's cheeks, chest and forearm, distinguishing it from the thinly painted background. Her ample bosom is the most thickly painted area. Delineated with a long, smooth stroke, the right arm extends back, while the left arm reaches downward, past the torso, and hovers above the groin. Quivering brushstrokes coalesce and blur. Evidently, this hand is not still.

Repeatedly, Charmy conveys sensuality through the intricacies in her handling of color and form, suggestive poses and gestures, shimmering pigments and idiosyncratic manipulations of the brush. Meanwhile, the genres of self-portraiture and the nude become interlaced in her oeuvre; Charmy's intense introspective regard is compounded with an intimate study of the female body. As Charmy probed *jouissance* in art, Colette pursued the theme in literature. Ecstasy and desire are primary and recurring themes in Colette's *The Pure and the Impure*. Colette delves into the topics of lesbianism and women's sexual satisfaction in the text through enigmatic prose. Sherry Dranch argues that the text is profuse with "unstated messages on some strongly censored experiences and desires."[137] Often, Colette trails off with an ellipsis further augmenting the elusiveness of what she is trying to describe. The author avoids terms which are directly explicit. In one such passage, Colette writes that the protagonist, Charlotte "barred me from the cavern of odors, of colors, the secret refuge where surely frolicked a powerful arabesque of flesh, a cipher of limbs entwined, symbolic monogram of the Inexorable ..."[138] Colette repeatedly lays emphasis on Charlotte's quest for sexual gratification as she reveals and conceals her character's sexuality.

Charlotte reflects her creator in appearance and mien, and so too does the woman depicted in *Nude on Red Sofa* (Plate 16). This painting along with *Nude Holding Her Breast* (Plate 17) could be self-portraits. Compared with *Self-Portrait with an Album*, the facial features in both nudes are similar. Not only was the regularity with which Charmy employed studio models uncertain, it is also hard to imagine a model holding such compromising poses without a trace of self-consciousness. Contrariwise, Seale, who knew the artist well during the last years of her life, states, "The model [in *Nude Holding Her Breast*] may have been Bianchini – or 'Bianc' as Charmy liked to call her – a bit-part actress of whom she was fond."[139] In her private nudes, the characteristically blurred brushstrokes hinder our ability to identify the woman. The question of whether these works are self-portraits or if a model posed for them is unknowable and should be left open to allow for the fictional latitude taken in the artist's self-representation.

As with many of Colette's protagonists, Charmy's nudes satisfy themselves independently. *Young Girl Undressing* (1927) presents a woman in a candid pose. Engulfed in an expanse of roughly painted cobalt, her ghostly pale flesh blends with the soft, white fabric of her undergarments. Together, the blue ground, black high heels, a mane of dark tresses and coarse outline delineating the visage all contrast with the figure's milky mass. With dots for eyes and nostrils, a daub for the lips and a raised eyebrow, her facial features are crudely rendered. The crimson lips stand out emphatically, with one small speck that appears misplaced, like smudged lipstick. The strap of her white slip hangs off the shoulder, and her stockings are pushed down past her knees where they dangle loosely. Her direct stare conveys a sense of brazen self-assurance despite her disheveled nudity. Her hand hovers over her lap between her gaped thighs, yet the blurred brushstroke conceals the hand and what it touches.

For Charmy and Colette, the mouth serves as a metaphor for female sensuality. Colette scholars have noted that this fetish, in psychoanalytic terms, "is an image obsessively repeated" in her prose.[140] Colette calls attention to the mouth in this description of the heroine Renée Néré in *The Vagabond*:

> Oh! ... suddenly my mouth, in spite of itself, lets itself be opened, opens of itself as irresistibly as a ripe plum splits in the sun. And once again there is born that exacting pain that spreads from my lips, all down my flanks as far as my knees, that swelling as of a wound that wants to open once more and overflow – the voluptuous pleasure that I had forgotten.[141]

Colette magnifies the suggestiveness of her description of Renée Néré's mouth through metaphor; she compares the cracked mouth to succulent fruit opening in the heat. Charmy's *Nude Holding Her Breast* (c. 1920–25) (Plate 17) displays a woman with tousled hair, her rouged mouth gapes open involuntarily revealing a blackened tooth, allowing the viewer to imagine a sharp pang disseminating throughout the body, like Renée Néré's "swelling as of a wound" that might "overflow." Charmy adapts the art historical convention of "speaking likeness" for her own purposes. The woman does not appear to be uttering any words, but instead seems to emit a rasping sigh as a sensation overwhelms her. One can almost hear a groan emitted from that dark orifice, sustained, and growing like a soprano's vibrato in a slow, melodic crescendo toward climax.

Charmy's work plays upon multiple sensory modalities, invoking a synesthetic experience for the viewer. In addition to her virtuoso artistic abilities, critics often noted the multisensory nature of Charmy's paintings. In an early and important book on the modern nude, Francis Carco noted an "orgy of colors" in Charmy's work along with an evocation of trembling movement. He writes, "With her, everything harmonizes and balances with fiery bursts of color. One would think that the material of paint still quivers on the canvas with the enthusiastic, exuberant gesture which precipitated it."[142] André Warnod surmises Charmy's oeuvre as featuring "flowers blooming with ardent sensuality, naked women, stretched out in voluptuous abandon like laughter that opens and offers the sumptuousness of their fragrant petals."[143] Just like her nudes, Charmy's still lifes are unapologetically sensual.[144] She transforms everyday objects into a heightened experience of optical, tactile and olfactory bliss. Color and paint handlings become vehicles for conveying the artist's sensorial perception. The dazzling hues and evocation of velvety and moist textures in the aforementioned *Still Life* from 1904 elicits the senses of sight, touch and taste with its lavish colors and whirling brushstroke. In *Still Life with Cherries*, Charmy amplifies the intensity of the hues and color contrasts, which are further set off by a darkened ground. The sanguine cherries are accented with bright specks of white pigment so that they glisten. Fused together, they seem to be transforming into liquid, as if melting into jam. Fruit and flora in Charmy's oeuvre may be seen as somatic metaphors.

Colette draws from her encyclopedic knowledge of plant life to describe a cornucopia of species in her writing, often in association with the female body. In "Nuit blanche" (Sleepless Night), a lyrical monologue from the anthology *Les Vrilles de la vigne* (1908), Colette relates the idea of a sleepless night of a couple in bed to a spring garden.[145] Calling upon multiple senses, including sight, taste and the olfactory, the garden comes to life like a lucid dream. The world of plants becomes an analogy for human anatomy as Colette names, with the acute knowledge of a botanist, specific plants, herbs and berries – blackcurrant, sorrel and sage. "Your knees are like two cool oranges … Turn towards me, so that mine can steal some of that cool freshness." Colette calls attention to lips, where "mingled" the "taste of alcohol and citronella."[146] Colette's resplendent use of adjectives and metaphor in her descriptions of flora elicits all the senses. The piece concludes with a delicately worded lovemaking scene, written in the future tense. Conveyed subtly, Colette reveals that the two figures sharing the bed are female.[147] Subliminal messages about female–female love and eroticism as seen in "Nuit blanche" are recurrent in Colette's writing. But when broaching lesbianism, she avoids same-sex terminology.[148] In fact, the word "lesbian" does not appear in her literature.[149] She also circumvents direct verbalization of women's organs or the sex act, utilizing what Dranch terms a "clearly stated covertness."[150] Sumptuous description, metaphor and ellipses – these are some of the devices Colette employs to instantaneously veil and unveil a multivalent female hetero- and homosexuality. The title of the book itself, *Ces plaisirs …*, originally included an ellipsis, reinforcing underlying implications. Counting a total of sixty-six ellipses in Colette's descriptions of Charlotte, Dranch wonders, "What is left out?"[151]

In a similar vein, Charmy renders female sexuality as variable and multidimensional, and her representations of the body are not overtly explicit. Rather than an unsparing portrayal, she employs certain tools of subterfuge with her brush to conceal the most revealing aspects. *Nude Holding Her Breast* is erotically impactful, yet this is not achieved through a full-frontal view of the woman's sexual organs.[152] The pudendum is casually marked with two thin strokes. It is the suggestively opened mouth and grasping hand that make this work so candidly sensual. At the same time, Charmy's blurred, spontaneous brushwork alludes to rather than directly represents woman's eroticism. The impression of a rippling and soaring sensation is caught in fluid paint. Enamored by stratums of seemingly moist matter, the perceptive viewer realizes that something imperceptible transpires. The agitated surface lends a sense of movement and sensuality, but her loose handling of paint shrouds the most intimate aspects from the viewer. The lack of precise detail engages the viewer's imagination to fill the void – to read between her brushstrokes.

In *Self-Portrait in an Open Dressing Gown* (c. 1916–18) (Plate 15), the private experience of self-pleasuring is intimated to the attentive viewer. The silk robe, painted in variegated shades of blue and grey, lackadaisically splays open. The woman's face is flushed pink and her lips part, mirroring the unfastened garment. In this presumed self-portrait, Charmy veils and unveils the body with her brush. One hand limply holds either a paintbrush or cigarette while the other provocatively recedes underneath a mass of fabric, shrouded beneath swirling strokes of matter. Charmy teases the viewer through the paint's viscosity. With her hand positioned somewhere between the stomach and the groin, this figure appears to be touching herself; however, Charmy obscures our view. She does not grant the viewer full access to the act taking place; she merely implies what *could* be happening.

Might Charmy's dripping paint, which dissipates before revealing too much, be compared to Colette's use of the ellipsis? It is analogously stimulating and elusive. It does not disclose the unmentionable; it merely evokes it. It also carries a sense of censorship and omission; Charmy's saturated brushwork obscures the image and dissipates before divulging all to the viewer, just as Colette's ellipses frustrate the reader, leaving the impression of an unstated subtext. Both hide a forbidden layer of carnality, without diminishing the erotic impact. In fact, the eroticism of their work is further underscored through secrecy and concealment.

Censorship

Censorship and spectatorship are critical for understanding Charmy's oeuvre. She seemed to have consciously made selective choices about which works she exhibited. Charmy refrained from exhibiting her most daring nudes, including those heretofore examined. *Nude on Red Sofa*, *Nude Holding Her Breast*, *Self-Portrait in an Open Dressing Gown*, *Large Nude*, *Young Girl Undressing*, *Nude Lying on Her Elbow* (c. 1920–25) and *Self-Portrait* (c. 1920–25) remained in her studio until her death.[153] No records indicate that these paintings were shown publicly during her lifetime – they do not appear in any of her exhibition catalogues before her death. She must have realized that certain nudes could have been controversial with ramifications such as censorship or accusations of pornography if displayed. Even at the end of her career, she exhibited nudes with discretion. Out of the twenty-eight works included in her last exhibition at the age of ninety-five, only two were nudes, *La Loge* (1902) and *Nude* (1936).[154] Examples of nudes which Charmy did exhibit are *Reclining Nude* (c. 1920), shown in 1921 at the gallery Art Ancien et Moderne, and *Large Reclining*

Nude (c. 1920), exhibited in 1922 at Styles gallery.[155] Painted on a grand scale, these nudes conform to the voguish female type: the *forme féminine.* As discussed in the Introduction, this was a highly stylized female form that appeared in art as well as fashion magazines in the 1910s and 1920s and appealed to bourgeois tastes. Perry contends that Charmy may have been aiming to create "marketable images of the female nude which reinforced a stylised, erotic image of fashionable femininity."[156] Charmy had practical reasons for painting these kinds of images: to attract patrons, to garner attention from the press and to sell her work. Moreover, Perry argues that the "marketable" nudes fetched higher prices than her work in other genres.[157] The lack of comprehensive records of Charmy's artwork sales in galleries makes it challenging to confirm this hypothesis.[158] Still, the chasm in scale and style of her exhibited nudes versus her private images points to a paradox in Charmy's oeuvre. Charmy may have acceded to her clients' bourgeois tastes in her exhibited nudes, but she also conceived intimate images through which she could express autonomous freedom and audaciously give voice to ecstasy in paint.

Juxtaposing Charmy's private and public nudes reveals striking stylistic differences. The majority of her exhibited nudes are lackluster. They are devoid of the kind of lucid corporeality evident in her private works. *Nude with Green Pumps* (c. 1920–25) and *Female Nude against a Pink Background* (c. 1921), exhibited in 1921 at the Parisian Galerie d'Art Ancien et Moderne, feature waiflike bodies subsumed in clouds of pink. Measuring over three by six feet, *Large Reclining Nude* was executed around the same time as her more modestly sized *Nude on Red Sofa*, perhaps using the same red couch. These works are so divergent, they appear as if painted by two different artists. In the former, the body is a sinuous arabesque which echoes the ruffles of the drapes framing the composition. The woman's entire form is visible, neatly positioned in the center of the picture plane. In *Nude on Red Sofa*, Charmy aggrandizes the body within the composition. Her ample figure, composed of generous mounds of flesh, represents more precisely how a woman might see her own body. This in turn, could facilitate an identification of a female spectator with the female body displayed. In a remarkable volte-face, Charmy employs a radically different facture as well; it is vigorous and agitated. Charmy's private works are as strongly tactile as they are visual representations of the body. Consequently, an encounter with these images is multisensorial, eliciting the viewer's sense of touch and sight jointly. More than mere depictions, they evoke sensuous experience in and of itself, through vision and touch. Furthermore, the nudes themselves are not idle objects but are active both physically and psychologically. Engrossed and absorbed, they turn their attention to the fulfillment of their own physical elation. In this manner, Charmy portrayed the female body in the act of touching, simultaneously leaving traces of her own touch on the canvas. This was transgressive, and Charmy knew it.

Tactility

Writers noted Charmy's accent on tactility during her lifetime. Critics frequently called attention to her deft ability to evoke textures through color and brushstroke in her exhibited works. In the catalogue of an important solo exhibition in 1921, critic Henri Béraud wrote,

> We look at a nude by Charmy; we taste the carnal beauty, these living reflections of light on the warm grain of skin, we feast with a slightly greedy eye. There is a kind of carnal gluttony here.[159]

Others viewed Charmy's thick applications of impasto as unfeminine. As formerly mentioned, Dorgelès wrote that same year, Charmy "sees like a woman and paints like a man."[160] Her forceful painting style befuddled critics who attempted to ascribe a "feminine" mode of painting to art by women through gendered rhetoric.[161] Charmy was aware of the vital significance of style and its gender ramifications in the minds of her contemporaries. The surplus of paint ran counter-current to contemporary codes of womanliness and expectations for female painters. In her book on women artists, Madeleine Bunoust (1936) called attention to the palpable quality of Charmy's nudes:

> The flesh, colored, elastic and moving, draws the quivering of the muscle, voluptuously stretches a spine, curves a neck, a torso, a bust of a young girl. We admire the epidermis of a hip or a breast, these carnal displays, this warm grain of skin, these amber colors of the flesh, these plays of lights that shiver on a female nude.[162]

The materiality of the paint medium is intrinsic to the reading of her depictions of the female body. With profuse impasto she concurrently heightens and conceals eroticism.

Flesh, muscle, skin: Charmy's nudes seem almost palpable. Close examination reveals a worked surface where paint has been massaged and stroked, applied in a rich creamy texture in some areas, thin in others, and, in certain spots, it dribbles. The thickly layered paint and textured surface become as important as the subject they depict. Meanwhile, flickers of color engage the eye. The shimmering liquid entices us while the absence of shadow in favor of full illumination gives visual prominence to each woman's body. Charmy consistently intertwines vision and touch in her private nudes. These works are marked by the *aesthetics of female jouissance*, a sensual play with matter and pigment that is distinctly her own. Through this rich application of paint, Charmy expresses pleasure.

Of course, tactility is a quality inherent in the medium of oil paint itself. Moreover, evoking touch through paint has a long tradition as a practice of male self-expression and sexuality. In representations of the female nude from the Renaissance onward, artists have often laid emphasis on touch as they strived to evoke the sensation of flesh on the surface of the canvas through delicate glazes, subtle shadow and luminous hues. Rubens, who painted corpulent and dimpled bacchantes, Boucher, with his carnal female forms whipped into confection by his brush, and Renoir, who portrayed voluptuous, dreamlike bathers with skin in radiant hues, are often designated as accomplished masters of the corporeal female form. The profound evocation of touch in Charmy's nudes would seem to align her work within this custom. However, her facture offers a markedly different effect from that of her male artistic forebearers and counterparts. Although at the time this would not have been a conscious strategy, the churned-up quality of her nudes underscores female eroticism and lends a feminist reading.

In her discussions of female sexuality, Irigaray has highlighted the role that the sense of touch plays in woman's *jouissance*. In *This Sex Which Is Not One*, she critiques the phallocentric privileging of male pleasure, marked by an emphasis on sight.[163] She contends that "The predominance of the visual, and of the discrimination and individualization of form, is particularly foreign to female eroticism." By contrast, "woman takes pleasure more from touching than from looking, and her entry into a dominant scopic economy signifies, again, her consignment to passivity: she is to be the beautiful object of contemplation."[164] According to Irigaray, touch is primordial to women's pleasure. Moreover, it is implicit in the very nature of woman's sexual anatomy; Irigaray argues that "woman 'touches herself' all the time, and moreover no one can forbid her to do so, for her genitals are formed of two lips in continuous contact." Woman, she surmises, "is already two – but not divisible into one(s) – that caress each other."[165] Her sexual makeup implies a sense of touch that is constant and limitless – her sex is irreducible to one. Through the analogy of the lips, Irigaray emphasizes woman's sexual bliss as tangible in nature as well as her connection to other women. The lips with their innumerable configurations can be read as a metaphor for autoeroticism as well as female homosexuality.

Irigaray's conception of woman's *jouissance* resonates deeply with Charmy's art. Characterized by viscous paint, blurred form, and a vigorous application, Charmy's facture highlights the touch of the figure portrayed in addition to the touch of the artist's own brush. The subject, the painter who painted it and the viewer who subsequently views it are all strongly entwined in an interplay of tactility. Charmy's nudes, shown in numerous poses, are captured in the act of touching themselves in various regions of the body. In manifold ways, she portrays women caressing themselves and experiencing enjoyment. The vivid hues ranging from vermillion to cobalt in expansive fields combined with accented minutiae in emerald or fuchsia add to the substantive sensorial impact of these paintings, while the magnified bodies, cropping, liberal paint applications and the uneven and faceted surface from smooth to granular lend a sense of corporeal proximity. Charmy's nudes exemplify the importance of touch that Irigaray stresses, as well as the limitless nature of woman's sexuality.[166] One might view Charmy's nudes in concert with Irigaray's words: "But *woman has sex organs more or less everywhere*. She finds pleasure almost anywhere."[167] In a diverse range of postures, gestures and viewpoints, Charmy demonstrates the boundless ways in which woman experiences *jouissance*.

Examining Charmy's *Nude Holding Her Breast* more closely reveals the tactile nature of the artist's painterly approach and its emotive impact. The nude is foregrounded before a warm ochre background thinly painted exposing the canvas weave. This coffee-hued tint peeks through the legs and other thinly coated sections. In certain areas, Charmy incises the skin and its boundaries with the edge of a palette knife or the butt end of the brush, evident on the right side just below the nape of the neck. Building outward, the flesh of the torso is applied copiously with a broad brush. The breast is given full plasticity, weighted in heavy layers of impasto, while the proximity of the grasping arm is emphasized by a particle of coagulated paint. The facial features are rendered in rudimentary detail. Her eyes, slightly cracked open, reveal a dark abyss. Her head is tilted back ever so slightly, the chin reduced to wavering strokes. She does not have two, but three flared nostrils, and this distortion, along with a blurred patch of black paint adjacent the nose, lends the sense of uncontrollable movement. As the head jostles, the body is static carrying a torpid, lethargic weight. The shoulders slope downward and one arm, sparsely painted, droops inert by her side and fades into the background. With the other arm, the nude reaches upward and grasps her breast, calling attention to her own sense of touch. One tiny flickering line catches the navel, and two lines delicately carve out the crease between the thigh and her torso. These lines casually intersect, intimating the triangular form of the woman's sex. The painting appears to be rapidly executed, as if Charmy were rendering a precise moment of fleeting euphoria.

Charmy's representation of the body is based as much on tactile as visual modes of perception. This approach brings to mind Cézanne's artistic practice, for which touch was integral. Richard Shiff discusses the issue of touch in relation to the artist's oeuvre. He argues that, rather than producing an illusionistic recreation of the objects he observed, Cézanne painted his perception of them. In so doing, he rendered the experience of seeing and touching the things he painted. Shiff notes, "His tactile gesture was never a matter of comprehending real objects by imaginatively tracing their contours, allowing a primitive application of touch (running the hand along a surface) to substitute for a more nuanced understanding."[168] He replaced line with color painted in "touches" (both *touches* and *taches* in French).[169] In her private nudes, Charmy denies line its usual tracing function. Forms blur and overlap, unrestrained by contours. Instead, line is used as accent. It draws attention to certain body parts: the navel, the nipple, the lips or thick strands of hair. Like Cézanne's, Charmy's method of modeling form "significantly departs from prevailing standards of iconic resemblance applicable to painting."[170] Critics have long noted Cézanne's so-called "constructive stroke" in which he placed strokes of pigment in various hues side by side to create a sense of volume. Charmy's own distinct techniques of execution are pronounced in her intimate works. She evokes the appearance of volumetric form differently. Employing glazes of varying densities, mass is implied through a buildup of paint. Ripples of silky flesh accumulate, from thinly painted thighs, to the softly dimpled belly, to the chest, where the richest lathering gathers. The paint is densely layered in certain areas, such as the bosom, and these strata give weight to the woman's form. Moreover, colors are choreographed to function metaphorically. Interspersed throughout, flecks of vivid hues scintillate on the surface signaling emphasis and directing our eye.[171] The splendor of multi-hued impasto becomes its own constituent element within the composition which generates meaning. The medium and its coloring serve as vehicles for expression, making the implicit explicit.

In Charmy's nudes, the acts of touching by the figure and the artist are evoked synchronously. Seen from afar, the illusory effect of the relief-semblance of form comes into full effect, but, with a close viewing point, the material substance cannot be ignored. One can imagine the painter's movement of the brush as she applies the paint in long undulating strokes, impetuously allowing particles to collect on the surface, even a fingerprint, and heedlessly permitting the stiff hairs of the brush to leave their mark across the surface of the canvas. This serves to represent Charmy's own touch within the work, or the authorial presence of the artist. As Charles Blanc wrote in the nineteenth century, "Touch is the [expressive] handwriting of the painter."[172] Cézanne's characteristic "touche" has been noted as just one device which signals his presence.[173] Likewise, in Charmy's work, there are myriad idiosyncrasies which index the artist's hand. For example, in *Nude Holding Her Breast*, areas of black are visible, seeping out from underneath the surface of pale skin. The painting appears unfinished – the woman's form is only partially rendered. The figure's left arm is incomplete, truncated at the wrist, and the thighs are so sparsely painted that they are almost translucent. Lines and scratches might at first be mistaken as unintentional marks or posterior damage. Stripes of yellow paint traverse the breast horizontally, intersecting with faint comb-like marks in grey running vertically like stretch marks. But these are not gaffes. Charmy employed the brush adeptly so that each stroke of paint, minuscule line and splash of color achieved a specific visual and symbolic effect. As the unexpected application of color and dynamic strokes compels viewers to approach the work and follow the tracks of her brush, on closer inspection, they become formidably aware that these are Charmy's own manipulations of *matière* (matter).

Charmy's idiosyncratic handling of paint is evident in her earliest nudes and self-portraits. In the aforementioned *Self-Portraits* from around 1910, Charmy constructs the face with thickened strokes of paint like makeup. A thick line encircles the face and delineates the eyes and eyebrows. It appears as if Charmy began the portrait by roughly outlining her silhouette with black paint, before building up successive layers of paint. The black contour remains visible in the completed portrait, articulating the jaw and hairline. In some areas, it blends with the upper layers of pigment, generating the impression of chiaroscuro modeling. Charmy employed this technique consistently. Two unfinished works including an undated, painted sketch and *Nu allongé sur draperie rouge* (c. 1920) demonstrate how she outlined the figure initially with black and then filled in the flesh with roughly textured paint. As for *La Loge*, an early work in which Charmy's unique facture and treatment are apparent, Charmy reworked the painting years later. X-radiography revealed that the black paint adjacent to the standing figure in the foreground was a subsequent addition.[174] A photograph of the *La Loge* in Charmy's Saint-Cloud studio circa 1906 demonstrates that the painting was originally vertical in shape, but was cut down to a near-square format.[175] Paradoxically, Charmy imprints this work with her artistic presence through abrasion and elimination, blotching out certain elements, scraping away others, and even going as far as to cut down the canvas. Her unusual process continuously draws attention to the surface, a constant reminder of the artist's hand.

Nude (c. 1920–30) (Plate 18) is a work that has been consigned to storage in a French public museum since 1963, unbeknownst to Charmy's descendants and scholars.[176] A thick black stroke demarcates the woman's back and legs, smudged by parallel applications of amber. There is a meatiness to the facture as it is smeared in varying densities across the canvas, conveying a sense of volume in the most saturated areas. Certain aspects are more finished than others, such as the nude's back, while other elements are incomplete – the woman's profile and her left foot are merely stenciled. The ivory-colored flesh emits a lustrous glow. The activated surface evokes the soft texture of skin, cloth and hair, but, more importantly, serves as evidence of the artist's process. The workings of the oil medium and its wavering degrees of thickness supersede the subject itself. More than a representation of a nude, this is a manifestation of Charmy's inimitable treatment of the physical properties of paint.

The nude and possession

The relationship between paint and flesh has long been discussed by academicians, critics and art historians. In France, it was broached frequently as part of a larger debate on *disegno* versus *colorito* in the academic system beginning in the seventeenth century with such figures as Roger de Piles and Charles Le Brun.[177] Only through color, it was argued, could an artist convey the sensation of flesh. “Impossible to represent by drawing, the expression of the flesh has always been the triumph of the colorists.”[178] Color elates the eye, but, when it is employed to render lifelike flesh, it equally entices our touch.[179] In her book on color in French classical painting, Jacqueline Lichtenstein writes:

> The emotion aroused by the successful imitation of flesh makes perception waver between surprise and caresses, giving the gaze a somewhat hallucinatory sensitivity: sight becomes like touch … Standing before the paintings of the great colorists, the viewer has the impression that his eyes are fingers.[180]

Thus, when a male painter succeeds in capturing the nuances of female flesh with his brush, vision seems to be granted a possessive power. The relationship between vision and touch – paint and flesh – goes hand in hand with issues of possession. Scholars have noted that male artists’ representations of the female body often imply grasping and controlling of the figure. Roger de Piles once wrote of a Rubens bacchanal, “The flesh of this bacchante and her children seems so real that you can easily imagine reaching out for them and feeling the warmth of blood.”[181] Likewise in sculpture, when marble is polished smoothly to resemble flesh, the viewer can perceive the textures and crevices of the body and may be granted the sensation of seizing the female form. In Bernini’s *Rape of Persephone*, the male spectator can identify with the fierce, muscular and intensely virile Hades, as he abducts Persephone, clenching her delicate frame with his sinewy hands and brawny arms. Writhing, the goddess vainly attempts to escape, but Hades grips her so tightly that her flesh hollows, cleaving under the weight of his fingertips. The nude within this tradition functions as an object to be gazed upon as it also entertains physical desires through the semblance of an imaginary possession.

Kenneth Clark, who surveys the history of the nude from Greek antiquity to the twentieth century in *The Nude: A Study of Ideal Form* (1956), describes the notion of sublimation as inherent in renderings of the nude:

> The desire to grasp and be united with another human body is so fundamental a part of our nature, that our judgment of what is known as “pure form” is inevitably influenced by it; and one of the difficulties of the nude as a subject of art is that these instincts cannot lie hidden, as they do for example in our enjoyment of a piece of property, thereby gaining the force of sublimation, but are dragged into the foreground, where they risk upsetting the unity of responses from which a work of art derives its independent life.[182]

The "instincts" Clark refers to are undeniably male. Lynda Nead offers a thorough analysis of his text, noting that Clark assumes a (heterosexual) male viewer, artist and connoisseur and a female nude. Moreover, she links the "desire to grasp" with Freud's theory of sublimation, or human activity "motivated by the force of sexual drives."[183] For Clark, to become "high art" the male sexual drives must be transmuted into male artistic creation, and the female body must be wholly transformed from a naked figure, deformed and deprived of clothes, to a "balanced, prosperous and confident" nude.[184]

The debate on the implications of a gendered possession of the female body surfaces frequently in discussions of early twentieth-century art. In a recent monograph on the sculptor Rodin, David Getsy situates Rodin firmly as a pivotal player within the development of modern art. According to Getsy, "He staged his own physical manipulation of the object, making it into something that … evinced Rodin's own touching."[185] Through touch, indicated by his rough, *non-finito* surface, Rodin's presence and sexuality are implied. In a similar vein, James Herbert argues that Matisse's proto-Fauve nudes, such as *Carmelina* (1903), demonstrate a "technology of gendered 'possession'" that "came to present itself as natural."[186] Echoing Shiff's analysis of Cézanne, he contends that Matisse's early approach to the nude was characterized by a "new form of naturalism based on tactile rather than visual correspondences between pictures and depicted objects."[187] He continues:

> Formulated early on in Matisse's paintings of the female nude, Fauve style matched method to theme: the canvas appeared to render the nude, to find the female form, as directly and naturally as men ostensibly looked at women (in fact, a highly mediated and enculturated act of viewing).[188]

In *Carmelina*, the sense of directness and immediacy is implied through a coarsely painted and rough picture plane, which draws attention to both the nude's physical presence and the artist's.[189] This is reinforced by the presence of Matisse himself; his reflection is captured in the mirror behind the nude, accented with crimson. The model's autonomy is thus undermined as the artist's presence is doubly affirmed. Hence, "Matisse's canvas brought the entirety of the sitter's existence under the purview of the controlling gaze."[190] Herbert's notion of "technology of gendered 'possession'" resonates with a statement Matisse himself made later. When asked by Aragon about his relations with his female models, he declared that, for him, each painting was like "*un viol*," a rape.[191]

Meanwhile, Matisse's rival ensnared the female body through draftsmanship. "The possessed woman, downed and engulfed, clings too close for seeing" writes Leo Steinberg in his description of Picasso's *The Embrace* (1933) in "Drawing as if to

Possess."[192] Picasso attempts to capture the carnal solidity of her form in a dizzying and disorienting way. Vanquished, sublimated and deformed, she is held firmly in the artist's grasp. Carol Armstrong later confirmed his "possessive and unabashedly phallocentric" drawing:

> Picasso is well known for the equation between drawing and sexual capture established in his nudes, where pencil or pen, etching needle, or paintbrush circle continuously around the forms of the female body, turning it on its axis in a kind of virtual sculpture, providing simultaneous views of front, back and side, breasts, belly, crotch, and buttocks, confident in the ability to have and to hold it all, graphically.[193]

One-sided domination permeates Western artists' representations of the female body, but it also extends to the field of philosophy. Irigaray argues that "for Western philosophers such as Jean-Paul Sartre or Maurice Merleau-Ponty, seeing is not a way of contemplating but of seizing, dominating and possessing, in particular the body of the Other."[194] She insists that touching and caressing, for these philosophers, always reinforces a subject–object relation, where the female assumes the role of Other.[195] Desire for "male philosophers generally evoke[s] sight and touch. Thus, like their hand, their gaze grasps, denudes and captures."[196] Linked to ownership, and even exploitation, it always comes at the cost of a subjugated Other.

Charmy's private nudes do not imply possession or represent a vanquished female body. Unlike in Matisse's *Carmelina*, there is no visible or inferred male presence in her pictures. Her private nudes were not even intended for a male audience. In Irigaray's words, they were not conceived for "entry into a dominant scopic economy" where they would be "[consigned] to passivity" as "beautiful object[s] of contemplation."[197] Concealed from view, they were created for the artist's own *jouissance*, as a means of sexual expression, and oriented toward a perceptive female beholder. The nudes themselves are emphatically self-aware. Fully conscious and in command of their own bodies, they do not feed male fantasies. Rather than inviting the male viewer to touch, they touch themselves. Their enjoyment is attained independently. The women are focused resolutely on their own elation in a manner which precludes the male viewer from imagining himself authoritatively in relation to them. The faceted surface, at times sculptural in its dimension and other times diaphanous, counteracts the mimesis of a body in the flesh. Moreover, the impasto in its denseness clouds our view of any erotic content. An imperceptible boundary is established between Charmy's nudes and the male spectator. These works unsettle presumptions of male sexual dominance embedded in the genre of the nude.

Rather than possession, Charmy's work resonates with Irigaray's theory of the caress, an alternate conception of female sexuality. Irigaray states, "The caress is an awakening to intersubjectivity, to a touching between us which is neither passive nor active."[198] The sense of touch between the artist and model, and the artist and her own body, is so intimately intertwined in Charmy's work that it becomes a relationship of reciprocity. There is no active–passive dichotomy, the subjectivity of Self and Other coexist. Moreover, the activated and vigorous movement of the brush along with the robust touches of color evoke the intense feeling of skin-to-skin contact, and, with it, "an awakening of gestures, of perceptions which are at the same time acts, intentions, emotions."[199] Charmy renders the sensations of the flesh with her paintbrush, "awakening" aspects often "inhibited" in everyday life.[200] In her analysis of Irigaray, Ofelia Schutte notes that there is no "compulsory heterosexuality" in the notion of the caress: "At the core of her description of love is an imaginary space where the two lovers are women."[201] Through the mingling of the genres of self-portraiture and the nude, and the merging of subject and object into a symbiotic rapport, Charmy's nudes evoke a complex and multifaceted female *jouissance*.

In Charmy's oeuvre, the materiality of paint and its resulting opacity masks elements so that they cannot be fully apprehended. A fluctuating degree of perceptibility marks her work: details are accented, alluded to, while others are altogether obscured beneath copious layers of impasto. This leads to a deceleration of the viewership process. Citing Merleau-Ponty's theory of "germination," Suthor writes that how, in Rembrandt's work, "the perception of the paint's materiality causes a delay … This slowing down of perception intensifies our sensitivity to the picture's sensory power."[202] Likewise, in Charmy's private nudes, perception is not immediate or obvious but a dynamic, emergent process that unfolds languidly, as a sensual charge builds. Her heightened emphasis on female eroticism is made enigmatic through her ample facture, which, through its opaqueness, inhibits a direct view of the subject and prolongs our reading of the picture. In many nudes by male artists, such as Camoin's *Saltimbanque at Rest*, Matisse's *Carmelina*, or bathers by Renoir, the beholder, with a mere cursory glance, is encouraged to fantasize possession of the female form suddenly and even forcefully. By contrast, in viewing Charmy's nudes, a steady crescendo of erotic feeling is signaled by a careful orchestration of pictorial elements which gradually stimulate our sensitivity to the picture's sensorial impact. Our eye is drawn as much to the subject depicted or intuited as to the physical qualities of Charmy's painterly practice.

Repeatedly, Charmy calls attention to the medium itself. Molding visual plasticity through a buildup of matter on the canvas, activated with seductive touches of vibrant color, she emphasizes flesh and her own *matière* simultaneously. She does not employ the requisite, time-honored techniques for rendering the body as a simulacrum for a real, warm, breathing being. Her bodies appear at once volumetric and transparent. Certain areas are impasto-laden, others are gossamer. The edges of her figures often appear liquefied; they are not reined in by academic modeling. This loose handling of paint does not allow viewers to fully ascertain the female form. Idiosyncrasies abound, such as her blurred, seemingly hasty strokes, dark underpainting and places where the brush seems to have slipped unintentionally lending authorial evidence to the work. Rather than superfluous, haphazard mistakes, the malformations and peculiarities signify the distinct mark of their creator. Like Cézanne and Matisse, Charmy proclaims her presence as artist, but with a different effect. She reminds the spectator that this is a pictorial representation of the body, and that pleasure is delimited to the picture plane. Furthermore, her distinct approach demonstrates a *jouissance* of a particular kind, differentiated from male desire – Charmy's own.

Intermingling the genres of nude and self-portraiture, Charmy occupied the roles of both artist and model; Self and Other are indistinguishable in her private nudes. This is enhanced by the tight field of vision, range of vantage points and large scale of the figures that often exceed the size of the canvas. In *Nude on Red Sofa*, the torso is pushed to the foreground of the picture plane, and her limbs extend beyond it. The body is amplified within the canvas, resonating loudly. Enlargement and fragmentation imply a sense of intimacy in these works, as does the extremely suggestive pose of the figures. The painting resonates with later investigations of self-portraiture and auto-affection by the feminist artist, Joan Semmel. In *On the Grass* (1978), Semmel captures her own viewpoint of her body from above, a glance caught without the use of the mirror. She depicts her bare breasts as she sees them, along with the ample folds of flesh on her belly and copious thighs. The rest of the body is truncated at the stretcher bars. With her hand extended across her lap, combined with the myopic focus, the insinuation of self-pleasuring is evident to a perceptive audience. Like Semmel's painting, the emphasis on proximity in Charmy's work lends the sense of the body observed not from the inquisitive eye of a voyeur, but from the eye of someone who knows the body intimately.

Charmy, like Semmel, contests the primacy of the flat mirror.[203] Displaying her own body or that of a model from an intimate first-person perspective, the resulting image departs from a two-dimensional likeness, a primary goal in traditional self-portrait practice. Irigaray addresses the static mirror in *Speculum of the Other Woman*. She contends that this two-dimensional flat object is insufficient for capturing the female subject. Instead, for better understanding woman's subjecthood and sexuality, Irigaray proposes the "speculum," consciously drawing an association with the convex mirror used in gynecological exams.[204] The speculum that allows the woman to see herself is an idea that runs parallel to Irigaray's concept of the lips, which evoke woman as continually touching herself.[205] This curved, reflective device enables the woman to see herself while reflecting the Other concurrently. Confounding the image of her own body with those of her models, Charmy represents a different type of reflection.

She does not portray a flat mirror image of the "Other" but a crossing of Self and Other that is irreducible to one; Self and Other coexist.[206] Just as the curved speculum breaks away from binary polarizations of subject and object, Charmy portrays a perplexing amalgam in which Self and Other are evoked at the same time. In this manner, she offers us a glimpse into an ambiguous and indefinable space beyond the mirror.

Painting in her seventies, in *Self-Portrait in Mirror* (c. 1950–55), Charmy displays herself as a mass of matter lathered thickly onto the canvas. This is a very late painting – done in the aftermath of numerous experiments in self-portraiture. She is ageless just as she is formless, her body vanishes into multicolored hues of orchid pink, peach and cornsilk with dabs of turquoise. Blurred beyond recognition, the image verges toward abstraction. The painting does not exude the descriptive function that the genre of self-portraiture normally demands. Ironically, this is the only self-portrait where the mirror is mentioned in the title, and it clearly denies the mimetic function of the reflective glass. As curator Matthew Affron notes, Charmy, "engages with an old metaphor of art as imitation." Her "large-texture strokes" blur and block, "effectively displacing the descriptive and mimetic mode."[207] In contrast with a figurative rendering of her appearance, a two-dimensional imitation of the reflection in the glass, her form is obscured by corpulent impasto which lends the image a quasi-three-dimensional form. Mass is built up and broken down with a free, gestural stroke. Over time, the thickened paint has fissured, literally and metaphorically adding a sense of decay in this old-age portrait. Through the mottled, crusty surface of viscous, coagulated paint, Charmy's form is as much intimated as it is erased. She treats her late nudes in an analogously haptic manner. In a pair of nudes from circa 1947, long undulating brushstrokes articulate the body's form in champagne and burnt umber hues, which dissipate at the extremities into the asphalt-colored ground. For one transient moment, the nude is a purely tactile phenomenon. But once it is perceived, form liquefies into an amorphous mass. Here, the nude loses its status as an object, literally, as it dissipates into flowing strokes of paint.

Could this be a nude self-portrait? Nothing about the figure's identity is discernible. Like the reciprocal touching of the lips through which woman touches herself, Charmy's private nudes represent the co-mingling of Self and Other. The body of the Self is reflected in the Other and vice versa, so that they become interwoven, like the very process of lovemaking Irigaray's lips imply. When the "two lips" touch there is an expression of intimacy.[208] The two lips join and mingle, becoming intertwined so that the position of subject and object is indeterminate.[209] For Irigaray, the exact identities of subject and object cannot be known as these positions are indistinguishable.[210] Rather than a single unit, they perform Self and Other in their infinite combinations. Like Irigaray's two lips which touch each other and themselves constantly, Charmy erases the usual active and passive roles. She recognizes her own subjectivity, still allowing for that of the Other to materialize. In lieu of the long-established, hierarchical binaries of artist and model, she presents something fluid or intermediary – something *in-between*. She depicts female desire without reducing the Self or Other to object status, creating an interstitial space, reflected metaphorically in the streams of interwoven paint. In disrupting these binary structures, she upsets the archetypal objectification of women in nude representation.

Female eroticism in art

Although Charmy's work may insinuate same-sex desire for certain female viewers, this is never explicit. In fact, she avoids showing more than one nude at a time. Often, when lesbian nude couples appear in works of art, they serve chiefly as male titillation: Toulouse-Lautrec, *In Bed: The Kiss* (1892) is a poignant example. As Toulouse-Lautrec's painting demonstrates, images of lesbians are often set in brothels, a space catered to male fantasies.[211] Lesbians, whether real or pretend, are acceptable in art when serving the fantasies of a male voyeur. Albert Marquet's *Les Deux Amies* (1911) depicts two lanky female nudes clad in black stockings. The nudes strike unnatural sleeping positions: one dozes on the floor with her torso propped up by the bed, the other reclines with her legs splayed casually. Marquet based the painting on visits to the *maisons closes* in Marseille.[212] He returned to this theme in a series of quasi-pornographic drawings and prints, published in 1930 to accompany a poem by Verlaine.[213] In these salacious images, Marquet's portrayal of lesbian sexuality derives from the male viewpoint and entails an amalgam of spectacle and secrecy.

Rarely does one see the representation of desire from a woman's perspective in Western culture before the 1960s. Even when painted by women, lesbian nudes are seldom shown "outside of the stereotypes of patriarchy that reduce them to sexual deviants," Nead asserts. Rather, they often conform to suit "male heterosexual fantasy."[214] The artists Louise Hervieu, Mariette Lydis and Tamara de Lempicka all depicted couplings of female nudes.[215] In Lydis's illustration for Lucian Samosata's *Le Dialogue des courtisanes* (1930), two female figures embrace, their bodies closely intertwined. Hervieu's *Lesbos* (c. 1920), an illustration for Baudelaire's *Les Fleurs du mal* 1920 edition, is a scene of female lovemaking set in a brothel. In Lempicka's *Les Deux Amies* (1923), two figures composed of tubular forms appear within an art deco urban landscape. Lempicka imbues her robotic bodies with a sense of erotic voluptuousness. One recumbent figure tilts her head sideways in an orgasmic gesture, and her darkened eyelids, cracked open, reveal the ghostlike whiteness of her eyes. These works fall within the theme of "Les deux amies," which Marie-Jo Bonnet describes as "a phenomenon specific to modernity" from 1905 onward.[216] She contends that, for female artists, the subject is an example of sexual emancipation.[217]

Conversely, as Marsha Meskimmon notes, "images of lesbians as 'oversexed' or as objects for male, heterosexual delectation" are common and are "difficult to defy."[218] When the intimacies between two women are shown or even hinted at, their sexuality risks being objectified for the male viewer regardless of who painted them. Indeed, these examples of lesbian scenes, created by women, seem to operate as delight for a male spectator.

Charmy's private nudes do not conform to heterosexual male standards of desire. Instead, they resonate with descriptions of feminine erotics in Colette's literature, where pleasures are implied through metonymy and metaphor rather than through detailed and direct descriptions. As we have seen, in "Nuit Blanche," Colette evokes intimacy and proximity between two figures without naming their gender, while linking their body parts with the scents, savors and colors of fruit and flowers of a lush garden. In *The Pure and the Impure*, dedicated to woman's sexual ardor, Colette reconnoiters the territory of female sexuality more openly. Yet, even in the most suggestive passages, she denies readers full access to the very act or object she is describing, veiling it with cryptic prose. Her repeated use of the ellipsis both conceals and accentuates the unspoken, enticing the viewer to imagine what lies outside the text. Charmy's brushwork can likewise be seen as a form of elision where opacity shrouds explicit elements, and the materiality of paint decelerates the process of viewership. Within the stratum of thickened impasto lies an aura of desire – subliminal messages about auto- or homoeroticism. Concurrently, Charmy paints an "autofiction" on canvas, akin to the mélange of autobiographical and fictional elements in Colette's prose. She erodes the distinctions between herself and her models, activity and passivity, and Self and Other. In so doing, she captures a subjectivity typically inaccessible for women of her era.

Charmy worked within a conventionally masculine art form – the nude – and with the traditional medium of oil paint. Yet, within this time-honored artistic practice, Charmy developed an alternative mode of visualizing female pleasure. She redefined the boundaries of self-representation and introduced a new subject to the history of art – the pregnant nude self-portrait. In these works, rather than emphasize fertility, Charmy accentuates pleasure. In other nudes, she portrays *jouissance* from a subjective viewpoint of a woman creating erotically impactful without the literal manifestation of sexual intimacies between *deux amies*. Charmy removed the female body from the aesthetic theater of sexuality construed for a male audience and represents female sexuality by other means. Rather than displaying the interactions between two subjects, she suggests the intimate relation between bodies through a close field of vision and the comingling of flesh with a canvas laden in textured paint. Charmy's images resonate with the intimate corporeal contact of Irigaray's lips and the caress along with the idea of feminine autoeroticism and homosexuality that they denote.

Moreover, by emphasizing tactility and eliding subject and object positions, Charmy expresses *jouissance* in all its complexity, *without* an object of desire. Like Colette's richly veiled meditations on lesbianism, she implies female eroticism without direct appellation. Charmy's oeuvre is as elusive as it is alluring; the exact nature of her desire remains masked under thick layers of luscious paint.

Notes

1 Henri Béraud, Roland Dorgelès and Louis-Léon Martin, *Emilie Charmy*, exhibition catalogue (Paris: Galeries d'Oeuvres d'Art, 1921). All translations by author.
2 Gill Perry, *Women Artists and the Parisian Avant-Garde* (Manchester: Manchester University Press, 1995), 2.
3 Nicola Suthor, *Rembrandt's Roughness* (Princeton: Princeton University Press, 2018).
4 Awarded the National Order of the Legion of Honor in 1926 and promoted to officer twelve years later. Matthew Affron, *Émilie Charmy* (Charlottesville: The Fralin Museum of Art, 2013), 31.
5 Charmy's biographical information comes from the following sources: Matthew Affron, "Charmy: the Artist in Her Time," in *Émilie Charmy*, 15–37; Edmond Bouche, "Ma mere," *Le Peintre*, 54 (December 1, 1952), 11; Edmond Bouche, untitled essay in *Émilie Charmy* (London: Patrick Seale Gallery, 1980); Sylvie Carlier, *Émilie Charmy* (Villefranche-sur-Saône: Musée Municipal Paul-Dini, 2008); Perry, *Women Artists and the Parisian Avant-Garde;* Patrick Seale, untitled essay, Musée Municipal Paul-Dini archives, Villefranche-sur-Saône.
6 Before becoming an artist, Charmy attended a private Catholic girls' school and École Supérieure. She played piano, sang and was offered a singing job in New Orleans, which her brother dissuaded her from accepting. She earned a teacher's certificate in Saint-Étienne and was offered a post nearby. She turned this down, choosing a riskier path in art. Seale essay, Musée Paul-Dini archives.
7 Both parents died in the 1890s leaving Charmy as an orphan by the age of fourteen. Perry, *Women Artists and the Parisian Avant-Garde*, 23.
8 Nelly Gabriel, *Histoires de l'école nationale des beaux-arts de Lyon* (Lyon: Éditions Beau Fixe, 2007), 93–7.
9 Friendly dedications written to him by Morisot, Puvis de Chavannes and Renoir were noted on their works in his collection. Maurice Bussillet and Veuve Blot, *Atelier du peintre Jacques Martin, catalogue des oeuvres de l'artiste et de tableaux … provenant de sa succession*, auction catalogue (April, [1920], 1919).
10 For more information on the turn-of-the-century Lyon art world, see Sylvie Carlier and Dominique Lobstein, *Le Postimpressionnisme et Rhône-Alpes (1886–1914): la couleur dans la lumière* (Villefranche-sur-Saône, Musée Paul-Dini, 2015).
11 The Musée des Beaux-Arts de Lyon was renovated and its collection enlarged beginning in 1878. Puvis de Chavanne's *Le Bois sacré* was installed in 1884 (Valadon posed for this). From 1900 to 1905, thanks to Mayor Victor Augagneur, late nineteenth-century artists were incorporated into the museum's collection, including Renoir, Manet, Alfred Sisley and Claude Monet. Ibid.

12 The closest translation to the word *intérieur* is "home." For a discussion of Morisot's depictions of interiors see Anne Higonnet, *Berthe Morisot* (Berkeley: University of California Press, 1995), 65.
13 Ibid., 68.
14 Ibid., 77.
15 Morisot's works listed in the auction catalogue from the sale of Jacques Martin's estate include: "paysage," watercolor (three studies in the same frame) and "paysage" (watercolor on glass). Both include a dedication by Morisot, "envoi à son ami Martin." Bussillet and Blot, *Atelier du peintre Jacques Martin.*
16 Exhibited later in 1908 Salon des Indépendants. Carlier, *Émilie Charmy*, 46.
17 Seale essay, Musée Paul-Dini archives.
18 Isabelle Collet and Dominique Lobstein, *Paris 1900: la ville spectacle*, exhibition catalogue (Paris: Petit Palais, Musée des Beaux-Arts de la Ville de Paris, 2014), 301; Carlier and Lobstein, *Le Postimpressionnisme et Rhône-Alpes*, 119.
19 Asti Hustvedt, *Medical Muses: Hysteria in Nineteenth-century Paris* (New York: W.W. Norton, 2011), 175.
20 Eugène Grasset's *La Morphinomane* (1897) and Victor Prouvé's *Opium* (1894) are two examples. See Victoria Dailey, *Tea and Morphine: Women in Paris, 1880 to 1914* (Los Angeles: Hammer Museum, 2014).
21 Perry, *Women Artists and the Parisian Avant-garde*, 31.
22 Perry was the first to analyze the work, arguing that it represents a brothel. Perry, *Women Artists and the Parisian Avant-garde*, 31. Sarah Betzer is more diplomatic, stating, "Charmy invokes the space – and subjects – of the brothel." Sarah Betzer, "Inhabiting the Modern: Charmy, Gender, and Genre" in Matthew Affron, *Émilie Charmy* (Charlottesville: The Fralin Museum of Art, University of Virginia, 2013), 52.
23 Perry, *Women Artists and the Parisian Avant-garde*, 31–2.
24 Sherry A. Dranch, "Reading through the Veiled Text: Colette's 'The Pure and the Impure.'" *Contemporary Literature* 24, no. 2 (1983): 177. Carlier, *Émilie Charmy*, 46.
25 Georges Seurat, *The Models* (*Les Poseuses*), 1888, Barnes Foundation in Philadelphia.
26 Black stockings, although commonly worn by women at the turn of the century, came to be associated with prostitution in art. Perry states that "knee-length black stockings" were "items of clothing which had become recognizable symbols of the trade of prostitution." Perry, *Women Artists and the Parisian Avant-garde*, 31. See also Abigail Solomon-Godeau, "The Legs of the Countess De Castiglione Photographed by Mayer & Pierson and the Commodification of the Feminine," *October* 39 (1986), 65–108.
27 Philippe Ariès and Michelle Perrot (eds), *A History of Private Life: From the Fires of Revolution to the Great War*, vol. 4 (Cambridge, MA: Belknap Press of Harvard University Press, 1990), 611.
28 Carlier, *Émilie Charmy*, 45. Although it is entirely possible that Charmy and her brother visited the *Exposition universelle* in Paris in 1900, there is no documentation in the archives to support this claim.
29 Eleven works by Manet were on view. *Catalogue officiel illustré de l'exposition centennale de l'art français de 1800 à 1889* (Paris: Ludovic Baschet, 1900).
30 Manet's *Olympia* was in the collection of Musée du Luxembourg from 1890 to 1907 before entering the Louvre's collection in 1907. Musée d'Orsay, "Notice de l'oeuvre:

Edouard Manet, *Olympia*," www.musee-orsay.fr/en/collections/index-of-works/notice.html?no_cache=1&nnumid=712. Accessed February 24, 2018.

31 Dominique Lobstein, *Dictionnaire des Indépendants, 1884–1914* (Dijon: L'Échelle de Jacob, 2003), 388–9.

32 Her addresses are listed in Salon des Indépendants catalogues, see ibid. By 1908, her studio was located at 88 rue de Clichy. It was rented by her brother, Jean, who had become an antiques dealer. Carlier, *Émilie Charmy*, 46.

33 The street address was 54 rue de Bourgogne. Bernard Bouche states that Charmy and her brother lived together until around 1910. Interview with Bernard Bouche, April 3, 2018.

34 Louis Vauxcelles, "Le Salon d'Automne," *Gil Blas*, October 17, 1905 [supplement à *Gil Blas*].

35 Lobstein, *Dictionnaire des Indépendants*, 388.

36 Ibid.

37 Vauxcelles, "Le Salon d'Automne."

38 Gill Perry, "Gender and the Fauves: Flirting with 'Wild Beasts,'" in *Art of the Avant-Gardes*, edited by Steve Edwards and Paul Wood (New Haven: Yale University Press in association with the Open University, 2004), 65.

39 Perry, *Women Artists and the Parisian Avant-garde*, 46.

40 Ibid., 49.

41 Perry, "Gender and the Fauves," 65.

42 Claudine Grammont, "Fauve sur nature," in *Charles Camoin: Rétrospective: 1879–1965*, edited by Grammont and Véronique Serrano, exhibition catalogue (Marseille: Musée de Marseille, 1997), 41.

43 Ibid.

44 Ibid., 43.

45 Marianne Le Morvan, *Berthe Weill: 1865–1951: la petite galeriste des grands artistes* (Paris: L'Harmattan, 2012), 72. Starting in 1902, Weill exhibited Matisse and Marquet, and then, from 1903, Puy, Camoin, Manguin and Dufy. A group show at her gallery in 1904 included Matisse, Marquet, Camoin, Puy and Manguin. See Grammont, "Fauve sur nature," 41.

46 Guillaume Apollinaire once called Laurencin a "fauvette among the Fauves." Apollinaire, *Le Petit Bleu*, April 5, 1912. Perry explains, "unable to accord her the masculine status of a Fauve, [Apollinaire] applied the diminutive feminised form of the word, which in French can also mean a type of singing bird or warbler. He positioned this female artist as a singing bird among the 'wild beasts.'" Perry, "Gender and the Fauves," 79.

47 Le Morvan, *Berthe Weill*, 61.

48 Her gallery was at 25 rue Victor-Massé and opened December, 1901. Ibid., 34.

49 Berthe Weill and François Roussier, *Pan! Dans L'oeil!: ou trente ans dans les coulisses de la peinture contemporaine, 1900–1930* (Dijon: L'Échelle de Jacob, 2009), 35.

50 Ibid., 107.

51 Ibid., 62.

52 Auguste Rodin, *Monument to Balzac* (1898), bronze, Musée Rodin, Paris.

53 Berthe Weill was a visionary. She saw potential in great artists at a time when they aroused confusion and laughter from audiences. Weill notes the reactions to the displays in her

gallery windows. "C'est certainement un c… qui a fait ça! mais encore plus c… celui qui l'a acheté! ... Pan! dans l'oeil de l'enfant!" Weill, *Pan! Dans l'oeil!*, 68.

54 Jean-Paul Crespelle, *La Vie quotidienne à Montmartre au temps de Picasso: 1900–1919* (Paris: Hachette, 1978), 217.

55 Le Morvan explains that Weill "finds in Charmy a bond that goes beyond their mutual interests. Both have a strong character, they understand each other by providing mutual support and quasi-familial attention." Le Morvan, *Berthe Weill*, 68.

56 Scholars disagree on the exact year when they met. Some state that they met in 1906 and traveled to Corsica and the south of France that summer. Grammont disagrees with this chronology. She dates their meeting to 1908 and states that they went to Lyon, Toulon and Porquerolles in 1909, and then Corscia in 1910. They probably crossed paths prior to 1908, as they were exhibiting regularly with Weill, with whom they were both friends. Affron, *Émilie Charmy*, 20; Carlier et al., *Émilie Charmy*, 46–7; Danièle Giraudy, *Camoin: sa vie, son oeuvre* (Marseille: La Savoisienne, 1972), 58; Claudine Grammont and Bruno Ely, *Camoin dans sa lumière* (Paris: Lienart, 2016), 154; Perry, *Women Artists and the Parisian Avant-garde*, 56; Perry, "Gender and the Fauves: Flirting with 'Wild Beasts,'"; Seale essay, Musée Paul-Dini archives.

57 Weill mentions Camoin and Charmy: "Ah! my poor Camoin! what a trio we make, you, Charmy and me! Like misery, we are filled." Weill, *Pan! Dans L'oeil!*, 97.

58 Claudine Grammont, *Correspondance entre Charles Camoin et Henri Matisse* (Lausanne: La Bibliothèque des Arts, 1997), 24–6.

59 According to Danièle Giraudy, Charmy posed for several works by Camoin including *Émilie à sa coiffure* (1906) and *Nu au jeu de cartes* (1906). Giraudy, *Camoin: sa vie, son oeuvre*, 60.

60 In an interview, Bernard Bouche stated that Charmy went to Corisca twice. The first voyage, which he believes occurred in 1906, may have been with or without Camoin. Interview with Bernard Bouche, April 3, 2018.

61 Discrepancies in the dating of landscapes are evident in both Charmy and Camoin literature. See: Affron, *Émilie Charmy*, Carlier et al., *Émilie Charmy*, and Perry, "Gender and the Fauves," and *Women Artists and the Parisian Avant-garde* versus Grammont and Ely, *Camoin dans sa lumière.*

62 Seale essay, Musée Paul-Dini archives.

63 For a description of Matisse's Collioure landscapes, see John Elderfield, *The "Wild Beasts": Fauvism and Its Affinities* (New York: The Museum of Modern Art, 1976).

64 Grammont and Ely, *Camoin dans sa lumière*, 91.

65 Corinne Charles, "Emilie Charmy, une expressionsite française?" in *Émilie Charmy* (Villefranche-sur-Saône: Musée Municipal Paul-Dini, 2008) 21. Matisee, *La rive* (1907), oil on canvas, Kunstmuseum, Basle.

66 Perry agrees: "I would argue that such images are more suggestive of the bold painterly expression of a so-called 'wild beast' than some of the Mediterranean landscapes painted by Fauve colleagues such as Manguin and Camoin from the same period." Perry, "Gender and the Fauves," 78. This was particularly evident when viewing Charmy's and Camoin's work side by side in the 2016 Camoin exhibition in Aix-en-Provence: Grammont and Ely, *Camoin dans sa lumière.*

67 Affron, *Émilie Charmy*, 35. Unfortunately, Charmy was not included in the centennial exhibition of the Armory show. Marilyn S. Kushner, Kimberly Orcutt and Casey Nelson

Blake, *The Armory Show at 100: Modernism and Revolution* (New York: New-York Historical Society, 2013).

68 Ibid., 187.

69 The painting was originally titled *Paysage*. Affron, *Émilie Charmy*, 35.

70 Interestingly, Charmy appears in the chapter entitled, "Virile-Impressionism." Arthur J. Eddy, *Cubists and Post-Impressionism: With 23 Reproductions in Color of Cubist and Post-Impressionist Paintings, and 46 Half-Tone Illustrations* (Chicago: McClurg, 1914), 191, 200.

71 Camoin, *Madame Matisse faisant de la tapisserie* (1904), Derain, *Madame Matisse faisant de la tapisserie* (1905), Marquet, *Madame Matisse faisant de la tapisserie* (1905), Matisse, *La Japonaise: Woman beside the Water* (1905), Museum of Modern Art, New York. Perry makes this observation, *Women Artists and the Parisian Avant-garde*, 56–8. For information on Camoin, *Madame Matisse faisant de la tapisserie*, see *Charles Camoin: Rétrospective*, edited by Grammont and Serrano, 28.

72 Interview with Bernard Bouche, December, 2021.

73 Matisse, *Femme au chapeau* (*Woman with a Hat*) (1905), oil on canvas, San Francisco Museum of Modern Art.

74 Camoin refers to the breakup in letters to Matisse in 1912. In June of 1914, Camoin destroyed eighty paintings in his studio. Grammont and Serrano, *Charles Camoin*, 192.

75 Ibid.; Grammont and Ely, *Camoin dans sa lumière*, 115.

76 Grammont and Ely, *Camoin dans sa lumière*, 30.

77 Camoin painted a series of nudes in brothels, including *Nu à la chemise mauve* (1908). Camoin often used prostitutes as models. See ibid.

78 Ariès, *A History of Private Life*, 590.

79 Rachel Mesch, "Sexual Healing: Power and Pleasure in Fin-de-siècle Women's Writing," in *Pleasure and Pain in Nineteenth-century French Literature and Culture*, edited by David Evans and Kate Griffiths (Amsterdam: Rodopi, 2008), 168.

80 Ibid., 159, 170.

81 Ibid.

82 Ibid., 160. Freud, like early sexologists, maintained that women were passive sexually, and engaged in sex solely for the purpose of having children. See Thomas Lacquer, *Making Sex: Body and Gender from the Greeks to Freud* (Cambridge, MA: Harvard University Press, 1990), 233–43.

83 Ariès, *A History of Private Life*, 593.

84 Ibid., 592.

85 Juliette Dade, "Exploring Sapphic Discourse in the Belle Époque: Colette, Renée Vivien, and Liane de Pougy" (Ph.D. dissertation, University of Illinois at Urbana-Champaign, 2009), 13.

86 Ariès, *A History of Private Life*, 605.

87 Ibid., 599.

88 Perry, *Women Artists and the Parisian Avant-garde*, 21.

89 Diane Radycki, *Paula Modersohn-Becker: The First Modern Woman Artist* (New Haven: Yale University Press, 2013), 172.

90 Paula J. Birnbaum, *Women Artists in Interwar France: Framing Femininities* (Farnham: Ashgate, 2011), 163.

91 In her book on Colette, Kristeva traces the history of European female authors who wrote about love and sometimes sex from the eleventh century onward. She positions Colette as central within this lineage, noting that it is not only the twentieth century when we learn more about female eroticism. Julia Kristeva, *Le Génie féminin: la vie, la folie, les mots* (Paris: Gallimard, 2004), 329.

92 Ibid., 38.

93 Sherry A. Dranch, "Reading through the Veiled Text: Colette's 'The Pure and the Impure'," *Contemporary Literature* 24, no. 2 (1983), 177.

94 See: Dade, "Exploring Sapphic Discourse in the Belle Époque"; Janet Flanner, "Introduction to Colette," *The Pure and the Impure* (New York: Farrar, Straus, Giroux, 1966); Jerry Aline Flieger, *Colette and the Fantom Subject of Autobiography* (Ithaca: Cornell University Press, 1992); Michael Lucey, *Never Say I: Sexuality and the First Person in Colette, Gide and Proust* (Durham, NC: Duke University Press, 2006).

95 See: Flanner, "Introduction to Colette," 9; Marks, *Colette*, 57; Lucey, *Never Say I*, 138.

96 Tirza T. Latimer, *Women Together / Women Apart: Portraits of Lesbian Paris* (New Brunswick: Rutgers University Press, 2005), 9. In today's terms, Brooks would likely have identified as a lesbian, although the artist and many of the women she painted recognized themselves as Sapphists. The vast vocabulary of terms that now exists, such as bisexual, queer, trans, cisgender, non-binary etc., along with gender-neutral pronouns, were not used during Brooks's lifetime. The term lesbian is consciously applied anachronistically by scholars.

97 Alison Oram and Annmarie Turnbull, *The Lesbian History Sourcebook: Love and Sex between Women in Britain from 1780 to 1970* (London: Routledge, 2001), 1.

98 Martha Vicinus, *Intimate Friends: Women who Loved Women, 1778–1928* (Chicago: University of Chicago Press, 2006), xix, and Elisabeth Ladenson, "Colette for Export Only," *Yale French Studies* 90 (1996), 29.

99 In twenty-first-century terms, Charmy might have identified as bisexual, as her son, Edmond, once suggested in an interview. Ultimately, these are speculations which bear little import in the reading of Charmy's art. Perry, *Women Artists and the Parisian Avant-garde*, 132. Jeanine Warnod also voiced this sentiment about the artist in a more recent discussion. Interview with Jeanine Warnod, December 5, 2017.

100 The term Sapphism was commonly used among lesbians of the upper and bourgeois classes to identify themselves in the nineteenth and early twentieth centuries. Dade, "Exploring Sapphic Discourse in the Belle Époque," 2.

101 See: Laurel Cummins, *Colette and the Conquest of Self* (Birmingham, AL: Summa Publications, Inc., 2005); Dade, "Exploring Sapphic Discourse in the Belle Époque"; Ladenson, "Colette for Export Only"; Lucey, *Never Say I*; Vicinus, *Intimate Friends.*

102 Colette, Preface to *Quelques toiles de Charmy, quelques pages de Colette* (Paris: Galerie d'Art Ancien et Moderne, 1921), n.p.; also published in "Sur l'album de la vagabonde," *La Revue de Paris*, 28 (November–December, 1921), 41–3; and in *Cahiers Colette* 12 (Paris: Société des Amis de Colette, 1990), 7–9.

103 Musée Colette, Saint-Sauveur-en-Puisaye.

104 Colette, *Quelques toiles de Charmy.*

105 Ibid.

106 Dana Strand writes, "Although at the end of the nineteenth and beginning of the twentieth century in France there was no shortage of literary movements whose doctrines a novice

writer might consider adopting, Colette avoided identification with the dominant literary schools of her time." *Colette: A Study of the Short Fiction* (New York: Twayne Publishers, 1995), 12–13.

107 Colette, *Quelques toiles de Charmy.*

108 See Colette, "Les Vrilles de la vigne," in *The Collected Stories of Colette*, translated by Matthew Ward et al. (New York: Farrar, Straus, Giroux, 1983).

109 Colette, *Quelques toiles de Charmy.*

110 Colette dismissed the Cubists as "'far too occupied … with driving the air from their paintings, with forgetting that mysterious, slightly divine thing called perspective, the miracle that, all of a sudden, four centuries ago … filled the portraits of trees.'" Colette quoted in Julia Kristeva, *Colette*, translated by Jane Marie Todd (New York: Columbia University Press, 2004), 347.

111 Henri Béraud, *Comoedia*, January, 1926.

112 Kristeva lists Colette's romantic female liaisons, concluding that "And, no doubt, there was a final lesbian affair with the painter Émilie Charmy." Kristeva, *Colette*, 59.

113 Colette would later become friends with Camoin when summering in the south of France. Camoin was in Saint-Tropez while Colette was in Treille Muscate. Grammont and Serrano, *Charles Camoin: rétrospective*, 197.

114 In the Charmy archives, correspondence with her husband and brother is also limited.

115 Bernard Bouche, Charmy's grandson, believes that this is a depiction of Colette. Interview with Bernard Bouche, June, 2013.

116 *Chéri* first appeared in serial form in the magazine *La Vie Parisienne* before it was published in 1920. Elaine Marks, *Colette* (New Brunswick: Rutgers University Press, 1960), 125.

117 Julia Kristeva, *Colette,* translated by Jane Marie Todd (New York: Columbia University Press, 2004), 59. Interview with Bernard Bouche, April 3, 2018.

118 Carlier, *Émilie Charmy*, 14. The collectors Bill and Pam Royall also stated this in an interview. Interview with Bill and Pam Royall, March 2018.

119 E. Gómez Carrillo, *Émilie Charmy*, Galerie André Pesson, Paris, June, 1919.

120 Edmond Bouche, "Ma mère," *Le Peintre* 54 (December 1, 1952), 11.

121 Affron, *Émilie Charmy*, 33.

122 Shari Benstock, *Women of the Left Bank: Paris, 1900–1940* (Austin: University of Texas Press, 1986).

123 Seale essay, Musée Paul-Dini archives.

124 André Warnod, "Un samedi chez Charmy," *Comoedia*, October 23, 1923.

125 Weiss founded *La Femme Nouvelle*, founded in 1934 with Cécile Brunschvicg, and advocated for a more prominent role for women in public life.

126 Louise Weiss, *Mémoires d'une européenne, II: Combats pour l'Europe, 1919–1934* (Paris: Albin Michel, 1968), 50, 276, 324.

127 Carlier, *Émilie Charmy*, 15.

128 Louise Weiss, Préface, *Charmy*, Galerie Marcel Bernheim, 1951.

129 Weill, *Pan! Dans L'oeil!*, 62.

130 Patrick Seale, "Émilie Charmy: une artiste renaît," in Sylvie Carlier, *Émilie Charmy* (Villefranche-sur-Saône: Musée Municipal Paul-Dini, 2008), 31.

131 Ibid.

132 Suthor, *Rembrandt's Roughness*, 13.

133 Ibid., 196.
134 Ann Rosalind Jones, "Writing the Body: Toward an Understanding of 'L'Ecriture Feminine," *Feminist Studies* 7, no. 2 (1981), 247–63.
135 Ibid.
136 Michel Pastoureau, *Rouge: histoire d'une couleur* (Paris: Seuil, 2016), 187, 189.
137 Dranch, "Reading through the Veiled Text," 177.
138 Colette, *The Pure and the Impure,* translated by Herma Briffault (New York: New York Review of Books, 2000), 24–5.
139 Patrick Seale, *Émilie Charmy* (London: Patrick Seale Gallery, 1980), 6.
140 Dranch, "Reading through the Veiled Text," 187. See also Jacques Dupont, *Physique de Colette* (Toulouse: Presses Universitaires du Mirail, 2003), 93.
141 Colette, *The Vagabond,* translated by Enid McLeod (New York: Farrar, Straus and Giroux, 1955), 126–7. *La Vagabonde* was originally published in 1910.
142 Francis Carco, *Le Nu dans la peinture moderne, 1863–1920* (Paris: G. Crès, 1924), 147.
143 Warnod, "Un samedi chez Charmy."
144 Still-lifes often have the capacity to evoke "sensuous pleasure." This was one of the major points of criticism of the genre, and one of the reasons why it was viewed as a "lesser genre" with regards to erudite history painting. During the nineteenth century, the genre was regarded as appropriate for female painters. Norman Bryson, *Looking at the Overlooked: Four Essays on Still Life Painting* (London: Reaktion, 1990), 174.
145 Colette, "Sleepless Nights," in *The Collected Stories of Colette*, translated by Matthew Ward et al. (New York: Farrar, Straus, Giroux, 1983), 92.
146 Ibid.
147 Ladenson, "Colette for Export Only," 35.
148 Flieger, *Colette and the Fantom Subject of Autobiography*, 110.
149 Ibid.
150 Dranch, "Reading through the Veiled Text," 179.
151 Ibid.
152 Gustave Courbet's *Origin of the World* (1866), Musée d'Orsay, Paris, might be seen as a counterexample.
153 Carlier, *Émilie Charmy*, 26; Perry, *Women Artists and the Parisian Avant-garde*, 130.
154 *Bouche Charmy: Peintures* (Paris: l'Hôtel Drouot, 1973).
155 Carlier et al., *Émilie Charmy*, 134, 139.
156 Perry, *Women Artists and the Parisian Avant-garde*, 129.
157 Ibid., 107–18, 127.
158 With no known extant private gallery records from Charmy's lifetime, it is difficult to know precisely which of her nudes sold and for how much. Auction records before Charmy's death are predominantly of portraits and still lifes. Until further documentation can be found, it is not possible to gage whether her nudes yielded more than her works in other genres. For a list of Charmy auction records, see Emmanuel Bénézit, *Dictionnaire des peintres, sculpteurs, dessinateurs et graveurs* (Paris: Gründ, 2006, vol. 3), 803.
159 Béraud, Dorgelès et al., *Émilie Charmy.*
160 Ibid.
161 Perry, *Women Artists and the Parisian Avant-garde*, 102.
162 Madeleine Bunoust, *Quelques femmes peintres* (Paris: Stock, 1936), 135.

163 "Woman's desire would not be expected to speak the same language as man's; woman's desire has doubtless been submerged by the logic that has dominated the West since the time of the Greeks." Luce Irigaray, *This Sex Which Is Not One*, translated by Catherine Porter (Ithaca: Cornell University Press, 1985), 25.

164 Ibid., 25–6.

165 Ibid., 24.

166 Paradoxically, Irigaray's theories on touch and female sexuality have been applied to discuss the seemingly erotic nature of Cézanne's nudes. Aruna D'Souza, *Cézanne's Bathers: Biography and the Erotics of Paint* (University Park: Pennsylvania State University Press, 2008).

167 Ibid., Irigaray, *This Sex Which Is Not One*, 28.

168 Richard Shiff, "Cézanne's Physicality: The Politics of Touch," in *The Language of Art History*, ed. Salim Kemal and Ivan Gaskell (Cambridge: Cambridge University Press, 1991), 146.

169 Ibid.

170 Ibid.

171 The result is strikingly different. Cézanne's and Charmy's works have little in common aesthetically, especially their nudes. This lends credence to the idea suggested by Shiff and others, that artists render their own distinct perception of the world on canvas. "Would a different type of social being have a different strategy for picturing objects?" Ibid., 138.

172 Charles Blanc cited in ibid., 146.

173 Ibid.

174 Interview with Charmy collectors Bill and Pam Royall, March 2018.

175 Affron, *Émilie Charmy*, 17.

176 Entered the collection of Musée Municipal de l'Evêché, Limoges (now Musée des Beaux-Arts de Limoges) in 1963. Fonds National d'Art Contemporain, catalogue interministériel des Dépôts d'Oeuvres d'Art de l'État.

177 Jacqueline Lichtenstein, *La Couleur éloquente: rhétorique et peinture à l'âge classique* (Paris: Flammarion, 2003), 161.

178 Ibid., 181.

179 Ibid.

180 Ibid., 182.

181 Roger de Piles cited in Susan Sidlauskas, *Cézanne's Other: The Portraits of Hortense* (Berkeley: University of California Press, 2009), 101.

182 Kenneth Clark, *The Nude: A Study in Ideal Form* (New York: Pantheon Books, 1956), 6.

183 Lynda Nead, *The Female Nude: Art, Obscenity and Sexuality* (London: Routledge, 1992), 13.

184 Clark, *The Nude*, 1.

185 David Getsy, *Rodin: Sex and the Making of Modern Sculpture* (New Haven: Yale University Press, 2010), 62.

186 James Herbert, *Fauve Painting: The Making of Cultural Politics* (New Haven: Yale University Press, 1992), 54.

187 Ibid., 13.

188 Ibid.

189 He contends, furthermore, that this same "technology of gendered 'possession'" carried over into Fauve landscapes, and subsequently into pastoral paintings, in which the two themes were elided. Ibid., 54.

190 Ibid., 64.

191 Matisse quoted in Hilary Spurling, *Matisse, le maître. II, 1909–1954*, translated by Paule Guivarch (Paris: Éditions du Seuil, 2009), 33.

192 Leo Steinberg, "Drawing as if to Possess," in *Major European Art Movements, 1900–1945: A Critical Anthology*, ed. Patricia E. Kaplan and Susan Manso (New York: Dutton, 1977), 194–5.

193 Carol Armstrong, "The Reflexive and the Possessive View: Thoughts on Ker, Brandt and the Photographic Nude." *Representations* 25 (1989), 57.

194 Luce Irigaray, *Conversations* (London: Continuum, 2008), 109.

195 Luce Irigaray, "The Wedding between the Body and Language," in *Luce Irigaray: Key Writings* (London: Continuum, 2004), 15.

196 Ibid.

197 Irigaray, *This Sex Which Is Not One*, 25–6.

198 Irigaray, "The Wedding between the Body and Language," 20.

199 Ibid.

200 Ibid.

201 Ofelia Schutte, "A Critique of Normative Heterosexuality: Identity, Embodiment, and Sexual Difference in Beauvoir and Irigaray," *Hypatia* 12, no. 1 (1997): 55.

202 Suthor, *Rembrandt's Roughness*, 177.

203 For a discussion of Semmel's self-portraiture in relation to the mirror and feminist theory, see Marsha Meskimmon, *The Art of Reflection: Women Artists' Self-Portraiture in the Twentieth Century* (New York: Columbia University Press, 1996), 1–7.

204 Luce Irigaray, *Reading Art, Reading Irigaray: The Politics of Art by Women* (London: I.B. Tauris, 2006), 72.

205 Rachel Jones, *Irigaray: Towards a Sexuate Philosophy* (Cambridge: Polity Press, 2011), 164.

206 Luce Irigaray, *Speculum of Another Woman* (Ithaca: Cornell University Press, 1985), 239.

207 Affron, *Émilie Charmy*, 33.

208 Cathryn Vasseleu, *Textures of Light: Vision and Touch in Irigaray, Levinas and Merleau-Ponty*. (London: Routledge, 1998), 67.

209 Irigaray critiques Merleau-Ponty's phenomenological theories for the continuing predominance of vision and the duality of the subject–object position. Luce Irigaray, *An Ethics of Sexual Difference*, translated by Carolyn Burke and Gilian Gill (Ithaca: Cornell University Press, 1993), 170.

210 Vasseleu, *Textures of Light*, 126.

211 Toulouse-Lautrec painted many nude female couples. See G.M. Sugana, *Complete Paintings of Toulouse-Lautrec* (Harmondsworth: Penguin Books, 1987), and *Toulouse-Lautrec: résolument moderne*, edited by Stéphane Guégan (Paris: Musée d'Orsay, RMN – Grand Palais, 2019).

212 Sophie Krebs, *Albert Marquet, peintre du temps suspendu*, exhibition catalogue (Paris: Paris Musées Editions, 2016), 62.

213 Ibid.

214 Nead, *The Female Nude*, 107.
215 See Birnbaum, *Women Artists in Interwar France*, and Marie-Jo Bonnet, *Les Deux Amies: essai sur le couple de femmes dans l'art* (Paris: Éditions Blanche, 2002), 159–279.
216 Bonnet, *Les Deux Amies,* 173.
217 Ibid.
218 Meskimmon, *The Art of Reflection*, 116.

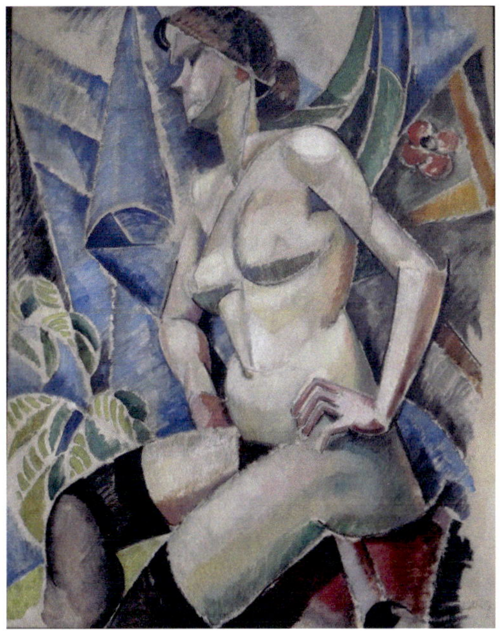

Plate 1 Marie Vassilieff, *Femme aux bas noirs* (*Woman in Black Stockings*), c. 1912–13

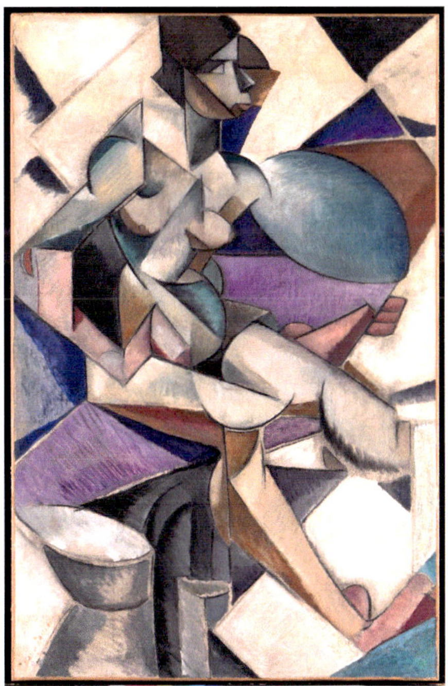

Plate 2 Marie Vassilieff, *Femme assise* (*Seated Woman*), c. 1913

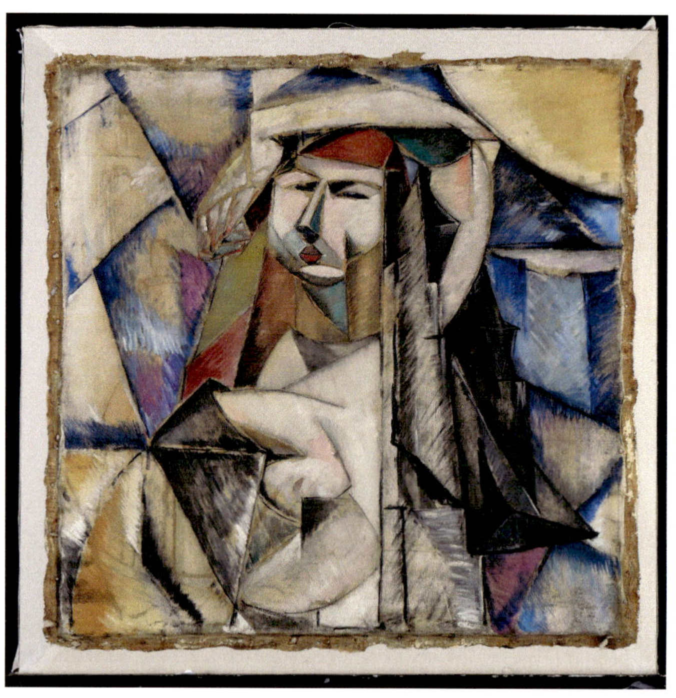

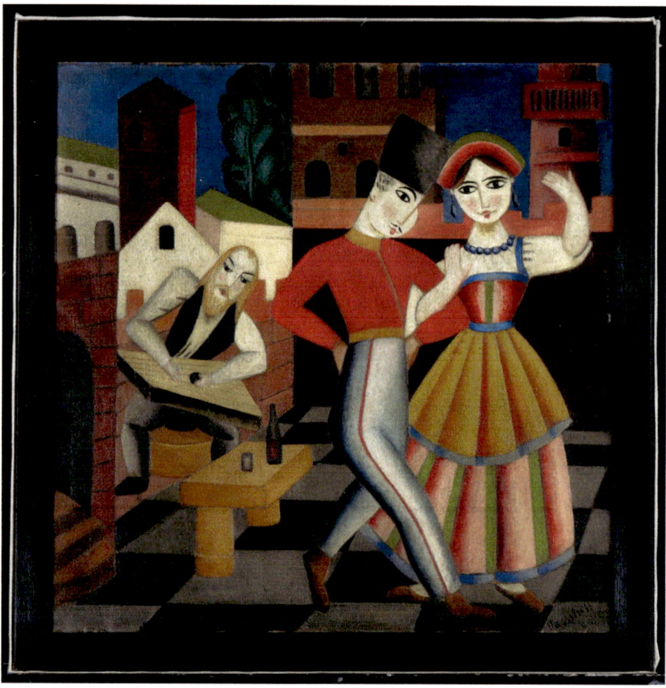

Plate 3 Marie Vassilieff, *Portrait de femme & la danse* (*Portrait of a Woman & The Dance*), c. 1913–14

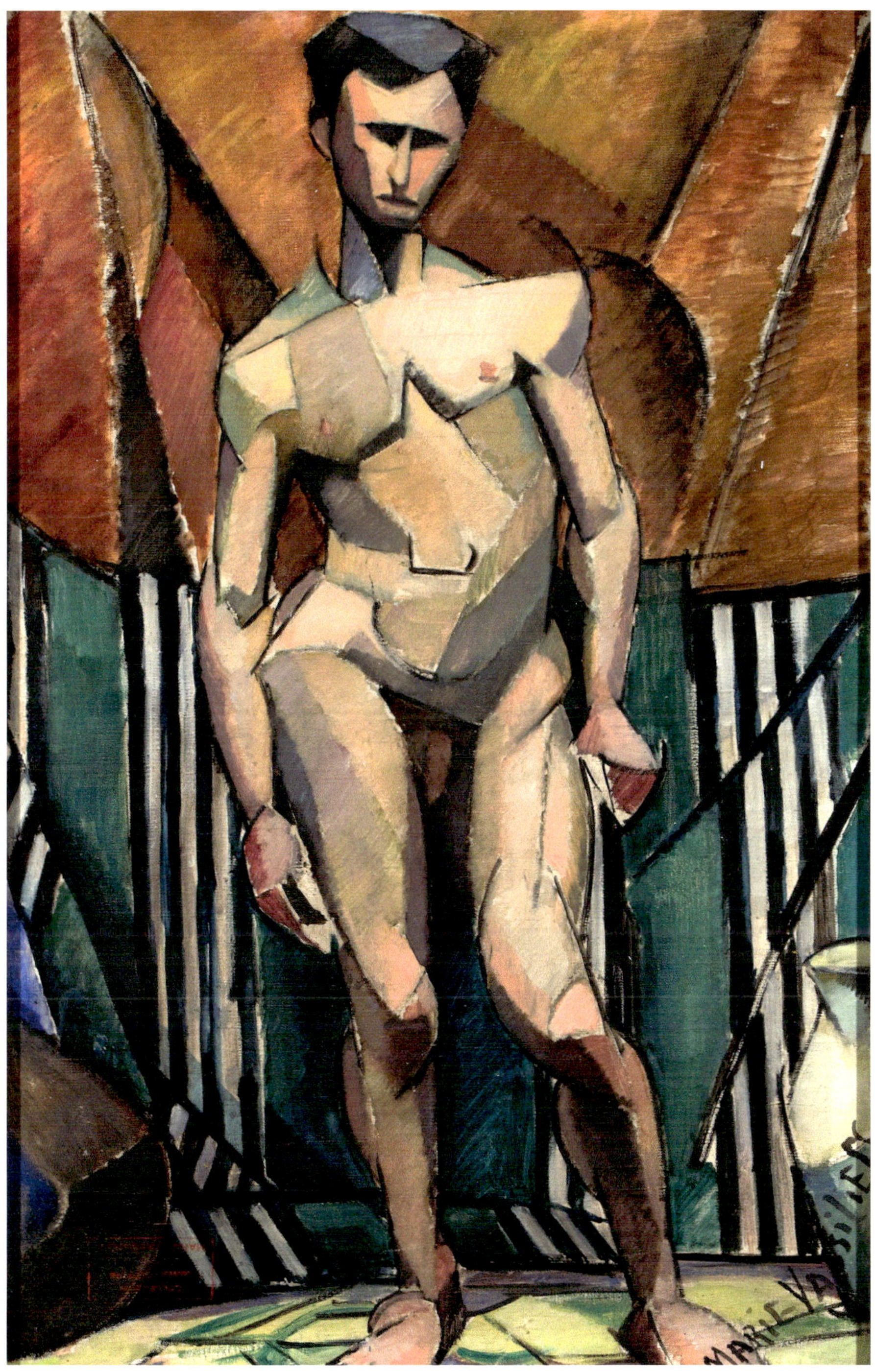

Plate 4 Marie Vassilieff, *Homme et femme* (*Man and Woman*), c. 1911–14

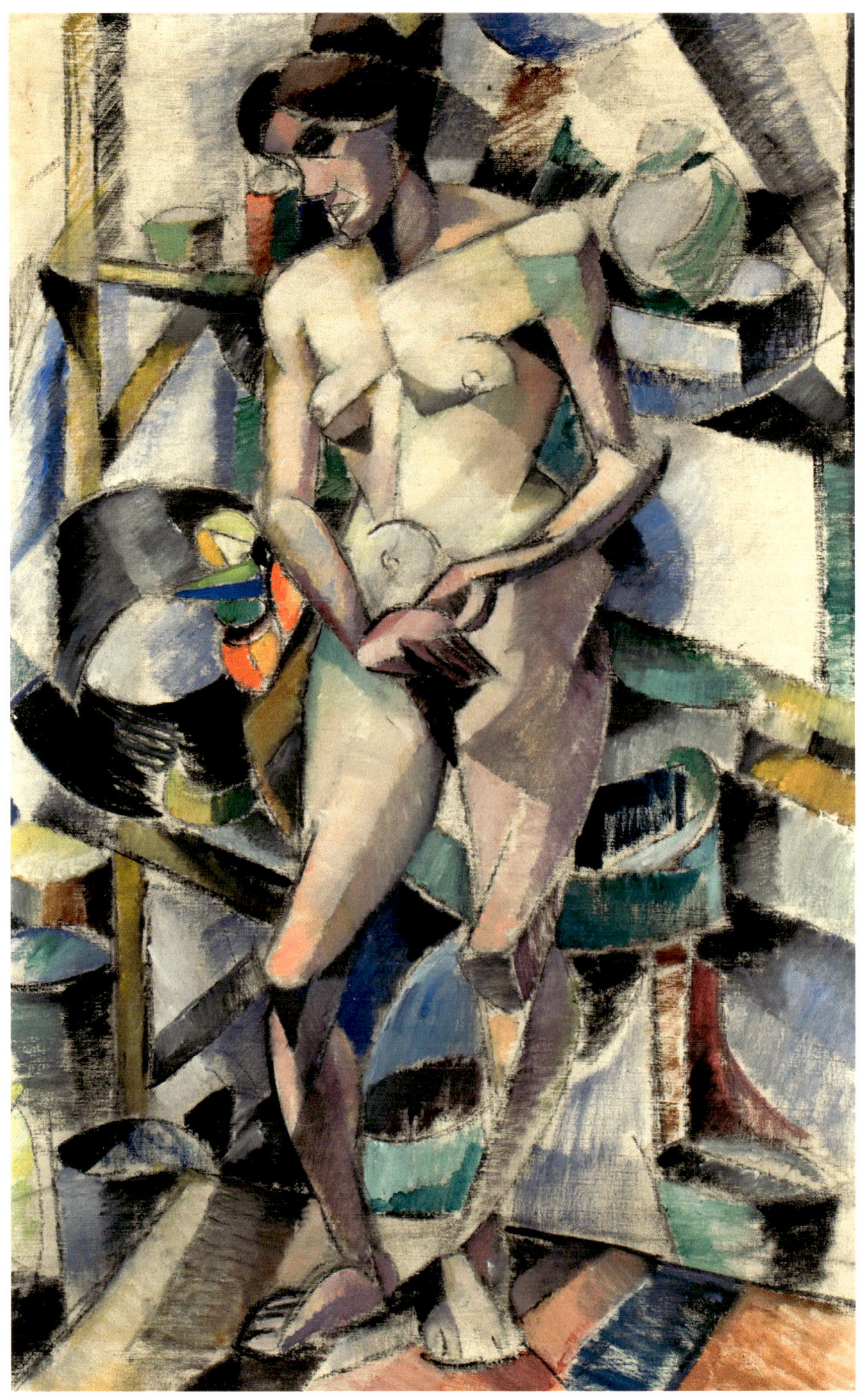

Plate 5 Marie Vassilieff, *Homme et femme* (*Man and Woman*), c. 1911–14

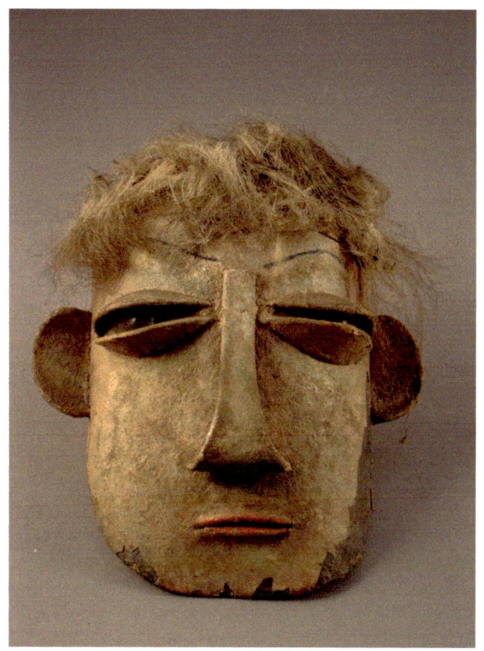

Plate 6 Marie Vassilieff, *Poupée-autoportrait* (*Doll Self-Portrait*), c. 1920–29

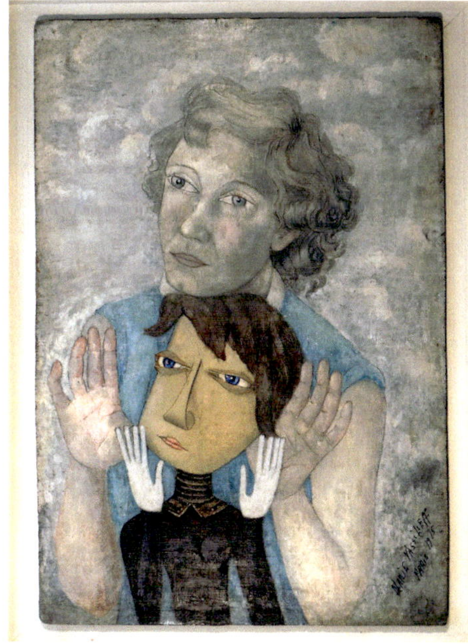

Plate 7 Marie Vassilieff, *Marie Vassilieff et sa poupée portrait* (*Marie Vassilieff and Her Doll Self-Portrait*), 1929 (antedated 1915)

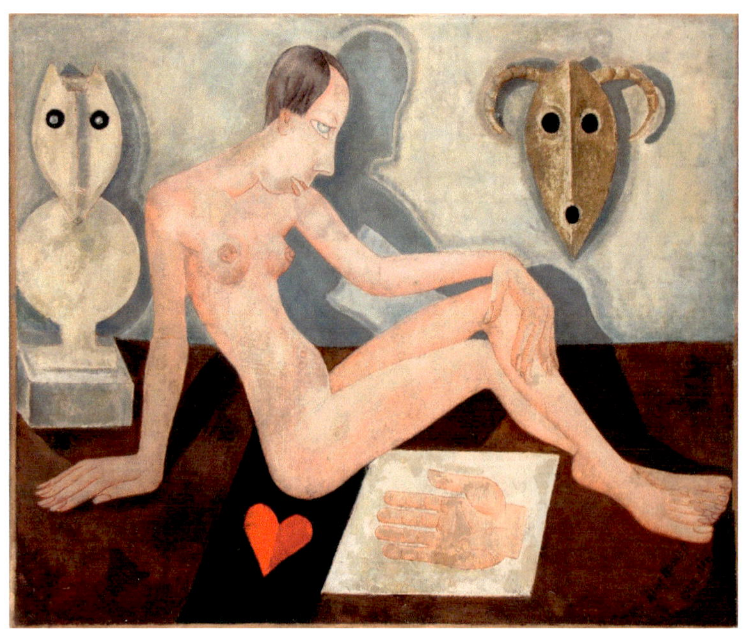

Plate 8 Marie Vassilieff, *Nu avec deux masques* (*Nude with Two Masks*), 1930

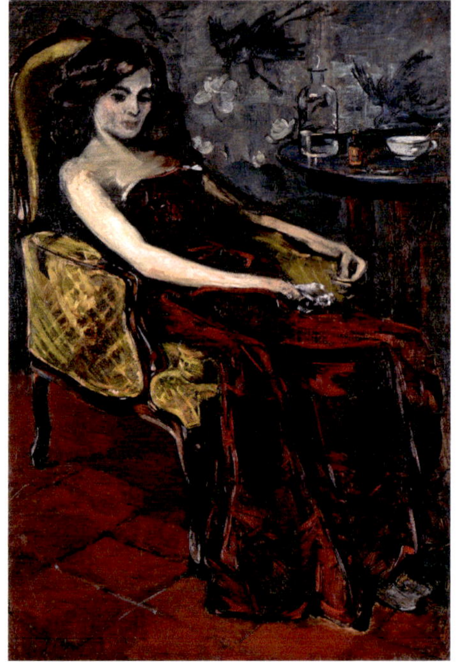

Plate 9 Émilie Charmy, *La Morphinomane*, c. 1897–1900

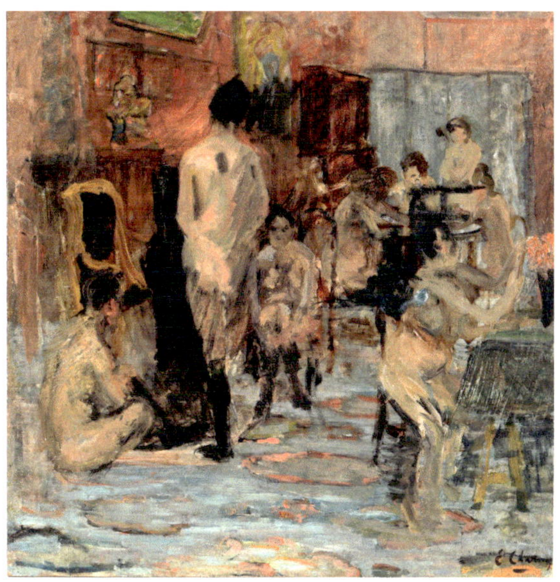

Plate 10 Émilie Charmy, *La Loge*, c. 1900

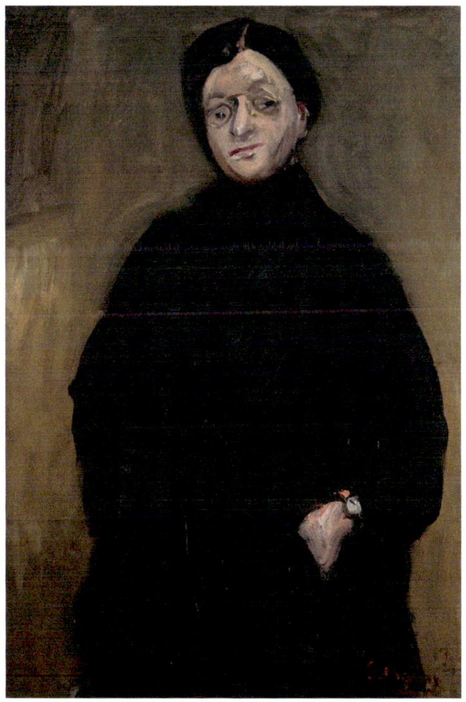

Plate 11 Émilie Charmy, *Portrait de Berthe Weill* (*Portrait of Berthe Weill*), c. 1910–20

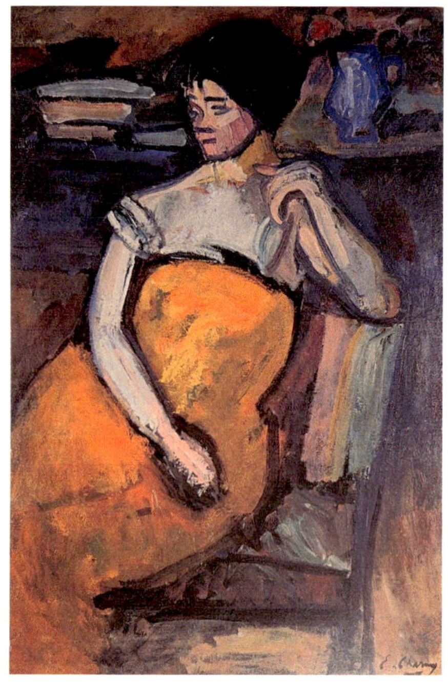

Plate 12 Émilie Charmy, *Jeune femme enceinte* (*Young Pregnant Woman*), 1906–7

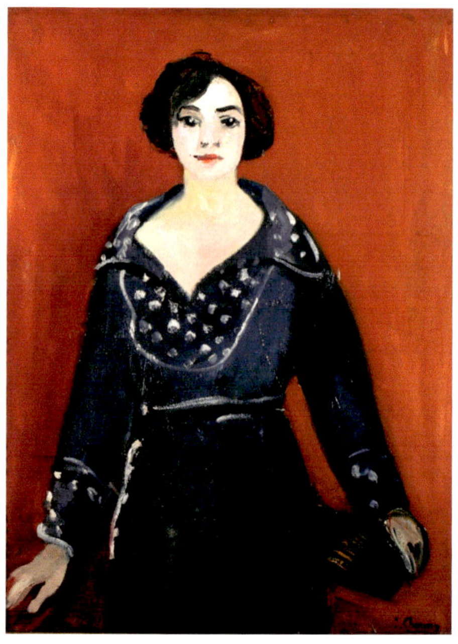

Plate 13 Émilie Charmy, *Autoportrait avec un album* (*Self-Portrait with an Album*), 1907–12

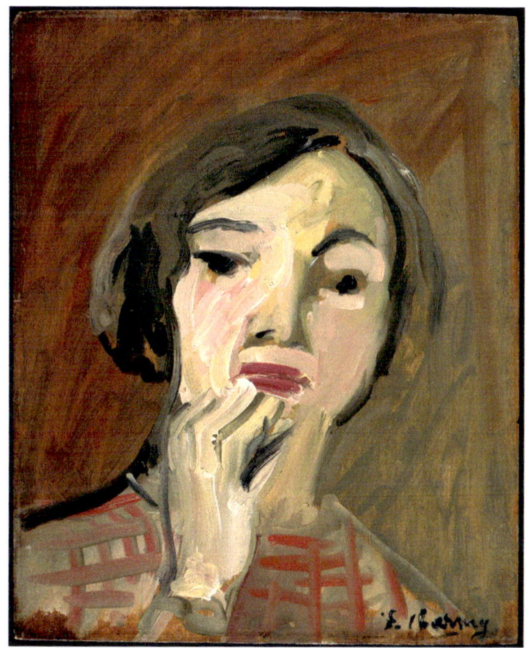

Plate 14 Émilie Charmy, Autoportrait (*Self-Portrait*), c. 1910

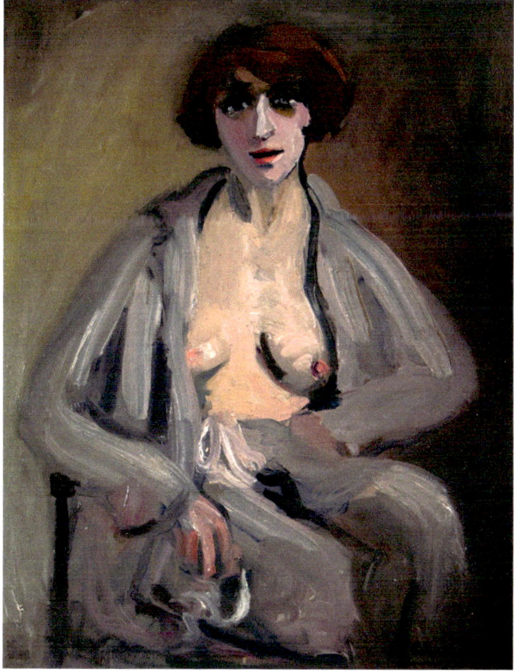

Plate 15 Émilie Charmy, *Autoportrait au peignoir ouvert* (*Self-Portrait in an Open Dressing Gown*), c. 1916–18

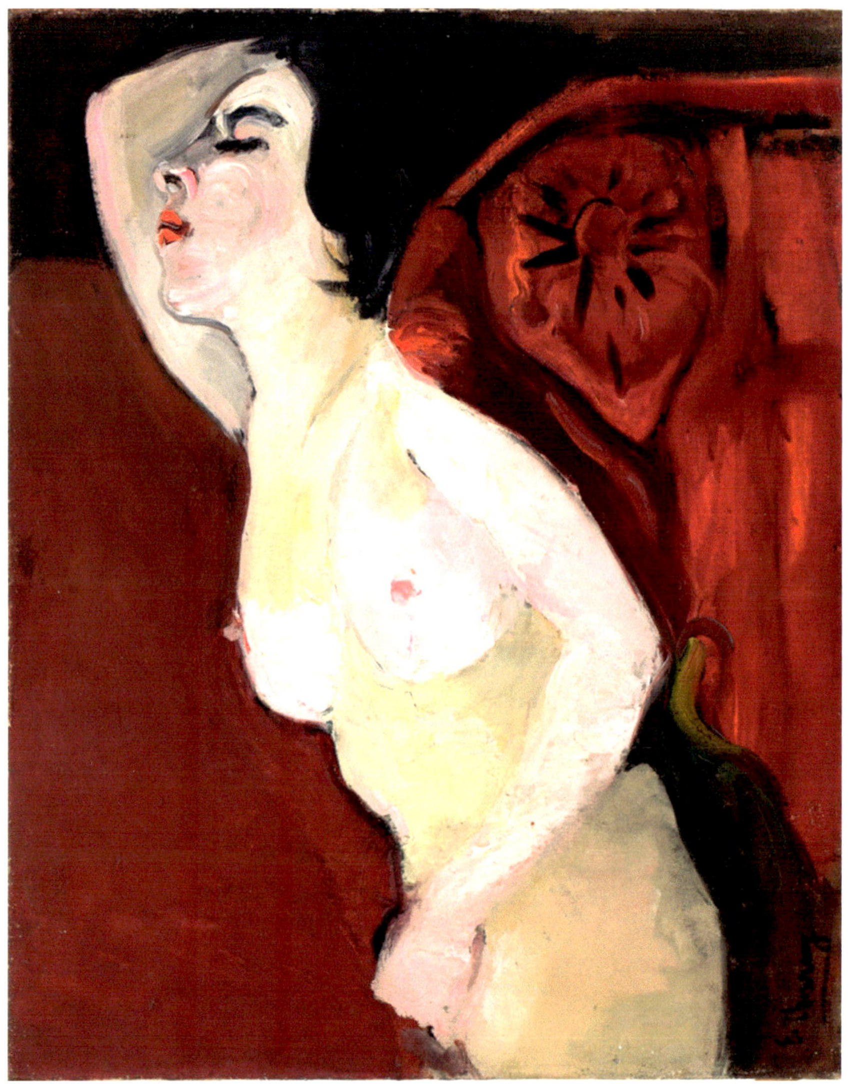

Plate 16 Émilie Charmy, *Nu au divan rouge* (*Nude on Red Sofa*), c. 1925

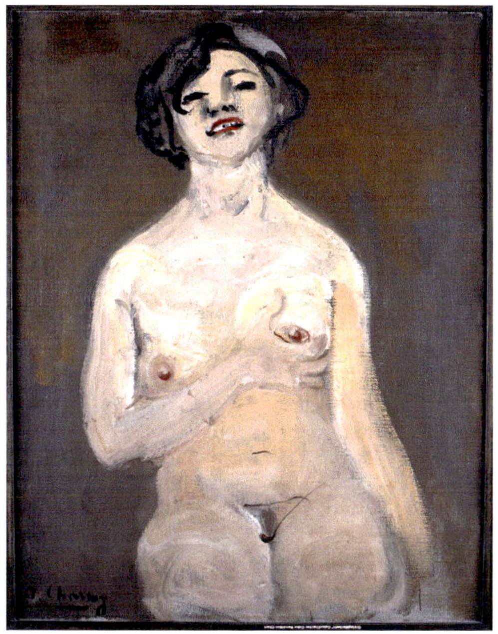

Plate 17 Émilie Charmy, *Nu tenant son sein* (*Nude Holding Her Breast*), c. 1920–25

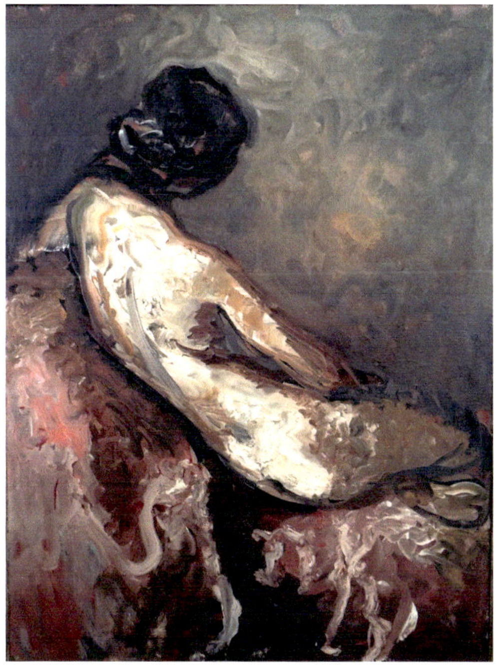

Plate 18 Émilie Charmy, *Nu* (*Nude*), c. 1920–30

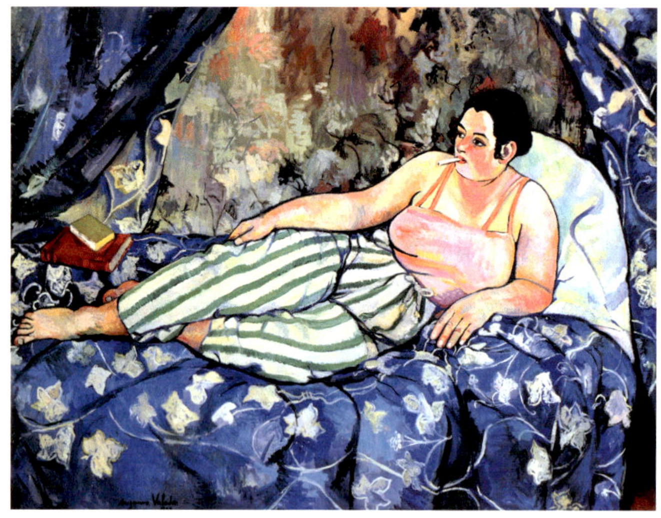

Plate 19 Suzanne Valadon, *La Chambre bleue* (*The Blue Room*), 1923

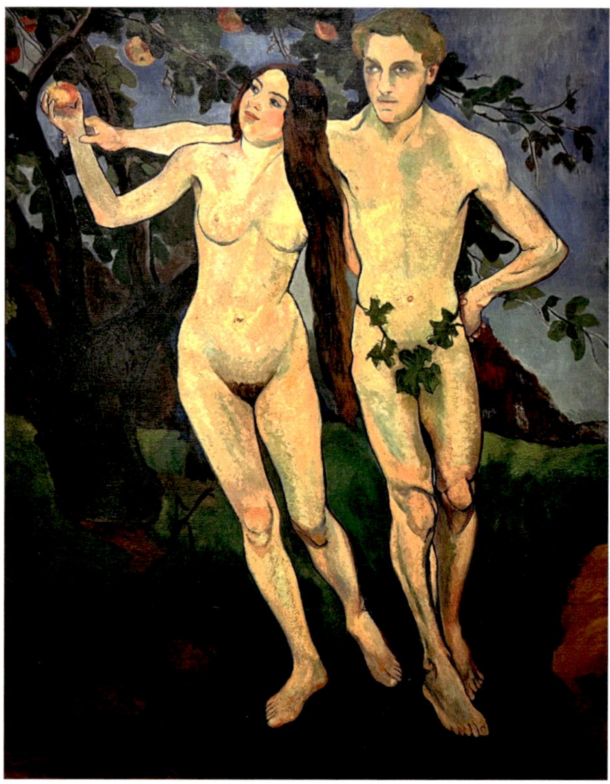

Plate 20 Suzanne Valadon, *Adam et Eve* (*Adam and Eve*), 1909

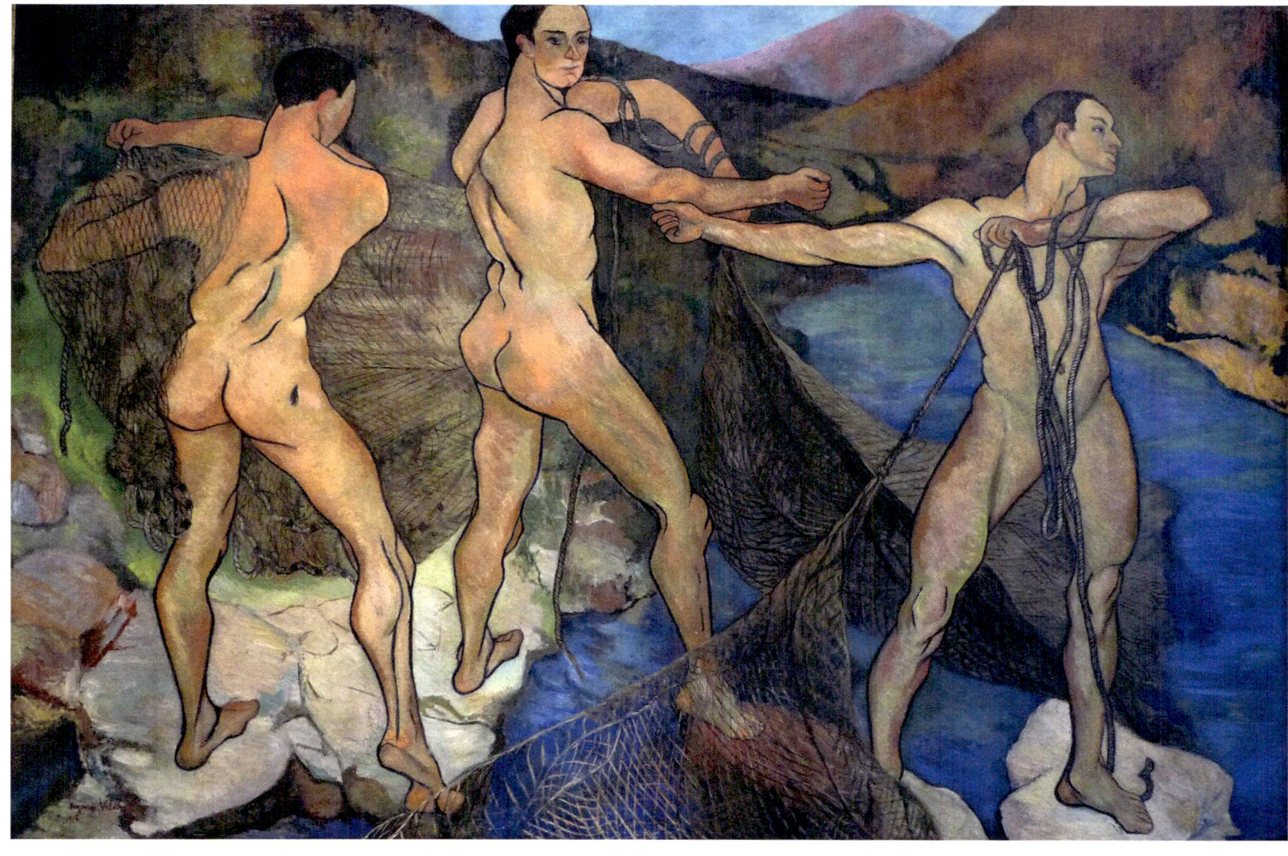

Plate 21 Suzanne Valadon, *Le Lancement du filet* (*Casting the Net*), 1914

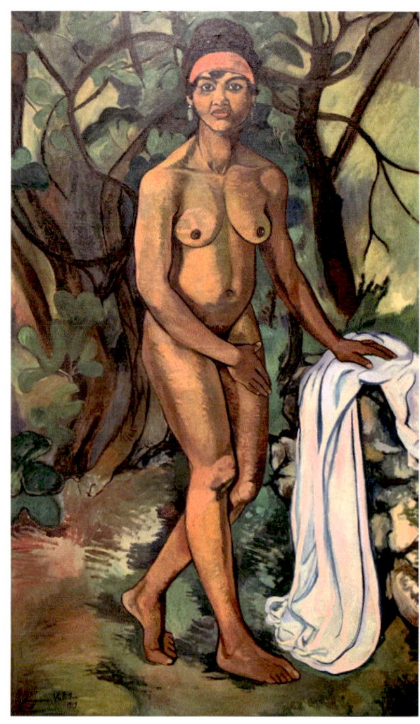

Plate 22 Suzanne Valadon, *Vénus noire* (*Black Venus*), 1919

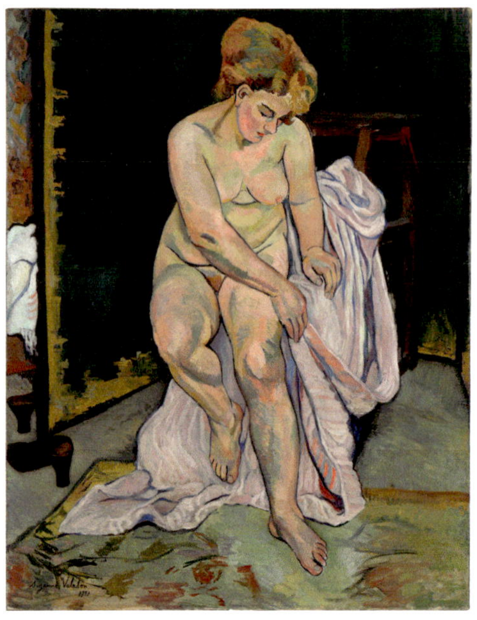

Plate 23 Suzanne Valadon, *Nu à la draperie* (*Nude with Drapery*), 1921

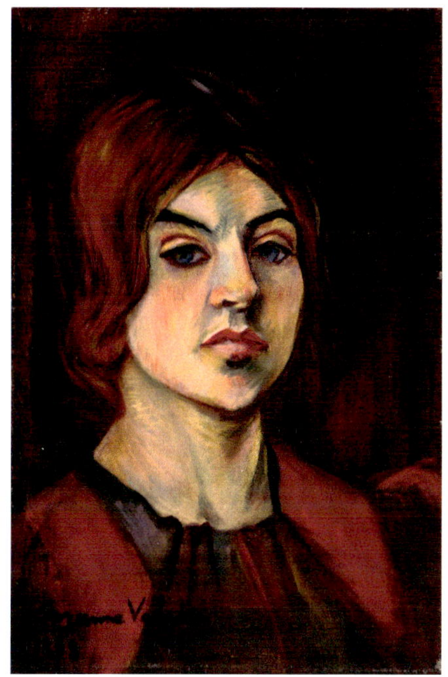

Plate 24 Suzanne Valadon, *Autoportrait* (*Self-Portrait*), 1898

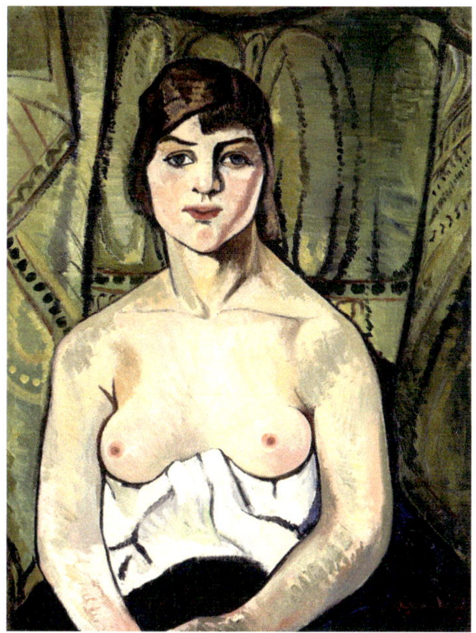

Plate 25 Suzanne Valadon, *Femme aux seins nus* (*autoportrait*) (*Woman with Bare Breasts, Self-Portrait*), 1917

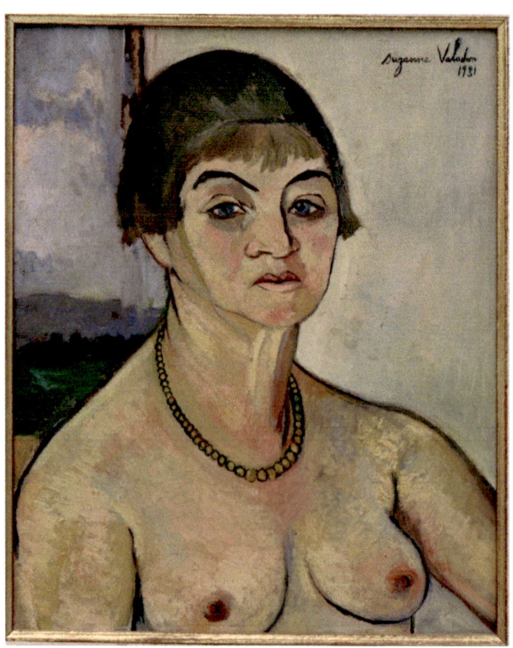

Plate 26 Suzanne Valadon, *Autoportrait* (*Self-Portrait*), 1931

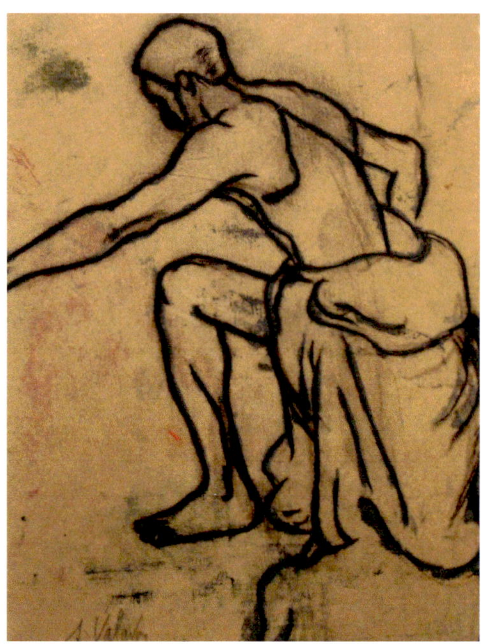

Plate 27 Suzanne Valadon, *Homme nu, de dos, tendant le bras gauche* (*Nude Male, from Behind, Holding Out His Left Arm*), c. 1910–14

3 Suzanne Valadon: a man as her muse

> For a woman to paint the male nude, as against being painted nude by a man, is a break with our whole art tradition.[1]

Defiance was Suzanne Valadon's modus operandi. She intrepidly disobeyed gender norms in her artistic practice as she opposed both traditional and avant-garde methods for the representation and display of the body. Through various styles and media, she captured different manifestations of the nude – idealized and unidealized, active and passive. She did not limit herself to one type of model, but instead depicted bodies of different ages, races and genders. She dared to explore the male nude, a genre which was largely off limits to female painters until the latter part of the twentieth century. Valadon confronted the subject head-on in several monumental paintings, a self-portrait and numerous drawings. Shunning patriarchal gender binaries and power relations, she displayed handsome and graceful male nudes at the Salon des Indépendants in 1914. Several years later in 1919, Valadon invited viewers to admire realistic and sensual portrayals of the Black female body. She tested societal attitudes about race, and at the same time exposed her own biases. From 1917 to 1931, Valadon depicted her aging form from an embodied perspective in a series of fiercely candid nude self-portraits. Focusing on key works in relation to issues of age, race, gender, embodiment and sexuality, this chapter sheds light on Valadon's polemic practice and demonstrates how she mobilized the nude as a vehicle for disruption. Her work exposes femininity and masculinity as socially constructed, and thus prefigures some of the ideas later presented in feminist, existentialist Simone de Beauvoir's *The Second Sex* (1949). Before the development of gender theory, and with varying degrees of success, Valadon subverted gendered hierarchies and upset the normative cultural frameworks for the representation of the nude. In certain works, she accomplished a profound sense of embodied subjectivity.

La Chambre bleue (*The Blue Room*) (Plate 19), a manifesto of modern womanhood and female intellectuality, exemplifies Valadon's unruly approach.[2] The artist made explicit her disruptive painterly aim, flouting contemporary stereotypes of femininity with an inelegant, sunburnt and smoking woman. Valadon offers her response to the hallowed nude genre. She depicts a supine figure on a bed in the manner of Titian's *Venus of Urbino* but replaces the loyal canine with a stack of books. Like Goya's *The Clothed Maja*, the woman is clad in trousers, except that, rather than smooth, lustrous silks, hers are rumpled and exaggerate her ample form. The background recalls the Odalisque's lair in Ingres's *Grande odalisque*. Yet, Valadon's female is neither elegant nor sultry, and, instead of a hookah, she smokes a cigarette. Surrounded by grapevines, the scene carries Dionysian undertones of revelry. Although the title may be a gesture toward Matisse's *Blue Nude*, the figure is not hardened into geometric shapes. Most visibly, *La Chambre bleue* is a response to Manet's *Olympia*. Still, Olympia is a courtesan who makes viewers aware of their gazes with her enduring stare. By contrast, Valadon's female is neither an ingratiating goddess, *femme fatale*, nor a demimonde *provocatrice*, but an educated bohemian.[3] She denies any tinge of eroticism with her unpolished and unsultry appearance. This "nu habillé" (dressed nude), as one French critic called her, does not conform to male fantasies.[4] Valadon depicts a woman who willfully asserts herself as an anti-object of desire, a differentially, defined self.

In *La Chambre bleue*, Valadon usurped the female nude from its patriarchal pedestal and dressed it shabbily. The painting is a bold retort not only to the lineage of nudes by male artists past and present, but also to those by her female contemporaries, Marie Laurencin and Jacqueline Marval, not to mention contemporary notions of femininity. In *La Bohémienne* (*The Bohemian*, 1921) Marval presents a sultry and excessively made-up woman – the epitome of girlish feminine appearance incarnated in the popular *forme féminine* of the 1910s and 1920s. Lying prone in a coquettish pose, her sensuous curves are accentuated by a long white plume. Marval displayed *La Bohémienne* at the Salon d'Automne in 1921, while Valadon exhibited *La Poupée délaissée* (1921).[5] Marval received numerous laudatory reviews that year: "How lovely it is to admire … an odalisque extending its stretched forms among the many shades of piled up cushions."[6] Critics applauded her sensual *Bohème*, comparing Marval to Berthe Morisot, the supreme compliment for a female painter at that time.[7] Conceivably as a rejoinder, Valadon exhibited *La Chambre bleue* in the Salon d'Automne two years later.[8] Valadon's bohemian must have appeared repulsive in comparison. One modish and flirtatious, the other brash and formidable, Marval's and Valadon's women are antithetical. With its enlarged form on the painting's foremost plane, Valadon's bohemian commands our attention. Far from fashionable with her sturdy frame and striped pants, her "female masculinity" resonates emphatically.[9] In *La Chambre bleue*, Valadon irreverently transgressed normative gender imaginaries, depicting a woman who for 1920s audiences was assertively masculine in appearance and manner, but is markedly gendered female.

To paint a woman with a cigarette wearing pants in the 1920s was to make a bold statement about gender.[10] Although it was common to see women smoking in advertisements, such as illustrations for Lucky Strike in the 1930s, cigarettes appear only occasionally in paintings of women where they may underline the sitter's intellectuality or modernity. Equally rare are women outfitted in pants in French art from this period. Exceptions in the domain of painting include Tamara de Lempicka's *Portrait de la duchesse de la Salle* (1925) and Romaine Brooks's *Una, Lady Troubridge* (1924). In actuality, only a small minority of women wore trousers in the 1920s and 1930s.[11] "Le pantalon," also called "le pyjama," was acceptable for certain functions, such as for sport or beach outings or in the privacy of one's home.[12] In the popular imagination, pants were considered an undergarment for women, as the lyrics of one pop song demonstrates.[13] Even Chanel, whose pared-down fashions liberated women's bodies, did not sell pants until later in the 1920s.[14] She once said, "a woman in pants will never be a handsome man."[15] A prophetic nod to the present, the comfortable attire in *La Chambre bleue* resembles athleisure today. But for the 1920s, Valadon's figure exemplified an unkept woman, unconcerned by aesthetics or physical appearance.

Therefore, while Marval's *La Bohémienne* could appease and delight audiences, *La Chambre bleue* posed a threat. Unsurprisingly, Valadon's painting received very little attention in the press.[16] Nonetheless, it was purchased three years later by the French government for the National Museum of Contemporary Art (Musée du Luxembourg) along with her *Adam and Eve* (Plate 20).[17] Displayed today in the Musée des Beaux-Arts in Limoges, the painting stands as a refusal of feminine stereotypes. Valadon's bohemian exhibits no qualms about her unstylish appearance. With her self-assured nonchalance, coupled with the stack of books, she prioritizes intellectual pursuits over a preoccupation with looks. Valadon's woman departs radically from early twentieth-century feminine ideals of beauty, and, with a cigarette pursed in her lips, she frankly couldn't care less.

Valadon did not paint to please. Her unvarnished nudes unnerved audiences. Resultantly, she faced hostile criticism and systematic exclusion. When Berthe Weill inquired about Valadon's obvious absence from the momentous exhibition *Cinquante ans de peinture française*, ancillary to the 1925 *Exposition internationale des arts décoratifs et industriels modernes*, the curator, Louis Vauxcelles, declared outright, "I don't like Valadon's painting; not more than Charmy's!"[18] When her nudes were shown at major salons and group exhibitions, some works sparked outrage while others left critics speechless. Her realistically rendered *Vénus noire* (Plate 22), exhibited in 1919, was met with aversion and disdain. In 1914, *Le Lancement du filet* (Plate 21), a spectacle of male nudes, offended bourgeois audiences. At a time when the expression of female sexuality in art was unacceptable, the painting provoked critical silence. Even Robert Rey's early monograph on the artist, which includes an illustration of *Le Lancement*, provides no analysis of the painting.[19] It is likely that male critics were threatened by Valadon's upfront display of sensual male bodies. They may have also seen in these works a dangerous reversal of the power structure. Silence and omission, in this case, are a telling response.

Over a century later, art historians have yet to break the silence. There is a dearth of information on Valadon's male bodies and Black female nudes.[20] The majority who have studied Valadon's oeuvre have focused almost exclusively on her representation of the white female body, which they have examined in relation to the theory of the male gaze.[21] Those who have mentioned *Vénus noire* celebrate the work as exemplary without elaborating on issues of race. To date, Ebonie Pollock is the only scholar who has provided a sustained analysis of Valadon's Black nudes within their colonialist context.[22] Meanwhile, the few scholars who have discussed her male nudes have provided cursory overviews and ignored her drawings. Such perfunctory analyses have led to misinterpretations of her work, which will be broached later in this chapter.[23] It is not my intention to critically dissect the feminist scholarship on Valadon, nor do I wish to belabor the most studied aspects of Valadon's oeuvre or her storied biography. Instead, employing interdisciplinary methodological approaches, I address the sheer diversity of her nudes and approaches.[24]

This chapter examines Valadon's most unusual and contentious works. Specifically, I consider her drawings of bathers, nude self-portraits, Black female nudes and male nudes. Avoiding broad generalizations about the entirety of her oeuvre, I examine key pieces in separate case studies, each of which yields distinct conclusions. Working in Paris during the transitional Belle Époque and interwar period, Valadon lived through a time of tumult. At the same time, as a lower-class white woman, she was not immune to the mores and notions of her era. Defiance is a trait found throughout Valadon's work, albeit unevenly. Acknowledging the inconsistent and paradoxical nature of her art and its cultured and gendered context, this chapter highlights the ways in which Valadon worked within and against the grain, breaching artistic currents, female respectability and conservative gender roles, as she determinedly negotiated the nude.

"That devil Maria"[25]

Born Marie-Clémentine Valadon in 1865 in Bessines-sur-Gartempe, a small town in Haute-Vienne, between Bellac and Limoges, Suzanne Valadon moved with her mother, Madeleine (Marie-Magdelaine Célina), to Paris around 1866.[26] Madeleine uprooted to the capital to escape the prejudiced views toward rearing a fatherless child only to struggle finding work as a housekeeper.[27] This necessitated Valadon, ill-equipped with only a rudimentary education, to begin working while still a teenager around 1876.[28] She tried numerous jobs, including a stint as a circus acrobat, before finally becoming an artist's model at age fifteen (around 1880).[29] Celebrated for her beauty, Valadon quickly gained renown within artistic circles as a model.[30]

Some of the artists for whom she posed included Henri de Toulouse-Lautrec, Jean-Jacques Henner, Guiseppe de Nittis, Renoir, Gustav Wertheimer and Federico Zandomeneghi.[31] When discussing her modeling career, Valadon frequently mentioned Puvis de Chavannes. She posed for him over a period of seven years.[32] This experience provided her in-depth knowledge of the classical treatment of the body. Observing how a multitude of artists recast her figure into a polished nude on canvas, she came to understand how the body is transformed from "naked" to "nude."[33]

As a model, Valadon became intimately aware of the process of figure painting. She witnessed the metamorphosis of her own body into an ideal form on canvas. In an interview with Adolphe Tabarant (an art critic, writer and socialist), she stated, "Puvis asked me to give him an attitude, a movement, a gesture. He transposed and idealized me."[34] In his work, Valadon appears sensual, curvaceous and delicately modeled, her unique features erased.[35] She noted the hours of arduous work posing entailed, "It was very difficult to assume the exact position that M. de Chavannes wanted and to hold it ... I cannot say how many hours I spent posing in the big workshop."[36] According to at least one account, Valadon was exceptionally proficient at modeling. An observer wrote, "She posed with intelligence and kept the pose for a long time, without ever showing the slightest sign of fatigue."[37] In Renoir's *The Large Bathers* (1887), she appears on the left, holding a precarious pose with one foot in the air.[38] In these grueling modeling sessions, Valadon learned the techniques for aligning and portraying the body. By contrast, Toulouse-Lautrec's *Female Nude* (1884) displays Valadon slouched nonchalantly in a chair. Rendered with stalwart realism, his serves as the foil to the traditional, idealized nude. Posing for diverse painters, from academic to vanguard, Valadon observed how artists set up their compositions, how they handled materials in the studio, and how they mixed paint. At the same time, the laborious task of posing granted her an enhanced bodily awareness. She was conscious of the position of her limbs, the balance of her body and her overall physiological state before the easel.

Transitioning from an artist's model to an artist, Valadon turned to her own image. Her first known work is a self-portrait: *Autoportrait* (1883). She portrays herself earnestly and without embellishment. Seen in three-quarter view, she shifts her eyes to meet ours, carrying a solemn expression. Her distinctive features are modeled with blue shading and yellowish-green highlights. At eighteen, she emanates a sense of poise and independence. It is reported that this self-portrait, proudly showcasing her signature and date on the upper right, is the first work she ever signed. After intentionally destroying her previous decade's drawings, she must have greatly valued this pastel. Through this self-portrait and the ones that followed, she asserts her evolving role, progressing from being an object of observation to becoming the observing subject and creator.

Degas, for whom she never posed, had a major influence on Valadon's work.[39] Exactly how and when they met is disputed by scholars, but it was likely through the combined efforts of Toulouse-Lautrec and the sculptor Paul Bartholomé.[40] In her interview with Tabarant, Valadon recalled how at the time she was living on rue Tourlaque near Toulouse-Lautrec and Zandomeneghi. Toulouse-Lautrec showed her work to his friend Bartholomé, who exclaimed, "We have to show that to Degas!"[41] Upon seeing her work, Degas purportedly responded, "You are one of us!"[42] The two became close friends, and Valadon visited him nearly every afternoon.[43] Degas, "equally fascinated by the ugly and the spectacularly beautiful," was fond of her drawings and hung her work in his dining room.[44] The two shared an appreciation for grotesqueness in art. Valadon later said to her son, Utrillo, "It can never be ugly enough."[45]

Valadon kept Degas's letters. This collection survives as a testament to their enduring friendship.[46] From their correspondence, it is clear that Degas constantly encouraged her to draw and inquired about new pieces. In one letter, he asked her to bring her work to his studio, "Come see me with some drawings. I like to see those thick and agile lines."[47] In a later note, the aging artist implored her once again to show him her work:

> My dear Maria. Your letter always arrives punctually, with its engraved and firm letters. It is your drawings that I no longer see. From time to time, in my dining room, I look at your red pencil drawing, which is still hanging; and I always say to myself: "That devil Maria had a genius for drawing." Why don't you show me anything anymore? I progress towards sixty-seven-years.[48]

Degas was one of Valadon's most fervent supporters and helped to launch her career. He may have arranged for her drawings to be shown in 1893 at the art gallery Le Barc de Boutteville in an exhibition, *4e exposition des peintres impressionistes et symbolistes*, alongside Toulouse-Lautrec, Camille Pissarro and Paul Sérusier.[49] In 1894, her work was accepted into the prestigious *Exposition de la Société nationale des beaux-arts*. The only female artist included in the exhibition, she exhibited five drawings of child bathers, one of which Degas purchased.[50] Degas made her art known to numerous dealers, including Ambroise Vollard who published her engravings and sold her work.[51] Degas himself would accrue a total of seventeen drawings by Valadon and three prints; these were noted in his collection after his death.[52]

"Drawn like a saw" – Valadon's early bathers

Valadon never received the rigorous academic training for successful "mastery" of the nude, but this did not impede her from exploring the subject. Her study of the body began with her own son, Maurice Utrillo.[53] Starting in the 1880s, she depicted him clothed and unclothed in numerous, candid drawings. Images of young Utrillo were among the first works she exhibited in 1894. In Valadon's catalogue raisonné, eleven nude drawings of Utrillo are documented.[54] In these sketches, she renders his angular spine, wiry limbs, and scrawny torso with a heavy outline of *crayon noir*. With minimal shading, she emphasizes his spindly form and paper-thin limbs. Valadon's probing gaze is ever-present in her drawings of her son, who conversely appears unaware of his mother's examining stare. Rarely, if ever, does Valadon depict herself with Utrillo in drawings, nor does she seem to convey a strong sense of maternal compassion toward him.[55] Her images of young Utrillo do not evince the kind of tenderness and affection manifest in many of Cassatt's scenes of children.[56] In her analysis of Valadon's sketches of young Utrillo and other children, Thérèse Rosinksy argues against any allusion to sexuality.[57] Courtney Hunt, on the other hand, takes the opposite stance. She contends that sexual undertones are present, although she notes that Valadon did not attempt to create an overtly eroticized image of Utrillo.[58] Often including his name in the title or the designation, "my son," Valadon underscores the fact that these drawings result from a mother's intimate knowledge of her boy's own body.[59] Her drawings of Utrillo resonate with Thomas Eakins's photographs and paintings of male youths from a decade earlier. Although Valadon would not have seen these works, there is an uncanny resemblance in their organic simplicity and unabashed nudity.

Apart from Eakins in Gilded-Age America, most artists in France had turned their attention primarily to the female form. Finding comparable examples to Valadon's young male bathers proves difficult. She may have seen Renoir's *The Boy with the Cat* (1868) or Gauguin's depictions of Breton adolescent bathers, such as *Nude Breton Boy* (1889). In Gauguin's work, the bony form, gauche recumbent pose and high perspective resonate with Valadon's depictions of Utrillo. Yet in Gauguin's and Renoir's paintings, the genitalia are elided. Neither of these artists treated adult male bathers.[60] *Maurice Utrillo nu allongé* (*Maurice Utrillo Nude Reclining*) echoes eighteenth-century academic studies of young men in supine pose, such as sketches by Louis de Boullogne (1654–1733). However, the linear boldness and blunt nudity of Valadon's figure diverges vastly from academic handling of line. Rather than modeling the figure with highlights and shadow to articulate the definition of musculature or the smoothness of skin, Valadon traces the rugged contours of her son's pre-pubescent body. Without camouflaging drapery, Utrillo's scrawny body appears exceedingly vulnerable. Valadon does not avoid rendering the male sexual organ in her images of the male form. Dated 1896, he would have been twelve or thirteen years old. In this image, Valadon tackles adolescent sexuality in an unsparing manner. With a dedication to Tabarant written on the back, she did not have qualms about sharing this image, at least among friends.

Valadon was liberated in the sense that she did not have to unlearn the laws of anatomy, perspective or modeling. Exploring a lexicon of body types outside of the conventional ideal, Valadon shed light on the rudimentary aspects of daily rituals of dressing, undressing and bathing for working-class individuals. In her early drawings of her son, friends and neighbors, Valadon's realistic and unidealized approach to the body is evident. Her figures are either lanky or heavyset. The model in *Catherine nue se coiffant* (1895) is amply proportioned with a protruding belly. Her plumpness is reinforced by bold contours which accentuate every mound and crevice. By contrast, the models in *Marie au tub s'épongeant* (figure 3.1) and *Fillette nue allongée sur un canapé* (1894) (figure 3.2) are sinewy and angular. While the profile view in the former image stresses the woman's curves, the oblique angle in *Fillette nue* amplifies the girl's angular rib cage, hipbones and budding chest. Strikingly, Valadon's images of bathing girls reflect her studies of Utrillo. *Fillette nue allongée sur un canapé*, for example, resembles *Maurice Utrillo à neuf ans* (c. 1892) and *Maurice Utrillo nu assis sur un divan* (1895) (figure 3.3). Both exhibit daydreaming children with wiry forms posed idly on couches within simple domestic settings. *Fillette nue assise* (1894) echoes such works as *Maurice Utrillo nu jouant avec un lance-pierres* (c. 1895) and

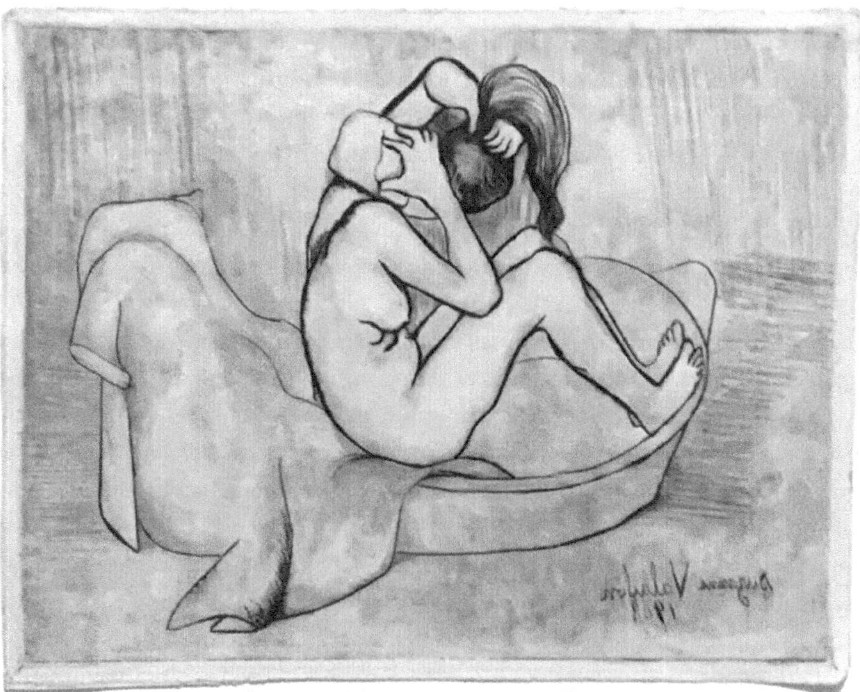

Figure 3.1 Suzanne Valadon, *Marie au tub s'épongeant* (*Marie Bathing with a Sponge*), 1908

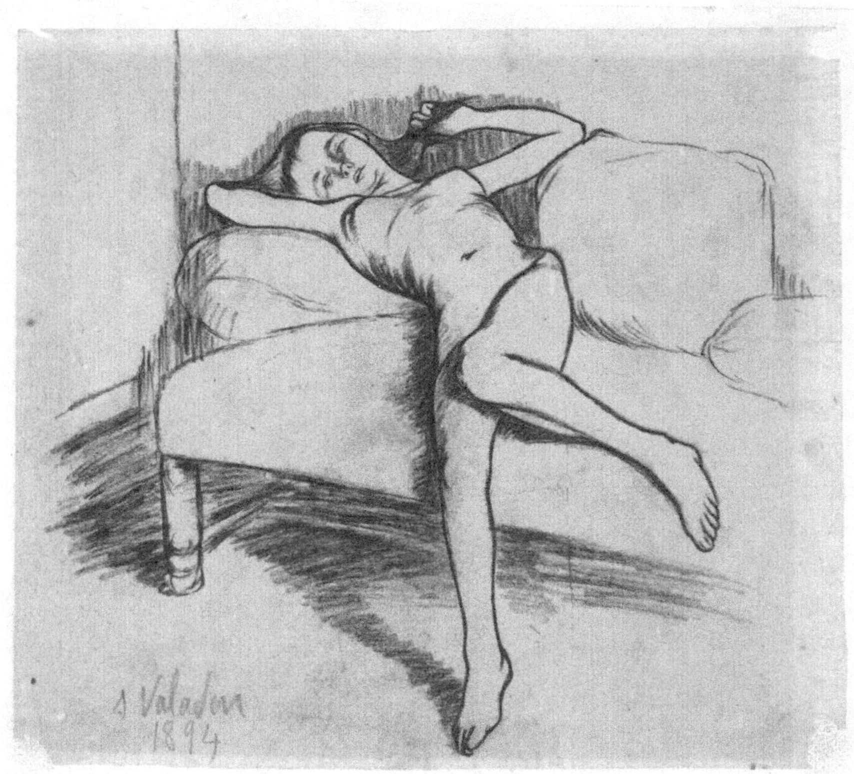

Figure 3.2 Suzanne Valadon, *Fillette nue allongée sur un canapé* (*Nude Girl Reclining on a Sofa*), 1894

Utrillo nu debout, jouant du pied avec une cuvette (1894). The girls and boys are isolated in barren environments, with only a table or floorboard to ground them. Like a photographer, Valadon hones in on the children's bodies from a high angle, with a downward gaze. The sketches are astonishingly raw. Gouged lines define their gangling forms and knotty joints as if incised not by charcoal but by burin. Valadon's incisive draftsmanship clearly demarcates the figures. The contours are so prominent that the bodies impress the viewer in a nearly tactile manner.

Valadon's bathers bespeak the influence of Degas, particularly in their unconventional techniques. When Valadon met the artist, he had already entered a late stage of his career. By 1886, with the Impressionism exhibitions coming to a close, Degas gradually began to retire from public life. He no longer exhibited his work regularly, unlike his Impressionist colleagues, Monet and Renoir. Nevertheless, as many scholars have demonstrated, this was an important period of production and innovation for Degas.[61] His penchant for experimentation was renewed with fervor. He returned repeatedly to the same motif, varying it slightly. His exploratory approach to the body

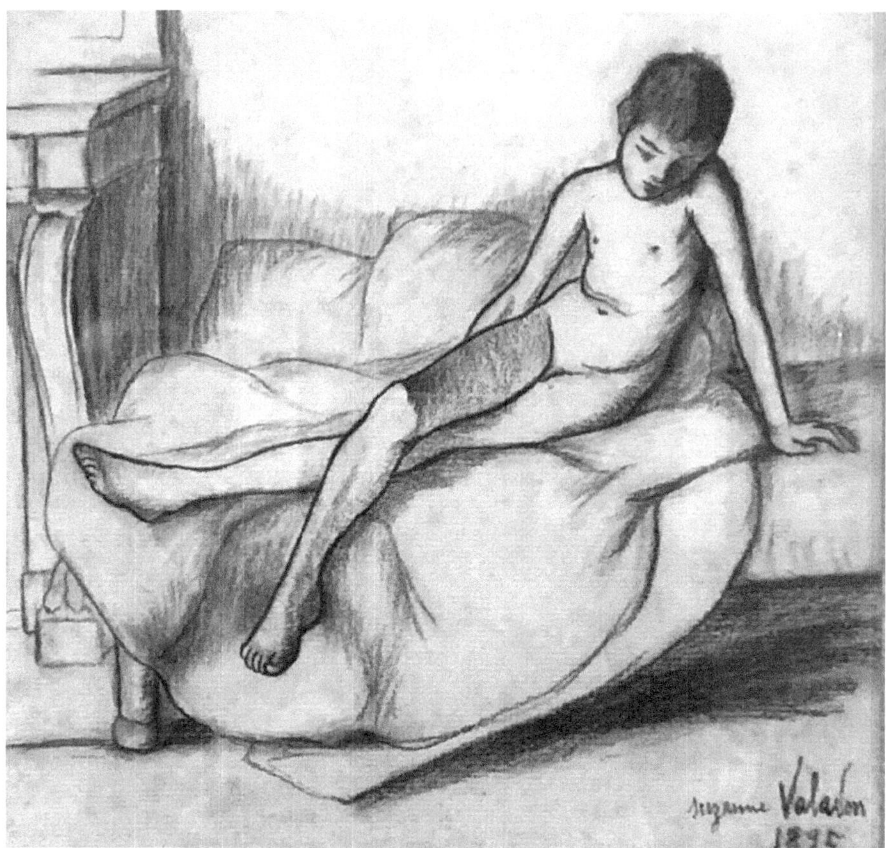

Figure 3.3 Suzanne Valadon, *Maurice Utrillo nu assis sur un divan* (*Maurice Utrillo Nude on a Couch*), 1895

would have a profound effect on Valadon.[62] In numerous works, she executes an analogous composition, varying it ever so slightly. In others, such as the aforementioned *Maurice Utrillo nu assis sur un divan*, she renders the same composition in reverse. These inverted drawings are likely *contre-épreuve* (counter proof), a technique that Degas employed in his late works. The process involved running a drawing attached to a moistened sheet of paper through a printing press, producing a reversed impression on the other sheet.[63] Her proclivity for repetition and novel practices substantiates a heightened interchange with Degas. As Richard Thomson surmises, "Duplication and multiplication, abbreviation and amplification, repetition and revision, formed the hub of Degas' late studio practice."[64]

Photographs in Degas's collection served as further stimulus for Valadon's bathers. *Après le bain* (1908) (figure 3.4), for example, closely approximates a gelatin silver print by Degas with the same title (1896). This photograph served as source

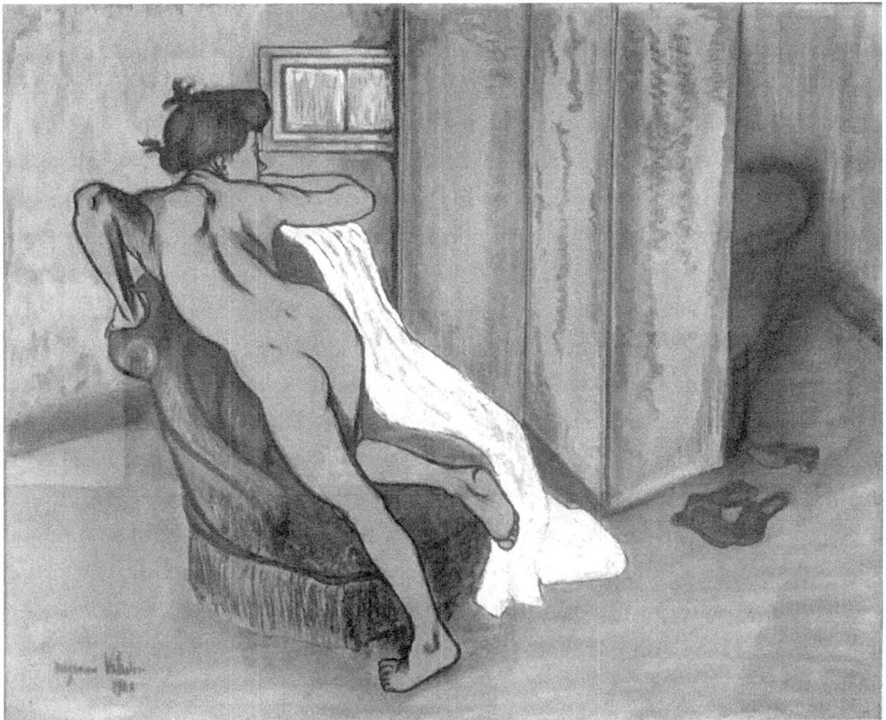

Figure 3.4 Suzanne Valadon, *Après le bain* (*After the Bath*), 1908

material for several works by Degas, including *After the Bath (Woman Drying Herself)* (1896). Valadon similarly reworks the composition in her pastel, inverting the figure's position and applying vibrant hues. A range of pulsating colors, including fuchsia, turquoise, cobalt, green and yellow, creates a striking contrast with the figure, which is left bare. A white towel cascades past the body, drawing attention to its naked state. The torsions of the limbs and curvature of the spine are accentuated, flanked by Venusian dimples. Her elbow and the sole of one foot jut outward forcefully. Yet, Valadon's image departs from the photograph in a few significant ways. In the gelatin silver print, the body tilts awkwardly over the sofa, as the woman stretches to one side. This pose appears contrived and unnatural. Her head is barely visible, engulfed by the surrounding shadows. By contrast, Valadon's nude does not lounge around languidly, but appears startled and alert. Her head is erect, and her profile is visible as she turns suddenly, as if surprised by an intruder. The possibility of a voyeur creates a heightened tension in the composition. It also demonstrates Valadon's awareness of the complexities of the gaze – both of the audience, whose gaze might be set into motion, and of the subject – who is conscious of a potential onlooker.

Like those of Degas, Valadon's bathing scenes are rooted in everyday life and capture a sense of the momentary. Still, hers depart from his in intention, meaning and affect. While in many of Degas's late bathers, the faces are obscured by shadow or cropped out of the image, Valadon does not habitually omit or distort her nudes' faces. She often reinforces her bathers' identities in lieu of their customary anonymity by including the first names of her models in the titles of her drawings.[65] Louise and Catherine are among the models she portrayed. Moreover, the settings are notably different. In Degas's *Femme sortant du bain* (1877), the seemingly bourgeois interior, with decorative wallpaper, carpeting and an armchair, recalls the garish décor of a *fin-de-siècle* brothel. In contrast, Valadon's figures appear in simple interiors bereft of ornamentation. The humble domestic environments reinforce the working-class status of the bathers. In *Catherine nue se coiffant* (1895), for instance, the room is sparse. Devoid of ornament, it contains only the essentials: an unadorned washstand, mirror and tub. The model poses awkwardly with her knees bent and her arms raised as she combs her hair. Seen from behind, the viewer catches a glimpse of an intimate moment, without a tinge of voyeuristic fantasy. In *Study for Children's Bath in the Garden* (figure 3.5), Valadon portrays children bathing and dressing outdoors with their caretakers. Attention is drawn to a young girl who attempts to button the back of her dress. Whereas the female helper is an indication that Degas's bathers are prostitutes, since "maids were an obvious part of the hierarchy of the brothel," the maternal or grandmotherly attendants Valadon depicts negate any such association (figure 3.6, figure 3.7, figure 3.8).[66] Finally, she draws upon a wider array of models of myriad sizes, shapes and ages, all in different states of awareness. Without exception, Degas represented only women in his bather series. Valadon portrayed children and adults of both sexes in analogous scenes, scenarios and poses.

In her numerous depictions of female bathers, Valadon evades the subject that so intrigued Degas and his Impressionist counterparts – prostitution. As a former model, she would have been well aware of the stereotypes associated with the profession. For a woman, posing nude was seen as a gateway into the sex trade. Placing men and children in analogous poses and settings lends credence to the fact that hers are not brothel scenes. While Degas's contemporaries assumed that his bathers were prostitutes,[67] critics did not perceive Valadon's work in this way.[68] Instead, they often mistook her realistic depictions of bathers as an aversion toward the female sex. Certain critics reacted vehemently to her work. Jean Vertex wrote:

> The sensuality with this fiery and implacable woman is expressed to the detriment of sensitivity ... She hates women and avenges the charms that they could have by condemning them by line, by such a faithful resemblance that not a detail is neglected, idealizing them as little as possible.[69]

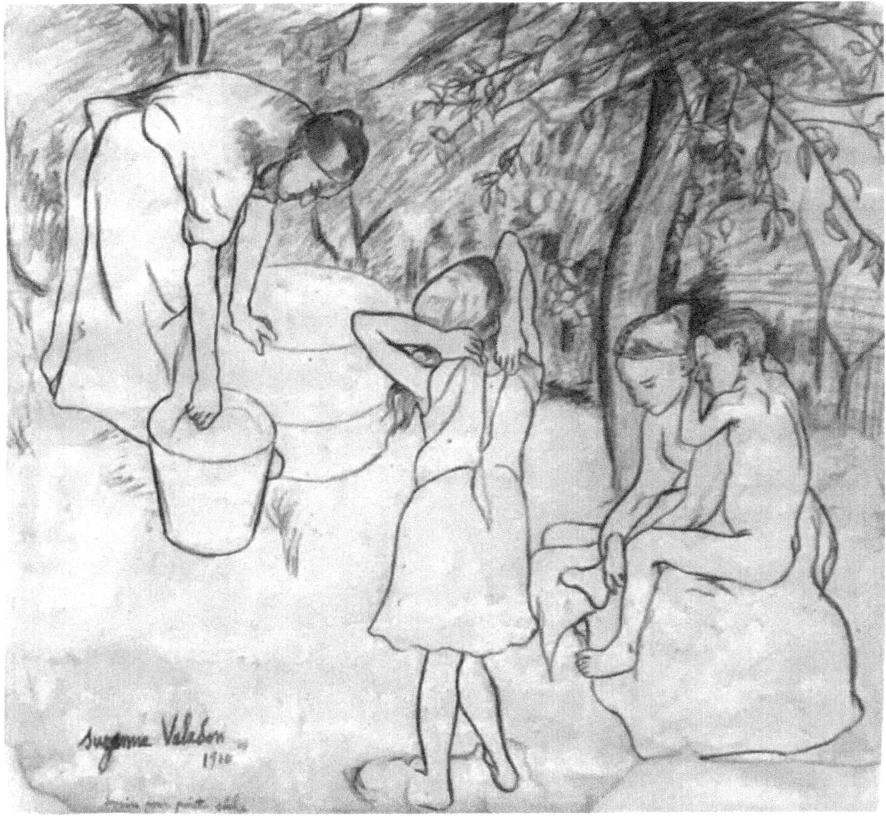

Figure 3.5 Suzanne Valadon, *Study for Children's Bath in the Garden*, 1910

Her bathers were exceedingly jagged and rough. Another critic described Valadon's approach as animalistic, "with the supple nature of an acrobat, a cat-like voluptuousness, attention that brings loving hatred, the human body in its most disgraced and animal state."[70] Her blunt and ostensibly unrefined style was mistaken as a debasement of the nude. Likely in response to such critical remarks, Valadon wrote, "You shouldn't put suffering in your drawings, but all the same, nothing is achieved without pain."[71]

Contemporaries repeatedly noted her bold and lyrical contours. Robert Rey wrote:

> She employs contours, the black and long line that creates a volume and unravels the plans already well established by the patient play of values. This contour is like a graphic pleasure and I also believe that it exists for the somewhat tactile eye of an Ingres, a Degas, a Lautrec.[72]

In Valadon's work, line creates volume, rather than the longstanding techniques of shading and modeling. Degas cited line as one difference in their approach.

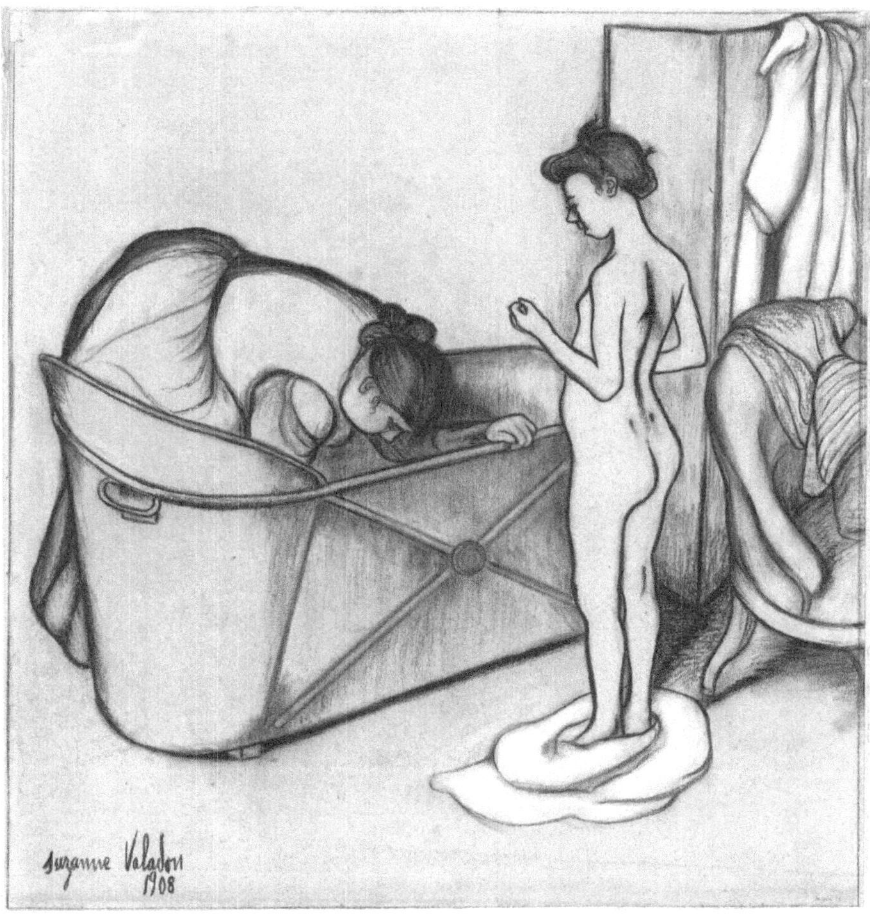

Figure 3.6 Suzanne Valadon, *Before the Bath*, 1908

He described in his letters to "terrible Maria" her "wicked and supple drawings." He remarked that her writing too, like her draftsmanship, appears "drawn like a saw."[73] There was something aggressive but also pliant in her work that enchanted him. He was also impressed by her sheer virtuosity. Later, in an interview with Marie-Anne Camax-Zoegger, founder of the Société des Femmes Artistes Modernes (FAM), Valadon claimed that she never used erasers.[74] She mastered and manipulated line with the skill and precision of a trained artist, which she never was.

All of Valadon's bathers, whether male or female, are incised by a heavy and coarse line. Degas's bathers from the 1880s and 1890s have been described in a similar manner. George Shackelford observes that "with their expressionistic simplification of form and tough, spare use of rich charcoal contours, they show the draftsman at his most bold and stand as indelible images of Degas's late transformation of his style."[75]

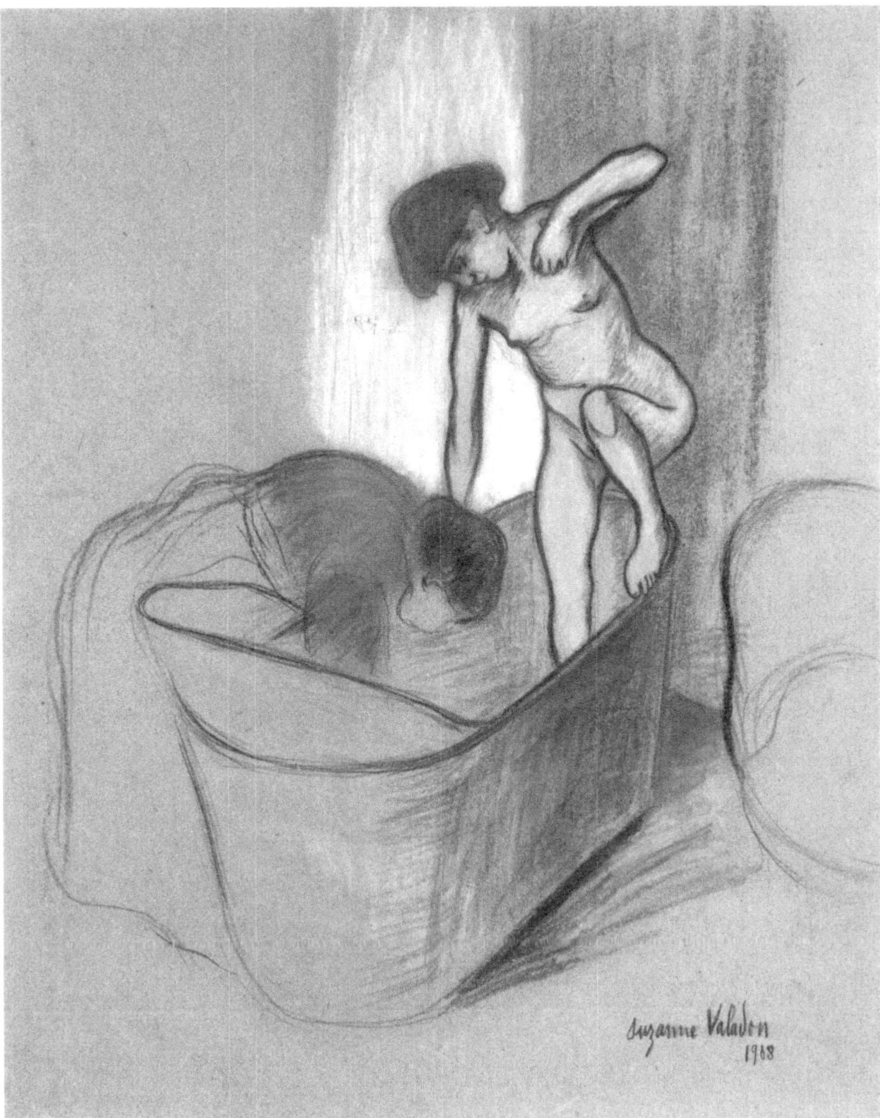

Figure 3.7 Suzanne Valadon, *La Toilette* (*The Bath*), 1908

Yet, Valadon's approach is marked by even greater rigor and sparser shading. In *La Toilette* (1908) she rigidly contours the girl's form. She traces the angular silhouette robustly, from the wrist to the scapula, spinal column and down to the fibula, ridding the image of suppleness. The flesh, uncolored, is denoted by the russet shade of the paper. The scrawny nude is an assemblage of knotty joints, an attenuated torso and gangly limbs. Degas depicted a related motif in *Bather Stepping into a Tub*, c. 1890.

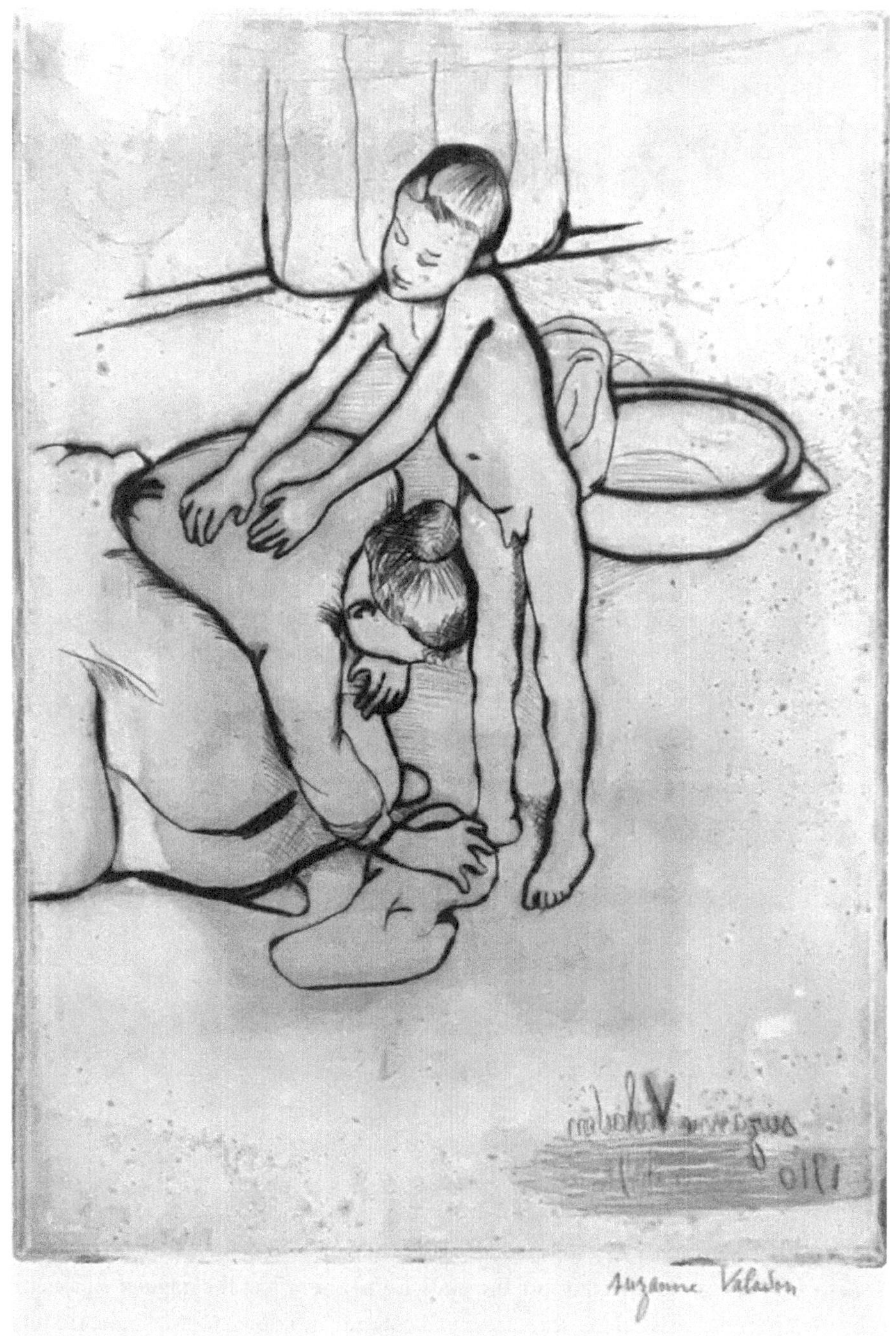

Figure 3.8 Suzanne Valadon, *Catherine et jeune garçon nu* (*Catherine and Young Nude Boy*), 1910

With greater proximity to the subject, and a repetitious, cascading pastel stroke, the figure's gaucheness is nearly canceled out by an emphasis on sumptuous flesh. Although Degas's bathers do not conform to contemporary standards of feminine beauty, they are not entirely devoid of sensuality.[76] By depicting the awkward contortions of the bather's underdeveloped body, Valadon rids the image of the kind of soft voluptuousness which lingers in Degas's pastels.[77] In grasping the idiosyncrasies of the human form, Valadon assembles as much as she disassembles the body. In some drawings, body parts seem dislocated or disjointed. Incising the bather as if using a "saw," she seems to be grappling with the body viscerally, attempting to seize all of the oddities and contortions, and lending each figure a strong sense of physicality. Valadon recognized her own emboldened, nearly physical approach to the medium: "I drew wildly so that when I could no longer see, I would have them at my fingertips."[78] With her pronounced heavy line, she carves out bodies that assert themselves from the surface like sculpture in the round.

In printmaking, Valadon's dense contours become even more prominent. She learned printmaking from Degas; there is mention of this in one of his undated letters.[79] Valadon created a series of twelve *vernis mou* (soft ground etchings) of bathers between 1895 and 1896.[80] These include images of Utrillo and his grandmother as well as female models. The emphasis on linearity and sense of spontaneity that marks her drawings is equally visible in her prints. She translated some of her drawings, such as *Catherine nue se coiffant* (1895) into soft ground etchings, mirrored in reverse. The continuous heavy line, hard-edged contours and overall austerity of her prints demonstrate her unwavering predilection for bold draftsmanship, no matter the media.

Degas exposed Valadon to the monotype, through which she reworked and revised several of her bather drawings such as *Catherine nue se coiffant*. Repetition and adaptation, mirroring and reversal – one motif could result in numerous variations. In this print and others, the gouged line gives plasticity and weight to the woman's rotund form. Around 1905, she also began executing dry points, including *Marie au tub s'épongeant* (*Marie Bathing with a Sponge*, 1908) (figure 3.1) and *Catherine et jeune garçon nu* (*Catherine and Young Nude Boy*, 1910) (figure 3.8). She depicts an adult female and a male child, respectively, nude and with a wash basin, bordering their bodies with a heavy line, a couple of millimeters in thickness. Claude Roger-Marx noted her powerful, "masculine" approach to printmaking:

> The engraved work of Suzanne Valadon brings to light the incomparable power of one of the only women painters who mastered the hard metal. No [other woman] dares to carry the pencil and the chisel like offensive weapons like men for it is also a war to imprison form ... and to give it a master.[81]

The critic compares Valadon's "incomparable power" in handling the burin with a soldier wielding a weapon. No other female artist "mastered the hard metal" in such a commanding way, according to Roger-Marx. He noted that Valadon's printer, Delatre, was astonished by the deep furrows she dug into the zinc plates when making dry-point prints, and compared her technique to that of a plowman.[82] As a woman artist, she contradicted the expected display of timidity, weakness and inadequate mastery. And as a printmaker, she embarked upon what was historically considered male terrain.[83] Her emboldened use of the chisel in her prints or *crayon noir* (black pencil) in her drawings lends her work a sense of immediacy and materiality rather than artistic finish. Her dark application of pencil, charcoal or engraved line which briskly accents the spine, buttocks, limbs and folds of flesh testifies to her assured and assertive hand. Valadon consistently employs line not simply to differentiate form but also to endow significance to the human figure. Her forceful draftsmanship and printmaking practice accents the corporeality and embodiment of her bathers. Adding to the images' impact is the fact that the nudes are caught in authentic, uncensored moments that are not especially flattering. This augments the sense of the everyday, lived experience.

Through their rough, unfinished linear quality combined with their impromptu poses, Valadon depicts her bathers in an intricate and evolving state of becoming, like the medium of drawing itself. According to the philosopher Alain Badiou, drawing is in a constant state of materialization or coming into being:

> It is that sort of movable reciprocity between existence and inexistence which constitutes the very essence of Drawing. The question of Drawing is very different from the question in Hamlet. It is not "to be or not to be," it is "to be *and* not to be." And that is the reason for the fundamental fragility of Drawing: not a clear alternative, to be or not to be, but an obscure and paradoxical conjunction, to be and not to be.[84]

Using the media of drawing and printmaking, Valadon emphasizes the embodied presence of her subjects. She captures a fleeting moment of an emergent body that is unstable and impermanent. This sense of the transient body is strongly present in all of her bathers – whether child or adult, male or female. Later, Valadon would apply the same stress on physicality to the grown, masculine figure in uncensored, quotidian moments. We shall see how these drawings upend the conventions for the representation of the male nude.

Painting the male nude

Valadon would not portray her son nude past early adolescence, but rather adopted André Utter as her muse. He would have a great impact on her art and career.

Utter states in an important, unpublished account detailing Valadon's career that she had executed around ten or so paintings when they met.[85] This is corroborated by the catalogue raisonné which includes apporximately fifteen paintings before 1909.[86] He encouraged her to paint and exhibit at the chief art salons in Paris – the Salon d'Automne and the Salon des Indépendants.[87] Valadon showed her work regularly at these venues starting in 1909. By the time she met Utter, she had already acquired considerable artistic knowledge, especially from her mentor, Degas, and was well connected in the art world. Still, she would benefit further from Utter's creative support, his impressive network of artists and intellectuals, as well as his deepened awareness of the latest artistic trends. An electrician by trade, he was also a self-taught artist with considerable art historical knowledge.[88] In his handwritten account, he mentions regular visits to the Louvre and other Paris museums, and later, his encounters with luminaries in Montmartre.[89] The first letter from Valadon to Utter dated 23 September 1909 mentions their proposed rendezvous at a museum.[90] Catherine Hewitt writes:

> Utter was not merely a shallow dilettante drawn towards the nearest party, but was a shrewd and informed connoisseur of avant-garde art. He studied and read assiduously and could legitimise any new or controversial idea he might espouse with a back catalogue of theoretical and historical knowledge.[91]

Equally, Utter had much to gain from Valadon's professional experience as both a model and an artist, as well as her art-world contacts. Paula Birnbaum notes that, although Utter was well connected, "it is likely that he looked up to Valadon … and that he viewed her as a mentor of sorts."[92] Paul Mousis, whom she had married in 1896, supported Valadon financially, allowing her to stop modeling, but Utter bolstered her with encouragement and expertise. She must have realized her potential when she renounced the financial security her bourgeois husband offered. She divorced Mousis in 1910 and married Utter four years later. Utter agreed to pose, and an intimate artistic dialogue ensued between them.

When they met in 1909, Utter was in his early twenties, only three years older than Utrillo, hence his gauche adolescent-like appearance in *Adam and Eve* (1909) (Plate 20), Valadon's first painting of a male nude. The work marks her passage full stroke into the realm of easel painting. Yet, she retains the hand of a draftsman, incising the figures with razor-sharp outlines of bluish-black paint. Her unidealized approach to the body clearly had its naissance in her sketches of young Utrillo. The painting shares with the bathing scenes a brazen, unflinching realism. His body is not heroically muscular but bony and emaciated. He appears limp, even Christ-like. Perhaps Valadon was looking to Crucifixion imagery, or at contemporary renditions, such as *The Yellow Christ* (1889) by Gauguin, an artist whom she openly admired.[93] The emboldened line defining Utter's body and the zones of unmodulated color in the landscape recall the Nabis technique of Cloisonnism, evident in *The Yellow Christ*. Valadon departs from Gauguin by accentuating the body with a wide range of hues. Layering gradations of white jade, amber and turquoise, she models the figure with luminous color. As a result, the skin does not appear smooth, but is richly textured. This painterly treatment of flesh would become a staple in Valadon's oeuvre.

Adam and Eve is not just a male nude. In this painting, Valadon audaciously portrays herself naked next to her partner, in a nearly life-sized nude self-portrait. Each figure's identity is immediately recognizable, although, at the time, critics did not outwardly name the models despite the explicit likeness.[94] Valadon subverts gendered codes by displaying the male and female body with the same steadfast realism. By 1909, the figure of Eve had become a symbol of modern womanhood. Birnbaum states that this biblical character served as "an archetype of modern femininity upon which popular sexologists, novelists, and visual artists inscribed larger conflicts surrounding the woman question."[95] Valadon wholly epitomizes "Modern Eve." Rather than modestly hide her own body, she shows off her youthful figure with her long hair swept to the side. She ignores the conventions of the male nude, by not transforming Utter into a timeless figure, but accentuating his unique physical characteristics. He appears awkward with his boyish figure and gawky limbs. They are not passive but moving forward, with arms interlocked. Valadon appropriates a time-honored biblical and art historical theme to stake her claim as a defiant painter of nude self-portraits and male nudes. In Valadon's version, there is no serpent, and the man is her accomplice as they reach for the apple together.

Now, imagine if there were no fig leaves. A preparatory sketch along with a photograph from 1909 shows the original version, in which Utter's genitalia are exposed in full-frontal nudity. Valadon added the fig leaves in order to exhibit *Adam and Eve*, over a decade later, at the Salon des Indépendants in 1920.[96] Although the exhibition was unjuried, it is probable that officials, stunned by the display of male nudity, required the painting to be censored. Even with the fig leaves, *Adam and Eve* lies far outside the boundaries of female propriety. Not only does the work exhibit a male nude, but Valadon is unabashed by her own naked body. Only Utter is covered; Valadon's pubic hair is shamelessly visible. This makes her appear even more confident. Utter seems self-conscious, leaning toward Valadon, who guides him assuredly forward. With his feet turned inward, there seems to be an awkward hesitation in his step. Beautiful and sexy, she depicts herself as a woman endowed with confidence and a libido. This painting bravely demonstrates a woman's sexual capacity and female heterosexual desire, something which was seldom professed in art by women during Valadon's lifetime. The artist inscribes herself in the history of art as an undaunted and sexually liberated female painter. *Adam and Eve* is an intrepid reshaping of both the nude genre and female self-representation.

There are no contemporaneous examples of exhibited male nudes by French female artists to compare with *Adam and Eve*.[97] While women artists engaged with the nude genre increasingly toward the end of the nineteenth century in France, they limited themselves to the female body. For a bourgeois woman to paint the male nude was considered socially objectionable.[98] During the second half of the nineteenth century, affluent women could enroll in private academies in Paris, which had fewer restrictions regarding life drawing.[99] Yet when faced with the nude, it was nearly always a female model or a fully or partially clothed male model.[100] The mere idea of a woman viewing a naked man in an art studio or classroom caused a great deal of anxiety amongst French artists and academicians in the 1880s and 1890s. Women's chastity had to be preserved.[101] What's more, it was believed that the presence of female students in life-drawing classes would negatively impact the male students' capacity to study the nude, thereby threatening the entire art system.[102] Women were thus banned from the prestigious École Nationale des Beaux-Arts until the very end of the century. This effectively prevented them from competing with their male counterparts, particularly in the important domain of history painting.

By tackling the male nude, Valadon was trespassing on a traditionally male artistic terrain. As Abigail Solomon-Godeau explains, "the ideal male body was the very linchpin" of French academic art and classical art theory.[103] Furthermore, "mastery of the representation of the male ideal was considered the most formally and intellectually demanding aspect of art practice, combining as it did the labor of mimesis with the requisite imagination to ennoble the raw material of brute nature."[104] Only men were considered capable of this arduous feat. Women's rootedness in their bodies hampered their attainment of the ideal in art.[105] Not only were they unable to transform a naked body into an idealized form, but they were also incapable of producing great art altogether. Garb notes:

> The capacity to create great art was conceived of as a function of the operation of the highest powers of intellect and imagination. It was improbable, in the light of contemporary medical and psychological understanding, that women could possess the characteristics needed for such an elevated practice.[106]

When women were finally admitted into the École in 1897, and granted equal state-funded art education in 1900, that institution's importance had greatly diminished.[107] At the same time, the male body, which had once populated canvases of neoclassical and academic art, had all but been replaced with the female nude. In a rapidly changing art world and burgeoning gallery system, women artists faced a new set of obstacles.

The genre of the nude was now a vehicle for expression of a male artist's "originality," virility, and sexuality – an endeavor from which women were once again excluded.[108]

To circumvent these restrictions, some women turned to their own bodies as prime subject matter. Just as Valadon was tackling her own image, so too was Paula Modersohn-Becker, a German artist who went to Paris several times and moved there in 1906 to pursue her career; she died in 1907 of complications from childbirth. Notably, Modersohn-Becker and Valadon both explored nude self-portraiture at the same moment without awareness of each other's work. The result, however, could not be more distinct. In *Self-Portrait on the 6th Wedding Anniversary* (1906), Modersohn-Becker displays herself with her arms enveloping her swollen abdomen as she gazes assuredly out at the viewer. She wears only a beaded necklace and a long skirt. Diane Radycki states that Modersohn-Becker "painted the female body from within its immanent life, a radical spectacle of skin and pubic hair."[109] Although she does not expose pubic hair in this self-portrait, she would do so in others. Any display of body hair on a female nude was taboo and prone to censorship in the early decades of the twentieth century. Modersohn-Becker's 1906 self-portrait is a highly innovative portrayal of the subject of pregnancy in paint (she was not pregnant at the time, but would become pregnant shortly afterward). With its playful self-sexualizing, *Adam and Eve* has little to do with the theme of pregnancy. Valadon exposes her naked body, pubic hair and all, in a pioneering display of female sexual consciousness and desire.

Valadon contested the exclusionary artistic establishment and male-dominated avant-garde in *Adam and Eve* and subsequent male nudes. Utter inspired another large-scale painting, *La Joie de vivre* (1911). Four female bathers appear in a landscape, unaware of a naked male onlooker.[110] The enigmatic context and eclectic poses of the figures recall Degas's *Scène de guerre au Moyen Age* (c. 1865). Valadon would have seen the painting in his studio where it remained until his death.[111] Unlike *Scène de guerre*, *La Joie de vivre* features a male nude. She exhibited *La Joie de vivre* in the 1911 Salon d'Automne where it largely went unnoticed.[112] Valadon's subversivism was difficult to comprehend by her contemporaries. Nevertheless, such a painting is a milestone for women artists. The feminist painter Sylvia Sleigh later noted the major impediments for women artists before her – restrictions on studying and painting the male nude and, consequently, the inability to compete within the esteemed category of history painting. She concluded, "One reason for a woman to do large figure compositions is to say, 'Look here, I can!'"[113] Although *La Joie de vivre* lacks a sense of aesthetic cohesion, Valadon aimed to validate her art within the "Grand Tradition," while simultaneously challenging it.

From 1909 to 1914, Valadon and Utter sketched and painted each other frequently. In *Suzanne Valadon se coiffant* (1913), the distorted perspective of the room, emphasis on geometric form and flat planes of vibrant hues demonstrate Utter's adherence to Modernist currents. Departing from nature, the panoply of loud colors on the body mirror those found in the tapestry in the background. Valadon appears again in Utter's *Trois nus* (c. 1913), where she poses from three angles. Her form is geometricized to a greater degree and her individualized characteristics are erased. Taking cues from Cubism, Utter reduces the body to cones and cylinders. Apollinaire took note of this painting (or one similar) exhibited in the 1913 Salon des Indépendants, stating, "Utter sends *Three Graces* with a probing realism; talent that develops."[114]

The two swapped roles for *Le Lancement du filet* (Plate 21). This time, Valadon represents Utter three times just as she had been portrayed. Like Utter, Valadon takes up the challenge of representing a modern nude. The figures are arranged at nearly the same angles as those in *Trois nus*. Shown from the back, side and front, the progressive rotation of a single figure in space recalls early cinema and also brings to mind Eadweard Muybridge's photography. In positioning Utter from various vantage points, she represents the male body as a passive object to be admired – just as she had been displayed countless times in art. An ambitious painting, colossal in scale, it measures around six and a half by ten feet. Valadon combines the Impressionist preoccupation of painting a figure *en plein air* with a Post-Impressionist palette. The painting was conceived during the couple's sojourn in 1913 in Corsica, where they visited the towns of Corte and Belgodère.[115] Valadon composed a number of sketches of Utter nude in the wild landscape, and completed the painting in her studio in 1914. After their return to Paris, the couple married and Utter joined the army.[116]

In *Le Lancement*, Utter is no longer maladroit and youthful as seen in *Adam and Eve*, but has been transformed into a robust figure. Valadon eliminates Utter's individual characteristics and adjusts his skin tone from an ashen, greenish hue to a golden bronze. The visage is generalized and has little in common with Utter's own facial traits. She pays greater attention to the body, which is highly idealized. The figures exhibit "proportion, symmetry, elasticity, and aplomb," the essential attributes for an ideal male nude.[117] Furthermore, two out of the three figures stand in a contrapposto pose, with weight shifted to one hip, giving a sense of naturalistic movement and rhythm. While Valadon does not render the genitalia, she suggests them by emphasizing the pelvic muscles. These strong lines, which divide the torso from the lower half of the body, are important "elements in the classical architecture of the human body" and assert the masculinity of the figure.[118] Rather than model the figure with chiaroscuro, Valadon creates a strong silhouette through a series of bold, flowing lines. Like a crenellation encompassing the body, they have a relief-producing effect. These contours emphasize the figure's athletic build, his powerful torso and slender but sturdy limbs.

While Valadon adheres to many of the rules for representing the male nude, she simultaneously includes a number of pictorial tools typically reserved for the female nude. She depicts man embedded in nature – an uncommon association. His figure is rendered with a kaleidoscopic palette of orange peel, salmon, ochre and olivine, applied synchronistically with short and vigorous brushwork. These hues mimic those found on the rocks and mountains in the background. Valadon's accent on vibrant and warm colors, as well as the livened facture, draws parallels between man and landscape. Rather than blend with their surroundings, the nudes take on a monumental presence within the composition. Larger than life-size, the central figure's head breaches the upper limit of the picture plane like the hyacinth mountain in the distance. Pushed to the foreground, the sequence of bodies reads like a classical frieze. In displaying the body from three angles, Valadon makes reference to the classical theme of the "Three Graces." As in Rubens's *The Three Graces* (1639), Utter stands gracefully in contrapposto pose, with arched feet. His arms are outstretched almost close enough to form an embrace. He holds the ropes of a net that wrap around his body in the same poised manner as the graces carrying their drapery. Like gauzy, flowing fabric, the net veils and unveils the body, further drawing attention to the figure's nudity. In form and pose, the nudes lure and seduce the eye.

Bathing, which was a common subject in art since antiquity, experienced a renaissance during Valadon's lifetime.[119] Many late nineteenth-century artists depicted bathing scenes to show the nude in a naturalistic setting removed from historical or mythological contexts. By the turn of the century, artists began tackling the subject to demonstrate radical stylistic innovations. But it was the female body that served as the subject of experimentation. There are only a few examples of outdoor male bathers in turn-of-the-century French painting, including Georges Seurat's *Bathers at Asnières* (1884) and Cézanne's *Le Baigneur au rocher* (1860–66) and *Baigneurs* (c. 1890).[120] Such images are notable exceptions in the seemingly endless pool of female bathers from this period.

Given its heightened popularity and her firsthand experience with it as a model, it is only fitting that Valadon would address this theme. She appears in a number of bathing scenes by these artists, including Renoir's *The Large Bathers* and Puvis's mural *Le Bois sacré* (1884).[121] In the latter, she posed for nearly all of the figures, both male and female: "I'm here, and then there, and almost all these figures borrowed something from me. I posed not only as women, but as young lads … Puvis asked me to give him an attitude, a movement, a gesture. He transposed and idealized me."[122] The harmonious proportions of the nudes in *Le Lancement* reflect the classical treatment of the body evident in Puvis's work. Moreover, the experience of modeling for both female and male figures would facilitate her association of male and female attributes in her own art. After having learned how to adeptly position her own body as a model, Valadon would apply these same skills as an artist, displaying Utter from the most complimentary angles. She effectively mobilized a career of posing her own body before male painters, tactfully transposing the masculine model into elegant and idealized figures on her own canvas.

Valadon's palette and brushwork depart from Puvis's and bespeak the influence of Gauguin and Cézanne. She would have seen their works in Degas's collection. In fact, Degas's house afforded Valadon the opportunity to study works by the masters and the newest generation of artists. An entire floor of his house served as a "museum" in which he displayed his collection.[123] In one of the only surviving written accounts by Valadon, she paid tribute to Gauguin and stated that she applied Pont-Aven techniques, "without a trace of aestheticism or artificiality, all with force of life."[124] Outside Degas's home, she could have seen Gauguin's work at the Volpini Exhibition held at the Café des Arts near the official art exhibition of the *Exposition universelle* in Paris, 1889, and later at his retrospective at the Salon d'Automne in 1906. In *Le Lancement*, the touches of violine and neptune green amongst patches of raw umber on the rugged landscape along with the shimmering, ultramarine-blue water recall Gauguin's liberal use of color. But as she herself acknowledged, her palette was not arbitrary; she never fully departed from nature in her use of color. At the same time, the visible constructive stroke and flat planes of color are reminiscent of Cézanne. She presumably saw Cézanne's images of bathers. However, his architectonic, frozen and malformed bodies are at odds with Valadon's luscious and sensual treatment of the male nude.

In composition and subject matter, *Le Lancement* most directly recalls Frédéric Bazille's *Le Pêcheur à l'épervier* (1868). This painting was exhibited at the Bazille retrospective at the Salon d'Automne in 1910.[125] Valadon showed her work at the Salon that year and thus would surely have seen it. In *Le Pêcheur* two male nudes appear on the banks of the Lez river, near Montpellier. Sunlight filters through the trees creating patches of light on the grassy riverbank. One figure stands next to the water holding a fishing net, while the other undresses in the background. As with *Le Lancement*, the work may be informed by classical iconography. The Hellenistic sculpture *Boy with Thorn* has been cited as a possible source for the seated nude's pose.[126] The standing figure is viewed from behind, in a comparable position as the left-hand figure in *Le Lancement*. Like Valadon, Bazille pays great attention to anatomy, articulating the muscles, backbone, shoulder blades and buttocks. In Bazille's image, the clothes strewn on the ground reinforce the naked state of the men and push the painting outside the realm of acceptable male nudity in art. While it is common to find the female nude undressed in nature with her clothes piled on the grass, the male nude rarely is portrayed this way.[127] The jury of the Salon may well have detected the erotic undertones, as they rejected *Le Pêcheur* from the Salon in 1869.[128]

Le Pêcheur and *Le Lancement* parade the male body in a manner normally reserved for female nudes. Both artists display the male body in nature, ignoring the time-honored principle that women belong to nature and men to culture.[129] Using nascent impressionist techniques, Bazille displays his nudes in a contemporary, *plein air* scene, firmly positioning his men within modern-day life. There is a notable absence of female bodies, which normally help to affirm the heterosexuality of the male viewer. Instead, the male body is the sole object of the viewer's gaze. Furthermore, the nudes are unaware of the spectator. This is especially pronounced in *Le Pêcheur*, which has voyeuristic undertones; the men are oblivious to the viewer as they relax naked on the riverbank. In *Le Lancement*, the figures' eyes are likewise averted from the viewers', while emphasis is placed on the athletic beauty of the male body. Both works plainly cast the male body as an object of desire.

Art historians have discussed this and other paintings of male bathers by Bazille in relation to homoeroticism.[130] A homoerotic image is one that permits male viewers to take pleasure in the male body. Michael Hatt lucidly explores the concept in an essay on Eakins's *The Swimming Hole* (1884–85), a painting inspired by Bazille's male bathers.[131] His analysis has also proved useful for Bazille's work and has been cited by Bazille scholars.[132] I contend that the issues of homoeroticism that pertain to Bazille's and Eakins's male bathers are obliquely related to Valadon's *Le Lancement*. Hatt states that "the homoerotic unproblematically marks a particular desire of one man for another, an expression of homosexual desire framed in a particular, perhaps subtle or covert manner."[133] The homoerotic image often does not reveal desire in a conspicuous way, but instead partly conceals that desire.[134] In both *Le Lancement* and *Le Pêcheur*, the male genitalia are fully hidden, and the figures engage in the manly activity of fishing. Furthermore, the figures do not interact directly with one another. Sexuality is insinuated in elusive ways by showing off the figures' muscularity and youthful forms, and, in Bazille's case, by including the piles of clothing. The homoerotic is normally concealed through the use of an allegorical framework. Traditionally, artists would legitimize the male nude with mythological or historical references and moral content.[135] Neither Valadon nor Bazille provides the necessary context for their male nudes – they fail to justify the nakedness of their male figures in any legitimate way. Their fishermen do not aggressively assert phallic power, nor do they illustrate a historical, mythological or biblical tale. Without narrative or moral structure, these images offer no defensible reason for spectatorship. Their male nudes are simply displayed as handsome bodies for the viewer's enjoyment.

A number of art historians have speculated about Bazille's possible homosexuality and its impact on his art, although never with any conclusive evidence. Any deviation from masculine, heteronormative sexuality seems to spark excitement and conjecture from art critics and scholars alike. For a woman artist, any display of sexuality at all transmutes her into an abnormality – it desexes her. Valadon's critical reception, biographies, and even recent art historical literature are riddled with gossip about her love life, while speculations on the identity of Utrillo's father add an additional element of intrigue.[136] Her libertine comportment is emphasized repeatedly, to the point of overshadowing her work.[137] Accounts ruminate about her liaisons with other artists, including Toulouse-Lautrec, Erik Satie and an unlikely affair with Puvis de Chavannes, forty-one years her senior.[138] Ultimately, whether the viewer is informed about Bazille's or Valadon's sexuality makes little difference. According to Hatt's definition, homoeroticism in art is not dependent on the artist's sexual orientation. Merely displaying the male body as an aesthetic object highlights pleasure and insinuates desire for it. Mary Manning elaborates upon Hatt's reading of the homoerotic in relation to Bazille's oeuvre: "Homoeroticism in visual representation need not be contingent on proof of the artist's homosexuality, and indeed, it cannot be contingent without delving too deeply into psychobiography or ahistorical definitions of sexual identity."[139] Thus, the sexual orientation of the artist does not need to be known in order for the work to be read as homoerotic.

One might object that issues of homoeroticism do not apply to an image of male nudes painted by a female artist. I argue the contrary. Spectatorship becomes a problem when the male nude is put on display regardless of who painted the image. Moreover, Valadon's eroticized bodies were addressed to a predominantly male audience at the Salon des Indépendants in 1914. Acknowledging the presence of women spectators, Solomon-Godeau insists that "the image of Man was always intended for the consumption of men."[140] The artistic environment during Valadon's lifetime was still overwhelmingly masculine in character. When confronted with a sensual body of his own gender, the heterosexual male is faced, consciously or unconsciously, with uncertainties about his masculinity.

The politics of looking are even more problematic with *Le Lancement*, as the male nudes are structured in accordance with the logic of female heterosexual pleasure – something, as far as we know, male viewers had never before witnessed at a public exhibition in France. Placing this enormous painting before heterosexual male viewers would be unsettling, since the eroticized gaze of the heterosexual female artist connects with that of the male homosocial realm. Once the viewer becomes aware of the fact that the artist is female, the painting becomes doubly threatening. Male spectators, accustomed to identifying with the position of the male artist while gazing at eroticized female nudes, could not identify with the female heterosexual painter without becoming embarrassingly aware of their own sexuality. Therefore, it is not surprising that *Le Lancement* received very little attention by critics.[141] One remarked that the painting evinced a lapse of judgment: "Valadon … has shown sometimes more sensitivity."[142] In a scathing review, the poet Arthur Cravan wrote, "Suzanne Valadon knows well the little recipes, but to simplify is not to make simple, old slut!"[143] Cravan's violent reaction, although tinged with satire, reveals shock and horror of viewing a male nude painted by a woman. Calling Valadon a "salope," the critic must have detected the erotic undertones in the painting. For a female artist to create such a work was lewd and wholly offensive according to Cravan.

As a member of Montmartre's avant-garde art world, former model and frequent observer and participant of the Salon des Indépendants and the Salon d'Automne, Valadon was acutely aware of the kind of response a painting of male bathers could ignite. If painting male nudes was already objectionable for a woman, exhibiting them was unthinkable. Valadon would have known that painting male nudes on a colossal scale and displaying them before a patriarchal viewership was a feat that no female artist had ever done before in France. She was cognizant of the fact that certain manipulations were necessary in order to avoid censorship or rejection from the Indépendants. Although the salon was unjuried, exceptions could be made if a work was too scandalous. In addition to idealizing her male nudes, Valadon avoided rendering the genitalia with the careful positioning of a dangling rope. Yet this did not fully diminish the overall erotic impact. Rotating two of the bathers so that they are shown from the rear, their derrières are showcased at eye level. With a sway in his hip, the leftmost figure becomes a twisted corkscrew that at any moment could bare all. While the overt sexuality of the female nude is accepted, the male nude must reject any eroticism.[144] Presenting the male nude as an expression of her own desires, Valadon broke with centuries-old assumptions about gender and sexuality. Provocation was in every way intentional.

Studies for *Le Lancement* reveal how she adapted and changed the orientation of the figures' bodies (figure 3.9, figure 3.10, figure 3.11). She originally orchestrated the trio of figures so that their bodies overlapped and their legs intertwined. In this manner, they appear even more like the canonical three graces dancing together in a spiraling motion while exhibiting their slender and muscular limbs. The preparatory drawings show how Valadon reworked the placement of the bodies and the ropes so that the genitalia would be covered in the final version. The same is true for her male nude in *La Joie de vivre*, completed three years earlier (figure 3.12). Valadon knew that she had to cover up her male nudes in order to have her works shown. If painting the male genitalia was a problem for a male artist, for a female artist this was even more controversial. Men assumed that merely the sight of the male body and exposed penis would have violated a woman, as "good" women were innocent and had no sexual desires.[145] If a woman painted the penis, it would be the acknowledgment of her own sexuality. The anxiety around a woman viewing and painting a naked man was based on more than just "the protection of women's chastity" in the interest of bourgeois society but, more importantly, the "preservation of masculinity."[146]

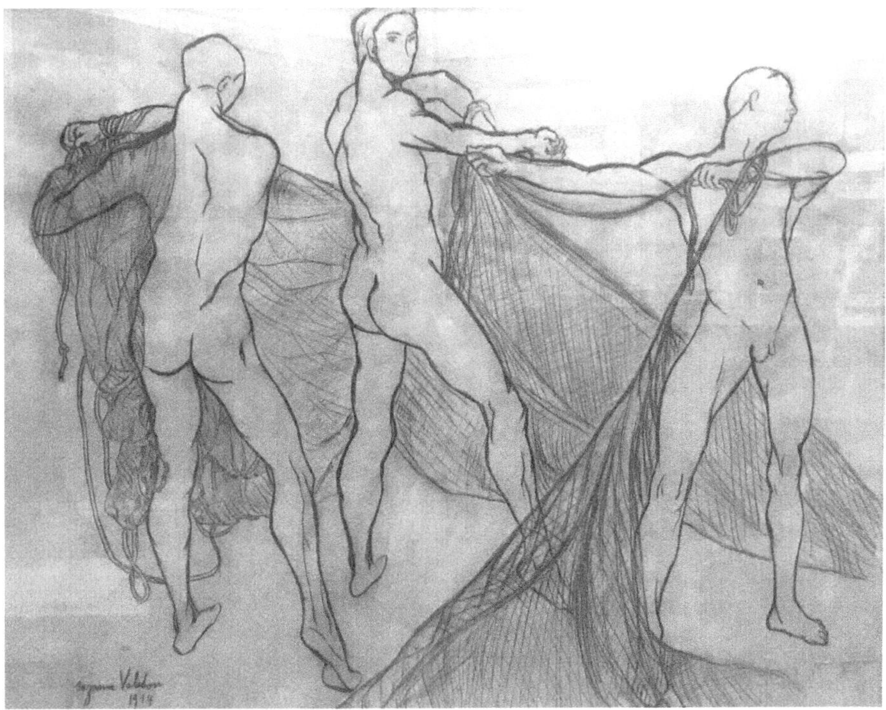

Figure 3.9 Suzanne Valadon, *Étude pour le lancement du filet* (*Study for Casting the Net*), 1914

Few art historians have paid attention to Valadon's *Le Lancement* studies. Heather Dawkins remains ignorant of her drawings of Utter altogether, stating, "Valadon appears to have avoided drawing adult men, and the conventions of art and propriety would have discouraged inclinations in that direction."[147] Those who have examined *Le Lancement du filet* have mistakenly described it as reserved. Margaret Walters attributes its timidity to its failure, stating that it was "too self-conscious to be fully successful … she carefully shields the genitals … she is inevitably over-conscious of the way she – former model and mistress – is turning the tables on men."[148] What Walters has failed to acknowledge is that Valadon would not have been able to exhibit this painting if she had not concealed the genitalia. From the preparatory drawings it is clear that only in the final image did Valadon cleverly position the nets to cover the male figure's groin. Lisa Tickner makes a similar error in assuming that "We cannot expect it to appear full-fledged in an alternative taxonomy of Man; as though there could, socially or pictorially, be a role-reversed equivalent to Degas' and Lautrec's brothel scenes".[149] The reason why Valadon does not paint the penis is not because she is embarrassed to, or because it is impossible for a woman to create a "role-reversed equivalent" to man's art, but

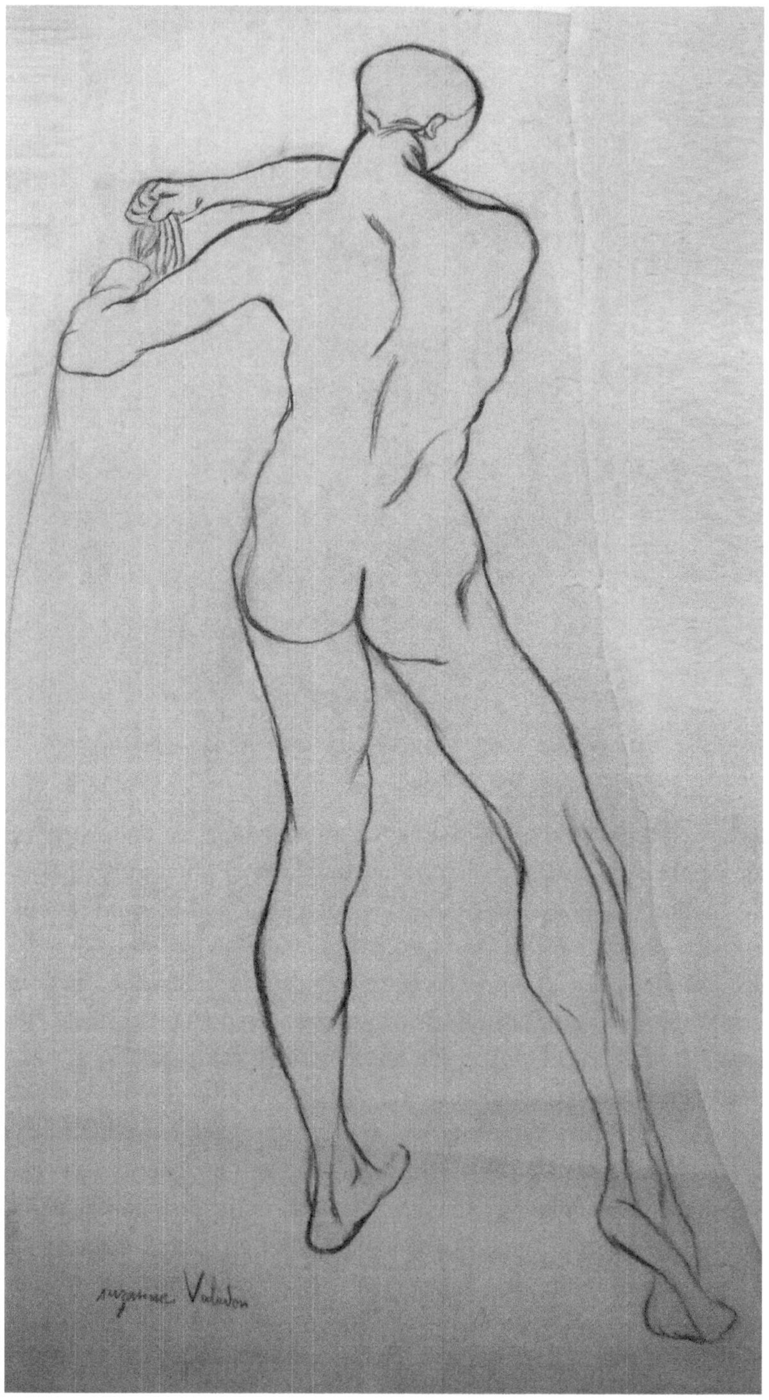

Figure 3.10 Suzanne Valadon, *Study for Lancement du filet* (*Utter from the Rear*), 1909

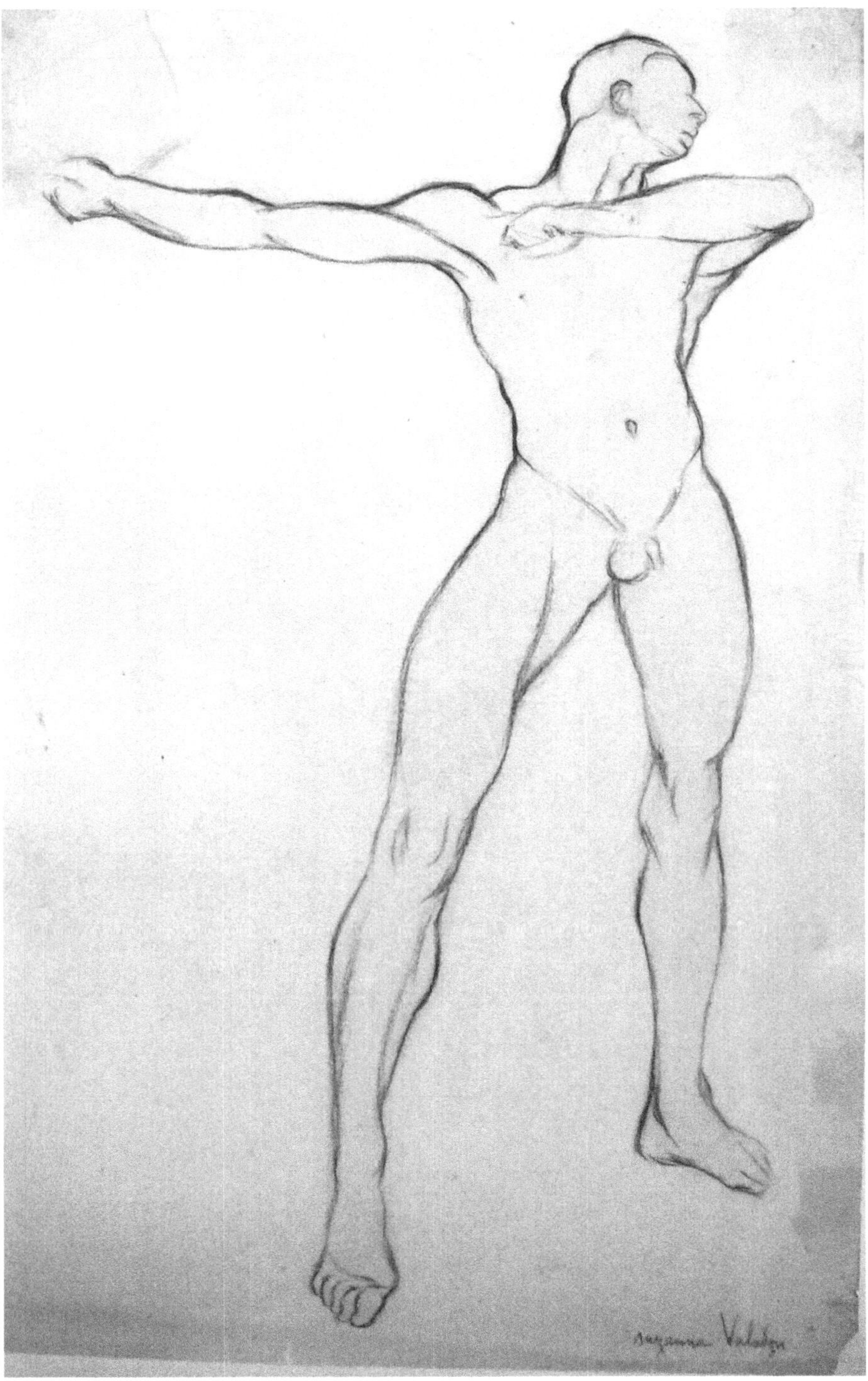

Figure 3.11 Suzanne Valadon, *Study for Lancement* (*Utter from the Front*), 1909

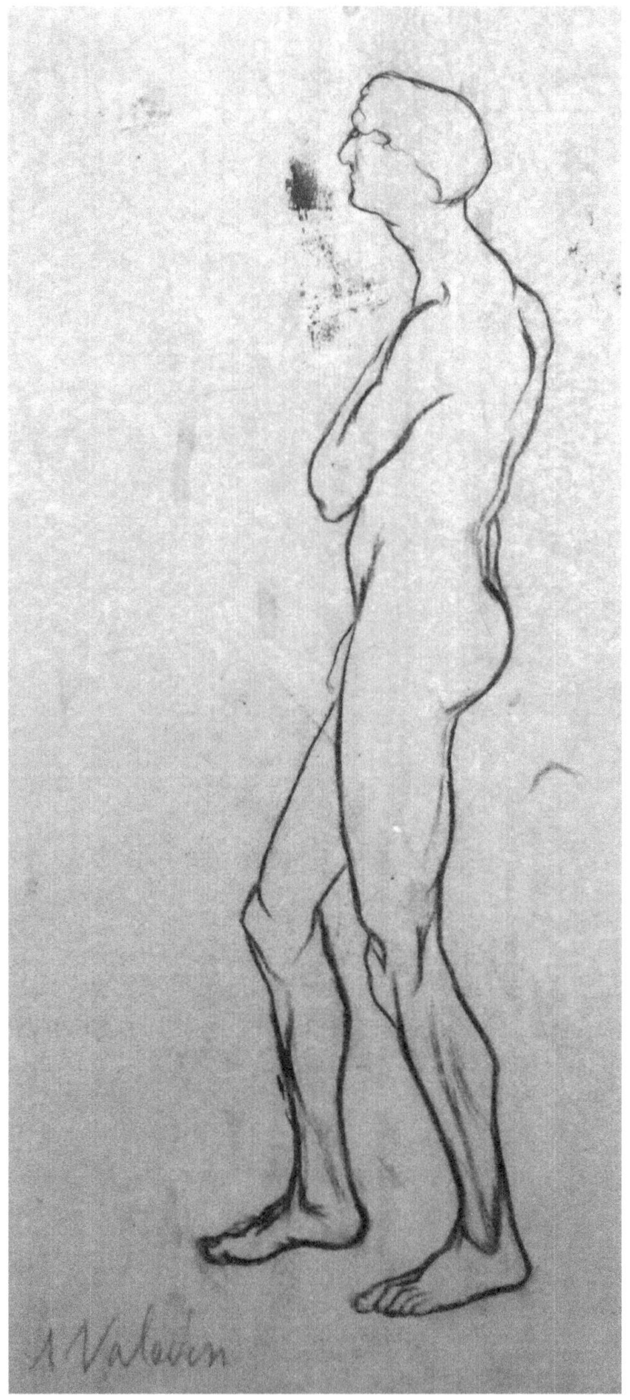

Figure 3.12 Suzanne Valadon, *Utter nu de profil* (*Utter Nude Profile View*), Study for *La Joie de vivre*, 1911

because she was forced to censor her work. Valadon, as these sketches reveal, was reluctant to conceal the eroticism of her male nudes.

Le Lancement was Valadon's last known painting of a male nude. This is likely due to the lack of a male model once Utter left for the Front in 1914 (he returned gravely wounded in 1917). Nevertheless, the painting would continue to be an important one in Valadon's oeuvre. It was exhibited multiple times during her lifetime, including in the 1935 Salon de la Société des Femmes Artistes Modernes. This time, two decades after its first showing, it received a laudatory response and Valadon was proclaimed "one of the foremost [women painters] of our time."[150] The greatest accolade came in 1937, when *Le Lancement* was purchased by the state.[151] Valadon paid homage to the work herself in a still life, *The Violin Case* (1923) (figure 3.13). This painting features a violin surrounded by sumptuous blue velvet, burgundy drapery, a multi-hued textile, vases and a bouquet of flowers. Behind this cornucopia of objects appears *Le Lancement*. This is a cropped view: only the net and the legs of two figures are visible, making the reference unintelligible without prior knowledge of the painting. The work is reminiscent of Cézanne's *Still Life with Plaster Cast* (c. 1894), which

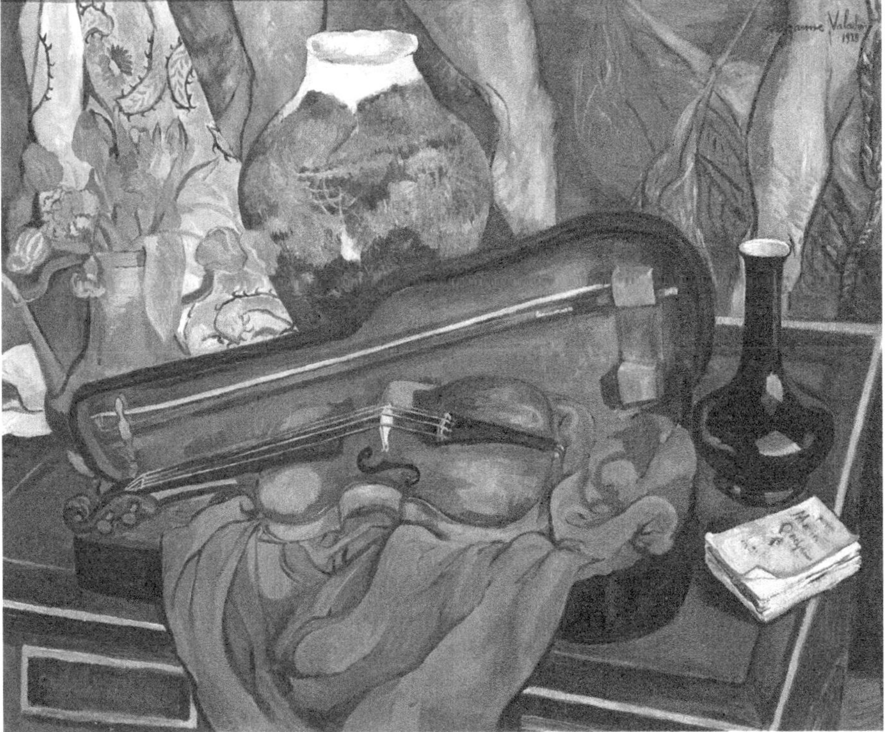

Figure 3.13 Suzanne Valadon, *La Boîte à violon* (*The Violin Case*), 1923

likewise exhibits male nudes in an artist's studio, in the form of a sculpture and a sketch. Yet Valadon's version is highly ambivalent. The appearance of men's hips and thighs in a still life is uncanny. With the frame hidden, it seems as if male nudes are presently standing behind the table. Meanwhile, the curvature of the men's legs rhymes with the shape of both the violin and the vase. The multicolored flesh corresponds with the pottery's decorated surface, while the flowing, red drapery mimics the ripples in the net. Combining female nudes with vases and fruit was a relatively common practice. Juxtaposing male body parts with curved and colorful still life objects was not. Once again, Valadon overturns expectations for the male body in art.

Valadon's *Vénus noire*

Departing from the male figure with the onset of World War One, Valadon tackled another unorthodox subject – the Black female nude. In *Vénus noire* (*Black Venus*) (Plate 22), Valadon presents a stunning woman, emerging from a dusky forest of tangled vines. Her piercing gaze arrests us. Elegantly coiffed, her hair is accentuated by a red headband which matches her full, crimson lips. With her torso positioned frontally, legs turned sideways, and heel arched, she is caught mid-movement, as if pausing momentarily before striding away. Valadon renders the golden highlights and violet shadows cast on the woman's form with her characteristically pronounced and textured brushwork, enlivening the surface with flecks of ochre, amber, mustard, mulberry and aubergine. The woman's prominent collarbone, muscular torso and wiry limbs convey strength. Her athletic form contrasts with Valadon's contemporaneous paintings of white females who are often voluptuous and fleshy (Plate 23). As in *Le Lancement*, the body is inscribed rigidly with firm contours which endow it with realistic plasticity and demarcate it from its surroundings. Yet, unlike *Le Lancement*, this nude stares back. The expressive force of her vigorous form, frontal pose and assertive gaze are at odds with her vulnerable state of nudity.

Vénus noire is one of the earliest known examples of a single, non-primitivized Black female nude in Western art. Valadon does not deform or geometricize the figure. She unveils the Black body in a manner freed from distortions of Cubism or Fauvism, and without a trace of caricature. Moreover, rather than the standard juxtaposition of white body/black body and hierarchical dichotomy of mistress/maid, Valadon shows the nude alone. She situates the figure within the canon of European art, as the Black model's elegant and graceful pose echoes ancient sculpture. In particular, her forearm covers the pubic region in a manner which recalls the classical *Venus Pudica*, an association further reinforced in the title itself. However, Valadon reformulates the motif and setting. Rather than a Mediterranean background, the lush forest exudes an exotic allure. The pose is not chaste per se – her left hand does not hide her breasts from an intrusive observer. Moreover, there is a sense of intention and strength in her gesture, rather than coy flirtation, as she forcefully presses her right palm against her thigh. In this manner, the nude is accorded a sense of agency, albeit subtle. Although Valadon hints at the woman's autonomy, she simultaneously undermines it – the identity of the model is unnamed in the title and she is set in a pastoral realm rather than a contemporary, Parisian milieu.

Vénus noire is an ambiguous image which invites correspondingly equivocal readings. Most Valadon scholars have acknowledged the painting but skirted the blaring implications of race which the work invokes.[152] In the spring of 2021, a group of art historians came together to tackle the painting's most contentious issues head-on. Spearheaded by Barnes curator, Nancy Ireson, a thought-provoking discussion ensued among the scholars, Adrienne L. Childs, Nancy Ireson, Denise Murrell, Ebonie Pollock and the author, and was published in the article, "Disrupting Tradition: Suzanne Valadon's *Black Venus*," transcribed and edited by Corrinne Chong.[153] I am indebted to this innovative dialogue. Following the viewpoints expressed therein, as well as in Pollock's critical examination of the painting in her thesis, "Suzanne Valadon's *Black Venus*," I concur that *Black Venus* cannot be read simply as an ennobling image of a Black woman. Like the other artists discussed in this book, Valadon was a white woman who was immersed in a rapidly evolving, yet doggedly unequal, imperialist and patriarchal French world. Therefore, we should not expect her perception of the Black figure to be entirely devoid of prejudice. Indeed, *Vénus noire* is problematic for myriad reasons. In highlighting the sensual nature of the nude and displaying her within an exotic realm, Valadon's nude accords with some of the stereotypes omnipresent in the colonialist mindset of the day.

As for discerning Valadon's intentions, we can neither ask her directly nor find any clues in her writings. No mention of the painting exists in her extant correspondence or interviews. In an effort to tease out the conflicting implications of the work, I examine its art historical sources, cultural context, position within Valadon's oeuvre, reception and provenance. Finally, I consider the titling of the work and the model's lack of identity. Not even for an instant have I pondered the baseless rumors that the model was the mistress of Utrillo (he was an alcoholic and was not known to have enduring romantic relationships). In this chapter, I limit my analysis to *Vénus noire*, one of the five images of the Black female nude recorded in her catalogue raisonné. Pollock recognizes all of these works collectively as the "Black Venus Series" due to the fact that they are "thematically and temporally linked" with the "shared model and their completion within the confines of a single year."[154] In the same study devoted entirely to Valadon's Black female nudes, Pollock effectively lays out the early twentieth-century French colonialist framework which informed Valadon's depiction. Egregious racism was rampant during this era, reinforced by appalling scientific studies, human exhibiting practices in world fairs and political suppression of non-ethnically-white groups, both in France and in its colonies. However, a comprehensive analysis of colonialism and racism in interwar Paris lies beyond the purview of this book.[155] While acknowledging the importance of broader socio-political currents, I limit my discussion to consider the most salient points. Moreover, I focus my analysis on the specific geographic and cultural milieu in which Valadon lived and worked – namely Montmartre, its avant-garde circles and its lower-class, bohemian community. Although Valadon was greatly influenced by the social norms of her day, I do not believe that her motivations were malevolent. Instead, I argue that she was seeking to address the absence of the Black body in the artistic lineage of the nude.

The Black Venus series stands out as an anomaly in Valadon's oeuvre – a short-lived experimentation in the representation of the Black figure. Like her depictions of Utter, this exploration is limited to one model studied over a relatively brief period of time. In the case of *Vénus noire*, the model's identity is undisclosed, an issue which I will address. As with *Lancement du filet*, Valadon was influenced by Bazille. At the Salon d'Automne in 1910, Valadon could have seen his representations of Black women in such works as *Young Woman with Peonies* (1870) and *La Toilette* (1869–70).[156] As in Bazille's *Young Woman with Peonies*, the white female counterpart is absent; Valadon foregrounds the solitary figure centrally. She depicts a Black woman who is neither enslaved nor a servant. Yet, while Bazille's flower seller belongs to the theme of modern-day life, Valadon does not depict a working-class woman in the Parisian metropolis. In addition to Bazille, Valadon was likely culling from a multitude of sources, neoclassical to modern, ranging from Marie Guillemine Benoist, *Portrait de Madeleine* (1800) (previously titled *Portrait d'une négresse*) to Manet's *Olympia*. Although she would have viewed the "Africanized" and primitivized nudes of Picasso, Matisse and Derain, her painting is stylistically distinct. Rather, there is an affinity to Gauguin's Tahitian nudes. The palette of *Vénus noire*, enlivened by striking applications of chartreuse, bespeaks his influence. As previously discussed, she would have seen his paintings from Tahiti at the Volpini exhibition in 1889. However, I agree with Pollock and Murrell that Valadon's representations of women of color yield different conclusions from Gauguin's.[157]

The most salient comparable for *Vénus noire* is to be found in Valadon's own oeuvre: *Adam and Eve*. Painted a decade apart, the works were exhibited within months of each other – *Vénus noire* in November 1919 at the Salon d'Automne and *Adam and Eve* in January 1920 at the Salon des Indépendants.[158] Valadon may have worked on these paintings simultaneously, as she was retouching *Adam and Eve*, adding the requisite fig leaves for its formal display. Both works are nearly life-sized, each measuring over five feet in height. The ambitious scale demonstrates Valadon's desire to have her work noticed. Rather than languorous nudes, these female figures are active and assume a monumental presence in the composition. In her self-portrait as Eve, Valadon conveys a sense of confidence with her forward-moving body. The same can be said of the Black model; her statuesque pose lends a sense of poise and self-assurance. In both images, Valadon daringly displays fully fledged nudes, replete with pubic hair. Despite her realistic treatment of the body, however, there is no verisimilitude to the backgrounds. Valadon positions the figures immersed in nature, in an ambiance that evokes a pre-Eden or exotic Utopia. Compared with her contemporaneous landscapes of the Rhône region and of the gardens and vineyards of Montmartre, the scenes are unspecific, evoking timeless, imagined realms beyond France. Although Valadon captures a definite likeness of herself and Utter in *Adam and Eve* and a specific Black individual in *Vénus noire*, neither Valadon nor her critics named or noticed the sitters' identities.

In *Vénus noire*, as in *Adam and Eve*, Valadon avoids the standard idealization of the female nude. She displays the unique facial features and physical traits of her model. Just as she had done in her earlier self-portrait, she renders the specificities and idiosyncrasies of the black figure with great care. She paints the expression lines flanking her mouth and pays attention to the minute asymmetries of the eyes. But in *Vénus noire*, she has clearly made strides in her own technique. Whereas *Adam and Eve* is rife with anatomical inconsistencies, *Vénus noire* is clearly the result of careful study and close observation of the human form. The latter displays a more advanced command of the nude, with careful attention to the model's musculature and bone structure, demarcated with Valadon's characteristic thick black contours. With her developed handling of paint and dazzling palette, she portrays the coloristic nuances of human flesh. In a eulogy to his mother, Utrillo later noted his mother's skill, "in magic colors, [of] blending natural tones, darker hues and pinks to paint Caucasians, sepia for Blacks (Black women to be precise)."[159] Utrillo's words echo the long-held notion that "the representation of flesh, because it is intimately connected to the living and expressive nature of the body, is simultaneously the highest achievement of the art of the colorist, and its unreachable limit."[160] Going along with this aesthetic convention were the polarities of transparency and opacity of female skin. In her discussion on the racial codification of skin in early nineteenth-century art, Cécile Bishop argues that "white skin is an index of individual sensibility, enabled by its transparency. Black skin, meanwhile, is a marker of race, an opaque surface invoked to justify the commodification and exploitation of black bodies."[161] Although painted over a century later, Valadon's Black nude is not fully divorced from this history. In his tribute, Utrillo clearly distinguishes "Caucasians" from "Black women" as subjects. Despite their stylistic congruencies, *Adam and Eve* and *Vénus noire* would not have been viewed as analogous by her contemporaries. There is evidently more at issue than

Valadon's technical proficiency at rendering lifelike female bodies and the chromatic qualities of varying skin tones. *Vénus noire* reflects larger societal shifts that Valadon was no doubt responding to, and signals the magnitude of race as a defining factor of modernity.[162]

During Valadon's lifetime, the demographics of Paris changed markedly. The city's populace evolved, as its diasporic communities grew. An array of working-class individuals of various backgrounds and ethnicities arrived seeking employment and opportunities. Among these was a steady influx of Black workers who settled in Paris.[163] Correspondingly, these individuals began to appear in works by Realists and Impressionists who aimed to show the shifting urban realm around them. In her groundbreaking exhibition and catalogue, *Posing Modernity: The Black Model from Manet to Matisse*, Murrell cogently argues how images of Black proletariats in the art of Manet, Bazille and other French painters reflected the growing presence of the Black figure in the Parisian metropolis.[164] This trend would accelerate following World War One, when, from 1918 onward, Paris witnessed the return of Black troops mobilized during the war, as well as the arrival of people of color from the colonies and the United States. These individuals brought with them their distinct traditions, including jazz. The onset of Negrophilia, the French vogue for Black entertainment and culture, was deeply felt in Paris, especially in the neighborhood of Montparnasse.[165] This phenomenon, which intensified during the 1920s with Josephine Baker's Parisian debut in 1925, led to a widespread celebration of Black culture, but also the propagation of pejorative stereotypes.

Ubiquitous colonial culture and flagrant racial ideologies were firmly in place in the nineteenth century and continued to persist during Valadon's lifetime. The dissemination and transformation of colonial attitudes is a complex and multifaceted topic beyond the parameters of this study. Nonetheless, Valadon was certainly not impervious to the all-encompassing colonial culture in France. Two key events which shaped her world were the invasion of Algeria in 1830 and the ethnological exhibitions, or human zoos, at the Expositions Universelles.[166] The latter debuted in Paris during the late nineteenth century and recurred through the twentieth, culminating with the Exposition Coloniale Internationale in 1931.[167] To combat this rampant racial discrimination and to promote the end of colonial rule, while endorsing human rights and economic equality, the Pan-African Congress was formed. Organized by W.E.B. Du Bois, the first conference was held in Paris in 1919, concurrently with the drafting and the signing of the Treaty of Versailles. As Pollock astutely points out, this momentous event took place the very same year in which Valadon exhibited *Vénus noire*.[168]

Beginning in the nineteenth century, the circus was an arena where the influx of the Black proletariat was pronounced. This was one place where working-class Black men and women could achieve a limited degree of success. In her essay on the acrobat Miss La La (Anna Olga Albertina Brown), a mixed-race Prussian circus star, Marilyn Brown states, "The circus was a hybrid space where class, gender, and race could intersect in performance."[169] Valadon likely saw Degas's painting *Miss La La at the Cirque Fernando* (1879), which was acquired after his death by the Courtauld Fund in 1925.[170] Some have speculated that Valadon worked at Cirque Fernando, the same circus where Olga performed.[171] Although *Vénus noire* shares no discernable visual analogies with *Miss La La*, it may be indirectly related through its title. In newspapers, journalists marveled at Olga's seemingly masculine strength, and also frequently referred to her as "Black Venus."[172] Coincidentally or not, the theme of the circus was on Valadon's mind at the time she painted *Vénus noire*. Just before executing the work, Valadon painted *L'acrobate* (c. 1918), an oil sketch on board, of a white female acrobat. Nevertheless, in Valadon's painting there is no actual reference to the circus, and it is in no way carnivalesque.

Valadon's title obliquely recalls another Black woman who was inhumanely paraded before European audiences – Sarah Baartman, commonly referred to as "The Hottentot Venus" in England, or as "La Vénus hottentote" in France. As Pollock and Denean Sharpley-Whiting assert, the term "Black Venus" was a commonly used archetype applied to Black women in the public eye.[173] This designation is evidently troublesome as it relates to these foremost examples of Black women put on display as spectacles of sexuality, pseudo-science and the grotesque for the entertainment and amusement of white Europeans.[174] Moreover, it conjures racist ideologies of the Black female body rampant at the time. Scholars have shown that, in the colonialist European mindset, the Black female body came to stand for sexual deviance.[175] Still, while Valadon's portrayal of a Black woman is fully nude, she is not overtly eroticized. Furthermore, her honest depiction differs greatly from the widely disseminated caricatures of Sarah Baartman in the early nineteenth century, as well as from the poster images of Josephine Baker which would follow.[176] Valadon evades the pronounced sexuality and animality evident in contemporaneous visual culture's display of the Black body.

In Montmartre, Valadon was immersed in a world of cabarets and music halls, where she would have encountered a sundry array of bohemian, intellectual and working-class individuals. She wrote that she was fascinated by the common laborers of Montmartre and painted them "to know them better."[177] The idea to paint a presumably working-class Black model thus falls within Valadon's objective to paint and understand fellow Montmartois. The shift in populace was felt to varying degrees in different arrondissements in Paris. The northern areas, including Montmartre, were home to growing numbers of Black workers.[178] A keen observer, Valadon would have witnessed this phenomenon firsthand. She may have rubbed shoulders with the model

Simone Luce, who was born in Montmartre in 1910. Her mother, Julie Luce, was a music-hall dancer who "took her daughter along with her everywhere to protect her from predatory men."[179] One popular cabaret venue was the Lapin Agile, down the hill from Valadon's rue Cortot studio.[180] It was at the Lapin Agile where Utter gathered in the evenings with André Salmon, an influential art critic who reviewed Valadon's work, the writers Apollinaire, Max Jacob and Mac Orlan, as well as the artists Picasso and Derain.[181] Picasso, Jacob and Orlan appear as fictional characters in Salmon's novel *La Négresse du Sacré-Coeur* (The Negress of the Sacred Heart), published one year after *Vénus noire* was displayed in the Salon d'Automne.[182] Aïcha Goblet, an artist's model of Flemish and Martiniquais descent, inspired Salmon's absurdly racist parody, where she assumes the role of Cora, an enslaved woman and mistress of a plantation owner of Montmartre. Bizarre references scattered throughout the text to Africa, the Amazon and beyond, within the terrain of Montmartre, reflect the racist elitism and cultural anxieties toward the Black figure shared by Salmon and his contemporaries.

Aïcha Goblet and Valadon had at least two things in common – they were both circus performers and models. Goblet, whose father had been a juggler, began performing at the age of six. She caught the attention of Jules Pascin during a performance and posed for him in the 1910s. Other artists followed, including Van Dongen, Kisling, Soutine, Modigliani and Foujita, as well as Matisse and Félix Vallotton. Just as Salmon projected his fantasized image of exoticism onto Goblet in his novel, so too did many of the artists who painted her. Playing on typecasts which blurred the French Caribbean colonies with Africa, she frequently wore a turban.[183] In the 1920s, Goblet became enmeshed in the artistic world of Montparnasse, frequenting the popular cafés such as Le Dôme, La Rotonde and La Coupole. Residing on the butte, Valadon was nevertheless connected with the Montparnasse community where "Negrophilia," the craze for everything "African," flourished during *les années folles*. In particular, she participated in the artist balls of Montparnasse, as her poster design for the 1927 ball hosted by L'Aide Amicale aux Artistes attests. Given Valadon's and Goblet's mutual ties to artists and writers, it is conceivable that Goblet posed for *Vénus noire*. However, due to the lack of archival evidence, this hypothesis cannot be confirmed.[184]

Valadon's *Vénus noire* compels us to look beyond the picture. We yearn to understand more about the woman who posed – her life circumstances, her relationship with the artist and, most essentially, her name. In her study of Valadon's Black Venus series, Pollock discusses Goblet and Luce, but she resists the temptation to speculate about the identity of Valadon's model. I applaud this approach. By maintaining the model's anonymity, the figure comes to stand for the countless Black women who worked as models in France whose names, never recorded, have fallen into obscurity.[185] Valadon's *Vénus noire* does not fully satisfy our twenty-first-century desire to decode an identity, decipher agency or read social progress and advancing perspectives on race. Indeed, her anonymity reflects the obscure and troubled status of the Black woman in Paris in 1919.

Recently, there has been a tremendous effort to identify the Black models in key works of art, instigated by Murrell's trailblazing research. This initiative came to the fore in the Orsay exhibition *Black Models: From Géricault to Matisse* in 2019 and has since motivated an impressive new body of scholarship.[186] But renewed attempts to determine who posed for *Vénus noire* proved unsuccessful due to a dearth of information both at the Pompidou and at the Musée des Beaux-Arts du Palais de Carnolès in Menton, where the painting is displayed. In the absence of primary sources, we cannot assume that, because she remains anonymous, the model was unimportant to Valadon. She also did not mention the name of the model who posed a few years later for *La Chambre bleue* in extant correspondence. Although some scholars have stated otherwise, the majority of Valadon's models remain nameless in the titles of her nude paintings.[187] Efforts to delve into finer details are foiled by an artist who did not write extensively and did not maintain copious records. It is uncertain whether or not she even maintained a notebook. None is found in the archives. The attempt to either lend agency to the model by finding her identity or, conversely, discredit Valadon for her lack of record keeping ends up missing the mark. Such approaches will always remain conjectural in the face of archival deficiencies.

In order to uncover more information on Valadon's *Vénus noire*, I pursued a different line of inquiry. Specifically, I examined the provenance of the painting. According to a Weill catalogue, it was exhibited in 1927 under the title "La Négresse." Charles Wakefield-Mori, a collector and friend of Valadon, was cited as the owner of the work. He was also the curator of the fine arts museum in Monaco. Valadon painted his portrait in 1922. He later donated Valadon's painting to the Musée National d'Art Moderne in Paris in 1939.[188] After his death, his widow bequeathed his entire art collection to the French state, forming the collection of the Musée des Beaux-Arts du Palais de Carnoles. Searching for clues, I inquired as to whether the museum had any of Wakefield-Mori's records or correspondence. Perhaps a mention of the painting in a letter could cast light on the painting. To my dismay, none of Wakefield-Mori's documentation is held by the museum. Meanwhile, combing through the archival material at the Pompidou did not reap any new information on the work or on the woman who posed. Alas, this enigmatic painting leaves us with more questions than answers.

I made one small discovery, however. *Vénus noire* was restored in 2012. The conservation report revealed an inscription written prominently in red on the upper-right portion of the back of the canvas. It reads, "N°1 / Vénus noire / s Valadon."[189] Comparing it with the signature on the front, the inscription appears to have been written by Valadon. The numeration supports Pollock's proposal to recognize this group of paintings as the *Black Venus* series. Moreover, the inscription indicates that the artist likely titled the work herself. Based on an archetype that implies savage sexuality, the title would have conjured stereotypes in the minds of Valadon's contemporaries. Problematically, Valadon's titles often changed numerous times over the course of her career. Perhaps these metamorphoses were driven by the art market. *Vénus noire* was alternatively titled *La Négresse* in several exhibition catalogues, while *Esclave couchée* was later renamed *Mulâtresse assise tenant une pomme.*[190] Another example is *Ni blanc ni noir* (1909). This work, which features two white female nudes, was originally named *Deux figures* when shown at the 1913 Salon des Indépendants. In the catalogue raisonné it appears under the titles *Après le bain* or *Ni blanc ni noir*, illogically calling attention to racial difference not evident in the painting. It is difficult to ascribe meaning to Valadon's work based on the titles alone, as they were frequently altered, and not always by the artist herself.

Valadon, or Utter as her manager, chose a far more derogatory title for the companion piece of *Vénus noire* – *Esclave couchée* (*Black Venus* – *Reclining Slave*). Such a title is baffling – it does not reflect the image itself, wherein the model does not appear enslaved, and thus seems incongruous with the painting. Unfortunately, though France had fully abolished slavery in its colonies by 1848, such antedated and inappropriate references were commonplace. Salmon's characterization of Goblet as Cora in his novel is one such example. The response to Valadon's work in the journal *Comoedia* evinces heinous racism in art criticism to match: "In front of Mme Suzanne Valadon's *Vénus noire*, in front of her *Esclave couchée*, we begin to think of Macbeth's witches and say with them: 'The beautiful is horrible, the horrible is beautiful.'"[191] Without actually describing the works themselves, the critic makes an extraneous association with the witches of Macbeth, effectively separating them from the tradition of the nude. Valadon's portrayal of a beautiful Black nude at the Salon d'Automne upset societal expectations of Black womanhood seen as dichotomous – in critics' eyes – to the "ideal" female nude. René-Jean's description supports Pollock's assessment that "Valadon's paintings would not have been received and interpreted as representations of beauty, as were images that depicted Western woman because the Black image usually carried with it encoded meaning and stereotype."[192] The critic continues, citing iconic nudes, from *Venus de Milo* to Ingres's *Grande odalisque*. In this manner, he denies a place for *Vénus noire* within Western art history. He even makes a dig at the artist. When stating, "There is a harmony of traits, a harmony of lines, toward which men of all races have reached" and the "pious hands of artists," he is referring not to Valadon, but to a male lineage: Correggio, Jean Goujon and Ingres. The critic's motives are twofold: to exclude both the Black nude and the woman artist from the canon of art. Other than this review in *Comoedia*, the press did not mention *Vénus noire.* Apparently, audiences were dumbfounded. Not sensual or savage enough, Valadon's Black female nude was out of sync with French racist notions.

It was not Valadon's intention to paint a monstrous, primitive or eroticized Black woman – far from it. Indeed, the nude's refined, classical pose, alertness and attractiveness defied pejorative associations which dehumanized the Black figure. Moreover, Valadon applied the same, if not greater attention and care to rendering this woman's body as she did with her white female nudes, and her own nude self-portrait. Valadon's composition reveals an attempt to insert the Black model within the tradition of the nude, just as the critical response inversely separates the work from the classical and "harmonious" nudes of the past.

Instead of criminalizing Valadon as a racist, I believe there is much more to be gained by considering the potential impetus of treating the subject. Given the scale of the work, allusions to the classical Venus prototype, similarities with her self-portrait, attention to the physiognomy of the model and prominent display in the Salon d'Automne, Valadon likely aimed to usher in a new kind of nude to the canon of art while breaking with the standard white female nude and ideologies of feminine beauty. She also seems to have endeavored to convey full respect for her subject. But this does not lessen the contentious aspects of the image. After all, a representation of the Black female body by a white female artist is in its very nature controversial. Valadon, a woman doubly marginalized by class and gender, painted another woman whose marginalization was compounded further. The result is unsurprisingly paradoxical. In venturing into the new genre of the Black female nude, Valadon posed numerous problems without clear solutions. As demonstrated by the 1919 review, Valadon's bigoted audience ostensibly would have perceived any naturalistic representation of the Black body as grotesque. Today, we can see Valadon's *Vénus noire* from an entirely new perspective. While we may be tempted to determine whether this is a fully humanist depiction of a Black woman or an objectifying portrayal of an archetype, it is perhaps more fruitful to consider how both seemingly incompatible readings are simultaneously possible. Valadon dignifies her subject while contrarily drawing from predominant stereotypes. She hints at the woman's subjectivity while undermining her autonomy. She lends the Black model as much agency as passivity. The Black model's beauty and distinct characteristics entice us as much as her anonymity disappoints. *Vénus noire* offers a vision in which subjugation and autonomy merge. The significant questions that the painting raises continue to preoccupy feminist art historians a century later.

The senescent and sexual body

At various stages throughout her career, Valadon disrobed and portrayed herself with striking realism. As we have seen, she depicted herself in a self-possessed manner in the guise of Eve. Valadon also appears nude in paintings not specifically designated as self-portraits, including *Jeux* (1910). Ultimately, Valadon ventured into uncharted territory and ushered in a new artistic subgenre – the old-age nude self-portrait. Self-portraiture holds an important place in Valadon's oeuvre (Plate 24). Sixteen self-portraits are listed in the catalogue raisonné, including a pastel, four drawings and eleven paintings. Among these, three nude self-portraits are documented from the mature phase of her career. Painted in 1917, 1924 and 1931, around the ages of fifty-two, fifty-nine and sixty-six respectively, these are the first known self-portraits by a woman that document the aging body.[193] In these works, Valadon shows herself from the chest up angled slightly in three-quarter view. The consistency in composition and pose allows these to be read as evolutionary studies of the artist's changing form and physiognomy. Never exhibited during her lifetime, they are introspective pieces which reveal intense examination and self-scrutiny. Although numerous painters had previously recorded the aging process in self-portraits, most notably Rembrandt, Valadon's decision to disrobe is unprecedented. She depicts her naked body unsparingly, with all of its imperfections highlighted and without a trace of narcissism. Through her pioneering nude self-portraits, Valadon reclaimed her own image while flouting societal attitudes and taboos about femininity, sexuality and aging.

In her *Autoportrait aux seins nus* from 1917 (Plate 25), Valadon faces the viewer squarely with her white blouse folded down, exposing her breasts. Her pale flesh is tinted with vibrant flecks of yellow and green, a shade lighter than the richly patterned drapery in the background. With rhythmic, hard-edged lines, Valadon emphatically articulates her features. A diagonal line of amaranth paint cuts across the left side of her face, accentuating her cheekbone. She stresses the minute asymmetries in her face and body: eyes which are somewhat off-kilter and breasts of slightly different sizes. Although women exposing their breasts are typically seen as objects of male desire, Valadon removes any erotic charge through an unapologetic directness. She is nude, but she is decisively not seductive. At fifty-two years of age, Valadon appears remarkably youthful. With her earnest gaze, she gallantly confronts the viewer, as if challenging them to see her as she really is – a sexually empowered woman.

In 1924, at the age of fifty-nine, Valadon painted herself bare-breasted again. In this image, she reduces her features to hard-edged geometric forms, imbuing a sense of asceticism. She demarcates the sternocleidomastoid muscle, which runs from her ear to her collarbone, with a thick, sharp line, further accentuating a sense of tension. Unfortunately, the current location of the painting is uncertain, and no color reproduction exists. Given its likeness to a clothed self-portrait from c. 1920, it is probable that she employed correspondingly strident colors. Valadon's expression conveys fierce determination. Although she was known for her beauty, she does not exaggerate her good looks in her self-portraits. Rather, she hardens her features and consistently exaggerates the jawbone, pursed lips, and untiring gaze, rendering an appearance more severe than that seen in contemporaneous photographs. Some art historians have described this work as masculine. Rosinksy states that this image is "sexless, her breasts still drooping and now shrunken, her shoulders squared, her features masculinized ... But the most disturbing factor is Valadon's choice of self-punishment. She turns her image into that of a man and obliterates all traces of prerequisite female softness."[194] Although I agree that Valadon effaces all "female softness," I depart from Rosinsky's assertion that she is "masculinized." Rather than distort, mangle or "masculinize," she intensifies her appearance with crude brushwork, loud accents of color and bold line. Baring her breasts, she does not conceal or deny her womanliness. Yet she willfully purges her portrait of any conventional signs of femininity. Valadon turns to her own image with the same rebuff for feminine labels as she had done a year prior in *La Chambre bleue* (1923). This is by no means a form of "self-punishment." Instead, her self-portraits portray a woman devoid of artifice and flattery. Just as some critics misinterpreted Valadon's nudes as cruel depictions of women, Valadon's mature, bare body, coupled with her stern expression, makes the viewer uncomfortable.

In 1931, Valadon returned one final time to her image, unashamedly documenting the aging process and boldly tackling the aged nude in art (Plate 26). Posing in an analogous manner as her nude self-portraits of 1917 and 1924, Valadon likely conceived the work to exhibit the transfiguration of her body over the course of time. She proudly signed and dated the work, making her actual age apparent – she was sixty-six. Painting herself naked from the torso up, she depicts the gradual deformations that occur with age – wrinkles, under-eye shadows, mouth creases, and a sagging jawline. In this unflinching portrayal of old age, she renders her weathered figure with no sign of self-pity. The painting echoes Valadon's own words, "You have to be hard on yourself, have a conscience, look yourself in the face. This surplus, this hatred and this narcissism, it must be purged."[195] Valadon turns to her own image with an honest and critical eye, purging her self-portrayal of two extremes – vanity and self-hatred. Rather than render herself as decrepit or inert, she depicts herself as an active painter, maintaining a contributory role in society. A glimpse of a canvas in the background indicates that she is in her studio. In fact, Valadon continued to paint until the very day she died in 1938.[196] Furthermore, with her petite, buoyant breasts plainly visible, accentuated by a necklace, her sexual capacity is still intact. Yet again, she portrays herself as a woman in touch with her sexuality.

Theories of embodiment prove useful in understanding Valadon's nude self-portraits. Embodiment contests the long-held division of mind from body, proposing that "subjectivity is the effect of human, corporeal existence in the world."[197] Rather than the body being viewed as a mere instrument of the mind, this phenomenological framework prioritizes the manner of living or inhabiting the world through one's physical body as a critical component to perception, cognition and action. In line with this concept, Valadon emphasizes corporeality as intrinsic to subjectivity and agency.[198] Resisting traditional artistic conceptions that distinguish theories of looking from touch, I consider concepts of viewership and embodiment as interrelated. They are equally indispensable to Valadon's self-portraits. She consistently stresses the physiological condition of the body, along with how she herself perceives and experiences it. I propose that Valadon, as a model turned artist, adopted a distinct approach in her nude self-portraits that might be termed a *model's gaze*.[199] Unlike the heterosexual male gaze that objectifies women as passive objects of pleasure, the model's gaze presents the body from a first-person perspective – as if from within and outside simultaneously. The model's gaze relates to the "female gaze," which has been described as the "empathetic closing of distance between the subject and object of the gaze," but it is enhanced by a more corporeal and even visceral awareness of the body.[200] The model's gaze is antithetical to the "medical gaze," theorized by Michel Foucault in *The Birth of the Clinic: An Archaeology of Medical Perception*, characterized by a distinct separation in medical practice between the body and the identity of the patient.[201] Rather, the model's gaze is an embodied mode of looking, informed by a full awareness of the body and the self. It stems from a phenomenological cognition of one's own physical form. Through the model's gaze, Valadon captures the sensation of inhabiting the body – a profound awareness of the body from within.

I wish to underscore here that I limit the notion of the model's gaze to Valadon's self-portraits. Although this theory may be relevant to other depictions of the female form, I assiduously avoid applying it broadly to Valadon's ample and diverse opus devoted to the nude. That Valadon's modeling career was an embodied experience which informed her depictions of the body is undeniable, but this complex phenomenon should not be reduced to simple or overarching claims. Some feminist art historians have affirmatively expressed how Valadon had a uniquely empathetic understanding of her models and that this influenced her work.[202] Whether or not Valadon's modeling experience enabled her to identify with her models is uncertain and unprovable. Others have emphasized that a different kind of feminine gaze typifies her female nudes.[203] In so doing, they have disregarded the multiplicity of Valadon's representations of the body. These blanket statements inevitably fail when extended to all of her work. I admire the recent scholarship of Yelin Zhao, who critically analyzes these convoluted and often contradictory arguments. Instead, she introduces a figure that she calls "the Model-Artist," exemplified by Valadon. She argues that "a modelling career has to be understood as a significant embodied experience, extended over a duration of years, and in Valadon's case over a decade."[204] I agree with Zhao that we can find "traces of articulation of this experience in Valadon's art." The impact of her modeling labor is strongly detected in her nude self-portraits. Years after relinquishing her modeling career, she poses for no one but herself. She emphasizes the way she sees and experiences her own body physically and psychologically.

Significantly, Valadon highlights the embodied experience of aging. Her nude self-portraits are about being in the world combined with the liminal process of growing older. She portrays the specificities of her aging body, achieving a more nuanced rendering of mature womanhood in painting. While aging is often associated with deterioration and decay, Valadon portrays a more optimistic and constructive view. In defiance of the frail, senescent body, she openly acknowledges the evolving biological states of her own form candidly with her brush. This flies in the face of widely held conceptions that the "biologically aging body … [precludes] agency."[205] Valadon articulates the agential nature of her lived body, even in advanced age. She scrutinizes herself through her untempered model's gaze, capturing the sensation of living in a mature woman's body. With unwavering and straightforward realism, Valadon achieved an embodied portrayal of the aged self.

Informed by her modeling vocation, Valadon found the space to re-examine herself before the easel and depict her body through an intimate and unassuming lens. Her self-portraits defy cultural norms that dictated the perception of older women during her lifetime as well as today. In a 2017 study on body image and aging in females, Sara M. Hofmeier summarizes Western society's biases towards old age:

> Aging is associated with unwelcome changes in physical appearance, increased dependency on others … and negative societal stereotypes. Thus, middle and old age are generally seen as period of decline in Western society, a problem with particular relevance for women due to Western society's long history of placing value on physical appearance, youth, and thinness.[206]

Scholars concur that aging has more serious consequences for women. Laura Hurd writes, "gendered body ideals emphasize the importance of being youthful, albeit by emphasizing different aspects of physicality in men and women."[207] Gender discrepancy in aging has been highlighted extensively by feminist scholars, including Susan Sontag in her concept "double standard for aging."[208] Aging is problematic for both sexes alike, but it is compounded for women, as they lose the characteristics which society values most for their gender: youth, beauty and sexuality. Without this, women serve little use within patriarchal society, becoming invisible. Thus, "signs of aging are greeted with distress as women are thought to lose the very qualities which give them the little representation they have."[209] This is reinforced in art, where youth and the nude go unquestionably hand in hand. Meskimmon notes, "old age in women contravenes the affiliation of beauty with youth in our culture and is associated with a loss of sexuality, with ill health and impending death."[210] Corresponding with this lack of visibility is the relative absence of representation of aging women in art and visual culture at the turn of the twentieth century. A rare example is Camille Claudel's *Clotho* (1893) which depicts one of the Three Sisters of Fate from Greek mythology, spinning the thread of life from her own hair. With unflinching realism, Claudel renders the ravages of time. Clotho's body is emaciated to a skeletal form, with sagging flesh dangling from her bones. Weak and frail, she struggles to stand upright under a mass of tangled, rope-like locks. Claudel's grotesque portrayal is at odds with Valadon's able-bodied mature self. Rather than an encounter with death, her self-portraits evince a sexually potent being, imbued with life and productivity.

Some feminist scholars argue that degendering takes place as one ages. The symbols of gender no longer carry the same weight for the senescent body. Therefore, the very fact that Valadon depicts herself as confident and dignified goes against cultural notions of age and gender. Hurd comments that women of the twenty-first century

> are perceived to become older at a younger age than their male counterparts and aging is especially detrimental to their social status. The onset of physical signs of aging such as age spots, wrinkles, sagging skin, increased weight, and gray hair progressively diminishes women's erotic capital.[211]

Rather than divorce her mature self from sexuality, Valadon stresses this in a venerable and realistic manner. She validates her "erotic capital" in her nude self-portraits. Without deformation, she retains poise and beauty. Rather than an appraisal of mortality, these self-portraits are endowed with agency and life. Valadon demonstrates that, even at an advanced age, she is a sexually conscious, able-bodied and productive artist. In concert with her truthful and reflective self-portraits, at the end of her life, Valadon summed up her career succinctly: "I found myself, I made myself, I said what I had to say."[212]

In 1931, Valadon had already exceeded the life expectancy for both men and women in France. When she was born in the 1860s, the average lifespan for a woman from birth in France was approximately forty-six years. During the twentieth century, life expectancy rose sharply (except during the two World Wars) to about sixty-three by 1930.[213] In France before World War Two, a woman in her fifties, considered middle-aged today, would have been seen as elderly. Mature women like Valadon faced bigotry and discrimination. Indeed, Valadon endured gender and age bias firsthand. She was subjected to countless defamatory reviews during the course of her career. Numerous critics attacked and insulted Valadon, describing her as old and unladylike, aging and degendering her simultaneously.[214] Cravan went as far as dehumanizing her, calling her an "old slut." At the time, Valadon was only forty-nine. In the face of derision, Valadon consistently renders her true and authentic appearance. At sixty-six, she seems to welcome, or at least accept, the changes in her physical appearance, and portrays this evolution positively. Moreover, in the 1930s, aging had yet to enter public consciousness as a topic of political debate or a feminist concern. Valadon addressed these blind spots within the realm of art.

Several decades after Valadon painted her old-age self-portraits, Simone de Beauvoir wrote about aging in *La Vieillesse* (*The Coming of Age*) (1970). She observed that, in France, old age is a "forbidden subject ... For society, old age appears as a kind of shameful secret which is indecent to speak about."[215] Beauvoir wrote about this proscribed topic, "to break the conspiracy of silence."[216] *La Vieillesse* resonates with *The Second Sex* in layout and argument.[217] Her overall premise is that "old age can only be understood in its totality; it is not only a biological fact but a cultural fact."[218] Like "womanhood," age, and the experience of it, are shaped by culture. Examining old age from various angles – biological, historical, literary and social – she draws parallels between the situation of the aged and that of women, insisting that both are marginalized positions of "Otherness." Furthermore, she reveals the ways in which ageism, like sexism, is entrenched in Western culture. In *The Second Sex*, she argued that women are divested of subjecthood by patriarchy. Following the same line of argument in *The Coming of Age*, she asserts that the aged are deprived of their subject status in Western societies. Anticipating Beauvoir's analysis and later theories on aging, Valadon shows the process as socially constructed and not intrinsically linked with physical debility.[219] Gracefully accepting her mature body with a sense of pride, she disavows adverse perceptions of aging as a state of decline, capturing instead a positive image. Through the model's gaze, Valadon affirmatively claimed her own subjecthood. She portrayed old age as an empowered state.

A work which resonates profoundly with Valadon's *Autoportrait aux seins nus* from 1931 is Alice Neel's *Self-Portrait* (1980), painted nearly half a century later. In her first and only nude self-portrait, Neel depicted her entire, wrinkled figure, replete with sagging flesh, on a monumental-sized canvas. Begun when she was seventy-five and completed when she was eighty, Neel fearlessly portrayed herself naked, stripped of everything except for the accessories of her trade: paintbrush, cloth and a pair of spectacles. Fully exposed, her pink flesh stands out against the striped blue and white armchair. Garb aptly describes the work:

> Not one to shy away from the truth, Neel chose to picture her unclothed, aged body without flattery or fiction to soften the effect of sagging flesh and swollen limbs. Nor did she hide her too ruddy cheeks and unflattering spectacles or her white, pulled-back hair. As an image of artistic identity, this one is truly revolutionary.[220]

Generations apart, it is uncertain whether Neel was aware of Valadon. Nonetheless, as mature artists, they dared to expose their bodies on canvas, an act that was truly rebellious.

In their self-portraits, Neel and Valadon radicalized the genre of the female nude, wresting it from the patriarchal structures of objecthood and voyeuristic viewership. Neel's portrait is informed by an awareness of second-wave feminist ideology and is conversant with the themes and ideas characteristic of the feminist art movement.[221] Valadon's work obviously predates these developments. Yet, from a twenty-first-century vantage point, the degree to which these images resonate with feminist theory is striking. She engaged with the problematics of gender, age and sexuality in the depictions of her own body in ways that are affirmative. She did not ingratiate herself, but turned to her self-image with exacting scrutiny, studying the complexities of the physical and psychological aspects of aging for a woman. She transgressed the boundaries of what was deemed acceptable subject matter, while subverting established mores about femininity, sexuality and the aged. Chiefly for Valadon, nudity was integral for capturing and asserting the self. Depicting herself naked, sexually empowered, but not eroticized, she reclaims the body and transcends the role of "Other." Beauvoir has shown that this position is assigned to women by patriarchy, but it can one day be surpassed. Laying her figure bare on canvas with a brutally honest eye, Valadon presents herself as an embodied human subject and defines self and sexuality on her own terms.

Male nude drawings

I would like to return to an unusual and overlooked body of work devoted to a formerly proscribed subject for a female artist – the adult male bather. For some art historians today, Valadon's drawings of Utter have been deemed of little artistic merit, warranting no sustained analysis or even consideration. I disagree for a number of reasons. First of all, it was a subject of great import to Valadon. Although she would only depict the male nude a few times in painting, she treated the subject repeatedly in her drawings. These works reveal an intense exploration of the male body in deliberate violation of artistic conventions. Their non-conformity would have offended public taste. She never exhibited them; they were made for her own private study and enjoyment.[222] I hypothesize that the extant drawings are only a small selection, and that many others are missing or destroyed. Like her female bathers, Valadon explored the male body without restraint and with disregard for artistic convention. While traditional artistic techniques stressed the transformation of the imperfect body into a perfect form, Valadon resists this practice in her bather images. She renders the human body straightforwardly in graceless poses and from unflattering angles. She shows the male figure in the most primitive states reserved for women: bathing, sleeping and relaxing unclad. Intrusively probing the male form in its most vulnerable condition, Valadon usurped the role of the active artist, normally ascribed to men. The male body now serves as the object of *her* gaze and *her* pleasure. Valadon's reversals of perspective materialize critiques of male dominance within the avant-garde art world and society at large.

André Utter, nu de face (figure 3.14) resonates with an earlier sketch of her son, *Utrillo enfant nu* (c. 1895), in composition and pose. Both drawings unapologetically exhibit the male form, undraped and unpolished without the requisite shading of an academic study. In *André Utter, nu de dos* (1909), Valadon captures the mounds and crevices of his lean and muscular physique. Valadon captures the mounds and crevices of his lean and muscular physique. Although she adds shading, she does not relinquish her deep lines and stern contours. The edge of a tub appears on the lower right – an odd accessory for a male nude. In these examples, Utter is shown alone, stripped of any context or narrative. The stark settings further amplify his exposed nakedness. He is not active, but passive, not classicized or heroicized but humbled and weak. Rather than the "balanced, prosperous, and confident body: the body re-formed" seen in *Le Lancement*, Valadon reveals the "huddled and defenseless body."[223] Valadon resists transmuting the masculine form into an expression of physical strength and virile power. Furthermore, she does not attempt to mask the erotic, but openly expresses it.

In *Nu couché* (c. 1909), Utter is recumbent, unaware of the artist's gaze. Positioned at a compromising angle, Utter is posed with one leg lifted, the ankle resting on the other knee. Valadon sketchily delineates salient elements of the body, including the genitals. In an unhindered exploration of the naked body, Valadon reveals its most intimate aspects, conventionally veiled or blurred. Sleeping, Utter is positioned like the traditional reclining female nude, his availability and vulnerability highlighted. Might Valadon's sketch then be an image for female enjoyment? The view of a man sleeping with genitals exposed pushes this image into the erotic realm. Such an image is unprecedented. As Linda Nochlin argues, "as far as one knows, there simply exists no art, and certainly no high art, in the nineteenth century based upon women's erotic needs, wishes, or fantasies."[224] The blatant sexuality of Valadon's image clearly positions the sketch as an erotic drawing for female pleasure.

Homme nu, de dos, tendant le bras gauche (*Male Nude, from Behind, Holding Out His Left Arm*) (Plate 27) is Valadon's most unusual drawing of a male nude. Utter is seated and viewed from behind. The chair is covered in white drapery, as he dries himself after a bath. This image hearkens back to Valadon's many images of female bathers, including *Catherine s'essuyant* (1895), *Après le bain* (1895) and *Nu à la draperie* (Plate 23). But it is clearly a reference to Degas's manifold variations on the theme of a seated female bather, such as *Femme s'essuyant le bras* (1885–95) and *Après le bain, femme s'essuyant* (c. 1890–95). This was unmistakably one of Degas's

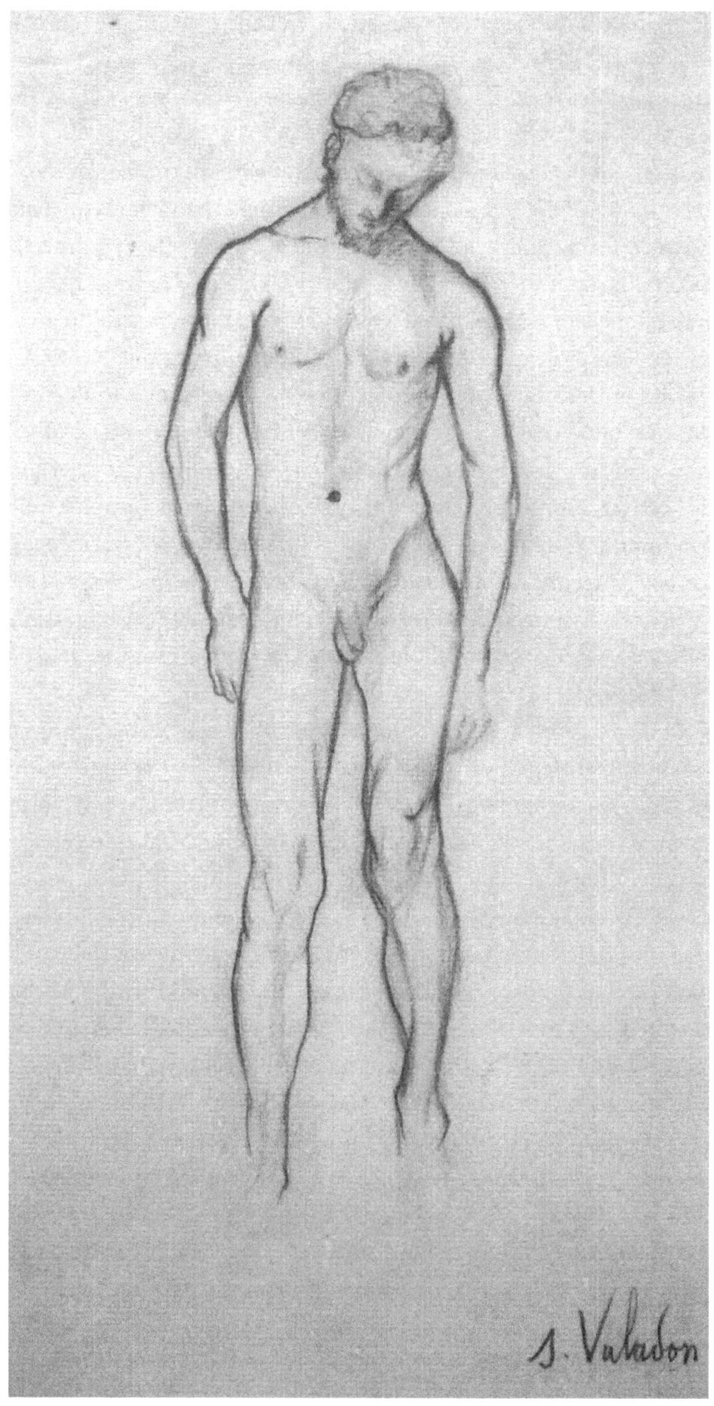

Figure 3.14 Suzanne Valadon, *André Utter, nu de face* (*André Utter Nude Frontal View*), c. 1909

favorite motifs in the 1880s and 1890s, the period in which he was in close dialogue with Valadon. She displays Utter in the same pose and in the most intimate moment of bathing and self-hygiene. The composition is remarkably similar to Degas's in a number of ways, from the angle of the chair, to the white linen and the forward-leaning body. Only the tub is missing. Like Degas, Valadon emphasizes the awkward contortions of the body. Outlining the figure with dark contours, she articulates the sharp angles of his shoulder blades, elbow and knee. Just as Degas captures the bather in movement, vigorously rubbing herself dry, Valadon depicts Utter in motion with one arm outstretched. Despite these artistic congruencies, the overall effect is not the same. With *Homme nu, de dos*, Valadon places the male body in the position of the female bather and shows the male nude from a woman's viewpoint. This female authorial presence lends a new meaning to the work. Valadon depicts the male nude in a pose that undermines his authority; Utter is de-masculinized.

Adult male bathers were seldom treated in late nineteenth- and early twentieth-century French art. Degas depicted only female bathers without exception. Representing a grown male nude partaking in ablutionary rituals broke with all manners of decorum. Bathing was considered a feminine task, Anthea Callen explains:

> Bathing was considered problematic for men … for different … reasons. The vanity (itself feminized) which was associated with all but the most perfunctory bathing was considered damaging to the masculine "esprit"; indeed, the dangers of warm water were such that it induced in initiates not only lasciviousness, but effeminacy.[225]

Indoor bathing, in particular, acquired gendered associations. It became linked in the popular imagination with prostitution, as it was customary for women sex workers to bathe in front of their male clients before sex.[226] Valadon completely ignores this distinction, erasing the boundaries between male and female hygienic practices.

While images of outdoor male bathers exist from this period, "intimate, interior scenes which might compare with Degas' *Bathers* are rare."[227] Gustave Caillebotte's *Homme au bain, se frictionnant* (1884) is an anomalous example of a male bather indoors. A male nude appears after the bath, vigorously rubbing himself dry. The work insinuates the homoerotic; just as in Bazille's *Le Pêcheur*, there is no narrative – only the context of modern, everyday life. The clothes dispersed around the room further emphasize his nakedness. In her analysis, Garb examines the positioning of the body, arguing that "the question of his 'masculinity' remains laden with anxiety. The view from the back constructs a potentially vulnerable image of the male figure."[228] And as Fionna Barber notes, the painting demonstrates that "issues of voyeurism apply to *both* representations of masculinity and femininity; this is not an issue merely confined to depictions of the female body."[229]

Nevertheless, Caillebotte's *Homme au bain* stands in stark contrast with contemporaneous images of female bathers. He presents us with a virile, muscular figure that stands firmly upright. Barber observes that the artist "seems to have been at pains to distinguish masculine bathing from that of the languorous and sensual activity of women."[230] Callen agrees. She notes that the title itself, *se frictionner* (to rub oneself) separates this male bather from Degas's females with the word *s'essuyer* (to wipe oneself dry) in many of the titles.[231] Although shown at his bath, his masculinity is so pronounced that his authority is not undermined. Caillebotte's nude "retains a dignity lacking in images of female bathers."[232]

Unlike Caillebotte, Valadon makes no attempt to mask the sensual nature of the male bather. In *Homme nu, de dos*, Utter is also viewed from behind, yet the position of Utter's body is far more effeminate. Rather than standing firmly with two feet squarely placed on the floor, Utter is seated. In the art historical canon, the seated back view of the female nude is common, epitomized by Ingres's *La Baigneuse Valpinçon* (1808). Standing, Caillebotte's male bather remains in control of his own body. Seated, Valadon's is powerless, weak and vulnerable. Here, we have an equivalent to Degas's bathers, but done by a woman. How many art historians have argued that such an image would have been impossible?[233]

Valadon adopts the keyhole viewpoint that Degas's critics, such as Gustave Geffroy, had identified in his work: "He wanted to paint a woman who did not know she was being watched, as one would see her hidden by a curtain or through a keyhole."[234] According to Callen, this vantage point is central to Degas's bather images and to "the iconography of voyeurism in which Degas' work is grounded."[235] The keyhole viewpoint implies distance, allowing the spectator to safely gaze at the female's body, while remaining invasive and controlling.[236] It implies physical contact through eye contact and "embodies masculine scopic power."[237] Valadon counters the voyeuristic male gaze with her own feminine one. Eyeing the male body at the most private moment, the male nude becomes synonymous with female desire. The female artist has now become the voyeur, watching and controlling the objectified and eroticized male body while taking sensual gratification in looking.

For feminist art historians, especially in the 1980s, the very act of looking was aligned with heterosexual masculinity. The male gaze, as Laura Mulvey first argued, objectifies women in cinema and the visual arts.[238] Art historians and feminist theorists have since expressed skepticism toward the idea of a woman reversing the gaze in accordance with her own desire.[239] Although there may be no direct female equivalent to the male gaze, Valadon demonstrates that a reversal is possible, and that it may occur to different degrees and in various manifestations of the male form. In *Le Lancement*, Valadon partially veils the sexual nature of her nudes, while still accentuating their muscular and graceful forms. The covert sexuality inherent in *Le*

Lancement aligns it with homoerotic works by Bazille and Caillebotte. In this way, the nudes are made available for the desiring male *and* female viewer. Such is not the case for her most intimate drawings of male nudes, which were created for Valadon's own exploration and pleasure. As such, the dominant subject/object dichotomy is destabilized completely; they reveal uninhibited *female* pleasure in viewing and depicting the male nude. Against all odds, Valadon became an agent of her own desire, expressing without inhibition her sexuality in the representation of the male body.

A closer examination of *Homme nu, de dos, tendant le bras gauche* reveals that there is more at stake than a reversal of the gaze. The materials show that Valadon was well informed of Degas's studio practices, and that she was experimenting with the male form in an unprecedented way. Significantly, the work was done on tracing paper. This is a material that Degas utilized in the 1890s for transferring an image to another surface. Employing tracing paper as a shortcut, the transparent material enabled him to see the drawing below, allowing him to trace over the original drawing repeatedly to create numerous variants.[240] Shackelford explains that the sheets were usually on a large scale and could stand on their own as individual works, some of them signed by Degas and sold. The majority of these remained in his studio and were discovered after his death.[241]

Valadon adapted Degas's methods for her own means. She employed tracing paper not only to modify a single motif, but also as a shortcut for transforming her drawings into paintings. Her catalogue raisonné reveals a handful of works done on tracing paper, each serving as a preparatory study for a finished painting.[242] Several of these pieces are cut or torn, perhaps in order to adjust the orientation of the objects and figures on canvas. Thus, *Homme nu, de dos* was most likely a preliminary drawing. Executed in graphite pencil and ink, there are extraneous traces of oil paint in varied colors on the surface. This residual pigment suggests that Valadon must have been reworking the motif into a painting.

Sure enough, she was. A black and white photograph of a painting entitled *Adam and Eve* or *Jeux* (1910) in the catalogue raisonné shows a male nude in exactly the same pose as *Homme nu, de dos*.[243] Toward the right edge of the canvas a man is seated, enveloped by a skirt of drapery, reaching forward with his left arm, this time to touch a female nude. His back is sliced by the edge of the canvas in a manner that recalls Degas's cropping techniques. The male bather motif conceived indoors is at odds with its *plein air* surroundings, and the presence of the female body next to it is unexplained. Digging further, I found that the painting had surfaced at a Sotheby's auction in 1988. Judging from a color reproduction of the painting, the work resembles *La Joie de vivre* from a year prior, in its color scheme of dark ochres, greens and yellows, grand scale and overall compositional incongruities. In the foreground, another set of male and female nudes appear and are recognizable as Valadon and Utter.[244] A playful reworking of the earlier *Adam and Eve*, the couple tease and flirt with one another. In a single image, Valadon materializes the male form as both active and passive, along with her own mobile body. In this peculiarly enigmatic work, Valadon unabashedly captures a euphoric display of female (hetero)sexuality and desire.

Valadon's humble *Homme nu, de dos* and its reiteration in paint demonstrates her aspiration to innovate, and it also shows that she was grappling with the male body with the same intensity as she extended to the female form. Valadon utilized charcoal, which was one of Degas's preferred drawing media, as it allowed him to achieve smooth, continuous lines and to smudge, wipe or even erase. Her use of the medium is more assertive. Just as seen in her female bathers, she articulates the male form with a thick, bold line, all the while depicting the body in a discomfited pose and from an unexpected viewpoint, as if trying to anchor the figure in space. Valadon insists on rendering the human form palpable with her hard-edged incisions. Her use of line is calculated and produces a semantic effect. With a vigorous charcoal silhouette, she portrays Utter in a continuous state of becoming. Her emboldened contours serve to metaphorically emphasize the corporeality and embodiment of the human figure.

In her depictions of male nudes, Valadon radically tests the power relations between the sexes. She not only contests the standard dynamics of looking, she also opposes male subjectivity as transcendent or disembodied. While it was the female that was traditionally seen as corporeal, Valadon insists on depicting the male form as similarly rooted in a physical body, rejecting Cartesian dualism. In regard to masculine-normative subjectivity, mind and body were conventionally divided. Meskimmon elaborates on this "divisive logic":

> Where an attainment of subjecthood relied upon the assumption of transcendence and a definitive rejection of corporeality, any sign of immanence, especially as "bodiliness," was eschewed. The corollary of this divisive logic was that the masculine (and white, middle-class, able-bodied – i.e. "normative") subject position became disembodied.[245]

In capturing the body, pose and physiognomy of the male form, Valadon renders the male figure as incarnate, made flesh and inherently embodied.

In Valadon's art, the notion of the subject, whether female or male, is not divorced from bodily experience. She painted the nude from the combined vantage point of seer and seen, as she portrayed the human subject as lived and materialized. This is most evident in her male nudes and nude self-portraits. In her series *Autoportrait aux seins nus* she represented herself as a fully fledged, substantive being and affirmed her role as an embodied subject. Examining herself with the model's gaze, Valadon exposed the artifice of cultural constructions of both femininity and age, as she pictured the body as it is lived, felt and seen by a woman.

In her bather images of Utter, Valadon revealed the adult male body as a fragile, weighty and physical entity, with the same sense of immediacy and vulnerability as her female bathers. Her male nudes opposed the "unilateral constitution of sexual myths" as encapsulated by Beauvoir in this citation from *The Second Sex*:

> The asymmetry of the two categories, male and female, can be seen in the unilateral constitution of sexual myths. Woman is sometimes designated as "sex"; it is she who is the flesh, its delights and its dangers. That for woman it is man who is sexed and carnal is a truth that has never been proclaimed because there is no one to proclaim it. The representation of the world as the world itself is the work of men; they describe it from a point of view that is their own and that they confound with the absolute truth.[246]

Brandishing her brush, Valadon audaciously exposed men who are "sexed and carnal." Of course, her works predate Beauvoir's writing as well as the feminist art movement, and thus cannot be viewed as specifically "feminist" in the historically sanctioned sense. Even without an overt ideological motive, Valadon ruptured conventions, challenging patriarchal models governing the depiction of the male body in art. With this complete role reversal, Valadon contested the time-honored definitions of gender and sexuality and anticipated a feminist revolution.

Notes

1 Margaret Walters, *The Nude Male: A New Perspective* (New York: Paddington Press, 1978), 314.

2 Numerous feminist scholars have discussed this work. See: Rosemary Betterton, "How Do Women Look? The Female Nude in the Work of Suzanne Valadon," in *Looking On: Images of Femininity in the Visual Arts and Media* (London: Pandora Press, 1987); Patricia Mathews, "Returning the Gaze: Diverse Representations of the Nude in the Art of Suzanne Valadon," *The Art Bulletin* 73, no. 3 (1991): 415–30; Gill Perry, *Women Artists and the Parisian Avant-Garde* (Manchester: Manchester University Press, 1995); Thérèse Diamand Rosinsky, *Suzanne Valadon* (New York: Universe, 1994); Yelin Zhao, "Ambitious Model, Ambiguous Artist: Three Case Studies of Victorine Meurent, Suzanne Valadon and Alice Prin" (Ph.D. dissertation, The University of Leeds, 2018).

3 I agree with Mathews that Valadon depicts a bohemian intellectual. Patricia Mathews, *Passionate Discontent: Creativity, Gender, and French Symbolist Art* (Chicago: University of Chicago Press, 1999), 207.

4 Marchesseau referred to Valadon's figure as a clothed nude, stating, this "nu habillé (dressed nude) … wears on her body all the traces of everyday labor." Daniel Marchesseau et al., *Suzanne Valadon* (Martigny: Fondation Pierre Gianadda, 1996), 123.

5 François Roussier, *Jacqueline Marval: 1866–1932* (Paris: Thalia Éditions, 2008), 246; *Salon d'Automne* (Paris: Société Française d'Imprimerie, 1921).

6 René-Jean, "Le Salon d'Automne," *Comoedia*, October 31, 1921, 3.

7 Etienne Bricon, "Le Salon d'Automne," *Le Gaulois*, November 5, 1921, 4.

8 Marchesseau, *Suzanne Valadon*, 262.

9 See Jack Halberstam, *Female Masculinity* (Durham, NC: Duke University Press, 1998).

10 Chadwick and Latimer state, "'Masculinized' feminine fashions, which afforded women new liberties literally and figuratively, spurred a hysterical level of debate in the contemporary press, which also periodically invoked nineteenth-century laws that prohibited women from appearing in public wearing masculine attire." Whitney Chadwick and Tirza Latimer, "Becoming Modern," in *The Modern Woman Revisited: Paris between the Wars* (New Brunswick: Rutgers University Press, 2003), 6–7.

11 Christine Bard, *Une histoire politique du pantalon* (Paris: Éditions du Seuil, 2010), 328.

12 Ibid., 325.

13 Bard quotes a song by Fred Gouin, 1924, "elle a perdu son pantaloon tout en dansant le charleston," ibid., 320.

14 Coco Chanel began designing pajamas sometime in the 1920s. Ibid., 321.

15 "A woman in pants will never be a handsome man." Chanel quoted in ibid., 321.

16 Art journals from 1923 revealed few responses to *La Chambre bleue*. One writer noted, "Suzanne Valadon is more opulent than ever; a radiant female body." Edmond Jaloux, "La Peinture," *Les Nouvelles Litteraires*, November 3, 1923. Valadon is mentioned in passing in reviews of the 1923 Salon d'Automne: *L'Intransigeant*, October 31, 1923, 2, and *Comoedia*, October 30, 1923, 4.

17 Paula J. Birnbaum, *Women Artists in Interwar France* (Farnham: Ashgate, 2011), 197.

18 Berthe Weill, *Pan! Dans l'oeil! ...* (Paris: Librairie Lipschutz, 1933), 294.

19 Robert Rey, *Suzanne Valadon: vingt-huit reproductions de peintures et dessins précédées d'une étude critique par Robert Rey* (Paris: Éditions de la Nouvelle Revue Française, 1922).

20 I first analyzed Valadon's male nudes in my master's thesis, "Defying Gender: The Nude in the Art of Suzanne Valadon" (MA thesis, Courtauld Institute of Art, 2011). Hunt has since added a perceptive analysis. Courtney A. Hunt, "Suzanne Valadon's Male Nudes" (Master's thesis, Hunter College, 2013).

21 Betterton, "How Do Women Look?"; Mathews, "Returning the Gaze."

22 Ebonie Pollock, "Suzanne Valadon's *Black Venus:* The Representation and Reception of the Black Artist's Model in Interwar Paris" (B.A. thesis, Washington University in St. Louis, 2019).

23 Heather Dawkins erroneously states, "Valadon appears to have avoided drawing adult men, and the conventions of art and propriety would have discouraged inclinations in that direction." Dawkins, *The Nude in French Art and Culture, 1870–1910* (Cambridge: Cambridge University Press, 2002), 88. Rosinsky discusses *La Joie de vivre* and *Le Lancement du filet*, but does not examine Valadon's drawings of male nudes. She incorrectly assumes that Valadon "did not ... represent him [André Utter] casually, as she did her female sitters." Rosinsky, *Suzanne Valadon* (1994), 84–9.

24 For a critical review of Valadon literature prior to 2018, see Yelin Zhao, "Ambitious Model, Ambiguous Artist."

25 Degas called her Maria while Toulouse-Lautrec renamed her Suzanne. The latter name relates to the Catholic tale of Susannah and the Elders. Toulouse-Lautrec suggested this designation because she was the model for a handful of older male artists.

26 The details of Valadon's early life are murky. Valadon and her mother found temporary housing on Ile Saint Louis, before renting a sordid room on boulevard Rochechouart near Place Pigalle. Thérèse Diamand Rosinsky, *Suzanne Valadon*, translated by Emmanuelle Delanoë-Brun (Paris: Flammarion, 2005), 29; Catherine Hewitt, *Renoir's Dancer: The Secret Life of Suzanne Valadon* (New York: St. Martin's Press, 2017), 33, 43.

27 Valadon's mother, Madeleine, had been a linen maid in Bessines, a modest but trained profession. She was unable to find employment as a linen maid in Paris, as these posts were highly sought after. Instead, she took on more general cleaning tasks as a charwoman. Hewitt, *Renoir's Dancer*, 14, 44.

28 Ibid., 61.

29 Valadon declares in an interview with Tabarant that she began posing for Puvis de Chavannes at the age of fifteen. Rosinsky notes that she likely posed for other artists first. The exact artist who first hired her as a model is unknown. Adolphe Tabarant, "Suzanne Valadon et ses souvenirs de modèle," *Bulletin de La Vie Artistique*, Paris, December, 1921, 627; Rosinsky, *Suzanne Valadon* (2005), 69, 77.

30 "Since she often posed and as we were among artists, I often saw her body which was admirable. Her skin was covered with a down that gave it gold glints. She looked like a statue." Georges Bonne, a friend of Valadon's, observed her posing for *Le Baiser de la sirène* by Gustav Wertheimer. Fonds Robert Le Masle, Kandinsky Library, Centre Pompidou, Paris.

31 Rosinsky, *Suzanne Valadon* (2005), 86, 95, 97.

32 Ibid., 77.

33 Kenneth Clark made this distinction in *The Nude: A Study in Ideal Form* (New York: Pantheon Books, 1956).

34 Valadon quoted in Tabarant, "Suzanne Valadon et ses souvenirs de modèle," 628.

35 For information on the traditional female nude see Clark, *The Nude*; Lynda Nead, *The Female Nude: Art, Obscenity and Sexuality* (London: Routledge, 1992); John Berger, *Ways of Seeing* (Harmondsworth: Penguin, 1972); Whitney Chadwick, *Women, Art and Society* (London: Thames & Hudson Ltd, 2007).

36 Valadon quoted in Tabarant, "Suzanne Valadon et ses souvenirs de modèle," 628.

37 Suzy Leudet, "Suzanne Valadon chez les pompiers," *Beaux-Arts*, May 16, 1938. Leudet was a painter who was studying in the studio of Hector Leroux in 1891.

38 Rosinsky, *Suzanne Valadon* (2005), 110; Auguste Renoir, *The Large Bathers* (1887), Philadelphia Museum of Art.

39 She insisted in an interview with Tabarant in 1921, "I never posed for him, although the opposite has been said a hundred times." Valadon quoted in Tabarant, "Suzanne Valadon et ses souvenirs de modèle," 628.

40 Valadon recounts to Tabarant in 1921 that it was either Lautrec or Bartholomé. Ibid., 629.

41 Ibid.

42 Utter, unpulished essay, Fonds Le Masle, Kandinsky Library.

43 Tabarant, "Suzanne Valadon et ses souvenirs de modèle," 629.

44 George Shackelford, "The Body Transformed: Degas's Last Nudes," in *Degas and the Nude*, edited by Shackelford and Xavier Rey (Boston: MFA Publications, 2011), 210.

45 Valadon quoted in Hewitt, *Renoir's Dancer*, 217.

46 Edgar Degas and Marcel Guérin, *Degas, lettres* (Paris: Bernard Grasset, 1945). Later, in 1912, when Degas was forced to move out of his home and studio on Rue Victor-Massé due to its impending demolishment, Valadon found a studio for him in on boulevard de Place de Clichy. Tabarant, "Suzanne Valadon et ses souvenirs de modèle," 629.

47 Degas and Guérin, *Degas, lettres*, 206.

48 Degas quoted in Marchesseau et al., *Suzanne Valadon*, 29.

49 Hewitt, *Renoir's Dancer*, 162.

50 She exhibited *The Toilet of the Grandson, Grandmother and Grandson*, and three studies of children. Jeanine Warnod, *Suzanne Valadon* (Norwalk: Easton Press, 1982), 9; Jacqueline Munck, Marc Restellini and Marie-Cécile Baudoin, *Valadon, Utrillo: Au tournant du siècle à Montmartre: de l'impressionnisme à l'école de Paris* (Paris: Pinacothèque de Paris, 2009), 19.

51 Warnod, *Suzanne Valadon* (Paris: Flammarion, 1981), 91.

52 Drouot, *Catalogue des tableaux modernes, pastels, aquarelles, dessins anciens et modernes ... faisant partie de la collection Edgar Degas* (Paris: Drouot, 1918).

53 Maurice's adoptive father was the Spanish artist Miquel Utrillo. Proud of his aristocratic heritage, Utrillo refused to marry Valadon, but he did agree to adopt her son and give him his name. The biological father is unknown.

54 Paul Pétridès, *L'Oeuvre complet de Suzanne Valadon* (Paris: Compagnie Française des Arts Graphiques, 1971). The illustrated sections of the catalogue are not paginated.

55 Valadon was a loving mother and taught her son how to paint as a treatment for his early-onset alcoholism. See Hewitt, *Renoir's Dancer*.

56 For a closer examination of Cassatt's images of children, see Griselda Pollock, *Mary Cassatt* (London: Universal Books, 1985).

57 Rosinsky, *Suzanne Valadon* (1994), 33.

58 Courtney Hunt, "Wicked, Hard and Supple: An Examination of Suzanne Valadon's Nude Drawings of Young Maurice," *Art Inquiries* XVII, no. 4 (2019), 412.

59 Ibid.

60 One example of Gauguin's depictions of adolescent male bathers is *Jeunes baigneurs bretons* (1888). Solomon-Godeau argues that "the prevalence of children, like that of unindividuated Breton women, masks something largely absent from the Bertonist vision – namely adult men and their activities" and reflects "a fantasmatic construction of purely feminized geography." She observes an absence of men in Gauguin's Tahitian paintings as well: "In the Polynesian pictures as in the Breton work, images of men are singularly rare." Abigail Solomon-Godeau, "Going Native: Paul Gauguin and the Invention of Primitivist Modernism," in *The Expanding Discourse*, edited by Norma Broude and Mary Garrard (New York: Westview Press, 1992), 317, 318, 327.

61 See: Shackelford, "The Body Transformed: Degas's Last Nudes", and Richard Thomson, *Degas: The Nudes* (London: Thames & Hudson, 1988).

62 The literature on Degas's bathers is vast. Feminist art historians, in particular, have shown a vested interest in these images. See, for example: Carol Armstrong, *Odd Man Out: Readings of the Work and Reputation of Edgar Degas* (Chicago: University of Chicago Press, 1991); Eunice Lipton, *Looking into Degas: Uneasy Images of Women and Modern Life* (Los Angeles: University of California Press, 1986); Richard Kendall and Griselda Pollock, *Dealing with Degas: Representations of Women and the Politics of*

Vision (New York: Universe Publishing, 1992); Anthea Callen, *The Spectacular Body: Science, Method and Meaning in the Work of Degas* (New Haven: Yale University Press, 1995).

63 Shackelford, "The Body Transformed: Degas's Last Nudes," 174.

64 Thomson, *Degas and the Nude*, 179.

65 First names are often included in the titles of drawn toilette scenes before 1909. See Pétridès, *L'Oeuvre complet de Suzanne Valadon.*

66 Eunice Lipton, *Looking Into Degas: Uneasy Images of Women and Modern Life* (Berkeley: University of California Press, 1986), 179.

67 Ibid., 174.

68 A century later, the discussion of Degas's bathers and prostitution became a heated debate amongst art historians. Lipton, *Looking into Degas*, 179; Martha Ward, "The Rhetoric of Independence and Innovation," in *The New Painting: Impressionism, 1874–1886*, edited by Charles S. Moffett and Richard R. Brettell (Geneva: R. Burton, 1986), 430–34; Carol Armstrong, *Odd Man Out: Readings of the Work and Reputation of Edgar Degas* (Chicago: University of Chicago Press, 1991); Norma Broude, "Edgar Degas and French Feminism, ca. 1880: 'The Young Spartans,' the Brothel Monotypes, and the Bathers Revisited," *Art Bulletin* (1988), 640–59.

69 Jean Vertex quoted in Warnod, *Suzanne Valadon* (1981), 73.

70 Luc Benoîst, quoted in Birnbaum, *Women Artists in Interwar France*, 197.

71 Suzanne Valadon, "Suzanne Valadon ou l'absolu," n.d., n.p. Fonds Le Masle, Kandinsky Library.

72 Rey, *Suzanne Valadon*, 12.

73 *Degas, lettres*, 216, 233.

74 Suzanne Valadon and Marie-Anne Camax-Zoegger, "Pour les futurs biographes de Suzanne Valadon et d'Utrillo," *Cahiers de France*, October, 1938, 86–7.

75 Shackelford, "The Body Transformed: Degas's Last Nudes," 188.

76 Broude, "Edgar Degas and French Feminism," 654.

77 Betterton makes a similar observation in "How Do Women Look?," 229.

78 Valadon, "Suzanne Valadon ou l'absolu."

79 Undated letter reprinted in Robert Rey, *Suzanne Valadon*, 9–10.

80 Pierre Georgel, *Suzanne Valadon* (Paris: Musée National d'Art Moderne, 1967), 90.

81 Claude Roger-Marx, "L'Oeuvre grave de Suzanne Valadon," *L'Art Vivant*, Paris, September, 1932.

82 Ibid.

83 For a discussion on gendered associations of printmaking see Christina Weyl, *The Women of Atelier 17: Modernist Printmaking in Midcentury New York* (New Haven: Yale University Press, 2019).

84 Alain Badiou, "Drawing," *Lacanian Ink* 28 (2011), 42–9.

85 Fonds Le Masle, Kandinsky Library.

86 Given that Valadon destroyed her drawings prior to 1883, she may have destroyed early paintings as well. Valadon, "Suzanne Valadon ou l'absolu."

87 Jacqueline Munck, "Suzanne Valadon's Painting (1909–1914): An Absolute Passion," in Saskia Ooms (ed.), *Valadon, Utrillo and Utter in the Rue Cortot Studio* (Paris: Somogy, 2015), 34.

88 According to Crespelle, Utter was an electrician working on avenue Trudaine in Montmartre when they met. Jean-Paul Crespelle, *Montmartre vivant* (Paris: Hachette, 1964), 163–4.
89 Fonds Le Masle, Kandinsky Library.
90 Fonds Le Masle, Kandinsky Library.
91 Hewitt, *Renoir's Dancer*, 214–15.
92 Birnbaum, *Women Artists in Interwar France*, 175.
93 Suzanne Valadon, "Suzanne Valadon par elle-même," *Promethée* (Paris: Editions littéraires de France, March, 1939), 53.
94 Birnbaum, *Women Artists in Interwar France*, 186.
95 Ibid., 174.
96 Ibid., 47.
97 Tamara de Lempicka painted male nudes in the mid to late 1920s as well as the subject of Adam and Eve in 1931. See Birnbaum, *Women Artists in Interwar France*, 176.
98 Eighteenth-century academic sketches of male nudes by French female artists have been identified, one by Marie-Anne Pierrette Lavoisier (1758–1836) in 1786 and others (undated) by Pauline Auzou (1775–1835). However, these studies show the male body from the back or with the model covered in some way. As Oppenheimer explains, "Even women such as Elisabeth Vigée Le Brun, who limited themselves to depicting female nudes, only showed partial nudity, and were never accused of drawing from the nude in mixed company, found themselves the victim of art critics who made suggestive comments and even hinted lewdly that they were used themselves as models." Margaret A. Oppenheimer, "'The Charming Spectacle of a Cadaver': Anatomical and Life Study by Women Artists in Paris, 1775–1815," *Nineteenth-Century Art Worldwide* 6, no. 1 (Spring 2007), 79.
99 Tamar Garb, *Sisters of the Brush: Women's Artistic Culture in Late Nineteenth Century Paris* (New Haven: Yale University Press, 1994), 80.
100 Ibid., 82.
101 Tamar Garb, "The Forbidden Gaze: Women Artists and the Male Nude in Late Nineteenth-century France," in *The Body Imaged: The Human Form and Visual Culture since the Renaissance*, edited by Kathleen Adler and Marcia Pointon (Cambridge: Cambridge University Press, 1993), 35.
102 Garb, *Sisters of the Brush*, 89.
103 Abigail Solomon-Godeau, *Male Trouble: A Crisis in Representation* (London: Thames & Hudson, 1997), 185.
104 Ibid.
105 Garb, *Sisters of the Brush*, 88.
106 Ibid., 101.
107 Ibid., 103–4.
108 See Carol Duncan, "Virility and Domination in Early Twentieth-century Vanguard Painting," in *Feminism and Art History: Questioning the Litany*, edited by Norma Broude and Mary D. Garrard (New York: Harper & Row Publishers, 1982), 293–313.
109 Diane Radycki, *Paula Modersohn-Becker: The First Modern Woman Artist* (New Haven: Yale University Press, 2013), 180.
110 Valadon's *La Joie de vivre* has been discussed by feminist art historians in relation to the male gaze. See: Rosinsky, *Suzanne Valadon* (1994), 85–8; Mathews, *Passionate Discontent*, 199–202.

111 Degas's *Scène de guerre au Moyen Age (Les malheurs de la ville Orléans)* was acquired by the Musée du Luxembourg in 1918 from the first posthumous sale of Degas's studio. Musée d'Orsay, "Notice de l'oeuvre: Edgar Degas, *Scène de guerre au Moyen Age*," www.musee-orsay.fr/fr/collections/catalogue-des-oeuvres/notice.html?nnumid=10028. Accessed April 12, 2018.

112 Warnod, *Suzanne Valadon* (1981), 91.

113 Sylvia Sleigh quoted in Dennis Adrian and Russell Bowman, *Sylvia Sleigh: Invitation to a Voyage and Other Works* (Milwaukee: Milwaukee Art Museum, 1990), 5.

114 Guillaume Apollinaire, "XXIXe Salon des Artistes Indépendants," *Montjoie!*, March 18, 1913. He also noted Utter's *Trois nus* from the same salon in a review in *L'Intransigeant*. See Apollinaire, *Chroniques d'art, 1902–1918*, edited by Leroy C. Breunig (Paris: Gallimard, 2002), 372, 379.

115 Georgel, *Suzanne Valadon*, 40.

116 Ooms, *Valadon, Utrillo and Utter in the Rue Cortot Studio*, 119.

117 Clark, *The Nude*, 34.

118 Ibid., 35.

119 Some examples include: Henri Matisse, *Bathers with a Turtle* (1908), oil on canvas, Saint Louis Art Museum in St. Louis, Missouri; and *Bathers by a River* (1909–16), oil on canvas, The Art Institute of Chicago; Jean Metzinger, *The Bathers* (1913), oil on canvas, Philadelphia Museum of Art; Maurice Denis, *Female Bathers at Perros-Guirec* (c. 1912), oil on canvas, Le Petit Palais, Paris; André Derain, *Bathers* (1907), oil on canvas, MoMA, New York; Picasso, *Three Women*, 1908, oil on canvas, Hermitage, Saint Petersburg.

120 Seurat, *Bathers at Asnières* (1884), oil on canvas, National Gallery, London; Cézanne, *Le Baigneur au rocher* (1860–66), oil on canvas transferred from plaster, Chrysler Museum of Art, Norfolk, VA; Cézanne, *Baigneurs* (c. 1890), oil on canvas, Musée d'Orsay, Paris.

121 Pierre Puvis de Chavannes, *Le Bois sacré cher aux arts et aux muses* (1884), Musée des Beaux-Arts, Lyon.

122 Valadon quoted in Tabarant, "Suzanne Valadon et ses souvenirs de modèle," 628.

123 Henri Loyrette, *Degas: Passion and Intellect*, translated by by Mark Paris (London: Thames & Hudson, 1993), 155–7.

124 Valadon, "Suzanne Valadon par elle-même," 53.

125 Michel Schulman, *Frédéric Bazille, 1841-1870: catalogue raisonné* (Paris: Éditions de l'Amateur, 1995), 180. Thanks to Christopher Green for drawing this to my attention.

126 Michel Hilaire and Paul Perrin, *Frédéric Bazille (1841–1870): la jeunesse de l'impressionisme* (Paris: Flammarion, 2016), 243.

127 One example is François Boucher's *Diana sortant du bain* (1742), Musée du Louvre, Paris.

128 Dianne Pitman, *Bazille: Purity, Pose, and Painting in the 1860s* (University Park: Penn State University Press, 1998), 151.

129 Solomon-Godeau, *Male Trouble*, 19.

130 See: Kermit S. Champa, "Frédéric Bazille: The 1978 Retrospective Exhibition," *Arts Magazine* 52 (1978), 110; Philippe Dagen, "Bazille, astre éphémère," *Le Monde*, July 17, 1992; Michael Kimmelman, "A Tragic Harbinger of the New," *New York Times*, November 13, 1992; Hilaire and Perrin, *Frédéric Bazille*, 143; Mary Manning, "Frédéric

Bazille and Masculinity between Paris and Montpellier, 1841–1870" (Ph.D. dissertation, Rutgers University, 2015).

131 Thomas Eakins, *Swimming Hole* (1884–85), Amon Carter Museum, Fort Worth, TX.

132 Michael Hatt, "The Male Body in Another Frame: Thomas Eakins' *The Swimming Hole* as a Homoerotic Image," In *The Body: Journal of Philosophy and the Visual Arts* 8, no. 21, ed. Andrew Benjamin. (London: Academy Editions, 1993).

133 Ibid., 11.

134 Ibid., 20.

135 Ibid., 12.

136 Hewitt examines these rumors in detail in *Renoir's Dancer*, 110.

137 As Rosinksy writes, "During that period, Maria took full advantage of the sexual freedom that prevailed in Montmartre and had fun adventures in the evenings. Sensual and accustomed from her earliest childhood to give free rein to her natural instincts, she savored the pleasures of life." Rosinsky, *Suzanne Valadon* (2005), 96. See also June Rose, *Mistress of Montmartre: A Life of Suzanne Valadon* (London: Metro Books, 1999).

138 Rosinsky, *Suzanne Valadon* (2005), 77, 96, 152, 179; Rose, *Mistress of Montmartre*; John Storm, *The Valadon Drama: The Life of Suzanne Valadon* (New York: E.P. Dutton & Co., 1959). Hewitt casts doubt on any sexual relationship between them in *Renoir's Dancer*, 81.

139 Manning, "Frédéric Bazille and Masculinity between Paris and Montpellier," 90.

140 Solomon-Godeau, *Male Trouble*, 198–9.

141 I consulted periodicals from 1914 at the National Art Library, Victoria and Albert Museum and Bibliothèque Nationale de France. As is customary, Valadon's name is listed among numerous other artists in the standard newspaper accounts which summarized the Salon des Indépendants each year. See Lucien Klotz, "Le Salon des Indépendants," *La Presse*, March 4, 1914, 2, and *Lemouzi*, April, 1914, 190.

142 Robert Kemp, "Au jour le jour: les Indépendants, II," *L'Aurore*, March 1, 1914, 1.

143 Arthur Cravan, "L'Exposition des Indépendants," *Maintenant*, 4 (March–April, 1914). In his review of the 1914 Salon des Indépendants, Cravan insulted almost every exhibitor, including Valadon. A boxer, poet and editor of his own review, *Maintenant*, he aimed to shock readers. He was greatly admired by Dadaists and Surrealists.

144 Hatt, "The Male Body in Another Frame," 12.

145 Walters, *The Nude Male*, 231.

146 Garb, "The Forbidden Gaze," 35.

147 Dawkins, *The Nude in French Art and Culture*, 88.

148 Walters, *The Nude Male*, 315.

149 Lisa Tickner, *Women's Images of Men* (London: Institute of Contemporary Arts, 1980).

150 V., "Les 'Femmes Artistes' et 'Les Universitaires,'" *Le Petit Parisien*, May 30, 1935, 4.

151 Bought by the state in 1937 with *Adam and Eve* and other works. Now in Centre Pompidou's collection, Paris, but displayed in Musée des Beaux-Arts de Nancy.

152 Most authors praise Valadon's *Black Venus* as a dignified portrayal, without carefully considering its potential racist undertones or colonialist milieu. Hewitt, *Renoir's Dancer*; Mathews, *Passionate Discontent*; Rosinsky, *Suzanne Valadon* (1994).

153 Adrienne L. Childs, Nancy Ireson, Lauren Jimerson, Denise Murrell, Ebonie Pollock, "Disrupting Tradition: Suzanne Valadon's *Black Venus*," transcribed and edited by Corrinne Chong, in *Suzanne Valadon: Model, Painter, Rebel,* edited by Nancy Ireson

(Philadelphia: The Barnes Foundation in association with London: Paul Holberton Publishing, 2021), 30–41.

154 Pollock, Suzanne Valadon's *Black Venus*, 5.

155 A selection of sources on colonialism in interwar France includes Jennifer Boittin, *Colonial Metropolis: The Urban Grounds of Anti-Imperialism and Feminism in Interwar Paris* (Lincoln: University of Nebraska Press, 2010); Elizabeth Ezra, *The Colonial Unconscious: Race and Culture in Interwar France* (Ithaca: Cornell University Press, 2000); Michael Goebel, *Anti-imperial Metropolis: Interwar Paris and the Seeds of Third World Nationalism* (New York: Cambridge University Press, 2017).

156 Frédéric Bazille, *Young Woman with Peonies* (1870), oil on canvas (two variations), National Gallery of Art, Washington, DC, and Musée Fabre, Montpellier, and Bazille, *La toilette* (1869–70), Musée Fabre.

157 Adrienne L. Childs, Nancy Ireson, Lauren Jimerson, Denise Murrell and Ebonie Pollock, "Disrupting Tradition: Suzanne Valadon's *Black Venus*," transcribed and edited by Corrinne Chong, in *Suzanne Valadon: Model, Painter, Rebel*, edited by Nancy Ireson (Philadelphia: The Barnes Foundation in association with London: Paul Holberton Publishing, 2021), 30–41. For a detailed discussion of Valadon's *Black Venus* in relation to Gauguin's Tahitian nudes, see Ebonie Pollock, "Suzanne Valadon's *Black Venus:* The Representation and Reception of the Black Artist's Model in Interwar Paris" (BA thesis, Washington University in St. Louis, 2019), 38–40.

158 *Vénus noire* was exhibited at the Salon d'Automne, November 1 – December 10, 1919, and *Adam and Eve* at the Salon des Indépendants, January 28 – Feburary 29, 1920, along with *Jeux*. *Salon d'Automne* (Paris: Société Française d'Imprimerie, 1919), 229; *Catalogue de la 31e exposition* (Paris: Société des Artistes Indépendants, 1920), 169.

159 Utrillo quoted in Hewitt, *Renoir's Dancer*, 383–4.

160 The politics of skin color in art is probed by Bishop in a revelatory essay on Guillemine Benoist's *Portrait de Madeleine* (1800), within its context of late eighteenth- and early nineteenth-century France. Cécile Bishop, "Portraiture, Race, and Subjectivity: The Opacity of Marie-Guillemine Benoist's Portrait d'une négresse," *Word and Image* 35, no. 1 (2019), 2.

161 Ibid., 5.

162 In her groundbreaking study, Murrell posits that, as much as gender and class, race underpins modernity. Denise Murrell, *Posing Modernity: The Black Model from Manet and Matisse to Today* (New Haven: Yale University Press, 2018).

163 See: Boittin, *Colonial Metropolis*; Tyler Stovall, *Transnational France: The Modern History of a Universal Nation* (New York: Taylor & Francis, 2015).

164 Ibid.

165 Petrine Archer Straw, *Negrophilia: Avant-garde Paris and Black Culture in the 1920s* (New York: Thames & Hudson, 2000).

166 See: Patricia Lorcin, *Algeria & France, 1800–2000: Identity, Memory, Nostalgia* (Syracuse: Syracuse University Press, 2006); Stovall, *Transnational France*.

167 Sandrine Lemaire and Pascal Blanchard, "Exhibitions, Expositions, Media Coverage, and the Colonies (1870–1914)," in *Colonial Culture in France since the Revolution*, edited by Pascal Blanchard, Sandrine Lemaire, Nicolas Bancel, Dominic Richard and David Thomas (Bloomington: Indiana University Press, 2014). On the French colonization of Algeria,

see: Jennifer Elson Sessions, "Making Colonial France: Culture, National Identity and the Colonization of Algeria, 1830–1851" (Ph.D. dissertation, University of Pennsylvania, 2005).

168 Pollock, "Suzanne Valadon's *Black Venus*," 40–1. On the Pan-African Conference see Tyler Stovall, "Black Modernism and the Making of the Twentieth Century: Paris, 1919," in *Afromodernisms: Paris, Harlem and the Avant-garde*, edited by Fionnghuala Sweeney and Kate Marsh (Edinburgh: Edinburgh University Press, 2013).

169 Marilyn Brown, "'Miss La La's' Teeth: Reflections on Degas and 'Race,'" *The Art Bulletin*, 89, no. 4 (2007), 744.

170 *Miss La La at the Cirque Fernando.* The National Gallery of Art, London, www.nationalgallery.org.uk/paintings/hilaire-germain-edgar-degas-miss-la-la-at-the-cirque-fernando. Accessed April 24, 2021.

171 Hewitt, *Renoir's Dancer*, 64–7.

172 Brown, "'Miss La La's' Teeth," 744.

173 Pollock, "Suzanne Valadon's *Black Venus*," 6. For more on this archetype, see T. Denean Sharpley-Whiting, *Black Venus: Sexualized Savages, Primal Fears, and Primitive Narratives in French.* (Durham, NC: Duke University Press, 1999).

174 Deborah Willis and Carla Williams, "The Vénus Noire," *Nka: Journal of Contemporary African Art* 30 (2012), 28–35.

175 Sander Gilman, "Black Bodies, White Bodies: Toward an Iconography of Female Sexuality in Late Nineteenth-century Art, Medicine, and Literature," *Critical Inquiry* 12, no. 1 (1985), 204–42; K. Sarah Yiu, "The Icon of the Hottentot Female and the Reclamation of Black Female Sexuality and Bodily Representation," *Footnotes* 2 (2009), 72–8.

176 Examples include Louis François Charon, "Les Curieux en extase ou les cordons de souliers," 1815, hand-colored etching, https://gallica.bnf.fr/ark:/12148/btv1b69543861. Accessed April 24, 2021; Paul Colin, "Revue nègre," 1925, lithograph. Henry Louis Gates and Karen C.C. Dalton, *Josephine Baker and La Revue Nègre: Paul Colin's Lithographs of Le Tumulte Noir in Paris 1927* (New York: H.N. Abrams 1998).

177 Valadon, "Suzanne Valadon ou l'absolu."

178 Murrell, *Posing Modernity.*

179 Michel Fabre, "Rediscovering Aïcha, Lucy and D'al-Al, Colored French Stage Artists," *S&F Online* 6, nos 1–2 (2007–8), 1, http://sfonline.barnard.edu/baker/mfabre_01.htm. Accessed April 24, 2021.

180 More scholarly work should be done to uncover the black performers of the Lapin Agile.

181 Fonds Le Masle, Kandinsky Library.

182 André Salmon, *La Négresse du Sacré-Coeur* (Paris: Nouvelle Revue Française, 1920).

183 *Index of quoted names.* Villa Vassilieff www.villavassilieff.net/?Index-of-quoted-names. Accessed April 24, 2021.

184 For a full list of archives consulted, see Bibliography.

185 Pollock, "Suzanne Valadon's *Black Venus*," 14.

186 Cécile Debray, Isabelle Bardon, Estelle Bégué, David Bindman et al., *Le Modèle noir de Géricault à Matisse* (Paris: Musée d'Orsay, 2019); Wendy Grossman, "Unmasking Adrienne Fidelin: Picasso, Man Ray, and the (In)Visibility of Racial Difference," 5 (2020), https://doi.org/10.26597/mod.0142.

187 See catalogue raisonné: Pétridès, *L'Oeuvre complet de Suzanne Valadon.*

188 *Suzanne Valadon, Vénus noire.* Centre Pompidou, www.centrepompidou.fr/fr/ressources/oeuvre/crb9y4. Accessed April 24, 2021.

189 Carole Husson, "Rapport d'intervention de Suzanne Valadon, *Vénus noire*, 1919," Dépôt du Pompidou au Palais Carnolès de Menton, 2012 (confidential condition report).

190 *Mulâtresse assise tenant une pomme* was sold under this title at Sotheby's in 2015. According to the Sotheby's condition report there is no inscription on the back.

191 René-Jean, "La Peinture et la sculpture au Salon d'Automne," *Comoedia*, 4 (November, 1919), 1.

192 Pollock, "Suzanne Valadon's *Black Venus*," 58.

193 Rosinsky, *Valadon* (1994), 79.

194 Ibid.

195 Valadon, "Suzanne Valadon ou l'absolu."

196 Valadon had a stroke while painting at her easel. Louis Vauxcelles, "Suzanne Valadon," *Le Monde Illustré*, April 16, 1938, 14.

197 Marsha Meskimmon, *The Art of Reflection: Women Artists' Self-Portraiture in the Twentieth Century* (New York: Columbia University Press, 1996), 76.

198 Betterton broaches embodiment in relation to Valadon's work before segueing into a larger discussion on other women artists' representations of the body. Rosemary Betterton, *Intimate Distance: Women, Artists and the Body* (London, Routledge, 1996), 7.

199 For a description of the "male gaze," see Laura Mulvey, "Visual Pleasure and Narrative Cinema," in *Visual and Other Pleasures* (Indianapolis: Indiana University Press, 1989), 14–26; E. Ann Kaplan, "Is the Gaze Male?," in *Women and Film: Both Sides of the Camera* (New York: Methuen, 1983), 23–35.

200 Armstrong describes the "female gaze" as such in Carol Armstrong, "This Photography Which Is Not One: In the Gray Zone with Tina Modotti," *The MIT Press* 101 (2002), 47.

201 Michel Foucault, *The Birth of the Clinic: An Archaeology of Medical Perception*, translated by A.M. Sheridan Smith (New York: Vintage Books, 1994), 8.

202 Rosinsky, *Suzanne Valadon* (1994), 89.

203 Betterton, "How Do Women Look?"; Mathews, "Returning the Gaze."

204 Zhao, "Ambitious Model, Ambiguous Artist," 184.

205 Ellen Matlok-Ziemann, "'Blue with Age,' Dis-and Dys-appearance of the Body in Eudora Welty's 'A Worn Path,'" in *Embodied Narration: Illness, Death and Dying in Modern Culture* edited by Heike Hartung (Bielefeld: Transcript Publishing, 2018), 105.

206 Sara Hofmeier, Cristin Runfola, Margarita Sala, Danielle Gagne, Kimberly Brownley and Cynthia Bulik, "Body Image, Aging, and Identity in Women over 50: The Gender and Body Image (GABI) Study," *Journal of Women & Aging* 29, no. 1 (2017), 3–14.

207 Laura Hurd, "Aging, Gender, and the Body," in *The Oxford Handbook of the Sociology of Body and Embodiment*, edited by Natalie Boero and Katherine Mason (New York: Oxford University Press, 2021), 184.

208 Susan Sontag, "The Double Standard of Aging," *Saturday Review*, September 23, 1972, 29–38.

209 Ibid.

210 Meskimmon, *The Art of Reflection*, 175.

211 Hurd, "Aging, Gender, and the Body," 185.

212 Exhibition wall panel with no citation. See *Suzanne Valadon: Model, Painter, Rebel*, edited by Nancy Ireson (Philadelphia: The Barnes Foundation in association with London: Paul Holberton Publishing, 2021).

213 Institut National d'Etudes Démographiques, "Life Expectancy in France," www.ined.fr/en/everything_about_population/graphs-maps/interpreted-graphs/life-expectancy-france/. Accessed May 16, 2021; Statistics Sweden, "Life Expectancy 1751–2020," www.scb.se/en/finding-statistics/statistics-by-subject-area/population/population-composition/population-statistics/pong/tables-and-graphs/yearly-statistics--the-whole-country/life-expectancy/. Accessed May 16, 2021.

214 Jacques Guenne describes an encounter with Valadon highlighting unladylike and hysterical behavior in "Hommage à Suzanne Valadon," *L'Art Vivant*, 14 (1938), 37.

215 Simone de Beauvoir, *La Vieillesse* (Paris: Gallimard, 1970), 7.

216 Ibid., 8.

217 Silvia Stoller, *Simone de Beauvoir's Philosophy of Age: Gender, Ethics, and Time* (Berlin: DeGruyter, 2014), 3.

218 Ibid., 19.

219 Matlok-Ziemann, "Blue with Age," 103.

220 Tamar Garb, "'The human race torn to pieces': The Painted Portraits of Alice Neel," in *Alice Neel: Painted Truths*, edited by Jeremy Lewison, Frank Auerbach, Marlene Dumas and Chris Ofili (New Haven: Yale University Press, 2010), 29. Garb overlooks Valadon when listing nude self-portraits by women predating Neel's. Bauer notes their similarities in Denise Bauer, "Alice Neel's Female Nudes," *Woman's Art Journal* (1994): 21–6.

221 Mary D. Garrard, "Alice Neel and Me," *Woman's Art Journal* (2006), 4.

222 Sketches for *Le Lancement du filet* and *La Joie de vivre* were exhibited as early as 1928. The majority of the male nude drawings including *Homme nu, de dos* were not shown until 1967 or later. Georgel, *Suzanne Valadon*, 76, 88.

223 Clark, *The Nude*, 3.

224 Ibid., 138.

225 Callen, *The Spectacular Body*, 145.

226 Fionna Barber, "Case Study 6: Caillebotte, Masculinity, and the Bourgeois Gaze," in *The Challenge of the Avant-Garde*, edited by Paul Wood (New Haven: Yale University Press, 1999), 152.

227 Ibid., 145.

228 Tamar Garb, *Bodies of Modernity: Figure and Flesh in Fin-de-siècle France* (London: Thames & Hudson, 1998), 50.

229 Barber, "Case Study 6," 153.

230 Ibid., 152.

231 Callen, *The Spectacular Body*, 145.

232 Ibid., 147.

233 "If it is normal to see paintings of women's bodies as the territory across which men artists claim their modernity and compete for leadership of the avant-garde, can we expect to rediscover paintings by women in which they battled with their sexuality in the representation of the male nude? Of course not; the very suggestion seems ludicrous." Griselda Pollock, "Modernity and the Spaces of Femininity," in *Vision and Difference: Feminism, Femininity and the Histories of Art* (London: Routledge Classics, 1988), 76.

234 Gustave Geffroy quoted in Broude, "Edgar Degas and French Feminism," 654.
235 Callen, *The Spectacular Body*, 109.
236 Ibid., 109, also see Armstrong, *Odd Man Out.*
237 Callen, *The Spectacular Body*, 109.
238 Mulvey, "Visual Pleasure and Narrative Cinema," 14–26.
239 See Mary Ann Doane, "Film and the Masquerade: Theorizing the Female Spectator," in *Feminism and Film*, edited E. Ann Kaplan (Oxford: Oxford University Press, 2000), 422.
240 Shackelford, "The Body Transformed: Degas's Last Nudes," 173.
241 Ibid.
242 Sketches for these paintings were executed on tracing paper: *Portraits de famille* (1912), oil on canvas; *Nature morte à la théière* (1914), oil on cardboard; and *Lancement du filet.* See Pétridès, *L'Oeuvre complet de Suzanne Valadon.*
243 Ibid.
244 Various painted studies related to this work and *La Joie de vivre* appear in the catalogue raisonné, ibid.
245 Marsha Meskimmon, *Women Making Art: History, Subjectivity, Aesthetics* (London: Routledge, 2012), 76.
246 Simone de Beauvoir, *The Second Sex*, translated by Constance Borde and Sheila Malovany-Chevallier (New York: Vintage Books, 2011), 162.

Conclusion: Subversive sexualities

> Woman's desire can find expression only in dreams. It can never, under any circumstances, take on a "conscious" shape.
>
> Luce Irigaray, *Speculum of Another Woman*[1]

At the conclusion of a tumultuous and revelatory year of heated gender debates and disclosures of sexual misconduct, an art scandal in New York City rocked the headlines. On Christmas Eve, 2017, Carolina Falkholt (b. 1977), a Swedish artist known for her feminist public art pieces, painted a four-story-high mural on a building on Broome Street on the Lower East Side. Manhattanites awoke to the sight of a towering, erect penis in fluorescent pink. A few days later, she painted a four-story vagina mural on a neighboring building in analogously vibrant hues. New Yorkers would thus have been granted a gender-balanced viewing experience – the male and female sexual organs were matching in scale and painted in an equally eye-catching magenta. In the end, this was not possible as the community protested the phallic display. Within a few short days, the penis mural vanished. The vaginal scene, though, was not removed.[2]

This contemporary artist has no relationship with the artists discussed in this book. However, the response that her art provoked demonstrates that there are several shared issues at stake. When women assert sexual agency through representations of the body, they seem to contravene societal mores and customs. Their work may be viewed as an assault on the patriarchal artistic tradition. Although no longer off limits for female artists, the male nude is still a controversial choice of subject. While the eroticized female body and its parts are common in Western art of the past century, the sexualized male nude is less frequently displayed, and representations of male genitalia are often deemed offensive to the eye.[3] When depictions of the nude are too transgressive, censorship intervenes. Falkholt was subjected to censorship, just as Valadon had been one century earlier.

As Vassilieff, Charmy and Valadon reimagined nude representation in art, they daringly turned to their own image. As we have seen, Valadon disrobed and depicted herself with equal realism and audacity as her other nudes. She offered thousands of viewers an unsparing view of her naked figure in the 1920 Salon des Indépendants, eleven years after its initial conception. Although, at the time, the painting was not acknowledged as a nude self-portrait by critics – the idea of painting one's body as a near-to-life-sized nude along with a naked companion, much less expose it, was inconceivable as much for a man as for a woman. Valadon made a claim to woman's artistic and sexual capacity by assuming the role of renewed Eve and modern painter simultaneously. Tracing her oeuvre, we discovered that, a decade later, Valadon heralded in a new artistic subgenre – the old-age nude self-portrait. These works evince a faithful study of physiognomy rather than a narcissistic portrayal. Through her inventive and fearless nude self-portraits, Valadon challenged societal attitudes and taboos about womanhood, sexuality and aging.

In Charmy's oeuvre, self-portraiture and the nude genre are embedded. Her self-staging was not prominent like Valadon's, but equivocal and at times, covert. In her nude self-portraits, the sense of the visceral is heightened, while the mark of the painter is pronounced. Her corporeal nudes combined with her unique painterly approach lend themselves to posterior theories of Luce Irigaray, who emphasizes the tactile nature of woman's sexuality. I have underlined Charmy's artistic individuality as it distinguishes her nudes from those by her avant-garde colleagues. Rather than a possessive grasping, her work implies a symbiotic relationship between artist and model, as well as beholder and nude. Roughness has long connoted maleness in art history, both before and during Charmy's time. It has also been claimed that individual expression and the unique mark of the painter's hand implies greatness, even ingenuity.[4] This argument is rarely extended to women artists prior to the late twentieth century. However, the sense of touch, as Irigaray reveals, is innately feminine. Charmy's cultivation of a unique painterly approach demonstrates how a woman's emboldened style can serve as intimate sexual expression.

I have also aimed to establish how androgyny is a tool not exclusive to male artists. In her nude self-portrait doll and its numerous iterations, Vassilieff explored gender as non-binary. She untethered herself from any fixed notion of early-twentieth century womanhood, with a mobile, androgynous body absent of clear sexual markers. Moreover, she abbreviated her features and incorporated those of an African Pende mask, prevaricating static conceptions of ethnicity and race. In other images, she cross-dressed in a suit jacket and tie, performing masculinity. Through these self-portraits, she pronounced her status as Other within her estranged Parisian milieu. She performed a disidentificatory process, as outlined by José Esteban Muñoz, paving new avenues of identification. Like certain postmodern and contemporary artists, her self-portrait practice is a complex process of recycling and remaking, as she countered hegemonic binaries and affirmed her identity and gender as pliable and transmutable.

In this book, I have examined how three early twentieth-century artists explored issues of race, gender, sexuality and the self in art and transgressed the boundaries of bourgeois propriety and femininity in unprecedented ways. Underlining the bold nature of their work and its public response proves difficult, however, since in most cases they did not exhibit their most daring nudes. Out of the three, Valadon took the greatest risks by displaying her work in major public venues such as the Salon des Indépendants and the Salon d'Automne. She tested the threshold of acceptable male nudity in art, experimenting with varying degrees of realism and idealization. In *Adam and Eve*, she exceeded the limits of decorum and was forced to censor her work. Later in *Le Lancement du filet*, she avoided censorship by idealizing the male form and carefully hiding the genitals. The resulting image seemed like a celebration of the male body painted by a desiring heterosexual female artist; it greatly disquieted viewers. In her drawings of male bathers, Valadon contravened laws of gender inherent in art and pronounced the "bodiliness" of the male figure. She depicted the male form as exposed and vulnerable, corporeal and embodied. She never exhibited these drawings; perhaps she suspected that they were too brazen for contemporary audiences. Charmy was lauded for her female nudes and her bravura brushwork, especially in the 1920s. But her contemporaries were not aware of the full breadth of her oeuvre. While painting delicate nudes in the mode of the *forme féminine*, she simultaneously mined the topic of female sexuality in a private body of work dedicated to the eroticized female nude and nude self-portrait. In these highly charged images, she found ways of expressing the sensuality of the female body without reducing the figure to her sex. Moreover, she alluded to lesbian desire without the literal representation of two female bodies, which might run the risk of becoming a voyeuristic spectacle for the heterosexual male viewer. It is uncertain whether Vassilieff ever exhibited her double-sided and inverted Cubist painting, *Homme et femme*. There is no record that indicates that it was shown publicly. This fact, along with the construction of the work itself, raises questions about viewership. Given its daring and unprecedented depiction of the male body, perhaps Vassilieff chose her audience selectively, as Picasso had done with *Les Demoiselles d'Avignon* (1907).[5] Rather than display it before a wide audience at the Indépendants and Salon d'Automne, it is probable that she showed the piece to colleagues and students at her academy and canteen. Regardless of who saw it, one thing is certain: Vassilieff created the work as a means of experimenting with the male and female nude simultaneously, and she merged and conflated their characteristics into forms that resist gender binaries.

Each of these artists approached the nude in a manner extraordinarily advanced for their time. With few exceptions, it was not until the latter half of the twentieth century that women would explore the male body, gender parity or female desire in representations of the human form. During the feminist art movement, the body became a battleground for women artists. They strove to topple the nude from its pedestal and wrest it away from patriarchy's tireless grip. Vassilieff, Charmy and Valadon did not live to witness this watershed movement. They were not feminists, and they could not possibly have been motivated by an agenda which had yet to be articulated. Even without an overt ideological motive, they ruptured conventions of the nude and pioneered modern body imagery. And before the advent of vocabulary or theory to effectively describe female sexuality, relationships or experiences, whether heterosexual, homosexual, bisexual, etc., they approached alternative sexualities in their work. The art of these three women is critical to the history modern art. Their work not only sheds light on early twentieth-century body politics, but can enhance our understanding of women artists thereafter. As Linda Nochlin once stated, "the work of women artists well before the momentous 1970s needs to be examined with specificity and critical insight in order to provide meaningful historical context for the work and ambitions of younger women artists today."[6]

It has not been my intention to elevate Vassilieff, Charmy and Valadon as eminent masters of greatness comparable to Degas, Matisse or Picasso. Moreover, I have made no effort to link any particular aesthetic to this trio or to women artists in general. Indeed, the sheer diversity across their oeuvres resists any single stylistic classification. Rather, I have investigated how three disparate artists explored a subject so essential to the art tradition, yet which had for centuries been regulated and restricted for artists of their gender. While access was granted at the turn of the twentieth century, for a woman to paint modern body imagery that challenged prevailing artistic and societal conventions was nevertheless a courageous act. My objective has been to spotlight women's novel engagements within this genre by studying select artists in relation to issues of sexuality, gender identity and modernity. I have re-engaged with questions first posed by feminist art historians in the 1970s and 1980s, which some scholars have since put to rest. I have been guided by the fact that, for women artists, the body and sexuality have long been important subjects, before and after they gained sanctioned access to the nude model. Finally, I have aimed to show how Vassilieff, Charmy and Valadon each forged distinct approaches for the expression of female subjectivity, desire and agency in art. As they explored the denied political and social representations of the body as well as the proscribed self-representation in the form of unclothed self-portraits, Vassilieff, Charmy and Valadon contested their exclusion from the avant-garde, engaged in the transformation of the nude made modern, and affirmed their identities as embodied and subversive selves.

Notes

1 Luce Irigaray, *Speculum of Another Woman* (Ithaca: Cornell University Press, 1985), 125.

2 Peter Libbey, "Lower East Side Murals Cause a Stir, and One Is Painted Over," *New York Times*, December 29, 2017, C3. Print.

3 See: Mira Schor, *Wet: On Painting, Feminism and Art Culture* (Durham, NC: Duke University Press, 1997), and Alyce Mahon, *Eroticism and Art* (Oxford: Oxford University Press, 2007).

4 See: Nicola Suthor, *Rembrandt's Roughness* (Princeton: Princeton University Press, 2018); Richard Shiff, "Cézanne's Physicality: The Politics of Touch," in *The Language of Art History*, edited by Salim Kemal and Ivan Gaskell (Cambridge: Cambridge University Press, 1991), and more examples in Chapter 2.

5 Picasso's *Les Demoiselles d'Avignon* (1907), oil on canvas, Museum of Modern Art, New York, was exhibited for the first time at the Salon d'Antin in 1916. Vassilieff's work was exhibited there simultaneously.

6 Linda Nochlin, "Women Artists Then and Now: Painting, Sculpture, and the Image of the Self," in *Global Feminisms: New Directions in Contemporary Art*, edited by Maura Reilly and Linda Nochlin (London: Merrell, 2007), 47.

Select bibliography

Archives, galleries and museums consulted

Archives, Musée Colette, Saint-Sauveur-en-Puisaye
Bibliothèque Nationale de France
Centre Historique des Archives Nationales, Paris (Fonds Picasso)
Claude Bernès, Paris (Marie Vassilieff archives)
Documentation from Charmy's descendants
Fralin Museum, University of Virginia
Kandinsky Library, Centre Pompidou (Fonds Constantin Brancusi)
Kandinsky Library, Centre Pompidou (Fonds Robert Le Masle – Archives of André Utter, Utrillo, Valadon)
Kandinsky Library, Centre Pompidou
La Maison de Colette, Saint-Sauveur-en-Puisaye (Les Archives Colette)
Musée d'Arts de Nantes
Musée d'Orsay
Musée de Grenoble
Musée de Montmartre
Musée des Beaux-Arts de Limoges
Musée des Beaux-Arts de Lyon
Musée des Beaux-Arts du Palais Carnolès de Menton
Musée Espace Valadon, Bessines-sur-Gartempe
Musée Municipal Paul-Dini, Villefranche-sur-Saône
Musée Utrillo-Valadon, Sannois
National Art Library, Victoria and Albert Museum
Société d'Histoire et d'Archéologie Le Vieux Montmartre
The Courtauld Institute, London (The Witt Library)

Art journals and newspapers consulted

L'Amour de l'Art
Art et Décoration

L'Aurore
L'Art Vivant
Bulletin de La Vie Artistique
Comoedia
Le Gaulois
Gil Blas
L'Intransigeant
Lemouzi
Maintenant
Le Matin
Le Monde Illustré
Montjoie!
Montparnasse
Les Nouvelles Litteraires
Le Populaire de Paris
La Presse
Soirées de Paris

Publications

Adamowicz, Elma, and Simona Storchi (eds). *Back to the Futurists: The Avant-garde and Its Legacy*. Manchester: Manchester University Press, 2017.

Adrian, Dennis, and Russell Bowman. *Sylvia Sleigh: Invitation to a Voyage and Other Works*. Milwaukee: Milwaukee Art Museum, 1990.

Affron, Matthew. *Émilie Charmy*. Charlottesville: The Fralin Museum of Art, University of Virginia, 2013.

Antliff, Mark. *Inventing Bergson: Cultural Politics and the Parisian Avant-Garde*. Princeton: Princeton University Press, 1993.

Antliff, Mark. "The Rhythms of Duration: Bergson and the Art of Matisse." In *The New Bergson*, edited by John Mullarkey. Manchester: Manchester University Press, 1999.

Antliff, Mark. "The Fourth Dimension and Futurism: A Politicized Space." *The Art Bulletin* 82, no. 4 (2000): 720–33.

Apollinaire, Guillaume. *Les Peintres cubistes: méditations esthetiques*, edited by L. C. Breunig and J.-Cl. Chevalier. Paris: Hermann, 1965.

Apollinaire, Guillaume. *Chroniques d'art, 1902–1918*, edited by Leroy C. Breunig. Paris: Gallimard, 2002.

Ariès, Philippe, and Michelle Perrot (eds). *A History of Private Life: From the Fires of Revolution to the Great War*, vol. 4. Cambridge, MA: Belknap Press of Harvard University Press, 1990.

Armstrong, Carol. "The Reflexive and the Possessive View: Thoughts on Ker, Brandt and the Photographic Nude." *Representations* 25 (1989): 57.

Armstrong, Carol. *Odd Man Out: Readings of the Work and Reputation of Edgar Degas*. Chicago: University of Chicago Press, 1991.

Armstrong, Carol. "This Photography Which Is Not One: In the Gray Zone with Tina Modotti." *The MIT Press* 101 (2002): 19–52.

Barber, Fionna. "Case Study 6: Caillebotte, Masculinity, and the Bourgeois Gaze." In *The Challenge of the Avant-Garde*, edited by Paul Wood. New Haven: Yale University Press, 1999.

Bard, Christine. *Les Garçonnes: modes et fantasmes des années folles*. Paris: Flammarion, 1998.

Bard, Christine. *Une histoire politique du pantalon*. Paris: Éditions du Seuil, 2010.

Barney, Natalie C. *Aventures de l'esprit*. Paris: Émile-Paul Frères, 1929.

Bauer, Denise. "Alice Neel's Female Nudes." *Woman's Art Journal* (1994): 21–6.

Beauvoir, Simone de. *La Vieillesse*. Paris: Gallimard, 1970.

Beauvoir, Simone de. *The Second Sex*, translated by Constance Borde and Sheila Malovany-Chevallier. New York: Vintage Books, 2011.

Becker, Jane R., and Gabriel P. Weisberg. *Overcoming All Obstacles: The Women of the Académie Julian*. New York: The Dahesh Museum, 2004.

Bell, Susan Groag, and Karen M. Offen (eds). *Women, the Family, and Freedom: The Debate in Documents. Volume One, 1750–1880*. Stanford: Stanford University Press, 1983.

Bénézit, Emmanuel. *Dictionnaire des peintres, sculpteurs, dessinateurs et graveurs*. Vol. 3. Paris: Gründ, 2006.

Benstock, Shari. *Women of the Left Bank: Paris, 1900–1940*. Austin: University of Texas Press, 1986.

Béraud, Henri, Roland Dorgelès and Louis-Léon Martin, *Émilie Charmy*, exhibition catalogue. Paris: Galeries d'Oeuvres d'Art, 1921.

Berger, John. *Ways of Seeing*. Harmondsworth: Penguin, 1972.

Bergson, Henri. *An Introduction to Metaphysics*, translated by T.E. Hulme. New York: G. P. Putnam's Sons, 1912.

Bergson, Henri. *Matter and Memory*, translated by N.M. Paul and W.S. Palmer. New York: Zone Books, 1988.

Bernès, Claude, and Benoît Noël. *Marie Vassilieff (1884–1957): l'oeuvre artistique, l'académie de peinture, la cantine de Montparnasse*. Livarot-Pays-d'Auge: Éditions BVR, 2017.

Bernheimer, Charles. "Manet's 'Olympia.'" *Poetics Today* 10, no. 2 (1989): 263.

Bertaut, J. "Réponse à une enquête sur la jeunesse." *Le Gaulois*, June 15, 1912.

Betterton, Rosemary. "How Do Women Look? The Female Nude in the Work of Suzanne Valadon." In *Looking On: Images of Femininity in the Visual Arts and Media*. London: Pandora Press, 1987.

Betterton, Rosemary. *Intimate Distance: Women, Artists and the Body*. London: Routledge, 1996.

Birnbaum, Paula J. *Women Artists in Interwar France: Framing Femininities*. Farnham: Ashgate, 2011.

Bishop, Cécile. "Portraiture, Race, and Subjectivity: The Opacity of Marie-Guillemine Benoist's Portrait d'une négresse." *Word and Image* 35, no. 1 (2019): 1–11.

Blanchard, Pascal, Sandrine Lemaire, Nicolas Bancel, Dominic Richard and David Thomas (eds). *Colonial Culture in France since the Revolution*. Bloomington: Indiana University Press, 2014.

Boccioni, Umberto, Carlo D. Carra, Luigi Russolo, Giacomo Balla and Gino Severini. *Les Peintres futuristes italiens*. Paris: Bernheim-Jeune & Cie, 1912.

Boero, Natalie, and Katherine Mason (eds). *The Oxford Handbook of the Sociology of Body and Embodiment*. New York: Oxford University Press, 2021.

Boittin, Jennifer. *Colonial Metropolis: The Urban Grounds of Anti-Imperialism and Feminism in Interwar Paris*. Lincoln: University of Nebraska Press, 2010.

Bonafoux, Pascal, Jorge Semprún and David Rosenberg, *Moi je, par soi-même: l'autoportrait au XXe siècle*. Paris: Diane de Selliers, 2004.

Bond, Anthony, and Joanna Woodall (eds). *Self Portrait: Renaissance to Contemporary*. London: National Portrait Gallery, 2005.

Bonnet, Marie-Jo. *Les Deux Amies: essai sur le couple de femmes dans l'art*. Paris: Éditions Blanche, 2002.

Bonnet, Marie-Josèphe. *Simone de Beauvoir et les femmes*. Paris: Michel, 2015.

Borzello, Frances. *Seeing Ourselves: Women's Self-Portraits*. London: Thames & Hudson, 2016.

Bouche, Edmond. "Ma mère." *Le Peintre* 54 (December 1, 1952): 11.

Bowlt, John, and Matthew Drutt (eds). *Amazons of the Avant-Garde: Alexandra Exter, Natalia Goncharova, Liubov Popova, Olga Rozanova, Varvara Stepanova, and Nadezhda Udaltsova*. New York: Guggenheim Museum, 2000.

Braun, Emily, and Rebecca Rabinow (eds). *Cubism: The Leonard A. Lauder Collection*. York and New Haven: The Metropolitan Museum of Art and Yale University Press, 2014.

Broude, Norma. "Edgar Degas and French Feminism, ca. 1880: 'The Young Spartans,' the Brothel Monotypes, and the Bathers Revisited." *Art Bulletin* (1988): 653, 654, 655.

Broude, Norma. *Impressionism: A Feminist Reading: The Gendering of Art, Science, and Nature in the Nineteenth Century*. Boulder: Westview Press / Icon Editions, 1997.

Brown, Marilyn. "'Miss La La's' Teeth: Reflections on Degas and 'Race.'" *The Art Bulletin* 89, no. 4 (2007): 738–65.

Bryson, Norman. *Looking at the Overlooked: Four Essays on Still Life Painting*. London: Reaktion, 1990.

Bucur, Maria. *Gendering Modernism: A Historical Reappraisal of the Canon*. New York: Bloomsbury, 2017.

Bunoust, Madeleine. *Quelques femmes peintres*. Paris: Stock, 1936.

Butler, Judith. *Gender Trouble: Feminism and the Subversion of Identity*. New York: Routledge, 1990.

Cachin, Françoise, Charles S. Moffett and Michel Melot. *Manet, 1832–1883*. New York: Metropolitan Museum of Art, 1983.

Callander, Margaret. "Colette and the Hidden Woman: Sexuality, Silence, Subversion." In *French Erotic Fiction: Women's Desiring Writing, 1880–1990*, edited by Alex Hughes and Kate Ince. Oxford: Berg, 1996.

Callen, Anthea. *The Spectacular Body: Science, Method and Meaning in the Work of Degas*. New Haven: Yale University Press, 1995.

Callen, Anthea. "The Body and Difference: Anatomy Training at the Ecole des Beaux-Arts in Paris in the Later Nineteenth Century." *Art History* 20, no. 1 (1997): 23–60.

Callen, Anthea. *Looking at Men: Anatomy, Masculinity and the Modern Male Body*. New Haven: Yale University Press, 2018.

Camfield, William A. "Juan Gris and the Golden Section." *The Art Bulletin* 47, no. 1 (1965): 128–34.

Carco, Francis. *Le Nu dans la peinture moderne, 1863–1920*. Paris: G. Crès, 1924.

Carlier, Sylvie. *Émilie Charmy*. Villefranche-sur-Saône: Musée Municipal Paul-Dini, 2008.

Carlier, Sylvie, and Dominique Lobstein. *Le Postimpressionnisme et Rhône-Alpes (1886–1914): la couleur dans la lumière*. Villefranche-sur-Saône, Musée Paul-Dini, 2015.

Carrillo, E. Gomez. "Émilie Charmy." Exhibition at Galerie André Pesson, Paris, June, 1919.

Catalogue officiel Illustré de l'exposition centennale de l'art français de 1800 à 1889. Paris: Ludovic Baschet, 1900.

Cendrars, Blaise. *Une nuit dans la forêt*. Lausanne: Au Verseau, 1929.

Chadwick, Whitney, and Dawn Ades. *Mirror Images: Women, Surrealism, and Self-Representation*. Cambridge, MA: MIT Press, 1998.

Childs, Adrienne L. Nancy Ireson, Lauren Jimerson, Denise Murrell, Ebonie Pollock, "Disrupting Tradition: Suzanne Valadon's *Black Venus*," transcribed and edited by Corrinne Chong. In *Suzanne Valadon: Model, Painter, Rebel*, edited by Nancy Ireson. Philadelphia: The Barnes Foundation in association with London: Paul Holberton Publishing, 2021, 30–41.

Chadwick, Whitney. *Women Artists and the Surrealist Movement*. New York: Thames & Hudson, 2002.

Chadwick, Whitney. *Farewell to the Muse: Love, War and the Women of Surrealism*. New York: Thames & Hudson, 2017.

Chadwick, Whitney, and Tirza Latimer, "Becoming Modern." In *The Modern Woman Revisited: Paris between the Wars*. New Brunswick: Rutgers University Press, 2003.

Champa, Kermit S. "Frédéric Bazille: The 1978 Retrospective Exhibition." *Arts Magazine* 52 (1978): 110.

Chenoune, Farid. *Les Dessous de la féminité: un siècle de lingerie*. Paris: Assouline, 2005.

Cirlot, J.E. *A Dictionary of Symbols*. Newburyport: Dover Publications, 2013.

Clark, Kenneth. *The Nude: A Study in Ideal Form*. New York: Pantheon Books, 1956.

Clark, T.J. *The Painting of Modern Day Life: Paris in the Art of Manet and His Followers*. Princeton: Princeton University Press, 1984.

Clarke, Jay A., and Marilyn McCully. *Picasso | Encounters*. Williamstown, MA: Clark Art Institute, 2017.

Clifford, James. *The Predicament of Culture: Twentieth-century Ethnography, Literature, and Art*. Cambridge, MA: Harvard University Press, 2002.

Cogeval, Guy, Claude Arnaud, Philippe Comar, Charles Dantzig and Collectif. *Masculin masculin: L'homme nu dans l'art de 1800 à nos jours*. Paris: Flammarion, 2013.

Colette. Preface to *Quelques toiles de Charmy, quelques pages de Colette*. Paris: Galerie d'Art Ancien et Moderne, 1921.

Colette. *The Vagabond*, translated by Enid McLeod. New York: Farrar, Straus and Giroux, 1955.

Colette. "Les Vrilles de la vigne." In *The Collected Stories of Colette*, translated by Matthew Ward et al. New York: Farrar, Straus, Giroux, 1983.

Colette. "Sleepless Nights." In *The Collected Stories of Colette*, translated by Matthew Ward et al. New York: Farrar, Straus, Giroux, 1983.

Colette. *The Pure and the Impure*, translated by Herma Briffault. New York: New York Review of Books, 2000.

Collet, Isabelle, and Dominique Lobstein. *Paris 1900: la ville spectacle*. Paris: Petit Palais, Musée des Beaux-Arts de la Ville de Paris, 2014.

Costlow, Jane T., Stephanie Sandler and Judith Vowles (eds). *Sexuality and the Body in Russian Culture*. Stanford: Stanford University Press, 1993.

Cottington, David. *Cubism in the Shadow of War: The Avant-Garde and Politics in Paris: 1905–1914*. New Haven: Yale University Press, 1998.

Cottington, David. *Cubism and Its Histories*. Manchester: Manchester University Press, 2004.

Crespelle, Jean-Paul. *La Vie quotidienne à Montmartre au temps de Picasso: 1900–1919*. Paris: Hachette, 1978.

Crespelle, Jean-Paul. *Montmartre vivant*. Paris: Hachette, 1964.

Cummins, Laurel. *Colette and the Conquest of Self*. Birmingham, AL: Summa Publications, Inc., 2005.

Dabrowski, Magdalena. *Liubov Popova*. New York: Museum of Modern Art, 1991.

Dade, Juliette. "Exploring Sapphic Discourse in the Belle Époque: Colette, Renée Vivien, and Liane de Pougy." Ph.D. dissertation, University of Illinois at Urbana-Champaign, 2009.

Dagen, Philippe. "Bazille, astre éphémère." *Le Monde*, July 17, 1992.

Dailey, Victoria. *Tea and Morphine: Women in Paris, 1880 to 1914*. Los Angeles: Hammer Museum, 2014.

Dawkins, Heather. *The Nude in French Art and Culture, 1870–1910*. Cambridge: Cambridge University Press, 2002.

Debray, Cécile, Isabelle Bardon, Estelle Bégué, David Bindman et al. *Le Modèle noir de Géricault à Matisse*. Paris: Musée d'Orsay, 2019.

Debray, Cécile, and Françoise Lucbert. *La Section d'Or 1912, 1920, 1925*. Paris: Cercle d'Art, 2000.

Degas, Edgar and Marcel Guérin. *Degas, lettres*. Paris: Bernard Grasset, 1945.

Delaunay, Sonia. *Nous irons jusqu'au soleil*. Paris: Éditions Robert Laffont, 1978.

Derouet, Christian. "Chronologie et bibliographie." In *Fernand Léger: une correspondance de guerre à Louis Poughon, 1914–1918*. Paris: Centre Georges Pompidou, 1997.

Derouet, Christian (ed.). *Fernand Léger: une correspondance de guerre à Louis Poughon, 1914–1918*. Paris: Éditions du Centre Georges Pompidou, 1997.

Derrida, Jacques. *Archive Fever: A Freudian Impression*, translated by Eric Prenowitz. Chicago: University of Chicago Press, 2005.

Doane, Mary Ann. "Masquerade Reconsidered: Further Thoughts on the Female Spectator" *Discourse* 11, no. 1 (Fall–Winter 1988–89): 42–54.

Doane, Mary Ann. "Film and the Masquerade: Theorizing the Female Spectator." In *Feminism and Film*, edited by E. Ann Kaplan. Oxford: Oxford University Press, 2000.

Dranch, Sherry A. "Reading through the Veiled Text: Colette's 'The Pure and the Impure.'" *Contemporary Literature* 24, no. 2 (1983): 177.

Duncan, Carol. "Virility and Domination in Early Twentieth-Century Vanguard Painting." In *Feminism and Art History: Questioning the Litany*, edited by Norma Broude and Mary D. Garrard. New York: Harper & Row Publishers, 1982.

Dupont, Jacques. *Physique de Colette*. Toulouse: Presses Universitaires du Mirail, 2003.

Eddy, Arthur J. *Cubists and Post-Impressionism: With 23 Reproductions in Color of Cubist and Post-Impressionist Paintings, and 46 Half-Tone Illustrations*. Chicago: McClurg, 1914.

Einstein, Carl. *Negerplastik*. Munich: K. Wolff, 1920.

Elderfield, John. *The "Wild Beasts": Fauvism and Its Affinities*. New York: The Museum of Modern Art, 1976.

Elliott, Bridget. "The 'Strength of the Weak' as Portrayed by Marie Laurencin." In *Reclaiming Female Agency: Feminist Art History after Postmodernism*, edited by Norma Broude and Mary D. Garrard. Berkeley: University of California Press, 2005.

Ezra, Elizabeth. *The Colonial Unconscious: Race and Culture in Interwar France*. Ithaca: Cornell University Press, 2000.

Fabre, Gladys. "Albert Gleizes et l'abbaye de Créteil." In *Albert Gleizes: le cubisme en majesté*, edited by María T. Ocaña and Vincent Pomarède. Paris: Éditions de la Réunion des Musées Nationaux, 2001.

Fabre, Michel. "Rediscovering Aïcha, Lucy and D'al-Al, Colored French Stage Artists." *S&F Online* 6, nos 1–2 (2007–8).

Fallaize, Elizabeth, ed. *Simone de Beauvoir: A Critical Reader*. London: Routledge, 1998.

Faure, Elie. *Histoire de l'art: l'art medieval*. Paris: G. Crès et Cie, 1921.

Fishwick, Sarah. *The Body in the Work of Simone de Beauvoir*. Oxford: Peter Lang, 2002.

Flieger, Jerry Aline. *Colette and the Fantom Subject of Autobiography*. Ithaca: Cornell University Press, 1992.

Foster, Hal. "The Artist as Ethnographer." In *The Return of the Real*. Cambridge, MA: MIT Press, 2009.

Foucault, Michel. *The Birth of the Clinic: An Archaeology of Medical Perception*, translated by A.M. Sheridan Smith. New York: Vintage Books, 1994.

Freadman, Anne. "Colette misogyne?" *French Forum* 31, no. 3 (2006): 45–75.

Gabriel, Nelly. *Histoires de l'école nationale des beaux-arts de Lyon*. Lyon: Éditions Beau Fixe, 2007.

Garb, Tamar. "The Forbidden Gaze: Women Artists and the Male Nude in Late Nineteenth-century France." In *The Body Imaged: The Human Form and Visual Culture since the Renaissance*, edited by Kathleen Adler and Marcia Pointon. Cambridge: Cambridge University Press, 1993.

Garb, Tamar. *Sisters of the Brush: Women's Artistic Culture in Late Nineteenth Century Paris*. New Haven: Yale University Press, 1994.

Garb, Tamar. *Bodies of Modernity: Figure and Flesh in fin-de-siècle France*. London: Thames & Hudson, 1998.

Garb, Tamar. "'The human race torn to pieces': The Painted Portraits of Alice Neel." In *Alice Neel: Painted Truths*, edited by Jeremy Lewison, Frank Auerbach, Marlene Dumas and Chris Ofili. New Haven: Yale University Press, 2010.

Garrard, Mary D. "Alice Neel and Me." *Woman's Art Journal* (2006): 4.

Georgel, Pierre. *Suzanne Valadon*. Paris: Musée National d'Art Moderne, 1967.

Getsy, David. *Rodin: Sex and the Making of Modern Sculpture*. New Haven: Yale University Press, 2010.

Gilman, Sander. "Black Bodies, White Bodies: Toward an Iconography of Female Sexuality in Late Nineteenth-Century Art, Medicine, and Literature." *Critical Inquiry* 12, no. 1 (1985): 204–42.

Giraudy, Danièle. *Camoin: sa vie, son oeuvre*. Marseille: La Savoisienne, 1972.

Gleizes, Albert, and Jean Metzinger. *Du cubisme*. Paris: E. Figuière et Cie 1912.

Goebel, Michael. *Anti-imperial Metropolis: Interwar Paris and the Seeds of Third World Nationalism*. New York: Cambridge University Press, 2017.

Golding, John. *Cubism: A History and an Analysis, 1907–1914*. Cambridge, MA: Belknap Press of Harvard University Press, 1988.

Gonnard, Catherine, and Élisabeth Lebovici, *Femmes/artistes: Artistes Femmes: Paris, De 1880 À Nos Jours*. Paris: Hazan, 2007.

Grammont, Claudine. "Fauve sur nature." In *Charles Camoin: rétrospective: 1879–1965*, edited by Grammont and Véronique Serrano. Marseille: Musée de Marseille, 1997.

Grammont, Claudine. *Correspondance entre Charles Camoin et Henri Matisse*. Lausanne: La Bibliothèque des Arts, 1997.

Grammont, Claudine, and Bruno Ely, *Camoin dans sa lumière*. Paris: Lienart, 2016.

Green, Christopher. *Léger and the Avant-Garde*. New Haven: Yale University Press, 1976.

Green, Christopher. *Art in France, 1900–1940*. New Haven: Yale University Press, 2003.

Green, Malcolm. *The Doll*. London: Atlas Press, 2005.

Grew, Rachel. "The Immortal Self: Surrealist Alter Egos." Queen's University Belfast, 2007, https://repository.lboro.ac.uk/articles/The_immortal_self_surrealist_alter_eg os/9335282. Accessed January 20, 2020.

Grogin, Robert C. *The Bergsonian Controversy in France, 1900–1914*. Calgary: The University of Calgary Press, 1988.

Grossman, Wendy. "Unmasking Adrienne Fidelin: Picasso, Man Ray, and the (In)Visibility of Racial Difference." 5 (2020), https://doi.org/10.26597/mod.0142.

Halberstam, Jack. *Female Masculinity*. Durham, NC: Duke University Press, 1998.

Hamnett, Nina. *Laughing Torso: Reminiscences of Nina Hamnett*. London: Constable and Co., 1932.

Harding, James Martin. *Cutting Performances: Collage Events, Feminist Artists, and the American Avant-Garde*. Ann Arbor: University of Michigan Press, 2012.

Hartung, Heike (ed.) *Embodied Narration: Illness, Death and Dying in Modern Culture*. Bielefeld: Transcript Publishing, 2018.

Hatt, Michael. "The Male Body in Another Frame: Thomas Eakins' *The Swimming Hole* as a Homoerotic Image." In *The Body: Journal of Philosophy and the Visual Arts* 5, no. 21, edited by Andrew Benjamin. London: Academy Editions, 1993.

Hauptman, Jodi (ed.). *Degas: A Strange New Beauty*. New York: The Museum of Modern Art, 2016.

Hemus, Ruth. *Dada's Women*. New Haven: Yale University Press, 2009.

Henderson, Linda D. *The Fourth Dimension and Non-Euclidean Geometry in Modern Art*. Cambridge, MA: The MIT Press, 2013.

Herbert, James. *Fauve Painting: The Making of Cultural Politics*. New Haven: Yale University Press, 1992.

Hewitt, Catherine. *Renoir's Dancer: The Secret Life of Suzanne Valadon*. New York: St. Martin's Press, 2017.

Higonnet, Anne. *Berthe Morisot's Images of Women*. Cambridge, MA: Harvard University Press, 1992.

Hilaire, Michel and Paul Perrin. *Frédéric Bazille (1841–1870): La Jeunesse de l'Impressionisme*. Paris: Flammarion, 2016.

Hofmeier, Sara, Cristin Runfola, Margarita Sala, Danielle Gagne, Kimberly Brownley and Cynthia Bulik. "Body Image, Aging, and Identity in Women over 50: The Gender and Body Image (GABI) study." *Journal of Women & Aging* 29, no. 1 (2017): 3–14.

Huffer, Lynne. *Are the Lips a Grave?: A Queer Feminist on the Ethics of Sex*. New York: Columbia University Press, 2013.

Hunt, Courtney A. "Suzanne Valadon's Male Nudes." Master's thesis, Hunter College, Department of Art, 2013.

Hunt, Courtney. "Wicked, Hard and Supple: An Examination of Suzanne Valadon's Nude Drawings of Young Maurice." *Art Inquiries* XVII, no. 4 (2019): 410–22.

Hustvedt, Asti. *Medical Muses: Hysteria in Nineteenth-century Paris*. New York: W.W. Norton, 2011.

Hutton, Marcelline. *Remarkable Russian Women in Pictures, Prose and Poetry*. Lincoln, NE: Zea Books, 2013.

Irigaray, Luce. *Speculum of Another Woman*. Ithaca: Cornell University Press, 1985.

Irigaray, Luce. *This Sex Which Is Not One*, translated by Catherine Porter. Ithaca: Cornell University Press, 1985.

Irigaray, Luce. *An Ethics of Sexual Difference*, translated by Carolyn Burke and Gilian C. Gill. Ithaca: Cornell University Press, 1993.

Irigaray, Luce. "The Wedding between the Body and Language." In *Luce Irigaray: Key Writings*. London: Continuum, 2004.

Jaccard, Paul-André. *Alice Bailly: la fête étrange*. Lausanne: Musée Cantonal des Beaux Arts, 2006.

Jimerson, Lauren. "Defying Gender: The Nude in the Art of Suzanne Valadon." Master's Thesis, The Courtauld Institute of Art, 2011.

Jimerson, Lauren. "Defying Gender – Redefining the Nude: Female Artists and the Body in Early 20th Century Paris." Ph.D. dissertation, Rutgers University, 2018.

Jimerson, Lauren. "Defying Gender: Suzanne Valadon and the Male Nude." *Woman's Art Journal* 40, no. 1 (2019): 3–12.

Jimerson, Lauren. "Les Nus et auto-portraits nus des pionnières du XXe siècle." In *Pionnières: artistes dans le Paris des années folles*, edited by Camille Morineau and Lucia Pesapane. Paris: Editions de la Réunion des Musées Nationaux – Grand Palais, 2022.

Johnson, Stanley R. *Cubism & La Section d'Or: Reflections on the Development of the Cubist Epoch: 1907–1922*. Chicago: Klees-Gustorf Publishers, 1991.

Jones, Ann Rosalind. "Writing the Body: Toward an Understanding of 'L'Ecriture Feminine.'" *Feminist Studies* 7, no. 2 (1981): 247–63.

Jones, Rachel. *Irigaray: Towards a Sexuate Philosophy*. Cambridge: Polity Press, 2011.

Juffermans, Jan. *Kees Van Dongen: The Graphic Work*. Aldershot: Lund Humphries, 2003.

Jullian, Philippe, *Montmartre*. New York: Phaidon / E.P. Dutton, 1977.

Kaplan, E. Ann. "Is the Gaze Male?" In *Women and Film: Both Sides of the Camera*. New York: Methuen, 1983.

Kemfert, Beate. "The Life of Natalia Goncharova." In *Natalia Goncharova: Between Russian Tradition and European Modernity*. Ostfildern: Hatje Cantz, 2010.

Kendall, Richard and Griselda Pollock. *Dealing with Degas: Representations of Women and the Politics of Vision*. New York: Universe Publishing, 1992.

Klein, Mason, and Maurice Berger. *Modigliani beyond the Myth*. New Haven: Yale University Press, 2004.

Kiblitsky, Joseph, E.A. Petrova and Juan Allende-Blin. *Paris Russe, 1910–1960*. Saint Petersburg: Palace Editions, 2003.

Klüver, Billy, Julie Martin and Édith Ochs. *Kiki et Montparnasse: 1900–1930*. Paris: Flammarion, 1998.

Krebs, Sophie. *Albert Marquet, peintre du temps suspend*. Paris: Paris Musées Éditions, 2016.

Kristeva, Julia. *Colette*, translated by Jane Marie Todd. New York: Columbia University Press, 2004.

Kristeva, Julia. *Le Génie féminin: la vie, la folie, les mots*. Paris: Gallimard, 2004.

Kushner, Marilyn S., Kimberly Orcutt and Casey Nelson Blake, *The Armory Show at 100: Modernism and Revolution*. New York: New-York Historical Society, 2013.

Lacquer, Thomas. *Making Sex: Body and Gender from the Greeks to Freud*. Cambridge, MA: Harvard University Press, 1990.

Ladenson, Elisabeth. "Colette for Export Only." *Yale French Studies* 90, Same Sex / Different Text? Gay and Lesbian Writing in French (1996): 25–46.

Latimer, Tirza T. *Women Together / Women Apart: Portraits of Lesbian Paris*. New Brunswick: Rutgers University Press, 2005.

Laude, Jean. *La Peinture française (1905–1914) et "l'art Nègre" (contribution à l'étude des sources du fauvisme et du cubisme)*. Paris: Éditions Klincksieck, 1968.

Léger, Fernand. "Les Origines de la peinture et sa valeur representative." *Montjoie!* May 29, 1913: 7 and June 9–10, 1913: 14–29.

Léger, Fernand. "Les Réalisations picturales actuelles." *Les Soirées de Paris* 15 (June 1914): 349–56.

Lehtinen, Virpi. *Luce Irigaray's Phenomenology of Feminine Being*. Albany: State University of New York Press, 2014.

Libbey, Peter. "Lower East Side Murals Cause a Stir, and One Is Painted Over." *New York Times*, 29 December 2017: C3. Print.

Lichtenstein, Jacqueline. *La Couleur éloquente: rhétorique et peinture à l'âge classique*. Paris: Flammarion, 2003.

Lipton, Eunice. *Looking into Degas: Uneasy Images of Women and Modern Life*. Los Angeles: University of California Press, 1986.

Lobstein, Dominique. *Dictionnaire des Indépendants, 1884-1914*. Dijon: L'Échelle de Jacob, 2003.

Loyrette, Henri. *Degas: Passion and Intellect*, translated by Mark Paris. London: Thames & Hudson, 1993.

Lucey, Michael. *Never Say I: Sexuality and the First Person in Colette, Gide and Proust*. Durham, NC: Duke University Press, 2006.

Lyford, Amy. *Surrealist Masculinities: Gender Anxiety and the Aesthetics of Post-World War I Reconstruction in France*. Berkeley: University of California Press, 2007.

Madeline, Laurence. *Women Artists in Paris, 1850–1900*. New Haven: Yale University Press, 2017.

Mahon, Alyce. *Eroticism and Art*. Oxford: Oxford University Press, 2007.

Malyševa, Tanâ and Isabel Wünsche. *Marianne Werefkin and the Women Artists in Her Circle*. London: Brill/Rodopi, 2017.

Manning, Mary. "Frédéric Bazille and Masculinity between Paris and Montpellier, 1841–1870." Ph.D. dissertation, Rutgers University, 2015.

Maor, Eli, and Eugen Jost. *Beautiful Geometry*. Princeton: Princeton University Press, 2017.

Marcadé, Jean-Claude. "Léger et la Russie." *Europe: Revue Littéraire Mensuelle* 75 (1997): 58–72.

Marcadé, Jean-Claude, and Valentine. *L'Avant-garde au féminin, Moscou, Saint-Petersbourg, Paris: 1907–1930*. Paris: Artcurial, 1983.

Marchesseau, Daniel. *Suzanne Valadon*. Martigny: Fondation Pierre Gianadda, 1996.

Marcilhac, Felix. *Chana Orloff, catalogue raisonné*. Paris: Éditions de l'Amateur, 1992.

Marcus, Sharon. *Between Women: Friendship, Desire, and Marriage in Victorian England*. Princeton: Princeton University Press, 2009.

Marks, Elaine. *Colette*. New Brunswick: Rutgers University Press, 1960.

Marks, Elaine. "Transgressing the (In)cont(in)ent Boundaries: The Body in Decline." *Yale French Studies* 72 (1986): 181–200.

Mathews, Patricia. "Returning the Gaze: Diverse Representations of the Nude in the Art of Suzanne Valadon." *The Art Bulletin* 73, no. 3 (1991): 415–30.

Mathews, Patricia. *Passionate Discontent: Creativity, Gender, and French Symbolist Art*. Chicago: University of Chicago Press, 1999.

McBreen, Ellen. *Matisse's Sculpture: The Pinup and the Primitive*. New Haven: Yale University Press, 2014.

McMillan, James F. *France and Women 1789–1914: Gender, Society and Politics*. London: Routledge, 2002.

Merrick, Jeffrey, and Bryant Ragan (eds). *Homosexuality in Modern France*. New York: Oxford University Press, 1996.

Mesch, Rachel. "Sexual Healing: Power and Pleasure in Fin-de-siècle Women's Writing." In *Pleasure and Pain in Nineteenth-century French Literature and Culture*, edited by David Evans and Kate Griffiths. Amsterdam: Rodopi, 2008.

Meskimmon, Marsha. *The Art of Reflection: Women Artists' Self-portraiture in the Twentieth Century*. New York: Columbia University Press, 1996.

Meskimmon, Marsha. *Women Making Art: History, Subjectivity, Aesthetics*. London: Routledge, 2012.

Middleman, Rachel. *Radical Eroticism: Women, Art, and Sex in the 1960s*. Berkeley: University of California Press, 2018.

Monroe, John Warne. *Metropolitan Fetish: African Sculpture and the Imperial French Invention of Primitive Art*. Ithaca: Cornell University Press, 2019.

Morineau, Camille. *Elles@centrepompidou: artistes femmes dans les collections du Musée national d'art moderne, centre de création industrielle*. Paris: Éditions du Centre Pompidou, 2009.

Morineau, Camille, and Lucia Pesapane. *Pionnières: artistes dans le Paris des années folles*. Paris: Editions de la Réunion des Musées Nationaux – Grand Palais, 2022.

Mullarkey, John, and Charlotte de Mille (eds). *Bergson and the Art of Immanence: Painting, Photography, Film*. Edinburgh: Edinburgh University Press, 2013.

Mulvey, Laura. "Visual Pleasure and Narrative Cinema." In *Visual and Other Pleasures*. Indianapolis: Indiana University Press, 1989.

Munck, Jacqueline, Marc Restellini and Marie-Cécile Baudoin. *Valadon, Utrillo: au tournant du siècle à Montmartre: de l'impressionnisme à l'école de Paris*. Paris: Pinacothèque de Paris, 2009.

Muñoz, José Esteban. *Disidentifications: Queers of Color and the Performance of Politics*. Minneapolis: University of Minnesota Press, 1999.

Murrell, Denise. *Posing Modernity: The Black Model from Manet and Matisse to Today*. New Haven: Yale University Press, 2018.

Natter, Tobias G., and Elizabeth Leopold (eds). *Nude Men. From 1800 until the Present Day*, translated by Ian Pepper and Bronwen Saunders. Munich: Hirmer Publishers, 2012.

Nead, Lynda. *The Female Nude: Art, Obscenity and Sexuality*. London: Routledge, 1992.

Nochlin, Linda. "Some Women Realists: Painters of the Figure." *Arts Magazine* 48 (1974): 33.

Nochlin, Linda. *Women Art and Power and Other Essays*. London: Thames & Hudson, 1989.

Nochlin, Linda. "Women Artists Then and Now: Painting, Sculpture, and the Image of the Self." In *Global Feminisms: New Directions in Contemporary Art*, edited by Maura Reilly and Linda Nochlin. London: Merrell, 2007.

Nye, Robert A. *Crime, Madness and Politics in Modern France: The Medical Concept of National Decline*. Princeton: Princeton University Press, 2016.

Olsen, Scott A. *The Golden Section: Nature's Greatest Secret*. Glastonbury: Wooden Books, 2009.

Ooms, Saskia. *Valadon, Utrillo and Utter in the Rue Cortot Studio: 1912–1926*. Paris: Somogy Editions, 2015.

Oppenheimer, Margaret A. "'The Charming Spectacle of a Cadaver': Anatomical and Life Study by Women Artists in Paris, 1775–1815." *Nineteenth-century Art Worldwide* 6, no. 1 (Spring 2007).

Otto, Elizabeth and Patrick Rössler (eds). *Bauhaus Bodies, Gender, Sexuality, and Body Culture in Modernism's Legendary Art School*. New York: Bloomsbury, 2019.

Pagé, Suzanne Jean-Louis Andral, Sophie Krebs, Gladys Fabre et al., *L' École de Paris 1904–1929, la part de l'autre*. Paris: Museé d'Art Moderne de la Ville de Paris, 2001.

Pastoureau, Michel. *Rouge: histoire d'une couleur.* Paris: Seuil, 2016.

Perry, Gill. *Women Artists and the Parisian Avant-Garde.* Manchester: Manchester University Press, 1995.

Perry, Gill. "Women Painting Women: Gender, Modernism and 'Feminine' Art c. 1910–c. 1930." In *Rethinking Art between the Wars: New Perspectives in Art History*, edited by Hans D. Christensen, Niels Jensen-Marup and Øystein Hjort. Copenhagen: Museum Tusculanum Press: University of Copenhagen, 2001.

Perry, Gill. "Gender and the Fauves: Flirting with 'Wild Beasts.'" In *Art of the Avant-Gardes*, edited by Steve Edwards and Paul Wood. New Haven: Yale University Press in association with the Open University, 2004.

Pétridès, Paul. *L'Oeuvre complet de Suzanne Valadon.* Paris: Compagnie Française des Arts Graphiques, 1971.

Pitman, Dianne. *Bazille: Purity, Pose, and Painting in the 1860s.* University Park: The Pennsylvania State University Press, 1998.

Pollock, Ebonie. "Suzanne Valadon's *Black Venus:* The Representation and Reception of the Black Artist's Model in Interwar Paris." B.A. Thesis, Washington University in St. Louis, 2019.

Pollock, Griselda. "Modernity and the Spaces of Femininity." In *Vision and Difference: Feminism, Femininity and the Histories of Art.* London: Routledge Classics, 1988.

Pollock, Griselda. *Mary Cassatt: Painter of Modern Women.* London: Thames and Hudson, 1998.

Pollock, Griselda. "Modigliani and the Bodies of Art." In *Modigliani Beyond the Myth,* edited by Mason Klein and Maurice Berger. New Haven: Yale University Press, 2004.

Pollock, Griselda. "Moments and Temporalities of the Avant-Garde 'in, of, and from the feminine'." *New Literary History* 41, no. 4 (2010): 795–820.

Radycki, Diane. *Paula Modersohn-Becker: The First Modern Woman Artist.* New Haven: Yale University Press, 2013.

Rey, Robert, *Suzanne Valadon: vingt-huit reproductions de peintures et dessins précédées d'une étude critique par Robert Rey.* Paris: Éditions de la Nouvelle Revue Française, 1922.

Richard, Julie. "Les Poupées de Marie Vassilieff (1884–1957): entre utopie et dystopie, les déploiements de l'effegie dans l'arts expérimental des avant-gardes historiques." Master's Thesis, Université du Québec à Montréal, 2016.

Rideal, Liz, Whitney Chadwick and Frances Borzello (eds). *Mirror, Mirror: Self-Portraits by Women Artists.* New York: Watson-Guptill Publications, 2002.

Riska, Elianne. *Medical Careers and Feminist Agendas: American, Scandinavian and Russian Women Physicians.* New York: A. de Gruyter, 2001.

Rivière, Joan. "Womanliness as Masquerade." *The International Journal of Psychoanalysis* 10 (1929): 36–44. Reprinted in *The Inner World and Joan Rivière: Collected Papers 1920–1958,* edited by Athol Hughes. London: Karnac Books, 1991, 90–101.

Roberts, Mary L. *Civilization without Sexes: Reconstructing Gender in Postwar France, 1917–1927*. Chicago: University of Chicago Press, 1994.

Roberts, Mary L. *Disruptive Acts: The New Woman in Fin-de-Siècle France*. Chicago: University of Chicago Press, 2005.

Robinson, Hilary. *Reading Art, Reading Irigaray: The Politics of Art by Women*. London: I.B. Tauris, 2006.

Rose, June. *Mistress of Montmartre: A Life of Suzanne Valadon*. London: Metro Books, 1999.

Rosinsky, Thérèse Diamand. *Suzanne Valadon*. New York: Universe Publishing, 1994.

Rosinsky, Thérèse Diamand. *Suzanne Valadon*, translated by Emmanuelle Delanoë-Brun. Paris: Flammarion, 2005.

Roussier, François. *Jacqueline Marval: 1866–1932*. Paris: Thalia Éditions, 2008.

Rubin, William, Hélène Seckel-Klein and Judith Cousins, *Les Demoiselles d'Avignon*. New York: Abrams, 1994.

Salmond, Wendy R. *Arts and Crafts in Late Imperial Russia*. New York: Cambridge University Press, 1996.

Schehr, Lawrence R. "Colette and Androcentrism." In *Entre Hommes: French and Francophone Masculinities in Culture and Theory*, edited by Todd Reeser and Lewis Seifert. Newark: University of Delaware Press, 2008.

Schneider, Pierre. *Matisse*. Paris: Flammarion, 2002.

Schor, Mira. *Wet: On Painting, Feminism and Art Culture*. Durham, NC: Duke University Press, 1997.

Schulman, Michel. *Frédéric Bazille, 1841–1870: catalogue raisonné*. Paris: Éditions de l'Amateur, 1995.

Schutte, Ofelia. "A Critique of Normative Heterosexuality: Identity, Embodiment, and Sexual Difference in Beauvoir and Irigaray." *Hypatia* 12, no. 1 (1997): 55.

Seale, Patrick. *Émilie Charmy*. London: Patrick Seale Gallery, 1980.

Semff, Michael, and Anthony Spira. *Hans Bellmer*. Paris: Centre Pompidou, 2006.

Shackelford, George T.M. "The Body Transformed: Degas's Last Nudes." In *Degas and the Nude*, edited by Shackelford and Xavier Rey. Boston: MFA Publications, 2011.

Sharp, Jane A. *Russian Modernism between East and West: Natal'ia Goncharova and the Moscow Avant-garde*. Cambridge: Cambridge University Press, 2006.

Sharpley-Whiting, T. Denean. *Black Venus: Sexualized Savages, Primal Fears, and Primitive Narratives in French*. Durham, NC: Duke University Press, 1999.

Shaw, Jennifer L. *Dream States: Puvis de Chavannes, Modernism, and the Fantasy of France*. New Haven: Yale University Press, 2002.

Shiff, Richard. "Cézanne's Physicality: The Politics of Touch." In *The Language of Art History*, edited by Salim Kemal and Ivan Gaskell. Cambridge: Cambridge University Press, 1991.

Sidlauskas, Susan. *Cézanne's Other: The Portraits of Hortense*. Berkeley: University of California Press, 2009.

Solomon-Godeau, Abigail. "The Legs of the Countess De Castiglione Photographed by Mayer & Pierson and the Commodification of the Feminine." *October* 39 (1986): 65–108.

Solomon-Godeau, Abigail. "Going Native: Paul Gauguin and the Invention of Primivitist Modernism." In *The Expanding Discourse*, edited by Norma Broude and Mary Garrard. New York: Westview Press, 1992.

Solomon-Godeau, Abigail. *Male Trouble: A Crisis in Representation.* London: Thames & Hudson, 1997.

Spurling, Hilary. *Matisse, le maître. II, 1909–1954*, translated by Paule Guivarch. Paris: Éditions du Seuil, 2009.

Staller, Natasha E. *A Sum of Destructions: Picasso's Cultures & the Creation of Cubism.* New Haven: Yale University Press, 2002.

Steinberg, Leo. "Drawing as if to Possess." In *Major European Art Movements, 1900–1945: A Critical Anthology*, edited by Patricia E. Kaplan and Susan Manso. New York: Dutton, 1977.

Stoller, Silvia. *Simone de Beauvoir's Philosophy of Age: Gender, Ethics, and Time.* Berlin: DeGruyter, 2014.

Stovall, Tyler. *Transnational France: The Modern History of a Universal Nation.* New York: Taylor & Francis, 2015.

Strand, Dana. *Colette: A Study of the Short Fiction.* New York: Twayne Publishers, 1995.

Straw, Petrine Archer. *Negrophilia: Avant-garde Paris and Black Culture in the 1920s.* New York: Thames & Hudson, 2000.

Suthor, Nicola. *Rembrandt's Roughness*. Princeton: Princeton University Press, 2018.

Sweeney, Fionnghuala, and Kate Marsh (eds). *Afromodernisms: Paris, Harlem and the Avant-garde*. Edinburgh: Edinburgh University Press, 2013.

Tabarant, Adolphe. "Suzanne Valadon et ses souvenirs de modèle." *Bulletin de la Vie Artistique*. Paris, December 1921.

Taylor, Sue. *Hans Bellmer: The Anatomy of Anxiety.* Cambridge, MA: MIT Press, 2000.

Thomson, Richard. *Degas: The Nudes.* London: Thames & Hudson, 1988.

Thurman, Judith. *Secrets of the Flesh: A Life of Colette.* New York: Ballantine Books, 1999.

Tickner, Lisa. *Women's Images of Men.* London: Institute of Contemporary Arts, 1980.

Tythacott, Louise. *Surrealism and the Exotic.* London: Routledge, 2014.

Valadon, Suzanne. "La Nature et la peinture." Archives docteur Robert le Masle, Bibliothèque Kandinsky, Centre Pompidou, Paris.

Valadon, Suzanne. "Suzanne Valadon ou l'absolu." n.d., n.p. Archives docteur Robert le Masle, Bibliothèque Kandinsky, Centre Pompidou, Paris.

Valkenier, Elizabeth K. *Russian Realist Art: The State and Society: The Peredvizhniki and Their Tradition.* New York: Columbia University Press, 1989.

Vasseleu, Cathryn. *Textures of Light: Vision and Touch in Irigaray, Levinas and Merleau-Ponty.* London: Routledge, 1998.

Vassilieff, Marie. "Mes poupées," *Montparnasse* 42, December, 1925.

Vassilieff, Marie. *La Bohème du XXe siècle* (unpublished memoir), 1929, archives of Marie Vassilieff.

Vauxcelles, Louis. *Histoire générale de l'art français, de la révolution à nos jours.* Paris: Librarie de France, 1922.

Vicinus, Martha. *Intimate Friends: Women who Loved Women, 1778–1928.* Chicago: University of Chicago Press, 2006.

Wagner, Anne. *Three artists (Three Women): Modernism and the Art of Hesse, Krasner, and O'Keeffe.* Berkeley: University of California Press, 1996.

Waldemar, George, Philippe Hupel and André Salmon. *Marie Vassilieff, 1884–1957, un peintre cubiste méconnu.* Paris: Galerie Hupel, 1969.

Walser, Hans. *The Golden Section*, translated by Peter Hilton and Jean Pedersen. Washington DC: The Mathematical Association of America, 2001.

Walters, Margaret. *The Nude Male: A New Perspective.* New York: Paddington Press, 1978.

Warnod, Jeanine. *Suzanne Valadon.* Paris: Flammarion, 1981.

Warnod, Jeanine. *Suzanne Valadon.* Norwalk: Easton Press, 1982.

Warnod, Jeanine, Saskia Ooms et al. *Valadon, Utrillo and Utter in the Rue Cortot Studio: 1912–1926.* Paris: Somogy, 2015.

Weill, Berthe and François Roussier. *Pan! Dans L'oeil!: ou trente ans dans les coulisses de la peinture contemporaine, 1900–1930.* Dijon: L'Échelle de Jacob, 2009.

Weiss, Louise. *Mémoires d'une européenne, II: Combats pour l'Europe, 1919–1934.* Paris: Albin Michel, 1968.

Weyl, Christina. *The Women of Atelier 17: Modernist Printmaking in Midcentury New York.* New Haven: Yale University Press, 2019.

White, Harrison, and Cynthia White, *Canvases and Careers: Institutional Change in the French Painting World.* New York: Wiley, 1965.

Willis, Deborah, and Carla Williams, "The Vénus Noire." *Nka: Journal of Contemporary African Art* 30 (2012): 28–35.

Wilson, Elizabeth. *Bohemians: The Glamorous Outcasts.* London: Tauris Parke Paperbacks, 2003.

Worms, Frédéric. *La Philosophie en France au XXe siècle: moments.* Paris: Gallimard, 2010.

Yiu, K. Sarah, "The Icon of the Hottentot Female and the Reclamation of Black Female Sexuality and Bodily Representation." *Footnotes* 2 (2009): 72–8.

Zhao, Yelin. "Ambitious Model, Ambiguous Artist: Three Case Studies of Victorine Meurent, Suzanne Valadon and Alice Prin." Ph.D. dissertation, The University of Leeds, 2018.

Index

Note: works of art can be found under artists' names